THE REALITIES OF AMERICAN–PALESTINE RELATIONS

THE REALITIES OF
AMERICAN–PALESTINE
RELATIONS

By FRANK E. MANUEL

Author, "The Politics of Modern Spain"

PUBLIC AFFAIRS PRESS
Washington, D.C.

To My Nephews—
Jeffrey and Steven

AUTHOR'S PREFACE

In the course of writing this history of American-Palestine relations a number of pious legends may have been destroyed and, likely as not, a few impious ones created. The author has preferred, however, not to engage in extended controversy with the originators of the legends. This obviated the necessity for scholarly polemic and the traditional substructure of footnotes.

The more pertinent sources for each chapter are indicated at the end of the book in such a manner that attempts to check specific quotations from manuscript sources will entail substantial archival search on the part of the curious. Transcription of Hebrew and Arabic names has in general followed the system devised by T. E. Lawrence. The learned will notice the absence of the diacritical mark under the *het* but those knowing enough to miss it can supply the lack in their mind's eye.

The staffs of the National Archives and the Library of Congress have been gracious and helpful. Dr. Lawrence Marwick, Chief of the Hebraic Section in the Library of Congress, has shared of his great knowledge beyond the call of duty, and my wife has contributed her labor to the preparation of the manuscript beyond the bounds of love.

To Robert Harvey of Public Affairs Press I am indebted for generous assistance on the index.

FRANK E. MANUEL, PH.D.
Washington, D.C.

CONTENTS

INTRODUCTION

This is a history of United States concern with Palestine from the time of the appointment of the first consular agent in Jerusalem in 1832 through the most recent troublous events. Diplomatic history in the accepted sense of the term consists mostly of verbal and written interchanges among sovereign states. Since prior to May 14, 1948, the Jews of Palestine had no government of their own, for more than a hundred years they were rather the objects of United States diplomatic interest than active agents in formal international relations.

Five distinct periods, of uneven duration, mark the development of United States involvement in Palestine:

1. The period of Turkish rule, during which we conducted sustained negotiations with the Ottoman Government about the condition of the Jews and their disabilities under Turkish law. The extraterritorial powers of European and American Consuls in Turkey created a unique and often grotesque international administration for the growing settlement of Jews.

2. The years following World War I when the Peace Settlement was being determined and for a time the United States was an active participant in the conferences leading to the disposition of Palestine.

3. The rule of the British Mandatory during which United States relations with Palestine were technically governed by the Anglo-American Treaty of 1924. In the last three years of this mandatory regime there was an abortive attempt at the formulation of a joint Anglo-American policy.

4. The period after the British deposited the Palestine problem in the lap of the United Nations and once more the political fate of the land became the subject of open debate in the comity of nations. Unlike the years following World War I, this time the United States could not shrug off responsibility for Palestine. There were divergent elements within the body politic, and their bitter dissension was reflected in a shifting policy, finally crystallized by events in Palestine itself.

5. The period since May 14, 1948, when a *de facto* Israeli Govern-

ment came into being and won immediate United States recognition.

American diplomatic policy is shaped by the interests of its people, interests which are varied, often sharply contradictory. The evolution of any major policy is thus rarely unilinear; it veers in one direction or another in accordance with the predominance of a particular group of interests. The historical unity of the national interest in foreign policy is a fiction, even though at moments of crisis there may be rallying of all forces towards a common objective. Such moments, until very recent years, have been limited almost exclusively to periods of declared war.

American Jews have always had a passionate interest in Palestine. At the consecration of a New York synagogue in 1818, Major Mordecai Immanuel Noah, a former United States consul in Tunis, hailed the prospect of the restoration of the Jewish nation to Palestine: "The signal for breaking the Turkish sceptre in Europe will be their emancipation . . .; they will march in triumphant numbers, and possess themselves once more of Syria, and take their rank among the governments of the earth."

His eloquent discourse was praised by the aged ex-Presidents John Adams and Thomas Jefferson, and the great Virginian philosopher of democracy wrote Noah a long analytic letter revealing his profound awareness of the inadequacy of mere legal safeguards against the persecution of the Jews even in a free government. "For altho' we are free by the law," said Jefferson, "we are not so in practice. Public opinion erects itself into an Inquisition and exercises its office with as much fanaticism as fans the flames of an auto-da-fé. The prejudices still scowling on your section of our religion, altho' the elder one, cannot be unfelt by yourselves."

Noah's plans for founding in a Jewish Palestine "a mild, just and honorable government accredited by the world and admired by all good men" were naive and utopian. They were soon forgotten. But once the United States established relations with Turkey and our consuls were sent to Palestine, both the "vice" of intolerance which Jefferson had castigated and the longing of the Jews for their ancient land became matter for American diplomacy.

In the nineteenth century the interest of American Jews in Palestine was humanitarian and religious. Their religious tie with the Jews of Palestine was in many respects far stronger than the bond of Catholics to the Papal establishment in Rome, because for most Jews it was underscored by a feeling of ethnic or racial kinship with other Jews. The humanitarian desire of American Jews, overwhelmingly refugees themselves from European centers of persecution, to alleviate the suffering of other Jews was natural, normal, and real. It was reasonable for them to use the instrumentalities of the United States government to further these benevolent purposes. There is no reason to regard such moral and spiritual interests as less valid, less worthy of being identified with the national interest, than the material interest of American businessmen seeking the protection of their government for commercial investments abroad.

The response of the United States government to the wishes of American Jews was varied. In the last years before World War I, when it appeared that economic concessions in Turkey would be jeopardized by our excessive concern with the fate of the Jews, our humanitarianism was somewhat attenuated.

With the emergence of Zionism as a political movement the humanitarian and religious interest of a substantial proportion of American Jews became associated with a definite viewpoint on what would be an acceptable political settlement in the Near East. The area was in a state of flux and migration of homeless Jews from eastern Europe to the land with which for two thousand years they had maintained a historical connection appeared a legitimate solution to the Jewish Problem in 1918–1919.

At the Paris Peace Conference, the Palestine problem became entwined with a hundred thorny issues of the international settlement and often as not it was lost in the underbrush. At Paris there emerged powerful groups who envisioned the Jewish National Homeland as a threat to their own interests, and who undermined American support for Zionism.

A group whose strength and subtlety have sometimes been ignored were the Protestant missionaries. They had built American universities and had become a dominant civilizing agent in the Near East. Apprehensive that the penetration of Palestine by a Jewish state would introduce into the Near East an element to compete with their own cultural concepts, they were vigorous antagonists to Zionism. When they unfolded before the policy-makers the vision of an Arab world under American tutelage, their interest was assuming forms akin to cultural imperialism, but it could not fail to be an attractive prospect to any nation.

The anti-Zionist Jews who on principle did not want a Jewish state to pose for them a problem of dual allegiance were in 1919 a potent interest. They counted in their ranks many of the leaders of the Jewish community whom the policy-makers could not overlook, even as they paid passing attention to those orthodox Jews who then despised a political solution of the Jewish problem as an invasion of the Messiah's prerogatives.

The interest of American Catholics was not as effectively organized at Paris as the Protestant missionaries, but fundamentally the Catholics too were a group who preferred to veto Jewish control in the land where their most sacred relic rested.

Finally, there were American business interests. At one time the Standard Oil Company, with its Turkish concessions in the Negev, felt that the special privileges forecast, at least on paper, for Zionist concessionaires under a British Mandate, would be inimical to its own development.

These various forces collided at the Paris Conference and they had changing fortunes. President Wilson's espousal of the Zionists' interest waxed hot and cold. By the time of his last positive diplomatic intervention in their behalf in February 1920, he was a sick man, no longer a power among the European statesmen, who proceeded to divide the world without him.

The clash of these interests at Paris had not been a violent one; for the most part it was even covert. But the end result was not favorable to the aims of American Zionists. In the Treaty of 1924, which governed Anglo-American relations during the mandatory period, business and missionary interests were explicitly protected in operating articles; the Zionist interest was relegated to an ambiguous inference, the inclusion of the full mandate with its Balfour Declaration as a preamble to the Treaty.

By the late thirties vast American oil developments and concessions in the Middle East introduced a new factor of great magnitude into our relations with that world area. Once war was declared, global strategy involved the United States militarily in the Middle East and produced a complete reorientation of policy entailing commitments of active responsibility in both its economy and politics. During the war Zionist interests, pleading for support, were time and again brushed aside in the name of military necessity and decisions which required the appeasement of potentially hostile Arabs.

The Zionist program emerged from the war with an appeal of far greater potency both to Jews and non-Jews than it had ever before enjoyed. The massacre of eastern European Jews had given tragic cogency to the argument that the Jewish remnants needed a plot of ground of their own. This sentimental interest was now backed by the full power of the organized Jewish community.

It came into sharp conflict with the world strategy of analysts in the War and State Departments who for reasons which they considered good and sufficient believed that United States policy had to support the "stable" rulers in the Arab world and their protectors the British. The existence of oil reserves along the Persian Gulf which came to be valued as the richest in the world and the threat of Russian imperialism strengthened the hand of the strategists. There was real division in the nation, during which all the accepted techniques of propaganda were used on both sides. The requirements of biennial election campaigns—the Jewish minority vote was heavily concentrated in specific metropolitan areas—and the less regularly appointed international crises both exerted their influence, buffeting the Executive now in one direction, now in another. Ugly passions were generated. During this storm the United States gave a display of kaleidoscopically changing policy which was not edifying. In the very process of careening towards a position the United States, to borrow from Machiavelli, landed on the same side on which it had started only by virtue of having reversed itself twice in the interim.

This is not a pleasant story. At more than one period the vulgar smell of anti-semitism obtrudes. It is replete with high-sounding phrases, for which we as a nation have become somewhat notorious, to cover the absence of a sense of responsibility.

But the tale has had a happy ending. There is a small Israeli state and the United States, with long lapses of indifference and even official hostility, had a hand in its creation. It is unfortunate that it could not have been born without war, with its wanton expenditure of men and material sorely needed to provide homes and a livelihood for the survivors of one of the greatest mass slaughters in western man's cruel history.

Chapter I

THE EARLY YEARS IN THE OLD SETTLEMENT

RUDIMENTS OF A PROTECTORATE

In the middle of the nineteenth century, United States interest in Palestine was primarily limited to consular relations with the various religious sects who dwelt in the old Jewish settlement of Jerusalem. The Jews in the old quarter, steeped in the medieval tradition of a persecuted minority eternally seeking a powerful protector, came to turn more and more to United States consuls as humanitarian emissaries of a new world outlook who could be relied upon to use their good offices in periods of crisis. The very remoteness of the United States from any conceivable involvement in Near Eastern politics bestowed upon our agents a prestige far greater than their effective influence.

Strands of a policy were visible from the very inauguration of the American establishment in the Holy Land. The Ashkenazic Jewish settlers were Europeans, and whether individual officials respected them or not, they were men from the West in the midst of barbarous Turks. The diplomatic tradition of the West, in which the United States had begun to participate, vouchsafed the Jews a right of pilgrimage and sojourn in the Holy Land.

By the end of the 1870's, there were about 250,000 Jews in the United States, a minority whose sentimental attachment to the Jews of Palestine dated from the appearance of the first Messengers of Charity to the prosperous Jewish synagogues of Newport and Norfolk in the eighteenth century. Our consular officials were able to take cognizance of this half-religious, half-ethnic bond of the American Jews without doing violence to other substantial American interests. The character of the early Jewish settlement in Palestine, however, was so turbulent, that the consul who managed to survive his term of office without stirring up an international incident involving the small though vigilant Jewish community of the United States, had performed his duties with rare circumspection.

Consuls at the Jerusalem post often intervened more actively in the affairs of the Jewish community than the State Department officially sanctioned. Under the system of capitulations with its extra-territorial consular justice, it was inevitable that United States representatives should be drawn into problems far outside a narrow definition of their functions.

MID-NINETEENTH CENTURY TURKEY

In 1799 President John Adams appointed an American mission to Turkey to arrange a treaty of amity and commerce with the Sublime Porte. After three decades of intermittent negotiations, the treaty, bestowing upon Americans privileges equivalent to the ancient capitulations enjoyed by the European powers, was finally concluded on May 7, 1830. The protracted discussion required to initiate formal relations between the two countries was characteristic of much subsequent diplomatic parrying. Pourparlers over specific issues between American Ministers and Turkish Grand Viziers dragged on for more than half a century, wound themselves into ever more confusing legal intricacies, and often lapsed without reaching a settlement. The Ottoman Empire was the true heir of Byzantine bureaucracy.

The impending collapse of the Ottoman Empire was foretold by mid-nineteenth century Ministers at Constantinople in grand Gibbonesque periods. They devoted the greater part of their despatches to the stifling corruption of the Turkish administration, the famines and the epidemics, the passing of economic power into the hands of the Christian rayahs, the widespread brigandage on the highways. The assassination of sovereigns and their ministers was accepted as the norm of Turkish political existence. On May 30, 1876, when Abdul Aziz was dethroned and Murad V was proclaimed Sultan, the United States proceeded to recognize the new ruler on the very same day. And when he in turn was done away with four months later by Abdul Hamid, our Minister hurried with congratulations to the latest incumbent.

American interest in Turkey was rather remote. With a continent of our own to exploit we could view with relative indifference and objectivity the disintegration of the Turkish Empire, the struggle of the European Powers for its choice remnants, and the concomitant religious conflicts of the Greek and Latin Churches. There was to be sure a living American tradition of hatred for kings, sultans, czars, and emperors; and since the people applauded every European nationalist independence movement, American diplomatic and consular agents in Turkey often voiced sympathy for the rebels when they were suppressed with excessive cruelty. But there was a counterweight to this love for the new Hellas and the other nascent nationalisms of the Balkans. Turkey granted religious liberty to all sects and a place of safety to the political refugees of 1848; her inveterate enemy was despotic Russia; thus, paradoxically, in mid-nineteenth century America there was born a measure of understanding even for the terrible Turk.

There were a number of thorny diplomatic issues outstanding between the United States and Turkey. After decades of discussion, we reached agreement on one of them in 1874: the United States accepted a protocol permitting its nationals to own real estate in Turkey, a concession which involved as a *quid pro quo* recognition of Turkey's right to tax their property. A naturalization treaty also was signed in Constantinople in 1875 setting forth conditions under which each would recognize the naturalization of the other's nationals, but a Senate amendment during the ratification debate was not acceptable to the Porte and the naturalized citizen remained a perennial problem of our diplomatic relations down to the First World War. Equally inconclusive was our vast diplomatic correspondence about the true text and meaning of Article IV of the Treaty of 1830, which lay at the core of the extraterritorial consular and diplomatic protectorate guaranteed our nationals in Turkey. The English, Turkish, and French texts of the Treaty diverged significantly; our *chargé d'affaires* at Constantinople had unthinkingly signed a note awarding primacy to the Turkish version, a document whose language was ambiguous enough to beget a score of varying translations. When the capitulations were abolished in 1914, there still was no consensus on the import of this critical provision of the Treaty.

For the rest American diplomatic agents spent their time protecting travellers in the wilds of Asia Minor, inducing the Sultan to issue firmans permitting archaeological expeditions, furthering the work of the Protestant missionaries and their schools, and protesting outrages against Christians and Jews. In a very genuine sense, they were the voice of nineteenth century humanitarianism on the shores of the barbarous East.

THE FIRST CONSULAR AGENTS IN JERUSALEM

Shortly after Commodore David Porter of Maryland was commissioned *chargé d'affaires* of the American legation in Constantinople in 1831, he chose as consular agent to represent the United States in Jaffa and Jerusalem one David Darmon, a Jew who was nominally a French subject and knew his way about the Levant. Named sight unseen upon recommendation of an American Jew who had just completed a journey through Palestine, Darmon gave his superior cause to regret the appointment almost from the inception of his tenure. Hardly five months after his assignment, Darmon sent the State Department directly—not through Porter—a number of ambitious proposals which included bestowing upon himself the title of Consul for Palestine. *En passant* he suggested that the United States should take immediate possession of the island of Cyprus. Commodore Porter soon complained to the Department that consular agent Darmon was not respected by the Christians in Jerusalem and that travellers returning to Constantinople had carried back with them accusations of malfeasance.

Since the Congress had not provided for an extensive consular service in Turkey and the agents at both Beirut and Jerusalem were not salaried personnel, it was common practice in the Near East to use foreigners as consular agents where American interests were not substantial; in such areas the primary function of the consul was to extend courtesies to visitors. In return the consular agent enjoyed a measure of prestige among the natives which was expected to bring him certain tangible rewards, since he was usually engaged in a commercial enterprise apart from his official duties. The practice was quite unsatisfactory, especially in Turkey under the capitulations and the Treaty of 1830, where a consular official exercised judicial functions over citizens of the United States. Commodore Porter was no happier about consular agent Chasseaud, a Frenchman whom he had appointed in Beirut with a jurisdiction which included northern Palestine, and he repeatedly urged the State Department to create a central salaried post at Jerusalem and subsidiary consular agencies at Jaffa and Beirut. His requests were not heeded.

When the *U.S.S. Delaware* on tour appeared in Syrian and Palestinian waters in 1834 Darmon welcomed Commodore Patterson and his men at Jaffa, and aroused in the naval officer an instant antipathy.

Patterson's letter to Porter describing his reception was couched in the standard vocabulary of modern anti-semitism, and included a portrait of the peculiar characteristics of the Jews as typified by the consular agent. He levelled specific charges against Darmon that he was hawking about American protection and called him a disgrace to the flag. When Commodore Porter received from a fellow naval officer this unsavory sketch of his consular agent, he promptly ousted him.

Darmon erroneously believed that his powerful secret enemies were the missionaries of Jerusalem whose advances he had resisted, remaining a "true Jew." His protest against his dismissal, written in fairly good French, its tone the Levant of the period, was an admixture of humble submission, pleas of forgiveness, flattery, demands for money to cover the extraordinary expenses incurred by his receptions in line of duty, and pointed threats that unless he received satisfaction from Porter he would appeal over his head to the President. Darmon's letter was set down by Porter as typical of Jewish character, when in truth it was the manner of the Levantine currying favor with powerful European or American foreigners. For almost a century thereafter, native employees of the diplomatic establishment—Greeks, Turks, Italians, Egyptians, Christian Syrians and Armenians—who were dropped from the service, invariably wrote long letters in a similar vein.

No replacement was appointed in Jerusalem for a decade after Darmon's dismissal and the Jaffa agency became a mere station subservient to Beirut. In December 1844 word reached Minister Carr in Constantinople that one Warder Cresson was going about Jerusalem proclaiming himself American Consul and issuing new consular seals for the Jaffa agency. "Among other things he is giving papers of protection to Jews and others not citizens of the United States," Carr reported. The Minister called him a madman, disavowed him to the Porte, and wrote Cresson that if he persisted, he would have the Turks expel him from their dominions. Lines of communication among officials of the consular and diplomatic service were hopelessly confused in this period: Warder Cresson actually had been confirmed by the Senate on May 17, 1844, as Consul at Jerusalem; but he never received an exequatur from the Porte, and no office was opened in Jerusalem under his auspices. Cresson himself stayed on in Palestine, was converted to Judaism, married a Jewess, who bore him children, and died in the land in 1860.

Warder Cresson was a strange man. In 1844 he published a variety of religious tracts, most of them of a Messianic character, such as *The Good Olive Tree Israel, showing the pre-eminence of Israel in the coming Dispensation.* Upon his conversion to Judaism he assumed the name Michael Boaz Israel, founded a Jewish agricultural settlement near Jerusalem, and distributed circulars in Europe and the United States pleading for support of his scheme for Jewish colonization of Palestine: "to facilitate the migration of such of them as desire to settle in the land given by the Almighty in Covenant to Abraham and his seed forever." His plans came to nothing, but he is an authentic nineteenth century precursor of later Zionist projects. Though his former fellow townsmen in New Hope, Pennsylvania, considered him a religious maniac, and wrote as much to Secretary of State Calhoun when they read of his appointment, there are many curiously realistic insights in his later writings on Palestine and the "Jewish Problem."

EARLY CONSULAR DESCRIPTIONS OF PALESTINE

Palestine was not a recognized administrative unit of the Ottoman Empire; the area traditionally known as Palestine was divided into three Sanjuks, strips of territory running east-west to the Jordan, with centers at Acre, Nablous, and Jerusalem—all in varying degrees dependent administrative units of the Vilayet of Beirut. By World War I Jerusalem was in effect an Independent Sanjuk with direct relations to Constantinople.

In 1856 the United States formally established two separate consular districts in Syria and Palestine, though they were not coterminous with any existing Turkish governmental units and their dividing boundary line, which ran through northern Palestine, was not sharply drawn. While the Jerusalem consular district was comprised of the Jaffa-Jerusalem area and the Beirut consular district included the Haifa-Galilee area in the north, through the years affairs touching the whole of Jewish Palestine tended to be concentrated in Jerusalem. Since the nineteenth century American consular service was only loosely integrated with the diplomatic service, these vaguely defined American administrative units overlapping Turkish units contributed their share of confusion to the conduct of ordinary business between the United States and the Sublime Porte.

The old consular agency at Haifa, under the Beirut consul, continued in existence through the First World War. For years the agent stationed there was Jacob Schumacher, head of the hard-working and prosperous German-American colony of Adventists in the Haifa area known as "The Temple," which had been founded in the early fifties. Since the two Jewish Holy Cities of Tiberias and Safed, nominally within his province, were a solid two days journey on horseback through treacherous Bedouin territory, the agent remained quietly at his post and only on the rarest occasions, when mayhem or other capital crimes were committed, did he venture forth into the communities on Lake Tiberias. The American consul at Jerusalem, living in the heart of the largest Jewish community in Palestine, was far more intimately drawn into their lives.

Jerusalem was not a commercial post of importance and originally the establishment of a consulate was regarded primarily as an aid to tourists and pilgrims. After the American consuls had turned in their records on imports and exports, the weather, the grain harvest and the fruit crop, they occasionally extended themselves with reflections about the land and its Turkish administrators. The consuls did not unveil any mysteries of the Ottoman Empire or of the Pasha's Palace in Jerusalem; but from time to time these agents of a young democracy at the other end of the world sent objective intelligence of the land.

On October 20, 1856, a Boston physician, John Warren Gorham, was appointed the first salaried American Consul in Jerusalem, and the next year he opened his office in rented quarters on Mount Zion. It was a sorry land, he found.

There was no harbor at Jaffa and even the anchorage was unsafe during the months of November to May. Export trade was insignificant, consisting of small quantities of grain, sesame, and oranges transported in French and Austrian bottoms. There was no commerce with America and he held out no prospects for trade until a harbor was constructed. Excavation of the old harbor to the north of Jaffa, which had been filled in with sand and planted with orange trees, would require purchase of the groves, and before the harbor could be made ready to receive shipping a costly sea-wall would have to be constructed as protection against the southwest winds of the winter months. There was no expectation that the Turkish Government would undertake any such innovations. Interior communications, beyond travel on horseback, did not exist. A railroad project for a line from Jaffa to Jerusalem had been abandoned and a private company's request for the right to build a carriage road between the two cities was awaiting approval somewhere in the labyrinth of the Turkish bureaucracy. Frequent Bedouin raids on agricultural areas rendered farming unprofitable and life was insecure even a short distance from the towns. The fellaheen planted wheat, barley, and doura, an Egyptian millet, and groaned under the oppressive taxation of the government and the exploitation of the factors who bought their produce. The Bedouin Sheikhs, continually at war with one another, kept the whole country in a state of turmoil.

There had been extraordinary construction activity in the European religious and national communities during the early fifties, with the consequence that the value of land, prices, and rents had quadrupled in the areas of Jerusalem and Jaffa. Christians had recently been granted the right to hold property in their own name though they rarely exercised the privilege outside of the cities. Russian expansion was the most striking among all the European nations. They had established a consulate on a grand scale; lands had been purchased, residences constructed for the bishop and the consul, and a hospice built for pilgrims. Other nations—the English, the Austrian, and the Prussian—were putting up lesser hospices. The Jews of Jerusalem had erected a new and elegant synagogue on Mount Zion which ranked with the Greek, Latin, and Armenian establishments. A New Orleans philanthropist, Judah Turo, had bequeathed money for the construction of a hospice for indigent Jews. The English benefactor of Palestine, Sir Moses Montefiore, executor, along with the Virginian, Kursheedt, of the Turo bequest, ultimately built a group of houses for the poor outside the city gates—thus creating the first new quarter of Jerusalem in modern times.

The Jerusalem consulate was not a desirable post. In the sixties and seventies, American consuls, complaining about the climate and their ailments, followed one another in rapid succession. They were plagued by filth and disease. Consul Gorham took refuge in drink and was retired. The great cholera outbreak of July 1865 in Jerusalem cost 3,000 lives; of a population of 20,000 about 15,000 of the poorest and most helpless remained, the more prosperous having fled the city.

In 1868 an Acting Jerusalem Consul, Lorenzo M. Johnson, sent the second general report on the district to the Secretary of State. (The annual report which was due from each district had long been neglected because of the frequent turnover of consular officials.) The land was still suffering from the burden of excessive taxation, especially the levy on individual trees which discouraged the culture of olives and figs. This was particularly unfortunate since it was commonly believed that a general growth of trees would restore the ancient fertility of the soil. One fifth of the grain produce was the legal tax, in addition to which the taxgatherers levied upon the peasants an indefinite amount for their own remuneration. The Bedouins continued to make incursions on the farming population and the Pasha of Jerusalem retaliated by organizing expeditions against them, seizing their sheep and their horses. Booty from these reprisals was not used to indemnify the peasants but to reward the Pasha for his exertions. The carriage road from Jaffa to Jerusalem had finally been constructed, though the consul was skeptical about its survival during the rainy season.

The completion of the Suez Canal in 1869 focussed new interest on the whole adjacent area of Asia Minor. In his annual report of September 30, 1870, Consul Beardsley delivered himself of a moving description of the desolation of the land, followed by a romantic vision of its potentialities. "The population diminishes, the plain becomes a desert and the mountain barren while the valley maintains its fertility in the face of the worse [sic] possible treatment. . . . With her climate, soil and geographical position, Palestine under favorable circumstances would become one of the most prosperous states on the Mediterranean. What she requires is a wise and just government which will protect instead of plunder her people, internal improvements such as roads and bridges to render her different parts of easy access and aqueducts to irrigate her thirsty soil and above all a patriotic spirit and national aspiration among her people. This last would naturally result in the course of time from a good government and then would commence the resurrection and rejuvenation of Palestine. She would rapidly advance in wealth and prosperity. Her desert wastes would again blossom as the rose and she would soon become one of the most favored countries in the world." Two years later, Consul Beardsley, less sanguine, wrote a trenchant account of the venal administrative policy of the Sublime Porte, which he held responsible for the plight of the land and its inhabitants. "Each successive Pasha . . . promises well, and we are always tempted to hope for better things, but each one follows in the beaten footsteps of his predecessor and leaves the province at the end of his term in a little worse condition than he found it. The fault, however, is not always with the Pasha, who is often sincerely anxious to ameliorate the conditions of the people and would like to distinguish himself in the wise administration of the affairs of his province. The fault is with the system of provincial administration which prevails throughout the Turkish Empire. A system which practically makes the Pasha a tax-collector and the government a machine to gather the revenues and transmit them to the Imperial Treasury. A Turkish Pasha is held in high repute by his Imperial Master in proportion as he is successful in collecting a large revenue from an impoverished district. His duty is to tax as much from, and return as little to the province as possible; and it is always desirable that he should be heartily disliked by the people over whom he is called to rule. To court the people by seeking to ameliorate their condition is interpreted as a sure sign of his ambitious aims and his fall and disgrace become more certain and imminent as he rises in the estimation of the people of his district. . . . Every year villages are deserted, the inhabitants flying to Egypt to save themselves and their personel [sic] effects from being seized for taxes. Hundreds of acres of the richest land in the world are given up to the desert annually because the exorbitant taxes cannot be paid. . . . Thus nine-tenths of the valley of the Jordan, the mountains and many of the villages of Judea, and large tracts of the plain of Sharon have not been cultivated for years."

During the seventies the long-drawn-out European power play over the Near East kept world interest in Palestine alive. Consul Beardsley heard rumors of an American Exploration Society organized to exploit the land; he approved of the venture because America would not be suspect of entertaining political ambitions in this area of the world. After the assembly of the first modern Turkish Parliament in 1877, the imminent reform of the Turkish administration became a general topic of conversation in Near Eastern diplomatic circles, but Consul Willson's informants in Jerusalem were dubious that any cleansing of the regime was feasible. "Raoul Pasha, Governor of Palestine, is in favor of reform; so is Joseph Effendi, Mayor of Jerusalem, both cultivated gentlemen, and apparently well-disposed, but as the Governor says: 'What shall I do? Every official almost takes backsheek, and if I remove one, and appoint another, he will repeat the offense, and the matter is no better but rather worse.' "

The administrative corruption was the more disheartening as the land itself inspired dithyrambs. The whole maritime plain was a natural wheat field, and the Esdraelon Valley scarcely inferior to the plains of Illinois and Iowa in Consul Willson's appraisal; the entire Jordan Valley could be irrigated. An American consul of the seventies, during the conquest of our own Far West, at first saw an expanding frontier even in barren Palestine and the physical impediments of nature as minor obstacles. "The world is waiting for the hour and for the man who shall call these dead industries into life, and make the resources of this ancient land . . . tributary and subservient to the wants and needs of the world's advancing civilization." But, like his predecessor Beardsley, after Consul Willson had stayed in Palestine for a few years, he altered his tone. The slowness of the East and its imperviousness to change made him far less enthusiastic in his outlook. He began to record that the population and wealth of Palestine had not increased in forty years and to notice that few of the projects talked about were ever undertaken.

The land lived in continual fear of the drought and the locust and the cholera. Sharp fluctuations of rainfall from year to year brought relative prosperity or starvation. When the rains were light, the cisterns of Jerusalem went dry; the harvests suffered, and the Jews huddled in their ancient quarter could buy food only at famine prices. When in the wake of drought locusts darkened the sky and stripped the earth, food had to be imported at costs higher than in a European metropolis.

The orthodox Jews of Jerusalem, living in their squalid district, blind to the physical aspect of the land and indifferent to the lot of the fellaheen, were nonetheless joined to their fate.

WARRING JEWISH SECTS

The Jewish community of the old settlement had a relatively stable character prior to the immigration movement of 1881. Though it was numerically insignificant in this period, its internal structure and dominant economic and social institutions already had definite forms which were to endure until the outbreak of the First World War.

The Jews of Palestine were divided into two primary groups, Sephardim and Ashkenazim. The Sephardim of Turkey were in part descendants of those Jews who had been received by the Sultan after their expulsion from Spain at the close of the fifteenth century (*Sepharad* is Hebrew for Spain). Through the years their numbers had been augmented by stray migrants from North Africa, Italy, Greece, Persia, and Afghanistan. By the middle of the nineteenth century, there were about one hundred and fifty thousand Jews living in the chief cities of the Ottoman Empire in Europe and Asia (exclusive of the Danubian provinces) who constituted a separate legal entity and led an autonomous existence. The Empire was divided into eight rabbinical districts—one of them Jerusalem—each with a rabbi at its head who exercised both sacerdotal and temporal functions. A district collected its own taxes, had law courts and meted out punishments. The rabbi was elected by the notables of the community and was subject to removal, an event which occurred often enough during internecine communal feuds. This merging of religious and lay functions was in harmony with the spirit of the Ottoman Empire whose ruler was both Caliph and Sultan. The Sephardic Jews tended to remain loyal to the Turkish sovereign during the rebellions of the various Christian sects and nationalities, a partisanship which earned them the bitter hatred of the Christian rayahs and the benevolent tolerance of the Turks. As long as public order was not disturbed the local pasha refrained from interfering in the Jewish affairs of his Sephardic subjects. For the transmission of general decrees to the Jews the Sultan had a Chacham-Bashi, a Chief Rabbi in Constantinople, who did not, however, exercise any supervision or authority over the other rabbinical jurisdictions, whose heads also bore that title. The Jerusalem Chief Rabbi had the additional honorific cognomen of First in Zion (*Rishon le-Tsiyon*).

By the mid-nineteenth century the infiltration into Palestine of a few thousand Ashkenazic Jews from central and eastern Europe had complicated the stable relations of the Porte and the Jews (*Ashkenaz* is Hebrew for Germany). In 1700 Rabbi Yehuda Hasid had led a movement of Ashkenazim to the Holy Land. It was the tail end of Shabbetai Zevi Messianism of the seventeenth century, and had spread from its original source in Poland to communities in Germany, Moravia, Austria-Hungary and Italy. About 1500 departed from their homes, of whom only 1000 reached Palestine. After their leader died, leaving heavy debts to the Moslems incurred in anticipation of contributions from the diaspora, many of the followers returned to Europe, or were converted to Islam or Christianity. A small remnant survived in Jerusalem and with the aid of an endowment from Austrian and German Jews, they were able to maintain a form of communal existence until 1721, when the Moslems burnt down their houses and wrecked their synagogue. For a century thereafter, the few Ashkenazim who did trickle into Jerusalem had to disguise themselves as Sephardim, until in 1816 a decree of the Sultan freed the Ashkenazim of the ancient debt of Rabbi Yehuda Hasid for which they had been held accountable as a community and allowed them to settle in their own right. In 1777 migrants from the provinces of Volynia, Podalia, and the Ukraine established themselves in the Holy City of Safed under the protection of the Russian and Austrian consuls. Through the early years of the nineteenth century there were intermittent group movements of a few score Jews from communities in central and eastern Europe.

The coming of the Ashkenazim introduced into the Turkish Empire alien Jews who were reluctant to place themselves under the jurisdiction of the Sephardic Chief Rabbi. In addition to differences of language, costume, Talmudic interpretation, and basic customs there were simple worldly reasons for the Ashkenazim to hold themselves aloof from the Sephardic community. Integration into that community would have meant adoption of Turkish nationality, payment of additional taxes, and liability for military service. After 1840, with the active intervention of the European powers in the affairs of Turkey and the establishment of resident consulates in Jerusalem most Ashkenazim sought to place themselves under the protection of one or another of the European flags and to enjoy the privileges of extraterritoriality: Russia for the Lithuanian, Polish, and Russian Jews; Austria for the Galician Jews; Prussia for the German Jews; and Britain for those of indeterminate nationality.

With the support of the European consuls the community of Ashkenazic Jews emerged as the equal of their Sephardic brethren; soon they surpassed them in influence because of the greater charity funds which flowed to them from Europe. Such monopolies as the exclusive right to slaughter *Kosher* meat which the Sephardic Jews had traditionally enjoyed were wrested from them in the sixties through the active intervention of the British and Prussian consuls. The Ashkenazim regarded the Sephardim as latitudinarian and easygoing; they seemed to have imbibed something of the temper of their oriental environment. The Sephardim considered the Ashkenazic rabbis grasping and intolerant, though they bowed to them in Talmudic learning. For the most part they kept their distance from each other; the bitterest discord was left for the Ashkenazic sects warring among themselves.

In mid-nineteenth century Palestine, the two main sects of Ashkenazim from Eastern Europe, the Prushim (Pharisees), who followed the strict-constructionist, rationalist, rabbinic doctrines of the Gaon of

Vilna, and the Hasidim, the mystical enthusiasts who were devoted to the teachings of the Baal Shem Tov, continued the same conflict on the soil of the Holy Land which they had been waging for more than a century in the Jewish communities of Poland and Lithuania. There was also an offshoot of the Hasidim called *Habad,* adherents of a cabalist deviation. In Safed before the great earthquake of 1837 the Prushim had harassed the Hasidim to the point where they were forced to abandon the Holy City and limit themselves to neighboring Tiberias. Christian travellers have left accounts of the bloody battles which were waged in Galilee between these rival communities over who should perform the ceremonial of the lighting of the bonfire in honor of the saints at whose graves both factions worshipped.

The Turks did not recognize the Ashkenazim in Jerusalem as a distinct juridic community, but in imitation of the Sephardim, and despite their internal sectarian squabbles, they chose a Chief Rabbi for themselves and formed a central committee under Meyer Auerbach in 1866. Though the rabbis of the various Ashkenazic sects differed on basic questions of doctrine and ritual, the Chief Rabbi, who came from the dominant Prushim, exerted great powers.

Since almost all Jews in Palestine lived on the *Haluka* (the literal meaning of the word is apportionment), collections of Messengers of Charity who begged for donations in Jewish centers on all five continents, their economic well-being was subject to a peculiar set of variables: the munificence of the Jews in the diaspora, the intensity of the cries of grief which reached the Jews of the world from the Holy Land, the virtuosity of the Messengers in depicting the sufferings of their brothers in Palestine, and the integrity of the Messengers. The Turks knew that the Jews lived on these alms from abroad and were confident that somehow the community would find means of paying—through frantic pleas to Europe and America—both the ordinary and extraordinary exactions which were levied against them without apparent system in accordance with the whim of local officials. During one of the pilgrimages of Sir Moses Montefiore to Palestine, he was begged by the Chief Rabbi in Jerusalem not to bestow too generous a gift on the synagogue when he was called up to the Torah lest the Turks hear of it and levy heavier taxes.

In addition to the main sectarian subdivisions of the Ashkenazim based on doctrine, there was a tendency for Jews from the same geographic area in Europe or Asia to group themselves together in a separate congregation. The major Ashkenazic sects had their strongholds in specific localities of eastern and central Europe: the Prushim in Lithuania, the Hasidim in Poland, *Habad* in the Libawiz area of Russia; hence a degree of parallelism between the geographic area from which the Jews of Palestine hailed and their doctrines. But when after 1850 the Ashkenazim reached a few thousand in number they tended to subdivide into even smaller congregations each with its own roots in a few European communities. The breaking away of a new congregation was usually motivated by the belief of a fraction that if they appealed directly to their own small home town or section for donations they would fare better than they did as a subsidiary to a potent group whose chief city emigrants tended to monopolize the funds for themselves. The Central Committee of the Ashkenazim, under the Chief Rabbi, by the same token fought these attempts at further segmentation because it reduced the power and monies available to the dominant group. The centrifugal tendency was marked throughout the nineteenth century. In 1856 the Austrian traveller Frankl found only eight separate congregations. In 1875 Sir Moses Montefiore received representatives of fourteen distinct congregations of new immigrants in addition to the old Sephardic community: Morocco; Gurgistan (Georgia) ; Wilna; Samut and Curland; Haradna; Carlin; Reussen; Warsaw; Minsk; Suvalk and Lounza; Volynian; *Hod* (Holland and Germany) ; Hungary; Austria. By 1902 there were twenty-five distinct congregations, the American group being one of the last to achieve independence.

These congregations of fellow countrymen formed the basis of the *Greater Haluka,* composed of charity collections from those districts of Europe from which the Ashkenazim had originally migrated and destined exclusively for the Jews of that area who had settled in Palestine. Recipients of relief were enrolled on area lists at birth and could be removed only by order of the contributory district which usually confirmed the decisions of the Jerusalem rabbi in control of the congregation. Thus in the hands of the Jerusalem rabbi was entrusted the awful power to grant or cut off sustenance. The *Smaller Haluka* consisted of monies collected everywhere in the world by those special Messengers of Charity who roamed the earth on missions for all the Jews of Palestine. There are detailed records of their travels and experiences in eighteenth and nineteenth century American communities.

This general fund was regulated by a pact made between the Sephardim and the Ashkenazim in 1871 to avoid competition among the rival Messengers in the same world areas. After deduction of as much as forty percent for the Messengers, the total intake of the *Smaller Haluka* was then divided into twenty-eight shares in accordance with the following bizarre formula: Sephardim, 11 and $\frac{1}{6}$ shares; Prushim, 6 and $\frac{3}{4}$ shares; Hasidim, 8 and $\frac{5}{6}$ shares; *Habad,* 1 and $\frac{3}{6}$ shares. The specific apportionment of these shares was constantly revised and there were long periods of open warfare when the sects refused to abide by any agreement.

The *Haluka* was no petty charity chest. Jerusalem bankers informed Consul Willson in 1879 that the Jews of the city received from eight to ten thousand pounds sterling a month from communities throughout the world. If distributed equally this was more than half a pound a month for every Jew in Jerusalem. To explain these generous contributions Willson coined an apt phrase, calling them "vicarious pilgrimages" on the part of the Jews who did not go up to the land. "This support therefore is deemed as a right as much as the support of the military in the Western Nations, or the Ecclesiastics of the Greek and Latin Churches."

The Prushim, the most powerful Ashkenazic sect, dispersed among the four holy cities of Jerusalem, Hebron, Safed, and Tiberias, belonged to one congregation, known as Kollel Vilna because the monies gathered for them from the whole of Russia were centralized in Vilna. Their *Haluka* was drawn up in two lists: the fund of souls *(Demai Nefesh)*, distributed equally among all individuals on the list, young and old, and the priority fund *(Demai Kadima)*, divided only among the worthies who had influence with the rabbis either in Vilna or Jerusalem. The transfer of the funds from Vilna to Jerusalem was a complicated transaction. Every year a Messenger was despatched from Vilna to Constantinople where he was met by a Messenger from Jerusalem, who turned over to the Vilna representative a corrected list—with new births and deaths entered—of those entitled to a portion of the *Haluka*. The Russian money was then exchanged into gold and brought to the Jerusalem comptrollers who distributed it through agents to the Jews of the four holy cities. Since Vilna was the center, control of the Prushim fund was firmly in the grip of the Lithuanian Jews, and the Polish Jews who were Prushim had reason to complain about their shares and to secede and form a separate congregation.

Ashkenazic Jews in the sixties and the seventies thus could fight among themselves on a geographic alignment—Polish versus Lithuanian Jews—or a sectarian alignment—Hasidim versus Prushim—or on a mere personal alignment, taking sides in partisan quarrels of rival rabbis over questions of precedence and dignity. The pious Jews of Jerusalem were no more spiritual in their warfare than the Catholic, Armenian, and Greek Orthodox clergy in their squabbles over who had the right to sweep the bottom step of the Church of the Holy Sepulchre. When conflict grew hot they dealt one another heavy, even mortal, blows. This was a turbulent, violent community.

In the sixties the Ashkenazic rabbis still on occasion administered corporal punishment to miscreants, including women, using the lash in accordance with Talmudic law, and they had erected a form of stocks where the guilty were vigorously pelted by the whole congregation. Every man was responsible for his neighbor; spying on evil-doers was encouraged; the literal letter of Talmudic law was enforced, often with cruelty.

The whole settlement was under absolute sacerdotal control and the rabbis administered justice within the body with an iron hand, their dreaded power of excommunication being no mean threat in this closed community. Evil tongues bore tales; letters were despatched to the comptrollers of the *Haluka* in Europe by rival groups, and the good repute and livelihood of the pious was destroyed by false rumor. In many respects this Jewish community resembled the early Puritan settlements in New England; though there was one vital difference— the Calvinist doctrine of work was alien to them. The Ashkenazic Jews of Jerusalem did not labor, which left them ample time for their devotions and their backbiting.

Before the great earthquake in Safed in 1837 there had been a sizable printing-press in that city where volumes of the Talmud were published; and there are accounts of a few Jewish farmers in Galilee; but workers among the Ashkenazic Jews of mid-nineteenth century Palestine were a small minority. The refusal of the Ashkenazic Jews to engage in productive labor engendered a great controversy when Montagu and Asher, a visiting committee of English Jews in 1875, wrote a derogatory report on the general slothfulness of the Jerusalem community. The head of the Ashkenazic rabbis returned with a counter-attack in an open letter addressed to Sir Moses Montefiore in which he denied the charge that they refused to labor when there was work, though he stalwartly maintained that prayer and study, not labor, was the prime purpose of their living in the Holy Land. The plans of Sir Moses Montefiore for agricultural settlements were not received with enthusiasm by either the Jews or the Turks. Neither were the settlement projects of the Englishman Laurence Oliphant, who, in terms almost identical with Theodor Herzl's politics, sought to associate the economic development of Turkey with the establishment of agricultural colonies for Jewish immigrants.

The tenor of Acting Consul Lorenzo Johnson's first general description of the Jews of Jerusalem sent to the State Department in 1868 is in the spirit of most Palestine travel literature of the period. They lived in idleness, he wrote, sustained by contributions from Europe and America. The learned among them studied only the Talmud. He knew of a number of proposals to connect the charity sent them with some industrial enterprise which would involve labor on the part of the recipients, but the rabbis were generally opposed to these plans, "preferring to enjoy the heavy percentage which accrues to them in the distribution of the money, to having it diverted to other channels." When two American Jews visited Jerusalem with considerable sums for distribution, the consul suggested that they sponsor the settlement of young Jews on lands adjoining the city in preference to the crowded and unhealthy quarters where they lived. The Americans approved of the plan and actually appointed a committee consisting of the Acting Consul Johnson, a banker, and a physician, to direct the distribution of any future funds sent from America with a view to extending the living area of the Jewish settlement. The rabbis who controlled the community through the distribution of charity funds were not partial to the project and nothing was heard about it subsequently.

In 1878, Consul Willson in his observations on the Jewish community, judged the Sephardim to be the most wealthy and the most numerous sect, occupying a higher social position than the Ashkenazim, though the Sephardim too had two hundred recognized relief families. His summary description of the whole community was similar to his predecessor's written a decade earlier—". . . poor, idle and apparently feeble physically as well as mentally. Jerusalem seems to be the rendezvous of a certain class of Jews, the *pious,* not to say the fanatical, the infirm, the unfortunate, the aged, in a word the disappointed, who come to Jerusalem to live on alms, and for prayers, spending their melancholy hours at the Wailing-Place and waiting for the coming of the expected Messiah."

THE AMERICAN CONSUL AND THE OLD SETTLEMENT

The American consuls initially were not particularly interested in the structure and internal squabbles of the old Jewish community in Jerusalem, no more than they were in the Greek Orthodox or Roman Catholic establishments and their battles over the guardianship of the Holy Places. Hence their descriptions of Jewish manners in the early decades after the opening of the consulate tend to be those of outsiders who are reporting merely what first strikes the eye. But under the system of capitulations it was the function of the American consul to administer justice to American Jews, and thus the consular court in the conduct of ordinary business was forced to bring within its purview the whole Jewish community. The relations of American Jews with all other members of the Jewish community among whom they lived intermingled of necessity put the consul's law court into contact with Jews from every nation in the world. From about 1890 on, the portion of total donations for indigent Jews in the Holy Cities of Palestine which derived from the United States became ever greater and the consul was drawn into controversies involving the distribution of these charities in fulfillment of the expressed will of the donors. Since the old settlement was a pauperized community, the fights among the recipients of relief over their just share were at the heart of their struggle for existence. The endless disputes over the division of the charities among the various rabbis and the sects and geographic areas they represented occupied their existence in between stated hours of prayer. Those without influence or favor with the head rabbis were beggars, subject to the humiliations of beggars. The internecine disputes among old residents of Jerusalem, with long standing on the relief rolls, and new immigrants who claimed a position of equality were bitter. And since American Jews and American charity were involved the consul had to settle cases which would have tried a Solomon.

The administration of *ad hoc* American justice in an ancient community swarming with pious rabbis who had spent their lives in the study of the refinements of Talmudic jurisprudence was not an easy task. Often enough the consul found that cases referred to him were rebounds, lawsuits where the rabbis had tried to effect a settlement among the rival claimants in accordance with Talmudic law and had failed to get acquiescence in their decision. The Jews of Jerusalem were no doubt a litigious group, a condition not surprising among people living in crowded quarters, hailing from all parts of the globe, and versed in a sophisticated legal system with a series of precedents that ran back more than two thousand years. American consuls often recoiled with dismay before their job; a few, blessed with an extraordinary judicial temper, took their work seriously and wrestled heroically with its details; hardly any of the consuls succeeded in pleasing all of the sects and cliques into which the old community tended to divide and subdivide itself. There was no formal procedure for appeal from the consul's decision and though there may have been theoretical resort to the United States, the whole field of consular justice was a legal limbo. Dissatisfaction with the practices of an American consul usually took the form of a protest from Jerusalem rabbis transmitted to American rabbis who appeared before the State Department which in turn questioned the consul. In most instances the Department was markedly less interested in the merits of a case than in the fact that the consul had provoked criticism.

Since the "new settlement," the Jewish agricultural colonies founded after 1881, had early developed arbitration boards of their own and the number of American Jews among them was insignificant, the consul's view of the Jewish community hardly ever extended beyond the old settlement prior to the outbreak of the First World War. Moreover, he dealt primarily with the Ashkenazim in the old settlement, who were the overwhelming number of immigrants from Eastern Europe and from the United States. Consular references to the Sephardim, whose Chief Rabbi was a recognized Turkish official and who were an integral part of the Turkish administrative system, were rare.

The limited vision of the consuls afforded them no insight into the mystical practices of the Jews of Safed and Tiberias at the graves of Rabbi Meir Baal Ha-Ness and Rabbi Simon Ben Yohai, the mourning at the Cave of Machpela in Hebron, or the wailing at the remnant of the Ancient Wall in Jerusalem. A number of the consuls dismissed the orthodox Jews as "fanatical." What there was in the religious life of the old settlement of authentic mystical experience, as distinct from the venality of some Messengers of Charity, distributors of alms, and the petty felons who were their hangers-on, rarely came into the consul's ken.

Since a substantial number of the immigrants were elderly and ailing the community had many aspects of an asylum, and this was all the consul saw. The old settlement appeared a miserable refuge in which dying men spent their days in prayer, supported by the Jewries of the world. In their midst lived a number of younger people who had been dragged along with the aged, and a few men of enterprise who had chanced upon Palestine as Jews might wander anywhere in the world.

CAUSES CÉLÈBRES, 1868–1876

In 1868 the American consulate became embroiled with the whole Jewish community over an issue which laid bare the underlying forces at play in the old settlement. Through the Sarah Steinberg case, which achieved world-wide notoriety, the problems of the jurisdiction of the consular court of the United States, relations with other consulates and with the Turkish governor became entwined in the war of the rabbis in defense of the faith against the Christianizing efforts of the English missionaries.

For some extraordinary reason the London Society for the Promoting of Christianity Amongst the Jews chose this orthodox community of praying Jews in which to expend a very substantial portion of its budget. Their hospitals were among the best in Jerusalem and their techniques of conversion were not too blatant, as they fed their patients *kosher* food and nailed *mezuzas* on the doorposts. A religious tract left by the bedside of the sick man was their only wedge into his soul. The rabbis of Jerusalem fought their activities with all the weapons at their command, spiritual and temporal. They excommunicated patients, threatened to deny them burial, and when such methods proved ineffective, they had visitors to the outpatient department beaten up and their medicine bottles broken. Each apostate Jew cost the London Society a considerable sum of money and conversion was so profitable to those who submitted to its patent spiritual risks that there were frequent lapses from grace, each requiring a new baptism and new funds. Since the London Society was under the protection of the British consul, he was usually in the unhappy middle between the rabbis and the missionaries and was accused of furthering their proselytizing. But in 1868 Victor Beauboucher, the new American consul, thrust himself into a controversy which his more experienced British colleague would have shunned. Perhaps the case itself would have attracted less attention if it had not become identified in Jewish eyes with the Mortara Affair of 1858 in Rome—that sordid story of a child's baptism while ill by a Christian nurse and the subsequent struggle with the Inquisition for its possession.

Before the Sarah Steinberg incident Consul Victor Beauboucher had enjoyed great favor among the Jews of Jerusalem. He employed a Jewish merchant and banker as his consular agent in Jaffa and he supported him vigorously against all the charges of peculation which G. W. Joshua Adams, leader of the "Jaffa colonists," a strange New England messianic sect with a tragic history, levelled against him. Perhaps less to the taste of the rabbis, he got an apostate Jew, Benjamin Finkelstein, the son of a Galician immigrant of 1846, appointed deputy consul even though he was an Austrian subject, and he wrote the Department in terms of high praise about Finkelstein's linguistic accomplishments.

Beauboucher was the first American consul in Jerusalem to initiate a system of non-citizen *protégés*, similar to the practice of the European consulates, of which the Jews were the prime benefactors; and for this grace the Ashkenazic rabbis showered their thanks upon him. But Beauboucher was not a calm man and he suffered from an improper amputation after a wound received in battle for the Union cause. Unwittingly, he got himself passionately involved, then carried away, in a dispute whose implications he hardly understood.

Two Jewish orphans, Sarah Steinberg, aged thirteen and a half, and her brother, aged twenty, had entered the Rothschild Hospital together. The brother, who had served as Sarah's guardian, died there. Their sister Deborah, who had been converted to Protestantism by the Jerusalem missionaries ten years before and was married to a Pole named Golupsoff, also an apostate Jew, was under the protection of the American Consulate. Sarah Steinberg and her brother appear to have been under the protection of the Prussian Consulate. Upon the death of Sarah's brother, the problem of her custody developed into a contest between her sister, who claimed family rights, and Arie Marcus, Rabbi of the Grand Synagogue of Jerusalem, a Prussian *protégé*, who claimed the right of the community to protect a Jewish minor from being abandoned into the hands of an apostate sister and condemned to baptism and eternal torments in the next world. Rabbi Marcus got to the Rothschild Hospital first, took Sarah Steinberg away, and hid her—"abducted her," was the later consular charge.

The Prussian consul Weber at Beirut was represented in Jerusalem by an acting consul who was the dragoman Daoud El Kardi, a timid man who had no desire to incur the enmity of the Jewish community by an untimely intervention. Deborah Golupsoff appealed to Beauboucher as her consular protector to help her obtain custody of her sister because she feared that the rabbis, in their anxiety to keep Sarah in the Jewish faith, would marry her off to a Jew even though she was still a child. Beauboucher was touched by what he considered the merits of the case and he called upon the Prussian acting consul to arrest his *protégé* Rabbi Marcus. The dragoman had been in the land long enough to realize that one did not proceed that precipitously against the Rabbi of the Grand Synagogue and he excused himself. Beauboucher, undaunted, led his cavasses with their scimitars into the Jewish quarter on a Friday afternoon to seize Sarah Steinberg in Rabbi Marcus's house. They came upon the rabbi preparing for the Sabbath, conducted a search, found nothing, and then summoned the rabbi to surrender the girl. When the rabbi refused, claiming that he was a Prussian subject, Beauboucher ordered him to proceed to the Pasha's Palace. Beauboucher's cavasses had to use force and a scuffle took place in which twenty Jews tried to protect their rabbi. Beauboucher later admitted that the cavasses had struck with the flat of their scimitars, but maintained that nobody was even scratched. Rabbi Marcus said that he was brought to the Palace half-dead. The Pasha had tried to avoid involvement, especially since it was Ramadan, but Beauboucher was on the march. The Prussian dragoman was summoned to the Palace, and to fill out the assemblage, the Spanish and the Austrian consuls appeared. Beauboucher took the formal position that he had not arrested Rabbi Marcus, only summoned him, since a Prussian *protégé* was outside of his jurisdiction. The discussion on the merits of the case dragged on aimlessly, and the rabbi was allowed to depart adhering to his original stand. When the dragoman would not arrest the rabbi, Beauboucher telegraphed the Prussian consul in Beirut demanding Marcus's imprisonment. Consul Weber acceded to his colleague's wishes and, acting under official orders, the Prussian dragoman at Jerusalem confined him.

Beauboucher thought he was performing an act of humanity in the face of one of the most fanatical men in Jerusalem,—"which is saying something," he reported. Rabbi Marcus considered himself a martyr suffering to save a Jewish soul in Israel from the clutches of the apostates and the missionaries, who had a special society with a large fund devoted exclusively to trying the faith of the small Jewish community. The Jews of Jerusalem saw their rabbi beaten and insulted like a common criminal while he was performing an act of devotion. Overnight telegrams poured forth from the rabbis of Jerusalem to Jews throughout the world. Rabbi Isaacs of New York addressed an inquiry to the State Department in the name of the Board of Delegates of the American Israelites. In the Prussian Diet the Government was interrogated as to why the American consul had been allowed to arrest a Prussian subject. Ultimately in the process of transmission and printing in newspapers, the story got garbled to the point where the unfortunate Beauboucher was accused of trying not only to convert Sarah Steinberg, but to elope with her.

Consul Beauboucher had to answer scores of official inquiries about the case. While he was *en route* to Constantinople to pursue in higher quarters a different quarrel with the Pasha of Jerusalem over the rights of travellers, his amputated leg became inflamed. When he learned of the more extravagant charges against him the sick consul was beside himself with anger. The Prussian consul Weber whom Beauboucher had dragged into the imbroglio explained to his Government that the American consul was an excitable invalid who had been provoked by tumultuous Jews. In the meantime, according to Beauboucher, the Jewish community paid Sarah's dowry to an Alexandrian Jew and married her off though she was still a child. This denouement, as described in the consular reports, was contradicted by Dr. London of the Rothschild Hospital in a letter to *Ha-Magid*, the Hebrew weekly published in Lyck, Poland. The case had become an international scandal. "I have come to fulfill my promise of the preceding letter to inform you about the incident of the Jewish girl and the American Consul and the confederates of the English Missionary Society. I have found it especially necessary to announce truthful things on the conclusion of this affair after I saw that anonymous people were publicly telling lies and falsehoods about it.

"Last month yet there came to us the wise gentleman, humanitarian, and man pure of heart who was known before by his brilliant writings, Professor Dr. Petermann of Berlin who is now appointed to rule over the affairs of the consulate of the North German Confederation. As soon as he came and the great outrage was known to him he hurried and freed Rabbi Marcus from his confinement and in public he said that the work of the girl's sister and the missionary her confederate was evil in his eyes. The girl he delivered, according to her desire, to one of our brethren of Israel, the head of a worthy family in the Holy City.

"And since the unfortunate girl has no other means of support but the bread of sadness of the *General Haluka* and since despite all the big talk that we heard about this case in Jerusalem not one of all our brethren the sons of Israel, even from among those whom God has granted the means, became aroused to pity this unfortunate girl, to clothe and shoe her, and to send her to school to learn what is necessary, therefore the above-mentioned Consul Professor Petermann bestirred himself and wrote a letter to the uncle of the girl who is living in Alexandria, Egypt, and he asked him that he should take pity on the girl and should bring her to his house to be his daughter (adopt her) and it is not yet known how the matter will come out. The consul also promised to turn, in the name of his government, to the American government with a cry of outrage on the doings of her consul in the affair of this girl and to demand satisfaction for the evil deed of the consul and his fitting punishment."

Victor Beauboucher presented his side of the case in an indignant despatch to Secretary of State Seward, November 25, 1868. Insisting that only humane motives and the earnest solicitations of the child's sister had prompted him to intervene in the case, Beauboucher declared that he had never arrested Rabbi Marcus, only brought him before the local authority; that the Rabbi's imprisonment on January 12, 1868, was the act of the Prussian consulate retaliating for Marcus's failure to turn over the child to the consulate as he had promised; and that all interest by the American consulate had ceased with the active entry into the case of the Prussian officials. Beauboucher noted that as a consequence of his abandoning the matter, after his departure from Jerusalem Sarah, a "victim of fanaticism," was married off to a "miserable person of Alexandria who received a few hundred piastres to complete the abomination." Beauboucher closed his letter with an outburst in which were commingled his resentment at the preposterous accusations levelled against him, and a determination to prove his innocence by continuing benevolence towards the Jews in his charge. "Catholic by religion, I am accused of wishing to convert a Jewish child by giving her to her Protestant Sister! My previous actions for which testimonies of profound gratitude etc. were lavished upon me by all the Jewish Committees of the Holy Land, Marcus himself, and well-known by the committees of New York, should have exempted me from imputations of fanaticism.

"It is by continuing to treat with the greatest benevolence such Jews as may need my assistance, that I shall demonstrate the puerility of this Jewish assertion, in respect to this matter.

"Newspapers of their society pretended that I had eloped with Sarah and left Jerusalem with her!

"I read these stories while ill and surrounded by my wife and child. At the same time Marcus and Co. justified the fears of Sarah's afflicted sister by sacrificing the former to one of their non scrupulous co-religionists."

Beauboucher had begged to be transferred for his health and the Consul-General at Beirut was glad to approve the request. Only one American Jew in Jerusalem, Mendel Goldstein, stood loyally by Beauboucher to the end and wrote him a testimonial in which he acidly commented that the 10,000 piastres which the telegrams of Chief Rabbi Auerbach and Rabbi Marcus had cost did not come out of their own pockets but out of the *Haluka,* the charity fund gathered for the poor of Jerusalem.

In the meantime a Rabbi Sneersohn of Jerusalem, dressed in flowing oriental robes appeared in the United States to lecture, to collect funds for Jerusalem charities, and to attack Consul Beauboucher. Sneersohn had a triumph, despite the fact (carefully noted by Beauboucher in despatches) that some Jews in Jerusalem accused him of keeping most of the funds of his previous Australian expedition. When Beauboucher was replaced, Sneersohn praised the Lord and President Grant, though he believed that his own efforts were in their small way also instrumental.

When Frank de Haas of New York City arrived in Jerusalem on December 16, 1873, to enter upon his consular functions as Beauboucher's successor, he found a middle-aged Jewish woman, the wife of Saul Benjamin Cohen, in the consular jail and he was immediately set in the midst of a quarrel between two Jewish factions which he likened to the Tweed trial in New York. The Acting Consul, Hardegg, had condemned Cohen to six months in prison, but he had been let out a few days previously, while his wife was detained until de Haas liberated her. It was a story of the *Haluka,* American charity, and Turkish justice. Cohen, originally an Ottoman subject, had been sent from Jerusalem as a Messenger of Charity to America. While on his mission he got himself naturalized and upon his return to Jerusalem he deposited his passport with the United States consulate. Reports went out in the Jewish community that he had returned with thirty thousand dollars which he had tried to avoid turning in to the charity fund by purchasing land in his wife's name. The rabbis who directed the *Haluka* formally ordered the Messenger to hand over the funds which he had collected and appealed to the American consulate for aid. While answering a summons to the consulate, Samuel Benjamin Cohen got into a fight with the cavass and he was sentenced to prison for his contumely by Acting Consul Hardegg. The consul could confine Cohen for striking the cavass but could not recover the embezzled funds tied up in lands because that involved civil law and the Turkish courts. Local Turkish judges had their palms greased with three thousand dollars, it was said, and it ultimately required a vizierial order from the Sublime Porte in Constantinople to get the property of the false Messenger of Charity transferred to the Jewish community.

In the years 1874 through 1876 the same Rabbi Sneersohn who while on tour in America had impressed President Grant at a public audience, became himself the subject of protracted, inconclusive diplomatic negotiations among most of the foreign missions in Turkey, following a murderous assault he suffered at the hands of the Jews of Tiberias. Sneersohn, like many other Messengers of Charity, had become a naturalized American citizen during his trip to the United States and the letters of recommendation he had diligently accumulated in America from prominent citizens impressed Minister Maynard enough to demand redress on his behalf in a *note verbale* to the Ministry of Foreign Affairs on January 25, 1876. The assault was obviously not a common felony but a violent Jewish communal punishment whose exact nature nobody inquired into, the Minister treating the affair as a simple criminal case. The bare narrative of the incident in the *note verbale* reveals the violent temper of this old settlement. "On the 28th of November 1874, the said Rabbi Sneersohn was set upon by certain Jews at Tiberias and robbed of a considerable amount and most shamefully maltreated by being imprisoned, stoned, stripped naked and in this condition ridden through the streets of Tiberias, insomuch that he barely escaped with his life to Jerusalem, where he was confined in hospital by reason of his said treatment about two months.

"After his recovery he applied for redress to the United States Consul at Beirut, who went in person to Tiberias and laid the matter before the Caimacam and Medjiliss. They took jurisdiction of the case and proceeded to have the offenders arrested. This was on the 27th of May 1875. One of the chief men arrested pretended to be under British protection and asked permission to go to his house for papers to establish his claim. This was granted him and he availed himself of the opportunity to mount a horse and escape.

"The friends of the arrested parties men and women assembled to the number of several hundred, overawed the Caimacam and Medjiliss, broke open the prison and released the prisoners. The Caimacam not having sufficient force to rearrest the parties the matter has remained until this time without further action. The injured party recovered his passport and naturalization papers but not the money of which he was robbed; nor have the offenders been punished; most of whom, and it is believed all, are unquestionably Ottoman subjects."

As described in the more detailed report of the Beirut consul, this is a wild tale of Sneersohn's appearance in Tiberias with gold napoleons, his attempt to advertise the loan of petty sums of money on heavy security, his fancy talk about proposing to found a new colony in Tiberias, and the cruel physical torture of the man at the hands of a mob outraged by his defiance of the mores of the community. The few Turkish officials in Tiberias were incapable of maintaining order since every participant in the riots had some vague claim to the protection of a foreign consul and every consular authority tried to wash his hands of the affair—all except the American consul at Beirut, who plunged in to defend his citizen. "Whether the Turkish authorities shall rule at Tiberias or the turbulent and lawless Jews . . . is not certain," Consul George S. Fisher at Beirut wrote the State Department, and he kept pursuing the case through a maze of negotiations with a score of European consular officials and Turkish authorities. The fantastic depositions of Sneersohn leave the definitive impression that he was something of a swindler; the descriptions of the violence he suffered bear out other testimony that the zealous piety of the settlers in the Holy City of Tiberias was often besmirched with avarice and an almost clinical sadism.

In September 1874, Jacob Schumacher, the United States consular agent at Haifa, had informed his superior at Beirut that Rabbi H. Z. Sneersohn, a citizen of the United States, intended to form a Jewish colony at Tiberias and had asked whether he could not serve as consular agent in that city. Sneersohn had had a book printed describing his colonization project and Schumacher, who was head of the Temple colony at Haifa, gave Sneersohn his support "since the undertaking was a noble one" and it was agreeable to him to have an agency established there. After the assault, Schumacher rued his early recommendation. He believed that the tumult had been brought on by Sneersohn himself. ". . . The establishing alone of the pawn institution, which you will notice in the report, would naturally cause a great deal of anger and brought him already at that time into conflict with the local authorities, which caused dislike, and among his fellow believers hate, and from that time, it seems to me, partly through imprudent words and behaviour matters were brought to a point the results of which of course were of a sad nature.

"That Sneersohn was beaten and robbed I believe, but that he was really robbed of such a sum of money, is a question with me as I could up to the present not gain the conviction that he possessed it, but of course it may be possible, that he did own such a sum.

"Sneersohn undoubtedly at times suffers from a disturbed mind, is easily excited and of a very nervous nature, it is undoubtedly a fact, that if difficulties once break out among fellow believers, especially among Jews, both parties run into extremes and this I believe to be the case with Sneersohn and the Jews of Tiberias, as it is a sad fact that most of them are an ignorant and degraded lot of people.

"Unless there is a commission appointed of the different Consulates under whose protection the Jews of Tiberias are, and make a thorough investigation I do not believe that the case can be settled."

Schumacher proved to be eminently correct.

THE FIRST AMERICAN CONGREGATION

On March 15, 1879, Consul Willson in Jerusalem reported the first organization of American Jews into a separate community with a synagogue of their own. The tendency of the various Ashkenazic Jews to band themselves into small synagogues based upon their country or district of origin before they had come up to the land was a normal one and it created individualistic groups who nevertheless all recognized the Chief Rabbi of the Ashkenazim. As with some of the other congregations, the secession of the American Jews had further implications beyond the mere gathering together of Jews into a separate synagogue. The Americans were determined to place themselves in direct communication with American Jews and to break away from the common fund of the Central Committee because they were convinced that their poor had been discriminated against in the apportionment and even excluded entirely from the *Haluka* despite the fact that a substantial part of the funds derived from America. The

United States consul had been told a story that an old Jew from New York had been ruled off the *Haluka* list because he had been absent from Germany for more than ten years and was thus disqualified as a recipient. There was no separate American list and the German congregation would no longer recognize him as one of theirs. If the Americans had a separate fund of their own they could take care of their poor. The American Jews proceeded to frame a constitution with by-laws, appoint a committee, acquire a seal and secure the approval of the consul. They adopted the name Community of Peace, the consul reported. The Committee whom they chose to represent them consisted of what the consul called the "better class of American Jew," a rabbi, a prosperous jeweller, a man living on his income. He was therefore pleased to transmit through the State Department their mournful plea in Hebrew for generous contributions addressed to Jews in the United States.

This first attempt of the American Jews in Jerusalem to form an autonomous unit within the greater body of the Ashkenazim and to break away from the central administration of the *Haluka* soon petered out, and was not renewed for almost two decades. Their number was too small in 1879 to stand up to the Chief Rabbi, who was reluctant to lose American contributions to the general fund.

THE DE HAAS PROTÉGES

Since European consuls in Turkey had traditionally accepted Jews and Christians as *protégés* even though they were not their nationals, the practice spread to the American consulates. In the early fifties many refugees from the nationalist and communist uprisings of 1848 fled to Turkey where they took advantage of the ancient practice under which envoys of European powers received "Franks" under protection, irrespective of nationality, if they had no other guardians of their interests. Many passports were issued in Rome to the Italian refugees by the American embassy there and in due time these papers came to be peddled about Europe. Minister Marsh in Constantinople was hesitant to assume responsibility for the refugees as bona fide American citizens but since it was contrary to tradition to abandon them he bestowed upon them a measure of protection even though he could not always vouch for their character.

One early American consul in Jerusalem, W. R. Page, resigned in 1861 over the promiscuous issuance of letters of protection in Con-

stantinople to what he called "hordes of spurious Americans." Consul
Victor Beauboucher had nevertheless approved of about a dozen
protégés who were not really naturalized citizens, until the turmoil
created by the Sarah Steinberg case confirmed the State Department
in its formal and absolute objection to receiving any aliens in Turkey
under its protection, and existing documents of protection which had
been issued under loose instructions were voided.

The duties of the American consul in Jerusalem were in the future
to cover only the full-fledged American citizens within his jurisdiction;
in January 1868 these comprised three Jewish families, three individual Jews, and a few remnants of the "Jaffa colonists" from New
England. In his instructions to the Minister in Constantinople on
August 21, 1868, Secretary of State Seward was most explicit in a
general policy statement limiting American protection to American
citizens. For naturalized citizens, he posited even further cautions. "In
case of naturalization the proceeding must not consist merely in a
preliminary declaration of intention, but must show a judicial process
fully complete and before the proper courts. . . . When the person
who demands protection claims it upon the ground simply that he is
a child of a person who has been naturalized in the United States,
you will look into the circumstances and see whether the claimant
has, by relinquishing his residence in the United States or by returning to Turkey or any other foreign country, practically waived his
legally acquired but provisional title as an American citizen."

In practice these stringent rules were not lived up to during the
period prior to the wave of immigration into Palestine in the eighties.
There were in Jerusalem only a handful of American Jews, among
them the family of Benjamin Lilienthal, a naturalized American citizen, and he and his children, many of them born in Palestine, were
annually recorded on the books of the consul and received his protection. No special inquiries were conducted into the intent of residence of the American Jews and even an apparently fraudulent
passport was overlooked.

State Department rulings have often enough been contradicted by
chance remarks of the President and violated by officials in action at
distant posts. At one of President Grant's public receptions in 1869,
Rabbi Sneersohn, the Messenger of Charity from Jerusalem, had made
a profound impression upon the gathering with his formal blessing
of the President, his description of the sufferings of the Jews of
Jerusalem, and his plea for protection. Even the office-seekers who

were crowding around Grant seem to have been moved and the President promised favorable consideration of the rabbi's request. By time an account of this "reception" got into *Ha-Magid,* reported in the flowery Hebrew style of the period, Sneersohn's interview with the President assumed an official character; to the sanguine Jews, living on exaggeration of each rumor from abroad, it seemed to portend a new role for America as protector of all the Jews of Jerusalem.

In July 1870, a formal plea was sent to the President through the Jerusalem consulate by the five heads of synagogues and the Chief Rabbi of the European Jews in Jerusalem, begging consular aid for those Jews who had no other protectors. The European Jews pointed out in their memorial that most of the eight or nine thousand Jews in Jerusalem were Russian Jews whose status had in recent months undergone a marked deterioration. During the Crimean War, when Russia became an enemy state, the British consul had accepted them as his charges. Immediately after the War, Russia refused to recognize any longer as its subjects Russian Jews who had stayed in Jerusalem for more than a period of five years without returning home. Since the primary drive of the migration of the orthodox Jews was enjoyment of the transcendent spiritual benefits of dying in the Holy Land, they had no intention of returning to Russia merely for a renewal of their passports, a long and arduous journey impossible for old men and women eking out their existence on charity. This decree of the Russian Government had left them without consular protection. Rabbi Hirsch Berliner, the Deputy of the British-protected Jews in Jerusalem, then interceded before Earl Russell on behalf of the Russian Jews and he was told that if upon the expiration of the five-year period they obtained a letter of release from the Russian Consulate, they would be accepted by the British. This promise had served the Jews well until 1870, when the Russian Consulate again changed its practice. While continuing to issue the certificate of release it refused to include a vital clause allowing them to go to the British consul for protection. Because of this alteration of the formula the British consul, in obedience to the rule as he understood it, saw fit to reject them, and each year a growing number of Jews were in danger of being abandoned to the caprices of Turkish justice. The rabbis therefore respectfully requested that the American consul be allowed "to receive under the protection of the United States such Jews as the Presidents and Representatives of the various Congregations shall recommend as honest and worthy persons, and who will never cause the Consul or Government any unnecessary trouble." American Consul Beardsley, in a despatch of August 5, 1870, approved the petition. While cognizant of the disfavor in which the State Department held the whole system of *protégés,* he believed, for charity's sake, that an exception should be made in this instance. An annotation on his despatch indicates that the Department did not agree with him.

During the early seventies there were only twelve or thirteen American Jewish citizens registered with the American consulate after the system of *protégés* as practiced by Beauboucher had been abandoned; by December 31, 1876, there were twenty-eight. But in 1875 a new wave of migration from Russia, estimated at 2000 in a year by Vice-consul Hardegg, poured into the land. This new immigration, which led him to write of the prospect of Palestine being repeopled at no distant period by the posterity of Abraham, brought to the American consulate a tumultuous problem. When the Russo-Turkish War of 1877 broke out, these new Jewish immigrants from Russia were left without any European consular protection and they frantically appealed to the new American consul, Frank de Haas to become his *protégés.* It had been published in the synagogues that all Jews without consular protection would be considered Turkish subjects and might be called up to military service. Many of the younger of the new immigrants had fled Russia to escape a service which was odious to them and here in the Holy Land they were suddenly confronted with the terrible fate of serving with the Turk. In a panic, rabbis and their parishioners, men and women, fled to the consulate, weeping and pleading for protection. Though de Haas knew of the Department's prohibitions against the system of *protégés* he felt that the emergency justified accepting about a hundred of them conditionally. "Some of them have resided in America, others were born there, but have no papers of citizenship, and nearly all are relatives in some way with the Jewish citizens connected with this consulate." The consul was moved, and there was no doubt some exaggeration in his statement of the facts. Other consulates had apparently taken on a share of the new immigrants. De Haas made it clear that he had promised protection only for the duration of the disturbed state of affairs and he hoped that the Department would approve his action "as the course we have pursued is in full accord with the genius of our Republican Institutions, and as this remnant of a once mighty nation are without any King, Government or Consul to protect them. . . . " For his generous action the heads of the Ashkenazic community praised de Haas in biblical terms in a petition in Hebrew and English which they sent to President Hayes.

The State Department had inadvertently led the Minister, Horace Maynard, into error about its policy of protecting Jews in Turkey during the war crisis. They had sent Maynard a copy of correspondence with the President of the Board of Delegates of American Israelites on the condition of the Jews in the theatre of war, particularly Roumania, and had directed him to secure the Jews in the Provinces a measure of protection in view of the peculiar exigencies of the situation. De Haas's interpretation of this policy in Palestine had involved granting actual letters of protection. Of this formal action the Department vigorously disapproved. Maynard therefore altered his orders to the consuls in the spirit of the State Department's more restricted view of protection. "In conformity with these directions you will instruct the consular officers of your jurisdiction to observe carefully the condition of the Hebrews within their consular districts and any instances of persecution or other maltreatment, to report without delay to the Legation, calling the attention to them unofficially, of the Governors or other Ottoman authorities. At the same time they will not take them under the charge of their consulates, or extend to them the protection due only to American citizens."

Through later instructions Secretary of State Evarts elaborated on his interpretation of American policy on the protection of Russians in Turkey during the war. "As a rule you will extend the protection of the U.S. only to persons who are native born or naturalized citizens.

"This rule is in accordance with long established policy of the government, and can only be departed from in exceptional cases when the representatives of the country to which the persons requiring protection owe allegiance request it, and the authorities of the country in which they are living consent to it. In such cases if no harm will result from the delay, the matter will be reported to the Department for instructions before action is taken, but where prompt action is required the representative is authorized to extend the desired protection, reporting the matter at once to the Department for its consideration."

Minister Maynard made it clear to the Department that he had instructed consuls to report instances of persecution and to make unofficial representations to local authorities, but not to protect Israelites as United States citizens.

A cipher telegram from the State Department had affirmed that de Haas's action was contrary to departmental policy unless there were "exceptional cases." But this had been precisely de Haas's definition of his *protégés,* according to his lights: in view of the fact that many of these Jews had lived in America and some had "served in the armed forces," they were exceptions.

The Department took a radically different view of the *protégés.* De Haas fell off a horse, was sent home, and in his stead came Consul John G. Willson to face the manifold implications of this new protection policy. At his very first interview the Pasha of Jerusalem questioned the new practice which had transferred a substantial number of Turkish citizens to American protection. The Turks had no desire to broaden the extraterritorial jurisdiction of the foreigners. The American consul was equally at odds with the Prussian consul, who claimed that before his departure the Russian consul had turned over his subjects to Prussian protection. Since neither passports nor approved and formal letters of protection had actually been issued to the Jews, they created a dilemma for the consul. The Jews inquired as to whether they were getting the protection as promised; if not, they wanted their money back, for they had apparently paid a registration fee. The only existing record of the whole transaction consisted of two lists drawn up by the Dragoman Joseph Gabriel, the first including 167 names of those who were supposed to have paid one napoleon; the second a list of 194 names of those who had paid half a napoleon. General rumor had it that the actual number of receipts issued reached 500.

As Consul Willson inquired into further details he learned that the papers of protection had been sold at various prices, "the matter arranged . . . by a ring of speculating Jews," and that many of the documents had been signed in blank by de Haas and later filled in by the dragoman. The practice had been generally condemned by the other consuls but Willson found extenuating circumstances for his predecessor in the atmosphere of panic which prevailed at the time of their issuance and the wild rumors that the Bedouins were marching on Jerusalem. Yet all these excuses did not solve his problem of what actually to do with the *protégés.* While Willson stalled off the Pasha, who had continued reluctantly to respect the letters of protection and had not hailed any of the *protégés* into a Turkish court, the Department was mute and sent him no instructions.

Ex-Consul de Haas wrote the State Department from New York on January 3, 1878, that he had felt justified in extending protection to the Russian Jews in the light of instructions from the Minister in Constantinople that the Jerusalem consul was "to observe carefully the conditions of the Hebrews . . . and report without delay any instance of persecution or maltreatment." De Haas, who was not a career man in the State Department, does not seem to have recognized the chasm between a reportorial function and a sweeping act which involved issuing unofficial letters of protection to hundreds of Jews. The money which the Jews paid de Haas for this protection had remained in his personal possession along with a copy of a receipt he had given Rabbi Mayer Meizel for ninety-six and a half napoleons, the fee for 193 "Russian Hebrews." He kept the money with his private funds and did not enter it on the consular accounts because he had personally promised the Jews that their money would be refunded if his actions were not approved. Finally, it was de Haas's contention that since the Jews had been promised protection only for the year 1877 the letters had in fact been fulfilled and the Jews had returned to their previous status. The Department took a much stricter view of this incident and decided that the money would have to be refunded, which de Haas expressed a readiness to do as soon as the consulate sent him a list of the *protégés*.

In March 1878, the new Jerusalem Consul received explicit orders to erase from the list of protected persons made by his predecessor the names of all who were not American citizens and to regard the certificates issued as cancelled.

When the war with Russia ended, Consul Willson was of the opinion that in effect the Jews had gotten their money's worth—provisional protection—though many of them had now begun to claim protection as a permanent right. No doubt during the issuance of the papers, the fine points of provisional protection and the other conditions which de Haas had set forth were not explained to the bewildered Jews. Willson warned that they would cause the Department some annoyance, but he was not worried until the Department informed him of its decision to have the money refunded. In terms as strong as his subordinate position would permit, he expressed his extreme reluctance to provoke tumult among the former *protégés* by trying to return the fees. It was his judgment that they "*were* protected. . . . The end was obtained by accident, or by the necessary delay incident to the Consulate correspondence." Thus ended the formal aspects of the case of the de Haas *protégés*—as the problem came to be known to the Department—in the Jerusalem consulate.

On the diplomatic level the de Haas incident was concluded by an absolute disavowal of the consul's actions in a *note verbale* to the Imperial Ministry of Foreign Affairs on February 28, 1878: "The Legation of the United States has the honor to acknowledge the note from the Imperial Ministry of Foreign Affairs . . . stating that the ex-Consul of the United States at Jerusalem in preparing a list of American citizens had included in it many Israelites who are Ottoman subjects, and asking that these names be effaced from the list.

"The subject was brought to the attention of the Department of State at Washington, and the facts ascertained by proper inquiry. The result is that instructions have been given to Willson the present United States Consul to regard as cancelled the certificates of nationality issued by his predecessor Mr. de Haas to others than American citizens in fact, and the names of all such will be erased from the list, having been placed upon it without our authority."

But the aftermath of the de Haas *protégés* continued to plague Consul Willson for years. If at times the United States consulate inadvertently became enmeshed in more affairs of the Jewish community than good policy might have dictated, it is also true that poverty-ridden, hardly literate, Jerusalem Jews were sometimes dragged without their understanding into the intrigues of the Levantines who surrounded most of the consulates in the Near East and held them in their grip.

Consul Willson had approved the dismissal of one Panyotti who had been dragoman of the consulate under Beardsley and de Haas. Since he failed to get himself reinstated through the compilation of a monumental compendium of lies and calumnies against his successor, he made tools of a few poor Jews—either American citizens or de Haas *protégés*—to support his cabal. In August 1878 he drafted two long letters of protest—the handwriting and the texts are patently his, though the signers may have salted them with a few complaints of their own—to the Minister at Constantinople and persuaded a group of Jews to sign them. It seems incredible that any person not deranged would imagine that techniques of this nature could be effective with men like Horace Maynard, but so complete is the mutual misunderstanding of divergent civilizations when they meet at the geographic crossroads of the world, that these maneuvers of Panyotti are characteristic rather than a-typical of the Levant of the period.

Minister Maynard sent a copy of the letters to Consul Willson, who proceeded with a meticulous denial of every charge they had made. American citizenship or protection far from being despised was highly prized and sought after. The complainants were troublesome but had always been treated with kindness. The First Dragoman against whom they levelled their shafts was competent, faithful, and honest. Willson had a private charity fund for cases of exceptional distress which he received from American Jewish donors, but any accusation that backsheesh was given to cavasses was infamous. Only those of the de Haas *protégés* were enrolled who had proper papers, though in a few cases he himself doubted their authenticity. Costs in lawsuits were borne in accordance with the rule book; the Fourth of July, contrary to their contention, was duly celebrated. Finally, he saw in the whole petition nothing but another one of the former Dragoman's exertions to oust his successor.

Consul Willson was no fool, as his Near East political analyses show, nor was he a bitter man. His judgment of the clients within his consular jurisdiction was mild, with something of the patron about it. "Of *'my Jews,'* as the Austrian Consul says of those under his protectorate, many are poor, some are querulous, not a few are beggars, and three or four are turbulent and malignant; but the great majority of them are quiet and give me no trouble. Generally I succeed in persuading them to settle their differences *amicably*. They are fond of being engaged in lawsuits about trifles. Three of them have been under arrest for assault and battery. Sometimes they are persuaded by designing men to sign letters or papers the import of which they *do not* understand. *Thus,* some of them have assigned their patrimony or allowance from the community, for months ahead, and then they come seeking redress *vainly* at the Consulate."

Panyotti had apparently organized an intrigue worthy of a broader stage.

"Panyotti was introduced into the office by Mr. Beardsley, unfortunately, as everybody knew but himself. Mr. De Haas knew it but knew not *how* to get rid of him, or where to get another. Mr. Hardegg as Vice-Consul dismissed him very properly. Panyotti labored for a restoration, worked against Mr. Hardegg, and flattered and carressed Mr. De Haas. *Money* was offered largely, promised by the man, who wanted Mr. Hardegg's place. The conspiracy was widespread and formidable.

"When this failed, Panyotti turned against Mr. De Haas. The correspondence was voluminous. One hundred and fifty pages were sent to me from Washington for examination."

Minister Maynard decided to back up the Consul and definitively put the quietus on Panyotti.

THE PROJECTS OF SIMON BERMANN

Into this fetid atmosphere of the old settlement of the seventies there came Simon Bermann, an American Jew of Polish origin with a plan for the agricultural colonization of Palestine. The man had a keen sense of the practical, a knowledge of agronomy, and a passionate love of the land which took the form of a mystical nationalism. In 1871, eight years before the founding of the first Jewish colony in Petach Tikva, he originated a project for an agricultural cooperative with individual holdings built along lines that show Fourierist influence, especially in the plans for intermingling agricultural and industrial labor in the colony. He was a contemporary of Montefiore, Rabbi Kalischer, and Oliphant and their Zionist projects, but unlike them, he was a man of the people who had tilled the soil with his own hands. His plan did not succeed, but many of the early Jewish immigrant colonists of the eighties have borne testimony that his Palestine travel book of 1879, which described his scheme, *The Travels of Simon,* was the work which stirred in them the first desire to go up to the land.

Simon Bermann had emigrated to the United States from Poland in 1852 and had spent eighteen years in the mid-west when, after a personal tragedy, he resolved to settle in Palestine in 1870. He had by that time experimented with community land settlements both in Poland and in the United States. En route to Palestine he established relations with the Jewish philanthropists in London, Paris, and Berlin, who had similar ideas and were planning the first agricultural school in Petach Tikva, but they reached no agreement. In the Jaffa area, Bermann visited the remnants of the American colony from Maine which had failed and the successful German-American "Temple" group who had taken over their lands. At Petach Tikva he tried in vain to convince Charles Netter, the representative of the *Alliance Israélite,* the French philanthropic society, to turn over to him a portion of their land, which he proposed to settle with about twenty Jewish families, in accordance with his scheme of colonization. In Jerusalem, through the intervention of the American Consul Beardsley, who supported his petition, he finally succeeded in obtaining authorization from the Sultan to purchase land and he started negotiations with the English Mission for a sale of a piece of their property.

In *The Travels of Simon,* he rendered thanks for the intervention of the American consul who had secured for him this permission to purchase land in Palestine from the Porte. "In Jerusalem we have consuls from the great powers of the world, hence also an American Consul named Mr. Birdsley (sic), a noble, friendly, and religious man, as is fitting for a true American gentleman. I often visited him and I was always very politely received. In order not to be negligent, I applied to the Turkish government to receive a permit for land to found a Jewish colony. My good consul used his good offices, stamped my request with the American seal, and sent it to the General Consul in Constantinople since I am an American citizen. The American Consul General handed it over to the Grand Vizier. About two months elapsed—I was then in Tiberias—when I received a copy of the decision from the consul in Jerusalem. It was favorable enough: if we wanted to purchase land the Sublime Porte would render us all possible assistance."

One of Bermann's letters of this period begging support from those German and Austrian rabbis who were interested in agricultural colonization in Palestine was published in the Hebrew weekly *Ha-Magid* by Rabbi Kalischer. It revealed the profound antagonism of the Jerusalem rabbis of the old settlement to the modernism of the prospective colonizers.

"I am fighting God's war and am speaking for an impoverished people, plagued by hunger, who hope for help and there is none. . . . With God's aid I have a good knowledge of agriculture. And I cast aside all my successes and the pleasures of this world in America and I made a great expenditure and I came here and I found a broad land and no one to work it properly. The Arab is docile with us. For three piastres he will work all day long. Also our poor people are seeking a livelihood. But when I began to engage in the affair I found enemies, in their sinfulness, among our own sons of Israel. Any man who has some authority in the congregation is opposed to the colony. And I saw that this is where its destroyers came from. Until now I have not asked and I will not ask to touch of their *Haluka.* To go ahead and expend everything I have for the settlement of Eretz Israel will not suffice. There is no time to delay or to be lazy. Since the Sultan gave permission to foreigners to buy land they will come from all parts."

The opposition of the heads of the *Haluka* in Jerusalem to any agricultural settlement was motivated by the simple fear that collections for this alien purpose would eat into their charity fund. Bermann therefore left Jerusalem for Tiberias where he was already known through the articles in *Ha-Magid*. He was commonly identified as the "American," and though his American clothes seemed strange amid the caftans of the eastern European Jews his piety was unquestioned. At Tiberias he was accorded a more sympathetic reception than in Jerusalem and he founded a Society for the Colonization of the Holy Land. One hundred and fifty persons joined in his plan for a cooperative settlement. Bermann was in favor of a first trial near Haifa where they could profit from the experiences of the prosperous German-American colony and be close enough to the sea to import agricultural implements and to export their produce. But the Jews of Tiberias insisted on remaining near their Holy City where, according to their tradition, the Messiah was to make his first appearance. They chose land on the Sea of Galilee near the village of Abu Shusha and waited for promised aid from Rabbis Kalischer and Gutmacher, those early adherents of Zionism. When the money was not forthcoming, Bermann left Palestine to rouse the people of the diaspora himself in support of the project. In 1881 he returned disillusioned to Palestine, where he died in a few years.

Chapter II

A CONFLICT OF PRINCIPLE: THE TURKISH IMMIGRATION LAWS

DEFENSE OF AN ABSOLUTE

In the last two decades of the nineteenth century United States diplomatic wrestling with the Turkish Exclusion Laws against Jews represented a defense of an absolute moral principle. Religious discrimination among United States citizens, native born or naturalized, was considered a violation of the letter of the constitution, and its spirit was carried over directly into foreign policy. The United States could not, without violence to its fundamental laws, countenance rules in foreign countries which differentiated among American citizens and it used forceful diplomatic measures to combat discrimination, whether it was in the great Austro-Hungarian or in the weak Ottoman Empire. Though in Turkey this position was further sustained by insistence on the Treaty rights of 1830, the legalities of the American position were only props for the abstract principle.

No doubt the appointment of Oscar Straus and then Solomon Hirsch as the protagonists of this policy before the Porte gave it added weight. The American Ministers at Constantinople who were Jews always insisted that their actions were solely in conformity with an American constitutional principle, but in practice when they fought against the disabilities faced by American Jews they invariably passed beyond the narrow confines of the protection of United States citizens to intercede for all Jews in Palestine. The pogrom migrations from eastern Europe after 1881 and the virulent recrudescence of anti-semitism in western Europe struck at the vitals of men like Oscar Straus; they were psychologically harassed by the Jewish Question even though they themselves had attained eminence and power in the United States.

The United States consular service was not immune to the anti-semitic virus, and in Consul Selah Merrill in Jerusalem the establish-

47

ment had a prototype of the prejudiced official. Jewish refugees from persecution have often borne the disease of anti-semitism with them. Towards the very end of the century there are a number of indications that Selah Merrill's annoyance at occupying himself with the Jews of Jerusalem was paralleled in the State Department. On the diplomatic policy level this took the form of relaxing somewhat the absolutism of the original American contention that no discrimination among United States citizens would be tolerated on any grounds.

THE OLIPHANT SCHEME

After 1870, when persecution of the Jews became bloody in the Danubian provinces and in the Balkan areas slipping from Turkish control, the United States envoys in Turkey were instructed to make diplomatic inquiries and informal representations in the name of humanity to both the Sublime Porte and the agents of the new semi-independent Christian states. In their despatches to the State Department on political conditions in these areas the American envoys contrasted the good fortune of the Jews under the old Turkish rule with their maltreatment at the hands of Roumanian and Serbian peasant leaders flushed with new liberties and power.

The pogroms of 1881, which broke out after the assassination of Alexander II, became the turning point of the modern history of the Jews, the sudden acceleration of a movement of oppression which had been gathering momentum for decades throughout eastern Europe and which knows no end in our time. Nationalism in Roumania had found its first aggressive expression in crushing the unassimilable element. Russia revived and extended imperial orders throttling the economic activity of Jews in the pale, the Ignatieff Decrees. The great pogrom migrations were set into motion: Russian Jews fled across the border into Roumania; Roumanian Jews poured over into Austria; Jews from all parts of Eastern Europe crowded into the slums of the cities of the West. The Jews in the isthmus of Europe between the Black Sea and the Baltic were thrown into turmoil and hundreds of thousands were driven from areas which they had inhabited for centuries.

The great question was, "Where to?" Many refugees from Russia and Roumania managed to push their way down through the Balkans by land to the Bosphorus; others crowded into Black Sea boats which carried them to Constantinople. There they camped in the streets of the Turkish capital waiting to be transported to an asylum. Palestine was a natural haven; Constantinople was on the regular sea route for Jewish pilgrims from eastern Europe to the Holy Cities. Intermingled with the material consideration that the Jews of Jerusalem had a recognized charity fund to which the refugees had contributed in other days was the elemental urge to find a more enduring resting place in a land they remembered in their daily prayers. This does not mean that the mass of orthodox Jews from the towns of Russia and Roumania were profoundly moved by the spirit of the Hebrew intellectuals, schooled in concepts of nineteenth century nationalist revivals common to all Europe, or by the preachments of the stray Palestine colonization societies which had sprung up in the larger cities. The ordinary people wanted a refuge anywhere—in western Europe, in the United States, in Palestine. The nationalist pioneers of the *Bilu* migration from Russia, young intellectuals prepared to till the soil of Palestine with their own hands and passionate devotees of a religion of labor on the land, were a small minority.

Of various schemes of mass emigration from Eastern Europe, the 1879 proposals of the English adventurer Laurence Oliphant for agricultural settlements in the rich Jaulon area across the Jordan (then considered a part of Palestine) attracted genuine interest both among Englishmen —Disraeli and Salisbury were said to have granted their approval— and among committees of Roumanian Jews who had previously conceived of projects along similar lines in their colonization societies. During his early contacts with the Porte Laurence Oliphant believed that success was imminent and that the Sultan was about to approve a charter for a settlement company elaborated by Turkish law advisers to "offer the most effectual guarantees for the just and satisfactory administration of the colony, and the interests of the shareholders, without in any way infringing upon the sovereign rights. . . ." But after an interview with the Sultan himself the protracted negotiations evaporated into thin air. The American Consul, Willson, reporting the failure, was generally skeptical about the success of such agricultural colonies. Apart from the Sultan's suspicion of all foreign proposals, Willson expressed the view that Bedouin raids as well as the climate, ill-suited to European labor, would render precarious the existence of any settlements. He noted the abandonment of the Jewish experimental station at Safed and the financial difficulties of the station near Jaffa. In December 1881 Consul Willson learned from Constantinople that the English and German philanthropists who had been sponsoring Jewish immigration into Palestine in the wake of the pogroms, had been informed by the Porte that the Jews would be allowed to establish themselves in separate communities in the Ottoman Empire only if they accepted Ottoman nationality without reservations. Moreover, Palestine was to be excluded from any area of settlement.

After his rebuff Laurence Oliphant published a diatribe against the Sultan's ministers and generally made himself unwanted at the Porte. England, involved in a conflict with Turkey over Egypt, became an unsatisfactory intermediary for any negotiations with the Sultan. It was necessary for the Jews to turn elsewhere for a go-between. Oliphant remained their protagonist. In June 1882, accompanied by a committee of Roumanian Jews, he approached the American Minister at Constantinople Lewis Wallace, Civil War general and author of *Ben Hur,* a man touched by Protestant Messianism, in a renewed attempt to persuade the Sultan to grant colonization permits in Syria—the precise definition of the geographic area covered by the term and the extent to which northern Palestine was included was left ambiguous. General Wallace was moved. On June 8 he sent a telegram to Secretary of State Frelinghuysen: "Refugee Jews starving here. Delegates ask good offices with Sultan to colonize Syria. May I act?" To which the Secretary promptly replied:

"The President will be much pleased if through your good offices used unofficially, you can secure a refuge for these unfortunate persons."

The next day a Reverend J. Mitchell of Atlanta, Georgia, sent the Secretary of State a letter recommending that the government advocate a "proposition to be submitted to the Porte for the purchase of the Holy Land by the oppressed Hebrews of all nationalities and the erection of a scheme of local self-government by them in Syria in virtue of such purchase." Frelinghuysen was disturbed at the thought that his telegraphic reply to Wallace be construed as blanket espousal of the Georgia preacher's purchase plan. He therefore explicitly disassociated himself from such a scheme in instructions sent to the Minister on June 20: "It does not appear that the propositions made to you are connected with Dr. Mitchell's project. On the contrary, your telegram excludes any other idea than that of urgently seeking asylum for certain necessitous refugees within the dominion of the Porte. While I should warmly sympathize with such a request and aid it so far as official propriety would admit, I could not commit this government to any proposal for independent colonization such as Dr. Mitchell describes. . . ."

Wallace was in complete agreement about the impracticability of the Mitchell plan. He had enough insight into the motive forces of the harassed Ottoman Empire to understand that while the Turks might be bought individually they would not dare as a government to part with a portion of the empire. Wallace wrote to the Department, "The Sultan and his official advisers were all too shrewd to dispose of Palestine by gift or sale. All the money of the Israelites would be no inducement to such an end." With the permission of his government Wallace was prepared to lend his good offices to a colonization scheme, but not to any fantasies. The Laurence Oliphant plan for the colonization of the Jaulon had, on the other hand, appeared realistic to him and he was generally impressed by the Englishman. Oliphant had aroused his sympathies with a description of the exodus of the Jews from Russia and the miseries they were undergoing. He himself had seen those who had reached Constantinople starving in the streets. During a further discussion with Oliphant and a Mr. Alexander, "both respectable gentlemen," who were acting as agents for the societies of Roumanian Jews, it was agreed that once Wallace had secured the permit from the Porte he would sever his connections with the whole enterprise, leaving the practical management of the immigration and the settlement of the colonists to them. The motives of Oliphant and Alexander were of course more ambiguous than Wallace knew; they were at once messianists and commercial adventurers. Alexander was agent not only for the Roumanian Jews but also for Edward Cazalet, an Englishman then negotiating a railroad concession with Turkey. In their plan the idea of Jewish settlement was neatly bound up with colonization along the route of the proposed railroad. Such convenient combinations of purpose will be found again and again in the unfolding of British imperial policy.

When Wallace called on the Turkish Minister of Foreign Affairs to espouse the Jewish cause he was informed that the proposal had already been discussed at a Council of Ministers and decided affirmatively; "that Jews from whatever parts could come and settle in Turkey; that there was a general law of immigration in force which must be taken for the guidance of such as choose to come; that they could come when they pleased; and would be settled in groups of two hundred or two hundred and fifty families; that they could settle in any unoccupied lands in Mesopotamia, about Aleppo, or in the regions of the Orontes river; that they could not establish themselves in Palestine, that the firman from the Sultan was unnecessary, for having once approved the law, he could not be called on to do so again; that every colonist was simply bound to become an Ottoman subject."

Although this policy was not fundamentally more liberal than that reported by Consul Willson seven months earlier, General Wallace was enthusiastic. When he saw the affair assuming vast proportions he thought it wise to receive some assurances in writing from the Minister of Foreign Affairs. But the Turks were chary about written documents. Artin Effendi, the undersecretary in the Ministry of Foreign Affairs, who was later to play a role of corruption and duplicity in Herzl's negotiations with the Porte, again assured Wallace that no further communication was required since the law of immigration stood unaltered. General Wallace was satisfied and concluded glibly that "there is nothing to prevent all the Israelites on earth from picking up and squatting in Asiatic Turkey. They shall not settle in Palestine—that is the only prohibition."

The terms of what the Turks called their Immigration Law were generous in certain respects; it was drafted in the general phraseology for which the Turks had a predilection and was made equally applicable to all foreigners. To the immigrants they granted free lands; freedom from taxes for six years in Roumelia and twelve years in Asia; the right to sell the property of the free grants after twenty years; freedom of worship. One requirement, however, if enforced literally, rendered any mass immigration prohibitive: the possession of a 1350 franc minimum by each immigrant family, a colossal sum to the refugees of eastern Europe.

The committees of Roumanian Jews made no formal applications for the allocation of areas of settlement under the provisions of the Turkish law. Apart from the fact that the minimum financial requirement was in itself absurdly high, the exclusion of Palestine from the area of immigration, which Wallace had passed over so lightly, was a major deterrent to the eastern European colonization societies, which were moved by the spirit of the Lovers of Zion movement. Even though there is reason to believe that the Turkish definition of Palestine did not include Transjordan and Galilee, the elimination of Judea and Jerusalem was enough to render the proposal worthless to the early Zionists. The fixation on the ancient heart of Palestine was absolute.

After the conquest of Egypt by the British there was a coolness on the part of the Turks to any Jewish colonization projects; they were not blind to the extent to which English intermediaries, active propagandists of British expansion in the Near East, had been proponents of these plans. In 1879 Edward Cazalet had forthrightly stated his view that there was an identity of interest between the Israelites and the British in this area of the world. Thus the well-intentioned Wallace intervention went the way of the Oliphant scheme. Received without enthusiasm by the Jews and with growing suspicion on the part of the Turks, it soon became a half-forgotten episode in the history of modern Zionism.

GENERAL WALLACE IN JERUSALEM

When General Wallace visited Jerusalem late in November 1882, at a consular reception thirty resident American Jews called upon him in a body and took the opportunity to complain that of thousands of dollars collected in America annually for Jerusalem charity not a cent ever reached the Americans in the community. They were certain that this discrimination was not known to the donors in the United States and that if only they could be informed of it, the wrong would be righted. The formal petition which they presented to Wallace on this occasion lamented that of the amounts donated by Israelites throughout the world, the poor of Jerusalem received only fifteen or twenty cents every three months, while the rest was lost among the Elders and Rabbis "who are generally considered a set of unhonest men." The American Jews closed the recital of their sufferings with a request that the Minister help them realize their plan for an American "House of Industry," to teach the young useful trades and to support the destitute with its profits.

Curiously enough, the petition had been composed by the same Simon Bermann who a few years before had tried to initiate agricultural colonization projects in Palestine and who now acted as dean of the American Jewish community in Jerusalem. This was more than the clamor of a Jewish sect for a greater share of the *Haluka;* it was in the spirit of Bermann's idea of making the Jews of Palestine productive men of enterprise. After Christian Americans in Jerusalem had verified the contentions of the petitioners, General Wallace promised to help them.

His communication of the complaint of the American Jews resident in Jerusalem was forwarded to a Washington Jew, "for the information of himself and the more influential of his co-religionists in the United States, and for such consideration as they may think the importance of the subject demands through the proper channels." But nothing came of the petition and the American Jews continued to live on the crumbs of the *Haluka* since they had no congregation of their own.

During this same trip General Wallace committed an outrage against the free press of Jerusalem about which the official dispatches of the period are silent. The Jews of Jerusalem had a defender at the Palace in the person of Joseph Krieger Effendi, the Jerusalem Pasha's interpreter and secretary, an elegant Levantine Jew much honored for his talents. According to protocol it had been his duty to lead the consular dragomans in welcoming Wallace outside of the gates of Jerusalem; but since it was Friday near sundown he hurried the ceremony in order to return home before the Sabbath and thereby earned the displeasure of the General and the American consular officials. The Jews believed, in the manner of the Levant, that the secret provocator of the Minister was the American consular dragoman, the son of an apostate Jew and a member of the Missionary Society in eternal war with the Jewish community. According to Jewish accounts the General, angered, complained to the Pasha about the conduct of his secretary, and the Turkish official, in terror lest the slight be reported back to Constantinople, ousted him. His removal caused great consternation in the Jewish community, who felt that they were losing their protector, the confidant of the Pasha. Frumkin, the editor of the Jerusalem Hebrew weekly *Havatselet* (The Rose), took up the cry in the spirit of crusading journalism and published a lead article entitled "A Republican and a Despot" in which he violently attacked the General and the American consular officials. This was a most flagrant affront to the worthy visitor and the Pasha had to punish Frumkin; it was said that the General himself demanded satisfaction. Whereupon the Pasha wrote Frumkin that he would have to suspend publication of *Havatselet* until final judgment on the editor was handed down in Constantinople. Upon reflection the Pasha refrained from sending the case to Constantinople and allowed the local magistrates to sentence Frumkin to forty-five days in jail during which time publication of his weekly was prohibited.

Frumkin suffered no great hardships in prison and his chamber became a reception room for the Hebrew intellectuals of Jerusalem.

Even the orthodox rabbis of the congregations who had hitherto bitterly fought Frumkin as a modernist were reconciled to the editor, who was now enduring trials "in the sanctification of the Lord."

THE DIPLOMATIC TRIUMPH OF OSCAR STRAUS

While the Law of June 1882 made the entry of Jews into Palestine illegal, it did not stop the flow of Jewish immigration. Many Palestine Colonization Societies in Russia and Roumania became discouraged at the prospect of wrestling with the Turkish legal bars and hundreds of thousands of Jews sailed across the Atlantic to the United States; but the law never stifled completely either the illicit colonization of the land by the Lovers of Zion or the helter-skelter flocking of orthodox Jews to the Holy Cities of the old settlement for want of another refuge. Compared to the main-current of migration to the American continent Palestinian immigration was a mere trickle, but never until the First World War did it dry up.

Eliezer Ben Yehuda, one of the early pioneers of the new settlement and father of the revival of spoken Hebrew in Palestine, has described in his memoirs the incredulousness with which the exclusion law was received by those Palestinian Jews who had hoped to rebuild the land with the pogrom refugees. "The few thousands of Russian Jews who came to Jaffa during the next two or three months literally crowded the streets and the lanes which were close to the shore, and the Arabs of Jaffa, who had never before seen so many Jews wandering around in groups day and night, filling the air of their city with a language that was so strange to them began to look upon them with an evil eye. . . . A few months later evil rumors reached us from the capital of the Empire that the central government was about to prohibit or had already prohibited Jews from coming into Eretz Israel. At first we did not want to credit these rumors. Afterwards we consoled ourselves with false hopes that it was the government's intent to close only the Jaffa coast to foreign Jews and that on other parts of the shore of the land the Turkish government would receive them with the same friendliness towards Jews which had heretofore characterized the Turkish government. Slowly the rumors began to materialize. . . ." The new law, as was typical with Turkish regulations, was not made clear at once, not even to the officials in Jerusalem. The customs agents at first merely separated Jews from other travellers and interposed technical difficulties to their landing. Then the prohibition became absolute.

In desperation the Jews resorted to baksheesh. As the rules grew more stringent the size of the payments increased. With time the whole transaction of clandestine immigration was clothed with recognized forms in which there were fairly stable rules of conduct. Intermediaries between the immigrants and the local Turkish officials had clearly defined functions. To his sorrow Ben Yehuda had to admit that the go-betweens were usually Jews who realized as much out of the deals as the Turkish officials. In a sense the most tangible result of the exclusion laws was a windfall for local officials and their Jewish confederates who were thus able to squeeze more and more baksheesh out of the immigrants. At first the Jews tried to use influence through local channels to get the rules abrogated and they appealed to their old protector, Joseph Effendi, the Pasha's interpreter. For a while he tried to help them, believing that the new rules had been established by subordinate officials for their own profit, but when he learned that the order had been handed down from the Sublime Porte itself he cautiously avoided further intervention.

Of the long struggle of surreptitious immigration, Ben Yehuda wrote with feeling: "From that day, the Ninth day of Ab of the year 5642 (1882) this decree remained in full effect for thirty-five years. From that moment on a war was declared between the Turkish government and us. For us this was a very hard war because we were not prepared and ready for a war of this character, and in our hands there was no weapon except the weapon of the diaspora—graft! With this weapon we fought with all our might, and we gained many victories with its aid and much of what we accomplished was achieved with this weapon. But the weapon did not always stand us in good stead. There were times when its edge was blunted and it could not perform its customary work. Then bad times passed over us, dark hours which almost made us despair."

The most trying days were those when the governorship of Jerusalem fell into the hands of a Turk who did not take graft, did not "bite." Petty officials failed to imitate his high principles; on the contrary, they only increased their demands and made the price of immigration almost prohibitive. Ben Yehuda has written pathetic accounts of this illegal immigration: old Jews hiding in the holds of vessels at the Jaffa anchorage while other passengers were taken off first, and then the secret smuggling of the Jews into the land by night.

In the early eighties the immigration into Palestine was kept alive only through extraordinary exertions. The pages of *Havatselet* are a contemporary record of this war to enter the land and the abject misery of those who could not afford to pay graft. From time to time the Pasha's police raided all inns and those Jews who had not found a place to lose themselves in the old quarter in Jerusalem were rounded up in Turkish jails. Jews caught at the Jaffa anchorage were deported to Cyprus and Alexandria, travelling sea lanes that Jewish refugees, clamoring to stay in Palestine, would know again in 1915 and again in 1947.

The Jews of the world were far from unanimous about the merits of Jewish immigration into Palestine and a controversy raged in Jewish periodicals and among rival philanthropic organizations. The issue of the relative advantages of immigration to the United States and Palestine were debated with passion. The *Alliance Israélite* ended by favoring the American refuge. Pious rabbis in Jerusalem were hostile to new immigrants into the Holy Land who might bring with them the "corrupting influences of the age"—such at least was the formal argument which concealed the fear of some lest the *Haluka* be stretched to feed many more mouths. The Lovers of Zion in eastern Europe and Palestine were outraged by the adherents of the United States and in *Havatselet* of Jerusalem violently denounced immigration to the United States as a death-blow to Judaism. *Havatselet* addressed a challenge to the *Alliance Israélite:* "Let us call to those who are sending the Russian refugees to America. Guarantee us! If you send our sheep to a new land then guarantee us that the same fate does not await them there that they suffered in the land from which they escaped."

The official Turkish position with respect to immigration was clear and defensible. Through three decades of negotiations, pourparlers, and the interventions of diplomatic officials and Jewish leaders it remained consistent with the original formulation of the immigration law of 1882 and the discussions with General Wallace. The Sultan Abdul Hamid would accept Jews to colonize the interior of Turkey in dispersed communities if they would become Ottoman subjects. He varied the details: at times he was willing to grant privileges of local self-government; he would bargain about the degree to which he would permit a concentration of the settlement; but he was suspicious both of a Jewish autonomous colony in Palestine which, he believed, would ultimately break away from the empire, and of large-scale immigration of individual Jews many of whom would seek and find the extra-territorial protectorate of the European and American consuls.

Abdul Hamid tried to hold together an empire that was doomed.

While he lost many provinces through inept political and military action, it was one thing to have lands wrested from the empire through the misfortunes of war and another for the proud Turk to alienate a portion of the domain through sale or concession. The Turks, who had been tolerant of the migration of stray groups of religious Jews into Palestine, became wary and antagonistic when, after the pogroms in eastern Europe, proposals for agricultural settlements and a restoration of the Kingdom of the Jews appeared with increasing frequency in the Jewish and European press, with scarcely a mention of the fact that the Sublime Porte was still sovereign of the land. The crowding of the Jews into the old quarters of Jerusalem, their sectarian bickering among themselves and their fights with their Christian neighbors had once been viewed with superior indifference by the Turks, but as soon as Jewish immigration assumed what they considered a political character, they bridled. Irrespective of the guise in which the colonization of Palestine was presented to the Turks or the character of the pleader—whether Oliphant, Rothschild's emissaries, or Herzl —they had a genuine fear of grave consequences for their empire. When Fernandez, the representative of the *Alliance Israélite,* went to the Turkish Minister of the Interior at the height of the panic of the pogrom migrations seeking aid for the colonization of Russian Jews, he was told in a forthright manner that the Turkish government, harassed by Greek, Armenian, Serbian, and Bulgarian problems, did not want to burden itself with the creation of a Jewish Question.

That this high policy of the Porte was nullified in practice by local officials who allowed whole colonial settlements of Jews to be built in flagrant defiance of the law was a characteristic reality of Turkish administration. The principles of the Sultan's decrees remained unsullied. The mechanics of exclusion were cumbersome and they involved the Porte in ceaseless controversies with the capitulatory powers. And decade after decade, the ambassadors in Constantinople sent verbal notes on the infringement of the Treaty rights by the immigration restrictions, the local officials filled their pockets with graft, and the Jews infiltrated into the land.

Until the seventies travel into the Turkish dominions on the part of "Franks" from Europe and America had been subject to no restrictions. Even the formal passport requirement had usually been overlooked. This facilitated the movement into Turkey of Russian espionage agents disguised as pilgrims, of common felons, of political refugees from the despotisms of Europe, and of Jews. Suddenly in

1878, to the bafflement of the American Minister, Horace Maynard, the Porte issued a stringent regulation governing passports, visas, and the control of travellers through the registries of inns and lodging houses. When, after 1881, the Jews began to land at Jaffa in great numbers, the existing rules were applied to their exclusion. In February 1883 Lewis Wallace informed the State Department that further rules had been promulgated by the Porte requiring all travellers to have their passports visaed by a Turkish diplomatic representative before they landed in Turkey. This worked to exclude Russian and Roumanian refugees who in flight rarely provided themselves with official papers; usually they had no knowledge of a passport or visa requirement; and if by chance they had heard of the regulations, neither Russian nor Turkish officials would exert themselves to make the documents available.

It was not until 1887 that the Sublime Porte made an all-out attempt to cut off the immigration tide of Jews. The juridical framework within which this restriction of immigration was to be effected was difficult to erect in a land where European powers enjoyed special status. Jews from Europe and America who disembarked at Jaffa with passports could always maintain that they were not settlers and were only making a pilgrimage to the Wailing Wall. Absolute prohibition of Jewish pilgrims would have been hard to enforce in view of the historic wars of the Christian nations with the Mohammedans over the rights of Christian pilgrims to visit the Holy Places. Any curtailment of Jewish pilgrimage was too proximate to the issue of Christian pilgrimage. Once the Jews landed nominally as pilgrims, or as guests —the circumlocution used by *Havatselet* in announcing the number of new arrivals—it was almost impossible to single them out from among the old residents.

Hence the Turks fell upon the idea of placing a time limitation of one month on any foreign Jew's pilgrimage to Palestine. Upon the expiration of this period Jews who were not Ottoman citizens would be subject to expulsion. Taken literally this order meant the deportation of all but the community of Sephardic Jews after one month. Consul Gillman, who had been given notice of the regulation by the Pasha of Jerusalem, reported to the State Department that though the general language referred to *all* Jews who were not Ottoman subjects, it really meant only the recent Russian immigrants. The new regulation was characteristic of the circumlocutions of Turkish legislation; its sweeping generality, far from achieving its ends through the artifice of limiting the sojourn of pilgrims, embroiled the Porte in years of diplomatic conflict with the envoys of the western nations. The Turks had built their juridical system more upon distinctions of religious than national communities. When they were developing their regulations on the exclusion of foreign Jews they no doubt aimed them primarily at the Russian refugees, but *en passant,* as a subsidiary intention, they were inclined to keep out all other Jews. The number of British, American, French, German, and Austrian Jews was not great, but the Turks had no desire to increase the colony of foreign Jews and in their eyes most of them were really Russian Jews who had recently been naturalized.

During the early eighteen-eighties the United States had retained a limited humanitarian interest in the fate of the Russian refugees, but it could hardly have intervened in the problem of Turkish passport regulations if their effect had been to exclude only Russian subjects. The restriction of the time allotment for all Jewish pilgrims posed a very different issue. Without fully realizing it, in passing these new rules against *all* Jews the Turks injured the dignity of Britain, the United States, and France, nations which had proclaimed doctrines of absolute religious toleration and had abolished religious disabilities. Whatever may have been the realities of social anti-semitism within those nations they could not permit a Turk to practice discrimination against their Jewish nationals. The official policy of the United States at this time was definite: it allowed for no discrimination among its citizens by foreign governments either in theory or practice. The mere act of passing a rule affecting American Jews as distinct from other Americans was intolerable.

Two years previously, in 1885, the United States position had been publicly formulated in a clear-cut manner which brooked no compromise. The Austro-Hungarian government had objected to the diplomatic appointment of A. M. Keiley of Virginia on the ground that his wife, being of Jewish parentage, was *persona non grata.* This gave rise to what became known as the Keiley incident in the course of which both Secretary of State Bayard and President Cleveland roundly rebuked the Austro-Hungarian government in a formal diplomatic exchange. Bayard's statement of policy was a most absolute formulation of the doctrine of the separation of religion and the state: "It is not within the power of the President nor the Congress, nor of any judicial tribunal in the United States, to take or even hear testimony, or in any mode to inquire into or decide upon the religious belief of any official, and the proposition to allow this to be done by any foreign government is necessarily and a fortiori inadmissible." In his first annual message to the Congress Grover Cleveland went out of his way to refer to the incident. "The reasons advanced were such as could not be acquiesced in, without violation of my oath of office and the precepts of the constitution, since they necessarily involved a limitation in favor of a foreign government upon the right of selection by the Executive, and required such an application of a religious test as a qualification for office under the United States as would have resulted in the practical disfranchisement of a large class of our citizens and the abandonment of a vital principle of our Government." With the appointment of Oscar S. Straus, a New York Jewish lawyer and scholar as Minister to Turkey in March 1887, this fundamental doctrine received concrete expression. Straus himself was particularly touched to be sent as representative of his country to the power which had dominion over Palestine.

Oscar Straus had received instructions from the Secretary of State before his departure to inquire into the restriction of Jewish pilgrimage. When, not long after his arrival in Constantinople, his intervention was requested by Dr. Kalmonovitz, acting as a representative of Russian Jewish philanthropists, Straus made it quite clear that whatever he accomplished in this affair he proposed to achieve as an American representative and not as a Jew. This was a distinction which he was always cautious to make to Jews who sought his intercession. When Straus called upon the Grand Vizier to make representations with respect to the "rumored expulsion" of Jews from Jerusalem, it was confirmed that a regulation had in fact been communicated by the Porte to the Imperial authorities in Jerusalem limiting the stay of foreign Jews to one month. At a subsequent interview he was told that the Council of Ministers was relaxing the provision and extending it to three months. The Grand Vizier gave two reasons for the regulations, one of a public order and one of a political character. At certain seasons of the year, such as Easter, the spirit of religious fanaticism rose to so high a pitch in Jerusalem that the Jews were forced to remain behind closed doors to avoid contact with Christians who would attack and perhaps murder them. The purpose of the regulation was to avoid such conflicts. The second reason was that report had spread that Jews throughout the world hoped to strengthen themselves around Jerusalem with the intention, at some future time, of re-establishing their ancient kingdom there. Straus replied that a strong police force would eliminate the first danger. As for the second compelling motive for the regulation, he assured the Grand Vizier that if the Porte would make inquiry it would readily satisfy itself that no such purpose actuated the Jews throughout the world. With respect to the discrimination in the Turkish law between American Jews and non-Jews, Straus adopted the spirit and language of Bayard and Cleveland in the Keiley incident. It was one of the fundamental principles of the United States government, he said, to make no distinction among its citizens based upon creed or race and uniformly in its relations with foreign countries the United States had denied their right to so discriminate among American citizens. He quoted relevant passages from Bayard's correspondence on this principle, referred to the capitulations, and claimed infringement of rights under the Treaty of 1830. The Grand Vizier assured him that should the local authorities threaten to expel any American citizen he would give due weight to the considerations Straus had outlined and would issue instructions accordingly. The response was characteristic of Turkish dealings with the powers: to avoid joining issues over abstract principles and await individual incidents.

From Jerusalem, Straus in December 1888 had received a circumstantial report by Consul Gillman which laid bare the bewildering cross-currents of opinion among the various consular officials and the local Jewish factions over the proper attitude with respect to refugees. Though Jews belonging to other nationalities had been expelled from Palestine, no American Jew had yet actually been deported during Gillman's incumbency. In all communications with the local Turkish authorities he had steadfastly held to the position that under no circumstances would he consent to, much less render aid in, the expulsion from Palestine of United States citizens who were Jews. He too had repeated the phraseology of Bayard in the Keiley incident. His outspoken refusal had incurred the displeasure of the Governor of Jerusalem, who had criticized his viewpoint in a written communication, followed by a verbal message in which Gillman was told that he was the only consul in Jerusalem who had denied assistance in carrying out the decree. Gillman had replied to the Governor that he had reported to his superiors and was awaiting further instructions. A British consular official had expressed surprise to Gillman over his friendship for the Jews and had initially aided the Turks in the enforcement of the decree, but after receiving instructions from his government the British consul reversed his stand and joined Gillman in withholding cooperation from the Turks. The hostility of the Russian consular officials to the Jewish refugees who were nominally their subjects was notorious. They had acquiesced in the deportation of a shipload of Russian Jews who had not even been permitted to land, Gillman reported, "entailing great misery on the unfortunate people who had been driven from their homes, many of them in poverty. Their condition was described to me as pitiable in the extreme; some of them being almost naked and without food, and suffering from sickness in consequence."

In the final section of his report to Minister Straus, Gillman referred with amazement to the antagonism of Jerusalem Jewish residents to the arrival of more Jews. The influx tended to increase the cost of living, added nothing to the wealth of the city, and reduced the proportion of charitable aid from abroad available to the old residents; this was Gillman's concise economic explanation of their hostility.

Gillman, who was a righteous man, thus saw himself standing alone with a thankless task, exposed at once to the disapproval of the Ottoman authorities, the animosity of his consular colleagues, and the opposition of some of the resident Jews.

Since the general issue had been brought to no conclusion with his oral intervention at the Porte, Straus resolved to visit Jerusalem himself to study the enforcement of the exclusion laws. There he used the subtle diplomatic technique of a carefully administered slight to express his disapproval of both the law and the manner of its administration by the Governor of Jerusalem. When he landed at Jaffa he declined the courtesy of an official conveyance and rode in a Cook's vehicle. Upon his arrival at Jerusalem he was besieged by a huge delegation of Jews, men and women with infants in their arms, who had come to plead for the release of four hundred refugee Russian Jews who had been imprisoned and were awaiting deportation. Straus was touched and he sent the Governor a message that he would decline to call upon him and would appeal to the Porte for his removal unless the prisoners were set free. He argued—with doubtful relevance—about the Treaty rights of the United States and the other capitulatory powers. The Governor was thoroughly frightened and within twenty-four hours ordered the Jews released. The following morning thousands of Jews appeared outside Straus's hotel and in the name of all the congregations of Jerusalem presented him with an embossed memorial of gratitude.

During this trip to Jerusalem Straus made efforts to discover what elements were arrayed against the Jewish immigrants and who had fanned the flames of Turkish suspicion against further colonization. Raoul Pasha, Governor of Jerusalem, expressed the opinion that the exclusion laws were the work of the French Catholics operating through their Minister in Constantinople; they feared that Jewish immigration, which meant land purchase, would disturb the status quo among the various religious bodies; they also accused the Jews of introducing typhus into the country. In his recollections Straus noted that both the Orthodox Patriarch in Constantinople and the dignitaries of the Roman Catholic Church had objected to the settlement of foreign Jews in Palestine and had brought pressure to bear on the Turks through the Russian and French envoys.

While Straus was travelling in Palestine the Turkish Minister at Washington had delivered to the State Department formal notice of the extension of the time limit for the sojourn of Jews in Jerusalem from one to three months with the proviso, however, that they were going to Jerusalem in the performance of a pilgrimage. When Straus returned to Constantinople he found instructions from Secretary of State Bayard to refuse acceptance of this Turkish evasion of the principle of the conflict. The British and the French had similar orders from their governments, but since they were waiting for new incidents on which to base their protests, which would have meant delay, Straus presented his own strong *note verbale* to the Sublime Porte without his colleagues. He first summarized his understanding of the Turkish position: "The Sublime Porte has decided only to authorize free access into Palestine to Israelites coming from foreign countries under the following conditions: their passports should expressly state that they are going to Jerusalem in the performance of a pilgrimage and not for the purpose of engaging in commerce or taking up their residence there. As regards their sojourn in Palestine, instead of one month, it cannot in any case exceed the space of three months. They must have their passports so drawn up (*libellés*), visaed by the Ottoman Consuls, and on their arrival, they will be bound to supply themselves with a *permis de séjour* issued by the Imperial authorities and couched in the same terms." Straus declared that it was impossible for his government to accede to any such conditions; he protested the brutal manner in which the regulations were enforced and he expressed the hope that the Sublime Porte would alter or revoke the odious rules in accordance with the broad principles of toleration which had been proclaimed throughout the Ottoman Empire first among the nations of Europe and the Old World and had been secured to all races and creeds under the capitulations and the treaties with the United States and other nations. In rejecting the new restrictions, Straus invoked doctrines of absolute religious liberty and individual freedom as guaranteed by the United States Constitution: "To require of applicants for passports which under our laws are issued to all citizens upon the sole evidence of their citizenship, any announcement of their religious faith, or declaration of their personal motives in seeking such passport would be utterly repugnant to the spirit of our constitution and to the intent of the solemn prescription, by the Constitution, of any religious test as a qualification of the relations of the citizens to the government and would moreover assume an inquisitorial function in respect of the personal affairs of the individual which our government cannot exert for its own purposes and could still less assume to exercise with the object of aiding a foreign government in the enforcement of an objectionable and arbitrary discrimination against certain of our citizens."

While Straus in Constantinople was formulating the position of the United States government, Henry Gillman in Jerusalem continued to hold to his resolve not to allow American Jews to be expelled from Palestine. In August 1888 the United States was confronted with an actual incident involving her citizens. Up to that time all protests had been based upon abstract principle alone and had often proceeded beyond the narrow legal confines of the protection of American nationals to make general humanitarian appeals on behalf of all Jewish refugees. On August 20, 1888 three American Jews who had landed at Jaffa were prevented from going on to Jerusalem because they had no Ottoman visas; they were held in a Turkish prison and were told that they would be deported on the next steamer. Reichmann, one of the three, escaped from Turkish custody and took refuge in the consulate in Jerusalem. This was the first time that the Turkish government had invoked the visa requirement against an American Jew. In Straus's absence on leave, the United States *chargé d'affaires* in Constantinople took a serious view of the case in his communication to Saïd Pasha, the Minister of Foreign Affairs. "The detention or expulsion of these American citizens would be in violation of long established rights; and their expulsion might lead to disagreeable complications. I therefore ask Your Excellency to give *immediate orders* to allow these men to go where they will without hindrance in the full enjoyment of their rights and liberties as American citizens, whatever their religious creed may be, who arrive furnished with American passports; because a repetition of such an occurrence will doubtless lead to a stringent protest on the part of my government."

The position of the United States was certainly clear.

By this time the English, French, and Austrian consuls in Jerusalem had, upon instructions, joined Gillman in protest against the deportation of their nationals. The Turks, adamant, fixed a date for a general expulsion of non-Ottoman Jews from Jerusalem, but the day set came and went without any sign that the Turks meant to enforce their threat.

New American arrivals kept up a peculiar game with the Turkish officials: they somehow disembarked at Jaffa, escaped to Jerusalem from the lax surveillance of the Turkish police, and remained there under the protection of their consul who refused either to surrender them or to sign any warrant limiting their stay.

Finally, in October 1888 a compromise formula was proposed to the envoys by the Turkish Foreign Office which purported to end the impasse on the Jewish immigration issue. Five months after the delivery of the original protests by the American, French, and British plenipotentiaries the Porte replied with a curt *note verbale* stating "that the measure concerning the Israelites going to Palestine shall not be applied except to those who emigrate in number (*en nombre*) and that no obstacle shall be placed to the sojourn of those who are not in this class. Instructions in this sense have already been sent to the Governor of Jerusalem." This was a formula much to the Turkish taste, a proposal which sounded eminently reasonable in Constantinople and was susceptible of broad local interpretation. Since American Jews who were either pilgrims or prospective settlers were hardly numerous enough to fall under the ban it was difficult to argue the issue. Theoretically it put a quietus on the Jewish colonization of Palestine, but that could not be considered a legitimate cause for American diplomatic intervention. Nevertheless, since the formula was an evasion of the principle that no rules affecting Jews *qua* Jews should be tolerated, the English ambassador was prone not to accept it. Straus adopted an attitude which showed that he could outplay the Turks at their own diplomatic circumlocutions; he decided neither to accept nor to reject the formula, reserving full freedom of action to take further steps in any particular case which might arise in the future.

In April 1889 Straus received another embossed memorial from Jerusalem: the Jerushalaim Lodge of the Independent Order of B'nai Brith praised him for having been instrumental in securing the abrogation of the law against immigration. "Considerable allowance must be made for the extravagant language in which the Memorial is couched after the manner of the east," was his diffident remark to the State Department when he transmitted it. Calling Straus the "first who shed glory upon the Jewish name as a statesman," the Memorial went on to heap praise and gratitude upon him for heeding the cries of his fellow-Jews and prevailing upon the Turks to repeal the exclusion laws. "It will always be remembered with deep satisfaction in the annals of the Jewish history that a man, chosen by the enlightened Government of the great American Republic to represent her important interests at the Sublime Porte, never forgot his suffering brethren. You not only came to Jerusalem, accompanied by your noble lady, to pay homage to the sacred memories of our glorious past, but having become acquainted with the restrictive measures taken against foreign Jewish emigrants you used all your influence with your colleagues, and with the well-intentioned Turkish Government and succeeded in having the exceptional law repealed. It is to you that we owe no more to witness the heartrending scenes of the unhappy emigrants being mercilessly driven from our shores. . . ."

Straus was obviously somewhat disturbed by the implication that he had acted on behalf of the refugees because he himself was a Jew; hence in replying to this testimonial he made the point explicit that any action he had taken "was in pursuance of and in strict compliance with the Department's Instructions, to protect American citizens abroad in their rights and privileges, irrespective of race and creed."

In the first years after the promulgation of the new formula the Turks construed the immigration law very liberally; Consul Henry Gillman reported in September 1890 that some hundred Jews at once landed without the least obstruction. Though Straus received the embossed memorial, Gillman in Jerusalem was convinced that it was primarily *his* efforts which had brought about the change in Turkish immigration policy. He saw himself as the agent of Divine Providence, ordained to facilitate the entrance into the land of the Jews who were being driven out of Russia by its harsh decrees: "The Russian consul affords them no protection; therefore this unfortunate and persecuted people are at the mercy of the Turkish Government if they choose to drive them out. The modified decree alone stands in the way."

The benign attitude on the part of the Turks did not long outlast the new wave of immigration in 1891.

SELAH MERRILL ON JEWS AND JEWISH COLONIES

In 1882 there had come to the Jerusalem consulate a former army chaplain, Selah Merrill, who was to occupy the post, with intervals, for almost three decades. Merrill considered himself an authority on all matters ancient and modern relating to Palestine and the Near East. Though he had graduated from a theological seminary, he preferred not to have the title reverend used and chose to describe himself as a scientist, naturalist and explorer. His travel books and antiquarian studies are in the popular style of the period and show no great distinction; but he had an inquisitive mind and, whatever his prejudices, learned and reported a good deal about the Jewish community in Palestine.

Shortly after his arrival, he recorded that despite the Exclusion Law, there had been a net increase of about 7,000 Jews in a year. Of this rise in the Jewish population of Palestine, he allotted roughly 4,000 to Jerusalem, 2,000 to Jaffa, and 1,000 to Hebron. Many more immigrants had departed because living conditions were too miserable in the crowded cities. The Turks kept the official figures of Jewish immigration low, at 4,000, but this was based upon known debarkations at Jaffa, while most Jews were resorting to less obtrusive routes. They arrived at Beirut or some other Syrian port and made their way overland.

Despite a good harvest in 1882 the sudden influx had pushed up prices by twenty-five percent. Building construction had increased and Jerusalem had an air of prosperity—though Selah Merrill was not deceived by the boom; all it meant to him was good-fortune for a small group of Jews amid the overwhelming wretchedness of the rest of the Jewish population. By 1883 Merrill, who had travelled extensively in Asia Minor, considered Jerusalem one of the most crowded cities in the East. Multitudes lived in stived houses, dens without ventilation. A number of families occupied a single room. He mentioned the purchase of land for Jewish colonization, but he was very skeptical about the prospects because of the Turkish government's hostility.

In July 1884, after the full impact of the pogrom migrations, Merrill set the Jewish population of Jerusalem at 20,000, a rise of about thirty-three percent in six years, which brought with it even more crowding in the hovels of the Jewish quarter. Proportionately, the Jews of Jerusalem still comprised half the inhabitants of the city as they had in 1869, the remainder being Mohammedan and Christian in equal parts. Three years later, in 1887, when Consul Gillman estimated the total population at 50,000, the three religions still preserved their old proportions and the Jews had increased to 25,000. The total population of the land, Gillman estimated at about 500,000, four-fifths of whom were fellaheen.

The number of American Jews tended to keep pace with the general growth of the old settlement. While the overwhelming number of Jewish immigrants to Palestine came directly from the Russian pale, most of the American Jews were only once removed from the same area. They had spent a varying number of years in the United States, had become naturalized and then had "gone up to the land" for reasons of health or religion. A few of the American Jews were retired businessmen with small incomes, but the majority had come to live on the same air of Eretz Israel as the other immigrants.

At the close of 1877 the consular records of Jerusalem residents recognized 75 American citizens, who almost without exception were Jews. By December 1879 the number had increased to 105, though Consul Willson felt that he was retaining under his protection persons who lacked adequate proof of citizenship merely because his predecessors had bestowed recognition upon them. In June 1879 he recorded 107 American Jews and one "native American"; at the end of 1880 their number was 115. By 1882 Selah Merrill counted 184 American citizens and six months later, 164 naturalized and 35 native-born Americans. In January 1891 Henry Gillman listed 317 American residents in Jerusalem who, with few exceptions, were all Jews.

When in 1891 Henry Gillman was succeeded at the consulate by Selah Merrill on his second term of service in Jerusalem, a man with a very different attitude towards the Russian Jews took over. Upon his return to the Jerusalem post after an absence of about six years, Merrill found a great many changes resulting from the Jewish immigration of the eighties, and much of what he saw irked him. There was incipient talk of a Jewish state, general excitement about Palestine colonization in the European and American press. Merrill resolved to set the Department straight on this problem in a long memorandum entitled *Jews and Jewish Colonies in Palestine*. Though opinionated in his views on the "Jewish Question," this report of

October 3, 1891 is thorough in many of its factual presentations of Jewish immigration. When it becomes highly colored with personal feeling, its very distortions are significant.

Merrill estimated that the influx of 1882–1883 had doubled the number of Jewish inhabitants in Palestine. During the following decade annual immigration fluctuated sharply, reaching a low ebb in the fall of 1891. "Respectable journals" had put the total Jewish population at 150,000; Merrill considered this a gross exaggeration, setting 50,000 as the top figure. Emigration had counterbalanced the early waves of immigration. Many Jews arrived, looked over the prospects of the country, and returned home. Within the year prosperous Jews had come, examined the investment potentialities of the land, and, after expressing their disappointment to Merrill, had sailed away. Poor Jewish tradesmen found the occupations they were accustomed to pursue in eastern Europe overcrowded, and after a brief stay, they too had departed. Even native Palestinian Jews or old-time settlers emigrated because the great influx of new Jews had made the competition hard. Finally, the Turkish government had expelled about 200 families in accordance with the provisions of their immigration law which they had begun to enforce again. The Jews had thus not found in Palestine the paradise which American and English enthusiasts imagined and Merrill condemned any further large-scale immigration as foolhardy: "To pour into this impoverished country tens of thousands of Jews would be an unspeakable calamity both for the country and for the Jews themselves. Mere enthusiasm of friends in Europe and America would not keep these poor immigrants alive."

Selah Merrill prepared an extensive survey of the Jewish population in Palestine in order to contradict exaggerated reports of their numbers. He was the first consul to make a serious attempt at accuracy and his results bear conviction. His figures were compiled not from official Turkish sources but from data furnished by the secretaries of the Jewish congregations, by the heads of the agricultural colonies, schools, pilgrim houses, hospitals, asylums, poor-houses, and by the various consuls with Jews under their protection. The geographic area covered roughly corresponded to the area of Palestine under the British Mandate and he paid no attention to the Turkish subdivisions of the Sanjak of Jerusalem and the Vilayets of Beirut and of Damascus. The total for cities and towns showed 40,353 Jews distributed in nine centers: Jerusalem, 25,322; Safed, 6126; Tiberias, 2900; Jaffa, 2700; Haifa, 1640; Hebron, 1200; Acre, 200; Ramleh, 166;

Nablous, 99. The eleven agricultural colonies reported a total of 435 families. Using an estimate of five persons per family as average—which he considered high for the colonies—he counted about 2000 Jews living on the land. Thus he arrived at a grand total of between 42,000 and 43,000 for the whole of urban and rural Palestine. The inflated figures in the newspapers he attributed for the most part to Jews who counted each Jaffa arrival as a family and each cluster of houses around Jerusalem as a colony.

The land boom of 1890 and the first half of 1891 was to be explained in part, Merrill believed, to predictions that Palestine was passing into "the control of the Hebrew race." Parcels of land which in the middle eighties had cost a few hundred dollars sold for ten times their original price. The plans for the Jerusalem-Jaffa railroad, extravagant talk that Palestine was being peopled with Jews, and rumors spread by "interested persons" in Russian, English and American newspapers to the effect that fortunes could be made in Palestine were all factors in the land price inflation.

Consul Merrill warned the State Department against the Blackstone Memorial which in March 1891 had been submitted to the President, bearing the signatures of a galaxy of eminent Americans who, though they were abysmally ignorant of Near Eastern politics, nevertheless sponsored a movement for the return of Palestine to the Jews. The Memorial was typical of American Protestant messianism. Apparently Reverend Blackstone had approached Secretary of State Sherman to ask whether the United States would join with the great powers of Europe in order to guarantee Palestine to the Jews on some basis acceptable to the Turkish government. Sherman went so far as to ask the American Minister at Constantinople, Solomon Hirsch, whether the Turks could be prevailed upon to pursue such a course of action; to which Hirsch had replied that the Turkish government would not part peaceably with any of its territory. "Turkey was not in the habit of giving away whole provinces for the asking," was Merrill's sharp comment. "They seem to forget that Turkey has a right to say who shall settle upon the soil."

In July 1891, the Turkish government had again stopped the immigration of Russian Jews and as a consequence the land boom was deflated; prices dropped by a third. This cut short the activities of the speculators who had migrated for easy business profit, not agricultural settlement. According to Merrill, the prime impetus to the issuance of the new order banning Jewish immigration had come this time from a petition of Mohammedans and Christians of Jerusalem sent to Constantinople in protest against the underselling practices of the new Jewish tradesmen. It was the same argument the Jews had heard throughout the world wherever they had migrated. "The older inhabitants . . . found their work taken directly out of their hands by a class whom the government allowed to reside here and whom it protected." Merrill saw in the whole new migration movement of Jews into Palestine only a duplication in Jerusalem of the Jewish quarters of New York, London, and Prague.

In the fall of 1890 Consul Henry Gillman had taken brief notice of the new agricultural colonies established, he wrote, "under the Rothschild patronage." Selah Merrill's report of 1891 on the Jews and Jewish Colonies was the first general consular evaluation of the colonization movement, and it was a derogatory estimate, often sarcastic, of the whole enterprise. Many of his strictures were nothing more than an echo of prevalent late nineteenth century anti-semitism with its fixed ideas about Jewish character. A few of his factual observations, however, are not unlike those of Ahad Ha'am's reports after his inspection tours of the land for the Odessa Committee of the Lovers of Zion. It was Merrill's conclusion that "1. Palestine is not ready for the Jews. 2. The Jews are not ready for Palestine." He did not believe that the Jews wished to colonize Palestine; the Jews did not want land, they wanted only cities "where they can live on the fortunes or the misfortunes of other people." The distribution of the Jewish population in Palestine was for him a concrete illustration of the manner in which Jews were drawn to urban areas. They had always gathered in the four sacred cities, Jerusalem, Hebron, Safed, and Tiberias; and more than half of them were in Jerusalem. Only in the late eighties did they spread out to Jaffa, Ramleh, Haifa, Acre, and Nablous, but these were also business centers. Of the latter group the overwhelming number of Jews had concentrated in the two seaport towns of Jaffa and Haifa.

Despite all the talk about the new agricultural settlements, Selah Merrill remained unimpressed. He had visited some of them and his picture was contemptuous. "Able-bodied men that have to be hired to be colonists are not the kind of material that is needed to make a new settlement flourish." According to his data, out of 439 families in the colonies, 255 were given a stipend of four dollars a month for each man, woman, and child by the Rothschilds. House rent was free, and so were schools, synagogues, doctors, medicine, and water. He contrasted these generous gratuities with the independent enterprise of the American settlers in the West and arrived at the conclusion that where a regular stipend is assured, individual initiative is not likely to be relied upon. In further contrast to the Jewish colonies, he pointed to the German "Temple Colony" near Jerusalem, "one of the most attractive places in Palestine," where a prosperous settlement was built through frugality and perseverance. One of the largest Jewish colonies which he visited (he did not name it) was a picture of dilapidation. "Houses were broken and patched, windows were stuffed with rags, dooryards were covered with litter, outhouses and fences were neglected, crops were poorly cultivated and weeds were growing abundantly everywhere."

Selah Merrill inveighed against Jewish clannishness, refusal to assimilate, "trifling observances," failure to establish themselves anywhere but in close settlements. He felt that there must have been some hidden justification for the persecution of the Jews in Russia, else that government would not have been so anxious to get rid of them. The fate of a Jewish Kingdom in Palestine would be disastrous. He used the standard argument for keeping people in bondage: that previous servitude unfits them for freedom. "It is only within a period of two or three generations that the Jews have been emancipated in the various countries of the world. After ages of bondage they have received their freedom and as a race they do not know what to do with it. When and where have they learned the art of self-government? The quickest way to annihilate them would be to place them in Palestine with no restrictions or influences from any civilized government, and allow them to govern themselves: they would very soon destroy each other." For the Jews Selah Merrill had remedies: the Jew had to rely on himself not bounties, stop early marriages which produce weaklings, and have real education beyond the Talmud which fits them "for nothing whatever."

While the haughty Merrill occupied himself with such splenetic utterances and foretold a miserable end for any efforts to colonize Palestine, more sanguine predictions came from other quarters. The *New York Daily Tribune* on May 31, 1891, ran an article entitled "Agricultural Colonization Promising Great Results," in which it praised the Jewish colonists and supported the idea of a Palestine rebuilt by the cruelly persecuted Russian refugees; the major deterrent, it felt, was the fear that Russia pushing down from the north would soon be master of Palestine and the Jews would again be in the hands of their oppressors. Several years later, on December 1, 1898, G. Bie Ravndal, the American Consul at Beirut, sent a despatch on the Jews of Palestine which gave the lie to Merrill's charges that the Jewish colonists were not men of fibre who could make a new settlement thrive. Ravndal wrote of the Jewish farmers: "The movement is . . . bringing out new qualities in the Jews residing in Palestine. They are no longer content with studying the Talmud and living on charity, but are waking to the fact, as the Hebrew would put it, that to till the ground is worship of God." When it was printed this favorable report did not fail to bring a sharp rejoinder from Merrill, who, despite the fact that the division between the Beirut and the Jerusalem districts ran "somewhere" south of Haifa, considered the whole of Palestine and its works to be his special bailiwick.

In May 1893 a Turkish order was issued, forbidding land purchases by Jews. It was the Turks' response to the wild land speculation of the immigrants which Ahad Ha'am had so bitterly condemned. But under the protocol of 1874 the United States had accepted for its nationals the right to acquire real estate, and since the new Turkish order covered all Jews, including United States citizens, it clearly again involved that issue of non-discrimination among American nationals which was basic to United States policy. Consul Merrill was not as fervent an exponent of this doctrine as his predecessor Henry Gillman had been, and he was not too much disturbed by the new order. He quoted with approval the claim of the Turkish government to a right of discrimination against what it considered an "objectionable class," just as the United States had passed special legislation against the Chinese. Moreover he had it on the authority of the Rutiger Company, Jerusalem bankers who participated in most Palestine land transactions, that the Turkish order would be annulled or at least amended. The modification, which Merrill reported on August 18, 1893, was in the spirit of the compromises effected between Turkish edicts and the Treaty rights under the system of capitulations, after a round of negotiations. Jews would be allowed to acquire freehold property locally, but all purchases of crown lands—the areas most readily available for colonization—would have to be referred to Constantinople. This would naturally lead to endless bureaucratic delays. The new order had been formulated in the Turkish manner, flexibly, so that local authorities could expand or contract its privileges with changing conditions or the payment of baksheesh. In apparent apology for the Turkish decision, Merrill made the point that the prohibition against Jews buying land was not "based upon any religious consideration . . . being solely on the ground that the proscribed persons were Jews of an objectionable class." Merrill did not exert himself in fighting the new regulation. In practice it made the acquisition of land by Jews cumbersome, though not impossible; the ancient remedy of baksheesh remained.

RENEWAL OF THE EXCLUSION LAWS

When Consul Edwin S. Wallace came to Jerusalem in 1893, the perennial problem of the immigration or residence of American Jews was again revived. It was extraordinarily difficult for the American consul to cope with the devious techniques adopted by Turkish officials in putting their discriminatory rules into practice. As far as the consul was concerned, the only known juridical prohibition against Jewish entrance into Palestine remained the *en nombre* formula, but in New York the Turkish consul, while visaing the passports of American Jews had written in Turkish a three-months limitation "according to regulation." This was a clear violation of previous commitments to our Minister Straus, and Consul Wallace was forthright in his statement of the American position. "I shall insist upon the right of an American to remain here as long as he wishes providing his behaviour is proper." The Department in its turn supported him in guaranteeing full protection of Americans "temporarily residing in Palestine," a somewhat diluted statement of the Treaty rights, a retreat from the absolute position of Grover Cleveland's day. The abstract pronouncements of the Department in any event afforded the Consul only limited guidance in his day-to-day haggling with the Turkish officials in Jerusalem. The grand generality of United States policy did not answer Wallace's pressing questions: What if the Jews were actually ordered to leave? How did Jews who were the sons of American citizens but born in Palestine fit into the "temporarily residing" formula? What about those Jews who had no intention of returning to America? What about Jews claiming protection on the ground that a husband or a father in the United States had been naturalized? There was growing evidence of a tendency to backslide from the hammer blows of the Oscar Straus notes to the Porte. The annoyance of Selah Merrill with the multiplication of his charges and the responsibilities they entailed were reflected in Washington.

In 1898, when Selah Merrill returned to his consular post for his third term of service, he found that the general Turkish restrictions on Jewish immigration were being applied to American Jews despite all previous agreements and promises. Jews were prevented from landing, had to give guarantees that they would not prolong their stay beyond thirty or ninety days, and were forced to resort to bribery to remain. Merrill was not a man to stomach contradictions between general rules and specific practices. He would not let the Department rest comfortably with vague agreements between the Turkish Foreign Minister and the American envoy at Constantinople. If it was lawful for an American passport held by a Jew to be stamped with a time limitation, then the Consul should support the Turkish government by helping to get the Jews out of Palestine after the expiration of the period allowed for their pilgrimage. If it was unlawful, then the United States government should clarify its position to the Turkish government.

Minister Straus, during his second mission, had written to Consul General Dickinson that it was his understanding from conversations with the Turkish Minister of Foreign Affairs that Jews could live, visit or travel at will and that the only restriction was against immigration *en masse* for purposes of colonization. This agreement by no means appeased Merrill, because he knew that the practice at Jaffa had nothing to do with the promises in Constantinople.

On the principle of the American right to visit and reside anywhere in the Ottoman Empire, Selah Merrill was a strict constructionist. He would not tolerate subterfuge. If American policy stood for non-discrimination then no time limitation should be entered by Turkish officials on the backs of passports either in the United States or elsewhere. This principle should be committed to writing on a diplomatic level and should apply to both individuals and families. Unless this final agreement was signed by the highest Turkish Ministers, Americans at Jaffa would continue to be molested by local officials and the consul in Jerusalem would bear the weight of endless disputes. Merrill complained to Washington: "While the Turkish Minister in Constantinople is talking pleasantly to our Ambassador and telling him that 'these regulations apply only to Jews who come *en masse*' and our Ambassador is writing to me that 'the arrangement is perfectly clear and sufficient,' the Turkish officials in Jerusalem and Jaffa, *By Order of This Same Turkish Minister,* are applying these restrictions rigidly to every individual Jew." The Department adhered to its general instructions and left Merrill to his dilemmas.

STRAUS'S SECOND MISSION TO TURKEY

In the closing years of the nineteenth century, the United States was again represented at the Sublime Porte by Oscar S. Straus. He had reluctantly undertaken a second mission to Constantinople in March 1898 at the insistent demand of President McKinley. Straus's chief task, as outlined to him by the Secretary of State, was the negotiation of an indemnity for the Turkish destruction of mission properties in Harpoot during the Armenian massacres of 1895. The United States, burgeoning as a great power, was in no mood to be put off by the disintegrating Ottoman Empire, and there was talk of war unless our demands were satisfied. Straus's instructions also included two issues which affected the lives of the American Jews in Palestine: the conclusion of a treaty or understanding mutually to recognize the full rights of naturalized citizens, and that perennial of American-Turkish relations, the interpretation of Article IV of the Treaty of 1830, which defined the extra-territorial rights of American citizens in Turkey.

The persecution of the Jews in eastern Europe, the dispersion of the refugees throughout the world, the rising wave of international anti-semitism, and the vision of Theodor Herzl had culminated in the assembly of the First World Zionist Congress in Basle in 1897. There a program had been adopted for the establishment of a Jewish homeland in Palestine predicated upon the grant of clear-cut autonomy by the Turkish Government. Through the Basle Congress the Sultan of Turkey was thus confronted with specific proposals touching his realm from an organized body of western and eastern European Jews whose real strength he could not accurately gauge. Zionism as an organized world political movement was novel, and its fresh vigor aroused hopes and fears in many parts of the globe. The mysterious travels of its leader Herzl were the subject of speculation in the chancelleries of Europe and their immediate import was often exaggerated. In 1898, in quest of a German protectorate for the Jewish homeland and a circuitous entrée to the Sultan's presence, Herzl was frantically trying, through a score of go-betweens, to gain an audience with Kaiser Wilhelm, the new friend of the Turk.

The publication of the Zionist program with its demands on Turkey placed a prominent American Jew who was our envoy at the Porte in a delicate diplomatic situation. En route to Constantinople in September 1898, Minister Straus stopped at Vienna, and there Dr. S. R. Landau, correspondent of the *London Jewish Chronicle* and editor of the official Zionist organ *Die Welt,* interviewed him about his attitude towards Zionism. Straus, a wary man, replied with a show of propriety that as the diplomatic agent of the United States, he had no opinions not related to his duties; Zionism did not fall within the sphere of those duties, hence he had no views official or unofficial to express on the subject. Having avoided this diplomatic pitfall Straus proceeded to Constantinople, to be welcomed warmly by the Sultan. Abdul Hamid, who was a complete personalist in his relations with the foreign plenipotentiaries at his court, had a genuine liking for Straus.

In October Kaiser Wilhelm paid a visit of state to Constantinople before continuing on his famous pilgrimage to Palestine. Herzl had come to Constantinople at the same time by prearrangement and was received by the Kaiser in an inconclusive audience whose significance the Zionist leader's fiery imagination inflated out of all relation to the realities of existing power politics. While Herzl hung on every whim of the German and Turkish imperial lackeys, Straus was a figure of eminence at the official reception for the Kaiser, and the newspapers of the day noted that Wilhelm marked him out for special attention.

After the Kaiser's departure, Straus threw himself into the maze of political manoeuvres at Yildiz Kiosk and in a few months achieved what were considered in Washington diplomatic triumphs on the missionaries' indemnity, their travel rights in Asia Minor, and the non-discriminatory treatment of all Americans, Jews and Christians alike, who were thereafter permitted to visit Palestine and Syria freely. These questions had hardly been brought to a successful issue when an incident occurred which was characteristic of negotiations at the Porte and which explains why apparently conclusive arrangements defining American Jewish and missionary rights of movement in Turkey were renewed every few years. The Minister of Foreign Affairs, Tewfik, frantically informed Straus that the Turkish Minister in Washington, Ferrouh Bey, had telegraphed the Sultan that he had amicably arranged with the Department of State to stop the entry of missionaries and Jews into Palestine and Syria. These agreements, Ferrouh Bey charged, had been upset by Straus when he wrested concessions on the missionaries' travel permits and the free immigration of American Jews into Palestine. By inference, thus, Tewfik was accused of incompetence and disloyalty. The Minister of Foreign Affairs was disturbed by the message because it had the earmarks of a cabal to oust him from his place. The Ministers at the Porte, as distinct from the Palace, had opposed Ferrouh's appointment and Tewfik called him an unreliable "canaille," and a drunkard who had nevertheless been appointed through Palace influence. According to Tewfik, the telegram was Ferrouh's vengeance, since he knew that such intrigues were not discouraged either by the Palace entourage or by the Sultan himself. Straus came to Tewfik's rescue, produced his last Instruction from Washington which showed that no such agreement had been made. He even wired Secretary of State Hay who despatched a detailed telegraphic reply in the same sense, which Straus handed to Tewfik. "I was glad to do him this service as he is a straightforward man and my relations with him are the best," Straus wrote in his diary. In any other country in the world except in this Wonderland—as Herzl named it—of Yildiz Kiosk, the Minister from Turkey would have been recalled. Instead, at Straus's next audience with Abdul Hamid the Sultan made a special point of praising his Washington Minister as a capable young man of whom he was fond and whom he had brought up. In the symbolism of Turkish administration this was to serve as a counter-balance to Tewfik's enmity for Ferrouh, of which the Sultan was well informed.

The following autumn Straus gave an official luncheon party to which Minister Ferrouh, on leave from Washington, was invited and there they continued their diplomatic duel. Ferrouh made the first thrust by informing Straus that he had many enemies in Washington, persons who would have liked to see war with Turkey and were opposed to his mission because it had brought about peaceful relations. They then parried about the mooted elevation of their respective missions to the status of embassies, Straus feigning indifference. Finally they touched upon the subject of Jewish immigration into Palestine. Straus said he thought it best that the immigration cease. Ferrouh took the opposite view; he was in favor of it, but "they" should have seen him first. "Evidently he thinks there would be some money in it for him," Straus noted in his diary. His summary description of the Turkish Minister in Washington could have been applied to half the creatures in the Turkish administration: "Ferrouh is very treacherous and tortuous in his character, but that is apparent in his face. He has intelligence and energy and does not seem to be embarrassed by scruples. Knowing this, I have no difficulty in seeing through him and believing what I like and guarding what I say."

On the eve of Straus's departure from Constantinople on leave in December 1899 the Sultan sent his Chamberlain with a confidential

message to be delivered personally to the Minister. He said that
the Sultan entertained the highest personal regard for Straus and
though no Minister had been more vigilant for his country's interests,
the Sultan considered him fair and just. Because Straus was an Israelite and not of the same faith as the hated missionaries, the Sultan
preferred him to a Christian envoy, and he promised that if he returned
to his post any pending matters would be amicably adjusted. The
Sultan reminded Straus that he always treated the Israelites in his
Empire with the greatest tolerance and that they enjoyed more liberty in Turkey than in most European countries. With this flattery
the bankrupt Abdul Hamid aimed to court favor with an American
Jew who presumably had influence with Jewish capitalists in Europe
and the United States.

HERZL AND THE MINISTER: AN ENCOUNTER

It was on Straus's journey homeward that he received Theodor
Herzl during a stop-over at the Hotel Imperial in Vienna. The interview had no momentous political implications at the time, but it was
characteristic of the cross-currents which were running through the
Jewries of the world during the pogrom migrations and the early
years of political Zionism. Both Herzl and Straus left long accounts
of the meeting in their respective diaries and since both were intro-
spective men with strange souls, the counterpoint of the two versions
affords an insight into the men and the viewpoints they represented.

On December 27, 1899 Herzl was waiting with frantic impatience
for a word from one of his paid intermediaries who was supposed to
arrange an audience with the Sultan during which he would make his
plea for a Zionist homeland in Palestine. "From Constantinople nothing, nothing, nothing. *Je me désespère.*" The newspapers reported that
envoy Oscar Straus was passing through Vienna; Gottheil, the American Zionist, had written that Straus would look him up; in 1895 Ben
Yehuda, reporting the interplay of political forces in Turkey, had
intimated that the American Minister was secretly a supporter of
Zionism. Though Herzl was anxious for a meeting, there were questions of precedence involved in calling on Straus about which he was
punctilious. He noted, "At any rate I think it fitting not to go to
him first." But the next day he succumbed to his eagerness and
through a third person requested an interview which was promptly
granted.

The Jewish literary man from Vienna, the visionary who had generated a world movement and was destined to be revered as the creator of a modern state, encountered the hard-headed American Jewish practical man of affairs who was equally successful as politician, ambassador, writer, and lawyer. Straus was obviously closer to the Sultan than any man Herzl had had access to in his international manipulations to get just one audience—years of feverish activity during which he had been mulcted of hundreds of pounds by all sorts of denizens of the diplomatic underworld and sycophants of the ante-chambers of the Palace. History has made of Herzl a far more imposing figure than the cautious knowing politician, but at the time Herzl was the suppliant.

They sized each other up. Straus described Herzl as above medium height, well-groomed, with coal black beard and hair and black eyes. "He is forty years of age, but looks even younger. He has the air of an active energetic man, keen expression, and looks what he is, a newspaper writer or rather theatrical critic and playwright. He is certainly not of appearance a man impelled by religious motives which he is not nor does he claim to be, nor has he the appearance of a leader or a philosopher neither of which he is."

Herzl noted that Straus was "smaller than middle height, with a thin reddish beard, hooked nose, Jewish *Hänkelohren,* sparse hair, about 48 years old, dry, *smart,* and yet immediately sympathetic because of his honest eyes."

After the first five minutes, Herzl wrote, they were intimate. Straus began cautiously, remarking that Herzl had a reputation for being indiscreet. Herzl expressed astonishment and in denial offered the fact that he had scrupulously refused, under every manner of pressure, to reveal the substance of his conversation with the German Emperor in Jerusalem in the fall of 1898. The real reason for this mystification Herzl took good care not to disclose: the Kaiser had promised him nothing and the secrecy was a veil for emptiness.

Straus at the outset again took the position that as an American official, accredited to the Sultan, he had no opinion to express on Herzl's movement or project. He had been told that Herzl was so devoted to his scheme that he would sacrifice all considerations of prudence to advance it. While Straus commended such devotion, he could not permit himself to be sacrificed on Herzl's altar. Herzl remembered a more complimentary version of the exchange. "He did not hold my recklessness against me because in so great a matter one could not spare individuals." In his diary, Straus explained to himself the subtle reason for his reticence on Zionism. "I certainly did not propose to cast carelessly aside with a veto the aspiration which Zionism embodied for the poor oppressed Orthodox Jews."

Herzl, probing, tried to learn whether the Sultan had ever spoken to Straus on the subject of Zionism. The Minister responded that he had not since Abdul Hamid very probably knew that it was not an American question. Zionism had come into the picture only in connection with the Turkish effort to exclude American Jews from Palestine because of the "Zionistic influx"; here Straus had always insisted on the rights of American citizens irrespective of their race or religion and had carried his point as each individual case arose. In his own mind Straus had created an absolute barrier between what he thought were his functions as a proper American envoy and any other considerations.

As the conversation with Herzl progressed, Straus was drawn into the cauldron of the Jewish Question and could not refrain from expressing his opinions as a Jew. He considered it unfortunate that so many poor Jews should crowd into Palestine when there was already dire poverty and no work in the land. "I had advised officially against further immigration," was his frank statement. Far from disagreeing with Straus, Herzl maintained that he too was exerting himself to prevent immigration until the rights of a Chartered Company had been obtained from the Sultan.

This was the cornerstone of Herzl's political edifice—violent opposition to any slow, illegal infiltration into the land. The seepage of Jews into Palestine only led to hostility and ultimately to the enactment of exclusion laws. Herzl's State was to emerge full-grown within a few years through a gigantic effort of world Jewry. In his grand design, the State would arise powerful from birth and in a brief period neighboring states would so benefit from its creation that they would give it their support. Before Herzl's viewpoint prevailed at the Basle Congress, some eastern and central European Zionists thought in terms of a slow penetration of Palestine by the Jews until they grew mighty enough to throw off the Turkish yoke, declare their independence, and gain the recognition of the Powers, as had the Balkan nations. Herzl deemed this approach futile and wasteful, insisting on a complete concentration of all energies on obtaining Palestine through a decree of the Sultan, in a manner recognized in international law. Herzl was an absolutist on this principle of a formal declaration from

the Porte. The further establishment of isolated colonies, ravaged by
disease, through the pittances of the Lovers of Zion or the paternalism
of the French Baron Rothschild were diversions of the Zionist main
effort, as long as there was no formal legal guarantee from the Turks.
After 1897 a group of Russian Jews led by Ahad Ha'am refused to
accept the Herzlian thesis that their slow plodding efforts should be
abruptly suspended while their "diplomatist" roamed the world negotiating with potentates in secret.

Minister Straus, though aloof from this inner Zionist controversy,
was of one mind with Herzl on the subject of Jewish infiltration
into Palestine. During his first mission to Turkey in 1887–1888 he,
more than any foreign envoy, had been responsible for the relaxation
of the Turkish Exclusion Laws, at least in practice, even though the
general principle was still enshrined in the confusion of Ottoman
legislation. By the turn of the century, during his second mission, he
had come to realize the utter impossibility of crowding more Jews
into the same miserable cities unprepared to receive them. The abstract principle of free Jewish immigration—whether of orthodox
Jews going to die in Jerusalem or Zionist colonists seeking to join
the new agricultural settlements—had to bow before the facts of a
poverty- and plague-ridden existence in Palestine. Straus never publicly attacked immigration because he was not the sort of man who
would defy a great traditional sentiment, but in private he had to
counsel against it.

As for Herzl's elaborate backstairs manoeuvres with the venal petty
officials of the Sultan, Straus was profoundly skeptical. Herzl cryptically informed the envoy that he was now in correspondence with
someone very near the Sultan and he had hopes of getting the Chartered Company approved. Straus tried to enlighten him about the
effectiveness of these so-called Turks of influence and their supposed
confidences. He told Herzl that he had been shown a letter written
by him to Artin Pasha, nominally under-secretary of State, but actually
the biggest rogue in the Empire, whom the Sultan kept in office because
he was an Armenian, for the express purpose of misleading and holding in check that poor oppressed people. Straus warned him against
Artin Pasha and expressed great doubt about Herzl's unnamed correspondent because in his books no one had influence with the Sultan
but the Sultan himself and if Herzl ever hoped to get any rights he
had better go to Constantinople.

In general Straus's estimate of Abdul Hamid was far more realistic than the popular image of the mad Red Sultan spread by Gladstone. When in 1901 Herzl finally did get his audience, after a delay of about two years, his famous description of Abdul Hamid gibed with Straus's in many respects. Yet despite his recognition that the Sultan alone kept all power and decision in his own hand, Herzl continued until his death to waste his energies on the Turkish scoundrels who were part of the scenery of Yildiz Kiosk and who were cannily used by the Sultan as an instrument of obfuscation. Herzl knew the character of his "agents" and in his diary he admitted to himself that he was being imposed upon; his recurrent rationalization was that *faut de mieux* he would use even these adventurers.

Though Straus had initiated the conversation with diplomatic reserve, according to Herzl he had ended by letting himself go, speaking in a blunt manner about the blackguards in and around the Palace. "The Ministers are idiots, cowardly and venal fellows. The Sultan does not care a fig for the whole of Turkey. Nothing is to be gotten from him through humanity and the like. Yes, if he could be shown money or other advantage he could perhaps be won over." Herzl thought that Straus was trying hard to get him to name his intermediary, but he kept silent to demonstrate his circumspection to the Minister. "He guessed here and there who it might be. I let him guess."

Herzl made an attempt to explain his great scheme to Straus, in essence the same one he later laid before the Sultan. The Zionists were to arrange to lend the Turks several million pounds—ten, or perhaps twenty (Straus could not remember distinctly)—in exchange for rights in Palestine. This was the heart of Herzlian politics: free the Sultan from the control of the French and British by refunding the Ottoman debt with a loan from Jewish capitalists. Herzl spent the last feverish years of his short life shuttling back and forth between the Sultan and his entourage in Constantinople and Jewish bankers in western Europe, now exaggerating to the Porte the ready availability of the money, now assuring the Rothschilds that the Charter from the Porte was about to be granted if only the money were forthcoming. The two elements never coalesced. Abdul Hamid always seemed to increase the tempo of his negotiations with Herzl when seeking more favorable terms in a French refunding agreement. The persecuted Jews of eastern Europe hung with bated breath on the consummation of the negotiations, and made of Herzl a demi-God. Such is the course of man that in the midst of these senseless negotiations in which Herzl was often enough the dupe, he created an international movement, the embryo of a State.

Straus pointedly refused to discuss the Turkish debt—the whole operation for obtaining the money sounded vague to him, he wrote —but the political realist, after two missions to Constantinople during which he had analyzed every aspect of Turkish administration, struck a body blow at the Herzlian conception. Straus could not see how these so-called rights of a Chartered Company in the English manner would secure the independent, stable concessions necessary for a Jewish State. How could Herzl prevent the recall of these rights whenever it suited the Sultan's purpose? Straus, with no reason to have faith in Turkish decrees, dismissed the significance of any papers signed at the Porte. Neither of them recorded a riposte to this argument. In defense of the Herzlian idea there is only this to be said: he had a contemporary Victorian notion that the Great Powers would force compliance with written commitments; and in his mind's eye he had a utopia, *Altneuland*. The whole settlement built up to vast power and magnificence in a few years would be able to defend itself. In July 1896 Herzl had even envisaged a Jewish army.

Straus perceived deep-rooted antagonism to the Palestine proposal in other quarters even more potent than the Turks. He pointed out that from the very inception it would encounter the hostility of all the Christian sects, Protestant, Roman, and Greek Orthodox. Herzl rejoined with historic insight that he considered only Rome as an opponent. In the diary, with characteristic Herzlian *esprit d'escalier*, he added: "The basic reason I forgot to tell him; it is because Rome is as oecumenical as Judaism. Rome is the rich brother who hates the poor one. The other churches are national and therefore do not need the Archimedes point of Jerusalem." Straus doubted from his own experience whether Herzl could get any support from Russia; he was obviously thinking of the close cooperation of the Russian Embassy with Turkish officials in the expulsion of Jews from Palestine in the 'eighties. Herzl disagreed and in this instance won the point historically. Ironically enough, the Russian Minister Plehve was the first representative of a great state who gave to Herzl an expression in writing—that longed-for piece of paper—of favor for a Jewish refuge in Palestine.

While he thought Palestine unattainable, Straus tried to persuade Herzl to the plan of colonizing Mesopotamia. It was a large territory inhabited only by nomadic Arab tribes, had been the most powerful country of antiquity famous for the hanging gardens of Babylon. All it needed was irrigation and the re-opening of the canals. He referred Herzl to the study of Professor Paul Haupt published some eighteen years before, which was aimed at German colonization. Herzl remarked that this was the Cyrus Adler plan, and remembered a brochure on the subject. Apparently a whole group of New York Jews, among them Judge Sulzberger, had studied the project and approved it. Herzl promised to regard the proposal more seriously since Straus considered Mesopotamian rights attainable. While to the eastern European Jews Palestine was the only Zion, the only refuge and homeland with historic ties, Herzl and many other leaders in western Europe were quite willing to experiment with new areas, which, though they may have lacked the same emotional bond, did not suffer from the political complexities of Palestine. Herzl was a pluralist in his diplomatic techniques. He told Straus that his movement could not rest on any single plan and that one always had to have another at hand in case the first failed. He mentioned, for example, Trietsch's Cyprus scheme, which, though he publicly opposed it, he had quietly encouraged. Straus knew of this project and had secured a letter of introduction for Trietsch from the British Ambassador O'Conor in Constantinople to the British Commissioner in Cyprus. Mesopotamia was particularly attractive to both Straus and Herzl because, with doubtful historical accuracy, they believed that it was the original home of Israel. "We could tie the mystical element in there," wrote Herzl.

They parted friends. Herzl recorded—though Straus did not—a promise that Straus would send him diplomatic hints which might be useful and opportune, under the pseudonym "Mesopotamicus." This was not too far-fetched; in Herzl's telegrams to his colleagues there were some really fanciful code names; Abdul Hamid was always "Cohn." Straus did not return to Turkey again until 1909, five years after Herzl's death, and there is no record of any further communication between the two in Herzl's voluminous diary.

After Herzl's departure from the hotel where they had met, Straus confided to his diary a final estimate of the Zionist leader. The political realist, with circumscribed vision, failed to grasp the seminal element of history in the man, or the iron historical chain which bound the Jews to Palestine. There is a melancholy in the conclusion of the successful Minister as in the last days of the nineteenth century he contemplated the wretched lot of the Jews throughout the world.

"I regret the movement has not a greater and wiser man at its head, who combines high aims with the character of a great leader. He does not measure up to the required standard. As the newspaper or even literary adjunct he would serve a better purpose. Herzl is not cast in the mold of such a cause. The leader will yet come forward and Herzl and Zionism will be cast aside. This new leader will head a band of colonists—from the land of their oppression to a new Zion —where I can't say—perhaps to the land of Ur in Chaldea, the birthplace of Abraham? Some such movement must come unless a greater measure of right and justice be accorded to oppressed Israel in the new century than has been theirs at the close of this one." In 1922 Straus in his published recollections revised his opinion of Herzl radically, though, after the manner of most autobiographers, he antedated his judgment. Writing of the Herzl interview he said, "It seemed to me that Herzl was one of those men who having capacity and idealism, attach themselves to a cause that appeals to their intellect or their sympathies and grow in spirit and effectiveness through the intensity of their devotion. Such men often develop extraordinary qualities of true greatness under conditions that impose weighty responsibilities, to an extent which they themselves did not realize."

Chapter III

THE COLONY OF AMERICAN JEWS
IN JERUSALEM

THE "JEWISH QUESTION"

In the last decade before World War I there was a marked decline of interest in the nineteenth century protectorate of the Jews of Palestine. The United States had emerged as a great economic power; and insofar as gratuitous involvements with the Porte over technical immigration rules for Jews—American and Russian Jews alike—were an impediment to the award of concessions, the diplomatic and consular representatives preferred to wink at the rigid principle previously enunciated. The Congress forced upon the State Department a break in diplomatic relations with Russia over travel restrictions against American Jews, but it was not accepted by most career men with favor. They considered the whole problem alien to expanding American business interests.

The Jews of the old settlement, who were the burden of consular relations in Palestine, showed all the ugly symptoms of decay. For Zionism and the new settlement ambassadors, consuls, and permanent officials in the State Department had nothing but contempt prior to the advent of Woodrow Wilson. American Zionists were considered a nuisance and the long-drawn-out disputes over the Turkish Exclusion Laws became a parochial interest with which officials preferred not to be bothered.

During this period there was a great controversy over the secession of an American Congregation of Jews in Jerusalem from the central body of the *Haluka*. It was an internal squabble in which Consul Wallace—one of the most benign and well-meaning men who ever held the post in Palestine—found himself embroiled against his better judgment.

In the legal sphere, after the passage of the United States Naturalization Act of 1907, the protectorate over Jews with a dubious status was first curtailed and then suspended altogether.

With Wilson's administration there was a complete reorientation of policy towards Palestine, the Jews, and Zionism. In a sense this was a reversion to the nineteenth century humanitarian conception. In Brandeis, the protagonist of the new policy in the Wilson administration, there was a far more powerful and effective protector for the Jewish settlement in Palestine than the Jews had had in any of the nineteenth century ministers or consuls.

THE STATUS OF AMERICAN JEWS

By 1884 the number of naturalized American Jews in Jerusalem had grown substantial enough to evoke a diplomatic exchange about their status between the American Minister and the Ministry of Foreign Affairs in Constantinople. The Turks still refused to recognize American naturalization, maintaining that when former Ottoman subjects who had changed their allegiance in the United States returned to Turkey they became Turks again. This affected a substantial number of *Haluka* Messengers who had utilized the opportunity of their charity missions in the United States to acquire citizenship.

General Lew Wallace informed the Turks in blunt, almost rude terms that naturalized American citizens enjoyed the full rights of native-born Americans. His warning to the Turks against maltreatment of naturalized Americans threatened action beyond mere diplomatic protest: "In accordance with these views the consul is instructed that if he finds in his jurisdiction many or few [such] Americans . . . they have a right to call upon him for protection, and it is his duty to protect them; and to that end he must exhaust the means usually of resort on such occasions; failing in them, he must close his consulate and come away, if possible bringing the threatened people with him and that I have no doubt the Government of the United States will have a vessel ready to receive him and them. These are in substance the instructions given, and I leave them to derive additional force and meaning from Your Highness' great intelligence and long experience in international affairs." The Turks had requested lists of American citizens in order to review the validity of individual naturalizations; General Wallace curtly refused, insisting that naturalized Americans had a right to live anywhere in Turkey under American protection as long as they went about their lawful business. The Turkish Minister of Foreign Affairs receded before this diplomatic onslaught and explained that he had referred only to delusive and fictitious naturalizations. Theoretically this ended the controversy. In practice, however, it became another perennial of American-Turkish relations, as the Jerusalem settlement of naturalized American Jews of Russian and Palestinian origin continued to increase.

During the visit of Minister Straus to Jerusalem in 1888 Governor Raoul Pasha complained that many Jews who enjoyed American consular protection were not Americans at all; to which the Minister replied with anger that if they had American passports they were Americans, and it was not the Governor's prerogative to question American documents.

The Porte continued to inveigh against the growing lists of American citizens in Turkey. For decades a naturalization Treaty was under discussion, but it could not be drafted to the satisfaction of both the United States Senate and the Sultan. The growth of foreign colonies subject to consular jurisdiction became a festering sore to the proud Turks. Every few years they attempted to emancipate themselves from the extra-territorial privileges of the foreigners and upon each attempt they had to yield to the united opposition of all the powers. When frontal attacks upon the capitulations proved futile the Turks tried harassment, calling into question the naturalization status of individual nationals under consular protection. It would be wrong to conceive of this as primarily a Jewish Question. In a sense the Turks were far more distressed about the extra-territorial status of naturalized Armenians who returned to Turkey as revolutionary agents of Armenian nationalism. In 1885 the Porte established a Bureau of Nationality, under whose rules any person residing in the Empire was to be considered a Turkish subject until he proved the contrary by presenting his documents for certification. American officials refused to impose any such conditions upon their nationals, and nothing happened.

In a despatch of November 26, 1887 to Secretary of State Bayard, Minister Straus made a comparative analysis of the various judicial practices of the nations in criminal cases under the system of capitulations. He arrived at the conclusion that the claims of the United States on behalf of its nationals exceeded those of all other powers. The English, Austrian, French, Italian, and Greek Governments allowed both trial and execution to remain in Turkish hands, though they insisted on approving the judgment. Russia and Prussia allowed a Turkish trial, but reserved execution of the sentence to themselves. The United States alone maintained exclusive jurisdiction over both trial and punishment. Straus would not commit himself on the merits of our interpretation of Article IV of the Treaty of 1830; he only added a confidential note that Turkish administration of justice in the provinces was still deplorable.

Through these many years of negotiation the United States never receded from its fundamental position on exclusive criminal jurisdiction. Thus it is quite understandable why American consular protection was prized above all others in Jerusalem. The immunities it bestowed made it worthwhile to risk falsifying naturalization papers and passports.

Henry Gillman, who came to the Jerusalem consulate in 1888, was an assiduous protector of the rights of individual American Jews who suffered injury at the hands of local Turkish officials. When a tax-collector proceeded violently against two Jerusalem Jews, Moses Angel and Shalom Kanstroon, with whom he had a dispute about real estate taxes, the Consul intervened firmly before the Governor of Jerusalem. A basic issue of consular justice was at stake, and Gillman refused to recognize a summons for the American Jews to appear in a Turkish court, at the same time demanding retribution for the physical attack on Moses Angel. Gillman used strong language: "Our citizens protest that their lives are not safe under an administration of the government which permits the military to be employed for the arrest and maltreatment of citizens of the United States, and that by a subordinate official and civilians, without due process of law, and contrary to our treaty and the direct commands of H.I.M. the Sultan, a worse condition than if we were in a state of insurrection, and the like of which has been hitherto unknown in the modern Government of Jerusalem." This was no doubt *un peu fort.* The Pasha returned his letter with the comment that he found no meaning for the expression a state of insurrection. In the end the Pasha paid the taxes out of his own pocket; to assess the injury of the alleged insults of Angel to the Turkish tax collectors, Gillman invited them into the consular court, to which no Turkish official would resort.

Minister Solomon Hirsch, Straus's successor, went to the Grand Vizier demanding satisfaction for Angel, and in June 1890 Henry Gillman received a formal apology from the Governor of Jerusalem for the assault on his national. Minister Hirsch made it clear to the Department that where rights of an American citizen were involved the gravity of the injury inflicted was less significant than the contest of the two authorities, Turkish and consular. Since prestige was at stake, the safety of American citizens for years to come depended on the outcome of minor cases. If consular officials should become somewhat less zealous in the defense of American Jews, the Turks would immediately sense the subtle change.

In September 1896, Consul Edwin S. Wallace in Jerusalem received a departmental instruction which signalled a new departure in the practice of the American protectorate over naturalized citizens as it had been interpreted by General Wallace in the eighties, though it was not out of harmony with Secretary of State Seward's earlier policy enunciated in his instructions to the Minister in Constantinople in 1868. The consul was ordered to withhold protection from those Americans reasonably suspect of not having the *animus revertendi,* the intention of returning to the United States. Consul Edwin Wallace, knowing the temper of Jerusalem, avoided official publication of this sharp change in American protection of its citizens, lest the Turkish officials descend all at once upon old Jewish residents who had long enjoyed American status. He communicated the new ruling to the American Jews verbally, as if to soften the blow.

As soon as the new rule became known in the Jewish community, there was general consternation. At a formal protest meeting they sent an appeal to the President, entitled "A Voice of Jerusalem," in which the policy was denounced. They described their community as composed mostly of aged Hebrews, many of whom were in Palestine for their health. They saw no reason why they should be deprived of consular protection from the caprice of Turkish law and attacked the order as robbing them of their American rights without trial.

Despite their fears, the new State Department instruction remained a dead letter for many years. The doctrine making United States citizenship dependent upon the intent to return to the homeland required, in every particular instance, a thorough judicial determination of an American citizen's status, an intricate procedure which the Embassy in Constantinople was most reluctant to have the local consuls undertake. The American Jews of Palestine did not present their passports for regular renewal, at which time they might have been questioned about their intentions. When an incident occurred involving the jurisdiction of the Turkish authority, the consul could not delay his intervention pending an elaborate inquiry into a citizen's *animus revertendi.* He had to act and thus *prima facie* to accept the citizenship of the old resident. Once he took a stand, a reversal which denied the American's status would cause the consul to lose face.

When Merrill reviewed the status of American Jews in his consular
district in March 1899, he discerned a marked debasement of their
juridical status since his first term of service in the Jerusalem Consulate in 1882. And he noted that this was true despite the protracted
diplomatic negotiations which had taken place at Constantinople, a
snide reflection on Minister Straus's activities, which were in their
day considered diplomatic triumphs. In at least four respects this
deterioration was evident to Merrill: 1. Formerly American Jews could
live in Palestine without residence restrictions; now time limitations
were entered on their passports. 2. Formerly American Jews could
buy land after a residence of three to five years; now they had to
provide proof of thirteen years residence, and endless bureaucratic
difficulties were placed in their path. 3. Formerly American Jews
occupied a special status; now they were treated like Russian Jews.
4. Formerly American Jews could obtain justice against Turkish subjects; now no American Jew could bring a complaint in a Turkish
court without having a counter-claim filed against him. Despite this
denial of rights, Merrill maintained that American Jews still enjoyed
more consular protection than the Jews of any other nation in Jerusalem. It did not occur to him that this decline was parallel with his
own incumbency during a substantial part of the period and that his
lack of zeal in pursuing specific cases may well have accounted for
the denial of capitulatory justice to American nationals.

Selah Merrill was a self-righteous man; both the general tone of his
reports and their lengthy apologies show it. If the status of American
Jews had sunk to a new low, it was, he maintained, due to the increasing number of fraudulently naturalized citizens who were entered on
his books. Merrill inquired of the Department how far he would be
supported in clearing the records of Jews with doubtful naturalization
papers or Jews who merely took out a certificate in the United States
and then left the country. "I call these people 'Russian Jews' because
that is their proper title. To call them 'Americans' is an insult to
American Civilization." He casually reveals, however, that the so-called
fraudulent naturalization papers were often as much a part of the
fabric of native American machine politics as the Jews' desire to get
themselves consular protection when they went up to Palestine. " 'I
was naturalized in the City Hall, Chicago,' reported one American
Jewish citizen, 'it was late in the night just before election.' "

Selah Merrill delivered himself of lengthy tirades against these
naturalized American Jews and their petty disputes which they tried

to exaggerate into "international importance." His unappreciated services to this class of "citizens" were "immense." He warned that when the United States Government kept insisting that these "naturalized Jews" be allowed to enter Turkey, it was only abetting the Zionist Movement and Jewish colonization. To deal with these Jews, Merrill suggested a requirement for a biennial passport renewal and proof that they did not intend to reside permanently in Palestine. He wanted a registration fee imposed because they paid no taxes and as tradesmen imported their goods from Europe. He had had 150 of them in 1882; 180 in 1885; by 1889 they numbered almost 800.

Merrill regularly filled his reports with examples of the dissimulation, fraud, bribery, and pleadings to which Jews had resorted in order to enjoy American naturalization status with consular protection. He had strong opinions about these naturalized Jews, and when he got hold of a visiting Congressman in 1902, during the period when immigration and naturalization legislation was under discussion in the United States, he tried to impress upon him the importance of stopping naturalization frauds, "some of them marvellous examples of ingenuity." He estimated that there were a thousand naturalized American Jews in Jerusalem in 1902 and voiced the opinion that had it not been for Turkish immigration restrictions, their number would have soared to eight or ten thousand.

In 1905 Merrill was still asking, "What is to be done with the army of naturalized Jews in Jerusalem and Palestine?" The Turkish Government was putting a "registration law" into effect in order to collect more taxes, and his office was besieged by Jews seeking protection. As Merrill went into his last period of service in the Jerusalem post, his hatred for Jewish clients became more violent. He could see nothing but their uncleanliness and their importunities. "In our case of documents we have a pile of Jewish Passports,—a remarkable collection, worn, tattered, and most of them offensive with Jew earmarks, namely, dirt. Every time we handle the pile we immediately wash ourselves with carbolic soap. The fact is that Jews take no pains whatever to preserve their passports neatly. I think these Jews ought to be taught a lesson in some way, but my admonitions to them are of no avail." Merrill grew ever more insistent in his despatches that some radical solution be devised, and his writing became charged with hysterical anti-semitism. "They are becoming a burden and a menace to our Government. . . . Our Jews are keen. They know we cannot compel them to apply for new passports. Hence they never apply for renewal of passports. These people have lived here anywhere from two to forty years. We are obliged to protect them. If this thing is not checked the Government will be obliged to establish here a special court with all the outfit, police, petty and supreme judges, prisons. . . ."

The United States Expatriation Act of March 2, 1907 was the answer to Merrill's prayer about purging the rolls of dubious Americans. It provided for the expatriation of citizens after long residence abroad. Under its rules, if a naturalized American, formerly a Turkish subject, returned to Turkey and resided there for two years, his status as an American would be presumed to have ceased. A naturalized citizen of other than Turkish origin would be presumed to have lost his American status after a residence in Turkey of five years. However, departmental circular instructions prescribed four conditions under which the "presumption of expatriation" could be overcome: if residence in Turkey was for commercial purposes; if there was an unforeseen exigency; if the citizen resided in a "distinctively American community" recognized as such by the Turkish Government; or if the citizen was a missionary of a recognized American Church Organization. It was necessary to establish specific facts and circumstances in each individual case, and mere assertions, even under oath, were not to be accepted. Copies of all documentary evidence had to be transmitted to the State Department.

The Expatriation Act of 1907 clearly applied to the overwhelming number of American Jews in Palestine who had arrived in the eighties and nineties, or who had been born in Palestine, naturalized in America, and had then returned to the Holy Land. But the real fears it spread among the Jews were only hinted at in official documents. Once the details of the process of naturalization of American Jews were investigated, irregularities would be discovered. To the Department in Washington this examination was justifiable to uncover fraud, but in Jerusalem, under Turkish administration, it would have convulsive consequences. Doubt cast on the status of one American Jew would put them all in jeopardy.

For three years a wise American consul, Merrill's successor, managed to delay enforcement of the Expatriation Law in Jerusalem through extra-legal arrangements with the American-Jewish community.

THE TURBULENT REVOLT OF THE AMERICAN CONGREGATION

In 1889 Henry Gillman, one of the consuls most sympathetic to the Jews of the old settlement, sent the Department a vivid description of the contentions and quarreling engendered by the *Haluka:* "Recriminations between the head rabbis and the members of the various congregations are incessant and prolific of the most acrimonious feuds. The chief accusations are that the Rabbis made an improper use of the fund, expending it upon themselves, their families, relatives and friends to a large extent, and using favoritism generally in its distribution. . . . There are about 200 synagogues in Jerusalem, and there are thousands of Rabbis, the majority of whom are far from being what they ought to be."

Eight years later, in the spring of 1897, the American Jews, whose number had risen to about a thousand and whose discontent with their treatment at the hands of the comptrollers of the *Haluka* had been smouldering for two decades, made a second attempt at establishing their independence as a distinct congregation, *Kollel America.* This new movement of the American Jews shook the whole structure of the old settlement in Jerusalem to its foundations. It was not of great moment to the rabbis who directed the general fund when Jews from a small province in Poland or Lithuania broke away, formed a congregation of their own, and sent Messengers of Charity to their district of origin begging alms for the Palestine Jews from that region alone. The American rebellion was a far more serious blow to the central rabbinical economy. American donations had by 1897 become a major source of income for the general fund gathered throughout the world and supposedly distributed among all the paupers of Jerusalem who had no congregations of their own. The autonomy of the American congregation would mean sending all donations from America only to American Jews in Palestine just as all collections from Suvalk went to Suvalk Jews. Rabbi Samuel Salant, head of all the Ashkenazim, and the General Committee of the Congregations would thus be deprived of the mainstay of their power; and the new arrangement threatened to eat into the portions of the paupers of Jerusalem who had no separate congregation from which to draw their *Haluka.* It was easy for the rabbis to arouse the poor European Jews to riot against the Americans who, in proclaiming their autonomy, were "robbing them of bread."

The Americans of course vociferously denied that they would by themselves consume all of the charity sent from the United States. They offered to distribute alms to other Jews, but funds of the American *Haluka* would have to channel through their organization. This method of distribution would have spelt the doom of the General Committee and presaged an ultimate transfer of power in the community to the Americans.

The Salant party mocked these "Americans" who had been born in Poland and Lithuania and who pretended, in the few years they had spent in the United States, to have learned the domineering ways of Americans. The Europeans pointed to the vast distinction between the establishment of a separate congregation among fellow townsmen of a Polish district and a congregation of the citizens of the "vast continent of the United States." The flame of controversy was fanned by the wife of Rabbi Diskin of Brisk, a Talmudic scholar whom the American leaders chose as their head; an ambitious woman who loved power she had the reputation of an intriguer in the community. When insults against the Salant party were reported in *Havatselet,* his partisans rejoined with clumsy, vulgar pasquils.

The communal strife in Jerusalem had repercussions in the Jewish communities in the United States when Messengers of Charity from both factions, the General Committee and the American Congregation, appeared to beg for alms. Donors in American cities became divided into partisans either of Salant or of Diskin. The merits in this characteristic struggle for power in the Jewish ghetto are not all on one side.

Havatselet, which formerly was a caustic critic of the dominant rabbis in the Ashkenazic community, had by 1897 been converted into their semi-official organ. During this battle of the *Haluka* it published weekly editorials of biting polemic against the Americans. "Do Not Separate Yourself from the Community!" posed the fundamental issues in brusque terms. It accused the Americans of destroying the peace of Jerusalem with their divisive schemes and of attempting to steal for themselves alone all the alms collected for the poor. At these "so-called Americans" *Havatselet* hurled deadly bolts of ridicule and contempt. "And so these Americans, natives and citizens of Lithuania and Poland, Samut and Reussen, have conquered the new world. They have swallowed it up as the Leviathan; they have wrapped it up in their bosom and have made it their property, for themselves and their children forever. As a sign and a witness for later generations, lest any stranger dare to approach their conquered world, they hung upon it their sticks and their sacks with which they had come out of Lithuania and Samut, Poland and Reussen, the places of their origin and their birth, saying wherefor do we now need these old sticks and sacks after we have become free men, finished gentlemen of the new world, which belongs to us and to us alone, and in which no stranger may have a portion.

"But, worthy gentlemen . . . is it allowable for you to separate yourselves away from the community more and more, to the point where you dare to snatch food from the mouths of the poor saying: 'To us belong America and all her alms which are sent to the Holy Land for we are the American congregation.' 'American Congregation!' Why you only arouse laughter with the name you have given to this new organization of yours. Is America like the city of your birth, Vilna or Kovno, Grodno, Pinsk or Suvalk? America is a fourth of the world with hundreds of thousands of people and many states and cities, and from one city in America, for example, New York, more donations are sent for the poor of the Holy Land than from whole countries like Roumania and Galicia. Do you intend to enjoy all of these donations, you few who have been living for a couple of decades in Jerusalem and who call yourselves with the name America only in order to eat her fruit and to be satisfied with her goods which are being sent to the thousands of poor in Zion? . . ."

Consul Edwin S. Wallace got himself involved in a feud with the chief Ashkenazic Rabbi, Samuel Salant, over this revival of the American separatist movement. Wallace had written a group of American Jews that in his judgment their charities were not being allotted as the donors had intended. This correspondence was reported back to Rabbi Salant, and the battle was joined. Salant wrote to rabbis in the United States and through them Wallace was accused before the State Department of partisanship and prejudice. He was charged with interfering in the internal affairs of the Jerusalem community and with favoring the new American Jewish Congregation. Wallace admitted to the Department that he had attended one of their meetings, at which almost the whole body of the American Jews were present, but he had not understood much of their proceedings since they were conducted in Yiddish. When the "new party" was attacked by the "old party" as swindlers and vagabonds in a circular letter distributed in the United States and Jerusalem by Rabbi Salant, it included as purported American signers one American not registered at the consulate, one dead man, and two American Jews who confessed to the consul that they had been forced to sign under threat of being cut off from the lists of the general *Haluka*. When Wallace refused to authenticate the document on the ground that those who pretended to be United States citizens were not really citizens, the "old party" thought it had specific proof of bias.

In self-justification to the Department, Wallace rehearsed the whole affair and quoted in extenso the original inquiry from the Denver Jewish Community in which the consul was asked about the rumored schism in the Jewish Community of Jerusalem. The Denver Community had heard that the rabbis had refused to include an American Jew, a recent arrival, on the lists of the *Haluka*. They felt that the funds should be distributed equitably, without prejudice against American Jews, since thousands of dollars had been contributed in America. Wallace had made the fatal error of writing back to the Denver Jewish Community that there had indeed been a "revolt" against the rabbis who had been receiving and pretending to distribute the funds.

Wallace's report provided many curious details of the "revolt": it had been initiated in secret by several "Jewish American gentlemen" who did not need charity but thought that the funds were being misused. This had brought down upon them the censure of Rabbi Samuel Salant, a man of power greatly feared by most of the Jews, for the uprising was unprecedented. "The stand for liberty which the American Jews made came as a shock to him. He had always had his own way and for anybody to oppose him or his methods was a novel experience." When Salant issued a formal rabbinic order demanding the submission of the American Jews, they refused. Diskin, whom the Americans had chosen as their rabbi, was greatly esteemed both in Jerusalem and America, and Rabbi Salant was confounded by his acceptance. When Rabbi Diskin's home was attacked by a group of Rabbi Salant's partisans the Governor of Jerusalem had to send police to disperse the mob. Wallace had contributed a consular guard for Rabbi Diskin's protection.

Unlike the abortive attempt of 1879 this time the independence of the American Jewish Community was firmly established, and the American Jewish notables in Jerusalem provided charity for their own poor.

In December 1897 representatives of *Kollel America* in the United States formed an organization to act as the opposite number of the Jerusalem *Kollel* (it was customary for each regional *Kollel* to have a body of supporters in its country of origin), and they received a charter from the State of New York with the right to collect donations for the support of the poor in the Holy Land. This led to violent reprisals from the beadles and elders who were representatives in the United States of the General Committee of all the Congregations in Jerusalem, and the two parties tore down each other's collection coin boxes in the synagogues and homes of New York. Lawsuits were instituted in both the rabbinic courts and in the secular courts in New York and the Yiddish and Hebrew press resounded with the rival contentions of the two groups.

When J. D. Eisenstein, a New York scholar and antiquarian, accepted the presidency of *Kollel America in America,* the movement assumed the character of a business-like attempt to reform the age-old abuses of the *Haluka* system. He offered the General Committee of the Rabbis a compromise which would have given *Kollel America* control of no more than a third of the total collections in the United States, but the "old party" at first refused to recognize the upstarts on any terms. In June 1900 Eisenstein again tried to settle the dispute and an agreement was signed leaving the General Committee in charge of collections in the United States, but recognizing the autonomous rights of the *Kollel America in Jerusalem.* After extended disputations they reverted to the first Eisenstein compromise and accepted a third of the United States take, leaving the rest to the General Committee.

Wallace remained a loyal partisan of the American *Kollel* after his return to the United States; he even lent them his services by lecturing on their behalf, and in his book, *Jerusalem the Holy,* published in 1898, he continued to plead their cause.

The war of *Kollel America* against the General Committee of Jerusalem is perhaps more than the minor sectarian quarrel it appears to be at first glance. *Mutatis mutandis,* one can already recognize both the issues and attitudes which in later years often divided American Jews from European Jews in the councils of the international Zionist organization.

CONSULAR JUSTICE

At the turn of the century communal life in the old settlement, the only one with which the consuls had dealings, sank to a low ebb. The crowding of ever greater numbers of new immigrants into the old quarters of Jerusalem gave rise to endless altercations. Selah Merrill was busied with the brawls of a strange misfit, Captain Samuel Johnson (formerly Mosche Goldstein) and his acts of violence when drunk. Jews within the American community ran to the consul bearing tales against one another, committing vain acts of spite, informing that American passports were fraudulent. Strife of this character is not rare in closed sacerdotal communities: witness the backbiting in seventeenth century New England settlements.

Selah Merrill, consul for his third term from 1898 to 1907, was annoyed by the pandemonium which the affairs of his litigious Jewish clients created in his office. "Papers are to be made out, petitions transmitted, complaints listened to, quarrels are to be settled, Kavasses must be sent to look after some trouble these people have had with their neighbors, there has been a fight, somebody has been beaten, somebody spit upon, something stolen, somebody has trespassed, contracts and agreements have been broken, wives have been ill-treated or turned out of doors, rent has not been paid. . . ." Merrill was the most acrimonious reviler of the Jews who ever occupied the post, and much of the tumult was engendered by his own faulty administration—a circumstance discreetly indicated by his successor—but there was a measure of truth even in these biased reports. This was the normal pattern of life in the poor quarters of all European and American peoples. Its existence in Jerusalem was a serious interference with the reverend's antiquarian studies. The self-portrait of a flustered administrative official is sketched in almost all of Merrill's reports, and his extended regime did not add to the felicity of the Jewish Community.

Thomas Wallace of Iowa, who followed Merrill in 1907, was a man of a different stripe, and his account of dealings with the Jewish community was incisive and balanced. His characterization of the role of the American consul in Jerusalem was knowing, marked by a deep consciousness of his official responsibilities. "The power he wields in these far off places is so autocratic that, in the hands of an ignorant and vicious person, the freedom and rights of the citizen are constantly endangered. . . ."

Thomas Wallace has left by far the most realistic description of the intricate problems of consular justice in its relations both with the Jewish community and with the Turkish officials. In accordance with the American interpretation of Article IV of the Treaty of 1830, the consular government maintained the exclusive right to try American citizens for all offenses committed in Turkey; the Ottoman Government claimed exclusive jurisdiction over the punishment of all crimes and never accepted the American position. This created an anomalous state of affairs which, Wallace thought, was so abnormal that he doubted whether anything analogous existed among civilized peoples. If there was a chasm between the basic principles of the Turks and the Americans, actual practice in day to day suits before the Turkish courts and the consular court of the United States came to resemble trials in Alice-in-Wonderland. If a Turk was injured by an American, the Turkish Government refused to intervene in the consular court, and the American consul would not allow American guilt to be determined in a Turkish court; hence the American went scot free. If an American was injured by a Turk, the consul brought an action in the Turkish court on behalf of his national. As a matter of normal procedure, the Turk retaliated by charging the American with prior aggression. This brought about an impasse: the Turkish court claimed the right to adjudicate both cases together, while the American consul steadfastly refused to allow his national to be tried in a Turkish court under any circumstances. Thereupon both cases were dismissed in the Turkish court and the Turkish defendant also went scot free. This seems to have been an airtight arrangement under which, in any conflict between a Turk and a protected national, neither side could ever be brought to trial. The American consul had only a few decorative guards and therefore no real power of enforcing punishment against Turkish subjects; the Turkish officials, for their part, did not often risk imprisoning an American in contempt of his consul. Thus the sanction of force was rarely used by either side. When a Pasha tried to break through the legal stalemate and seized an American national, the case inevitably resulted in protracted and inevitably inconclusive diplomatic negotiations in Constantinople.

Thomas Wallace was not a man prejudiced against Jews, hence his account of the abuses in which American citizens indulged under this grotesque system of law bears credence. Some Americans became receivers of stolen property which it was almost impossible for the native *fellaheen* to retrieve. Americans would slaughter their animals in the heart of the crowded old quarter of Jerusalem and leave a dreadful stench of refuse in violation of the few Turkish sanitary regulations which did exist on paper. When a quantity of counterfeit coins were put into circulation and the felons were caught, the two Turkish Jews apprehended were sentenced to hard labor but the American

Jew who was their confederate continued his business without a day's delay.

It had been the opinion of former American consuls at the Jerusalem post that the machinery of the consular court could not be put into operation unless an aggrieved foreign national actually brought a complaint, and if he was a Turk no justice was done. As a natural result of their favored status American Jews were much sought after in partnerships, and whenever any violation was charged to the association by the Turks, the American Jew claimed immunity for the whole enterprise on the basis of his participation. Consul Wallace took a very different view of the role of his office and proceeded to summon Americans into the consular court on his own initiative in cases which drew his attention. This apparent legal immunity of American Jews in civil and criminal affairs was of course counterbalanced by unpunished acts of violence by the native Moslem population. It was uneven justice because the victims of Moslem vengeance were not often the sharpers.

Thomas Wallace's report of 1908 includes a good description of the securely established rabbinic power in the Jewish community of Jerusalem: "Two chief Rabbis are at the head of the different sects or divisions. They have a thorough organization, and usually conform to the rules governing them as a religious body, and submit to the findings of their committee on spiritual affairs and on business matters when it is satisfactory. The men forming the organization which looks after the political and diplomatic interests of the Jews are shrewd and intelligent businessmen, subjects of the great powers of Europe. Active, vigilant, and aggressive, they are ready at all times to take advantage of any occurrence or incident happening that may be turned to the benefit of their co-religionists." But in defense of what he considered the rights of individual American Jews, Thomas Wallace did not hesitate to question the action of the Chief Rabbis and the charity committees, even in minor cases of injustice. He quoted as typical of the detail attended to by his office a letter from a Safed Jew who wanted his *Haluka* money sent directly to him from Jerusalem and not to an intermediary who monthly robbed him of a dollar and made him sign a receipt for the whole amount. Wallace did not see how he could adjust such countless petty complaints without examining general charges against the charity committees, and contrary to the dominant opinion of his predecessors, it was his final judgment that as a rule the committees were reasonable.

When Wallace assumed office in 1907 he found marked "discrimination against Jews" in the practice of consular business, a carry-over from Selah Merrill's regime. Jews were kept standing in line for hours, waiting for the one dragoman who dealt with them, even when there were unoccupied chairs in the room. Wallace changed all this, told the Jews to be seated and transacted the business himself. "One of the women, American-born, with a smile, said: 'This is going to be an American office now.' The answer was that it is an American office. The business that brought these people to the office was of a simple character, and all were disposed of within an hour. . . . The clerks were informed that in the future no more lines were to be formed of American citizens, because of their race or religion, and that all were to be treated alike, and that it would go hard with them in the future if discriminations were made against any American citizens. . . . There are no more lines formed, and the office is never crowded except in case of some controversy, while the Jewish people have been profuse in their thanks for this act of justice shown them."

There is a striking contrast between the frantic tenor of Selah Merrill's despatches and the judicial equanimity of Thomas Wallace. Upon such changes in the personalities of the American consuls hung the fortune of the community.

THE YOUNG TURKS

The uprising of the Young Turks in 1909 and the abdication of Abdul Hamid II gave rise to expectations for a time that Turkish governmental practice would undergo a thorough reform. The slogans of the revolution preached love, amity, and participation in power by all the peoples of Turkey. But Consul Thomas R. Wallace's description of the administration of Palestine in his report to Ambassador Straus on November 26, 1909, indicates that in practice the upsurge of Turkish nationalism took the form of barbaric maltreatment of all foreigners, especially Jews. This is the more remarkable in view of the rumors, current in European chancelleries, that the *Noumé* of Salonika, Jews who were descendants of converts to Islam but retained their group identity, had been among the chief financial supporters and organizers of the Revolution.

In their new-born nationalist pride the Young Turks were deeply resentful of the special privileges granted foreigners under the system of capitulations, and Jews in Palestine were ready targets for their anger since many of them enjoyed consular protection. The young Turkish prosecuting attorney who had been brought to Jerusalem by the new movement displayed vigorous activity against non-Moslems and condoned criminal acts committed against Jews. Whenever a Jew filed a complaint, was beaten up, or was robbed, he was immediately accused of having insulted the Prophet, and the plaintiff was turned into a defendant. Wallace detailed numerous incidents of mob violence against Jews in cities and towns. This represented a diversion of the militant religious prejudice of the native Mohammedans from Christians to Jews. During the Russo-Turkish wars of the nineteenth century, the American consuls would report riots created by the ravings of a dervish against the local Christians; in the early years of the twentieth century, after the increase in Jewish immigration and the Young Turk revolution, the Moslem population of Palestine turned against the Jews rather than the Christians. (This new alignment of the three religious communities continued through the first decades of the twentieth century.) In the nineteenth century, the great menace was the Bedouin raid on isolated agricultural settlements; in the first decade of the twentieth, insecurity spread to the towns, and the Turkish police countenanced the attacks of ruffians against foreign Jews. "Though constitutional law has been proclaimed," Wallace wrote, "yet injustice and brutality have increased, causing both life and property to be insecure. For some time there have been daily occurrences of violence and robbery committed in open daylight, almost in front of the Seria, without the least effort on the part of the authorities to suppress such deeds or punish the miscreants."

Ambassador Straus, now on his third mission to the Porte, called the attention of the Turkish Minister of Justice to conditions in Palestine, and there were a number of changes in bureaucratic personnel. The Governor of Jerusalem resigned, the Judge of the Religious Court was discharged, and half the local police force was dismissed from the service. But later despatches bear ample testimony that this administrative shake-up had no more than a passing influence on Turkish law enforcement. Neither the Revolution of the Young Turks nor the establishment of the forms of municipal organization in Jerusalem had any lasting effect on the essentially corrupt character of Turkish governmental practice. Neither the Party of Union and Progress nor the Party of Union and Liberty and the introduction of the mechanics of party politics imitative of western Europe altered the temper of the regime.

Straus's interpretation of official departmental instructions for his third mission betrayed a completely new American orientation in dealings with Turkey: ". . . I conclude," he wrote, "that the chief influence should at present be centered upon substantial advancement of our prestige and commerce." In fulfillment of his mission, Straus sent despatches on the construction of warships for Turkey and the "political phases of commercial questions as illustrated by Railway Concessions and Consequences." Thereafter American consuls and ambassadors joined actively in the fight for concessions which accompanied vigorous capitalist penetration into Turkey. Along with the other great powers, American capital made its bid for railway, harbor, and oil monopolies, and the Embassy in Constantinople regularly reported on the spoils of our European rivals as well as our own limited triumphs. In the free-for-all scramble American envoys were not loath to bargain away some of their formal extraterritorial legal rights under the Treaty of 1830 for the more immediate and tangible award of economic controls.

Palestine was not one of the great prizes of the Empire, but it had its patrons. The Standard Oil Company got concessions for oil and minerals in the vicinity of the Dead Sea in 1913, and the French got concessions for the ports at Jaffa and Haifa in 1914. War came before they could be exploited in earnest.

REGISTRATION OF AMERICAN JEWS

For three years after the passage of the Expatriation Act of 1907 no registration or investigation of the status of individual American Jews in Palestine had taken place in accordance with the prescribed regulations, nor had the Department sent inquiries to the Jerusalem Consul on his laxness. On January 10, 1910, Consul Thomas R. Wallace addressed a long memorandum to the Department in which he enclosed petitions from American Jews in Jerusalem and Jaffa who hoped to induce the Consul to postpone for an even longer period the contemplated registration of Americans in his consular district.

Wallace was most sympathetic with the petitioners: "The petitions present a picture of conditions not overdrawn. They are exceptional and peculiar to the land. No one can realize the full import and significance attached to an enforcement of the Order, except those who reside here and are well informed of the treatment meted out to aliens, especially those of the Hebrew race, who are not protected by the power of some foreign government. The horror of the Adana massacre brings to their minds the terror and despair of their own helplessness should they be abandoned. With scenes enacted before their eyes of cruelty and injustice against their kind, upon those who are unprotected, they beg me to leave the matter of re-registration as it is, hoping for better conditions here, or that our government will exempt American citizens from the enforcement of the Order who reside in a country where barbaric acts are permitted to go unrebuked, when committed upon an alien."

The Consul justified the three-year delay in the registration of the American Jews; his lame excuse was the pressure of other consular business and the pleadings of Jews who knew that once the registration was initiated, the greater number of them would be dropped from the rolls. It seemed to Wallace an act of inhumanity against the aged, the defenseless, and the weak to leave those "who were looked upon as our fellow citizens to conditions that would be imposed upon them but slightly removed from barbaric." Many of the Jews would return to the United States if they could; others wanted to spend their remaining years in prayer and to lay their bodies in holy ground with the fathers of their race. "It seemed cruel and unnecessary to turn these over to the heartless mercies of those who hate them. . . ." Under strict construction of the rules, Wallace thought that those who came to Palestine for their health or because of racial or religious sentiment would have to be repatriated if they wished to retain their citizenship. Wallace could see no moral justification for such an action. Most of the Jews were beyond the age of usefulness. At first he had procrastinated in the hope that the new Turkish regime would improve its administration. "This hope has not been fulfilled, the conditions getting worse as time passed after the first outburst of fraternal feeling had subsided."

Wallace had come to an informal understanding with the American Jews in Jerusalem that the Consulate would not occupy itself with picayune disputes on their behalf, but that, if it afforded them freedom from annoyance by Turkish officials, the registration would be deferred. The arrangement had worked out satisfactorily. "The Americans are known and recognized as such by the officials and the community in general, and are not disturbed or mistreated. Should a change be made and some parties be dropped from the registration, it would soon become known (bad news flies swiftly in Jerusalem), and they would soon be subjected to the mistreatment they dread."

But Wallace, who had held up the registration for three years, was afraid that further delay would bring censure from the Department, and he therefore submitted a proposal for a formal exception from the general order. "It is hard to convey in mere words scenes common to this office, such as women in tears and with wild supplications begging for official interposition in cases where husband, children, or other dear relatives are involved, and influential men of the community, personal friends and others, entreating us to save some one who is barred by law from our protection."

The petitions of the Jews of Jerusalem and Jaffa which Wallace transmitted to the State Department expressed the hope that the regulations of 1907 would not be applicable to them since they were a "separate American community" living in the Holy Land. They had not left America with the intent of abandoning their country and never expected to merge "into the society of these barbarous natives. . . . The Jew here suffers most when deprived of the protection of a powerful foreign government. Other races and religious denominations, even the Turkish subjects are more or less enjoying some protection through their officially recognized spiritual chiefs or by reason of having the same religious belief or being of the same race. But the unprotected Jew is subjected to every kind of unjust exaction from officials. Should he resent attacks or assaults upon him he may be cruelly beaten and then arrested upon some trumped-up charge and imprisoned. There is no hope of his obtaining justice in either the civil or criminal courts as now conducted in this land."

In reply to Wallace the Department referred to its instructions on the Expatriation Law, particularly those sections in the April 19, 1907 circular which touched on the health of citizens and the section on residence in a "distinctively American community recognized as such by the Turkish Government." These might be applicable to some of the American Jews of Jerusalem. The Department was, however, adamant in its requirement of a full registration of all citizens with detailed documentary proof in each individual case. "The Department is not disposed to be unduly technical or severe in its attitude toward those Jews who went to the Holy Land in their old age, especially if it appears that they spent many of the years of their active life in this country, but each case must be decided upon its peculiar merits. You should extend such protection as is necessary and proper to persons who present evidence of American citizenship, unless it has been finally decided by the Department that they have expatriated themselves."

A long period of registration followed, during which the individual records of American Jews were sent to the State Department for examination, and often a re-registration was required. In October 1911, Consul Coffin finally reported that nearly all Americans in his district had registered. The registration raised a host of thorny, often insoluble, legal problems about citizenship and swamped the consulate and bewildered the American Jews of Palestine for the remaining years until the outbreak of the war.

THE RED RECEIPT

Selah Merrill was transferred to Georgetown, Guiana, but the immigration and pilgrimage problems of the American consular protectorate remained the same for his successors. In 1909, when American Jews arrived in Jaffa their passports were taken up at the port, and they received a red receipt. At the end of three months, the Turkish officials would demand that the consul compel his nationals to depart. The consul would formally refuse, and nothing would happen. As for the sequestered passports, it became the general practice that Jewish firms, acting as intermediaries, made arrangements with Turkish customs officials to have the passports surrendered at a price fixed in accordance with the individual Jew's ability to pay. Against this practice Ambassador Straus made his customary representations at the Porte but there was no reply; the temper of negotiations with foreign envoys had changed since "the good old days" of Abdul Hamid. Thus lightly were erased the triumphs of his first two missions to Turkey.

In 1913, a year before the Turkish abolition of the consular protectorate, the tug-of-war between the American consul in Jerusalem and Turkish customs officials over the passports of American Jews continued unabated. The Jews had been retrieving their passports at the port of entry through the payment of baksheesh, until a new Kaimakam came to Jaffa—a "bad one" someone in the State Department noted—and he had the passports sent to his own residence, withdrawing them from the Customs House where many hands could lay hold of them. An incident was created when an American consular representative was not allowed to view his own nationals' passports. After protests were delivered in Constantinople, the Governor of

Jerusalem was ordered to stop the practice of collecting the passports of foreign Jews and issuing a red receipt permitting a three-months' stay. But at the very same time the Governor was advised to take appropriate measures preventing the settlement of Jews in Palestine. Since the Governor of Jerusalem now had a local council, in the spirit of the New Turkey, he asked their advice on the manner of enforcing the decree; whereupon they came up with the time-worn proposal that each foreign Jew should be required to furnish a bond that he would leave Palestine within three months. Vice-Consul Edelman explained to the Governor that the United States would be embarrassed—a new American approach—if any such order were issued. The Governor understood and agreed to ask only for the addresses of Jews during their stay. "This, I think is a fair concession," commented Edelman, "considering the absolute fear which the Ottoman Government has of that section of the Zionist movement which has for its object the creation of a Jewish state in Palestine." The "solution" was really the old face-saving compromise which the Turks and Americans had gone through time and again for decades. The prohibition against Jewish immigration remained in effect; the passport was stamped with the date of arrival and then it was up to the Governor to see that the Jew left. Once he was in the land the American Jew came under the capitulations, and the Consul could decide "according to the peculiar merits of the case." A pragmatic formula had replaced the uncompromising principles of Secretary of State Bayard.

After thirty-five years of active negotiations over the Turkish immigration laws and restrictions on Jewish pilgrimage which affected American Jews as well as their less protected Russian brothers, nothing fundamental had changed.

Nominally, American Jews had in 1913 won a point in the cessation of a practice which had been a source of deep injury to their pride—the red receipt, a badge of humiliation like the yellow patch of the middle ages, had been abolished. But in reality, nobody's abstract principle had a consistent triumph in this immigration battle. The Turkish Exclusion Laws remained in effect and the Jews continued to find their way into the land. American Expatriation Laws were interpreted and re-interpreted, and the old Jewish community of Jerusalem had its American citizens of many years residence who enjoyed consular protection and who, through their associations, extended a protecting arm over other Jews.

The persecuted Jews of eastern Europe had long since learned to grasp any momentary advantage of official venality, and in the face of the frequently emended Turkish decrees the new settlement of Zionist agricultural colonies was built up. While the aged of the old settlement were dying off, Jewish immigration into Palestine continued. In a multitude of disguises they stole into the land. Viewed historically, the interminable negotiations in Constantinople between our Ambassadors and the Porte were not as futile as they may have appeared to the men who had to conduct them. They were a façade behind which the immigration and the purchase of land somehow went on.

Herzl's absolute pre-condition for Zionist settlement, political rights recognized in public law, had never been granted; but in the last years before the war the "practicals" as contrasted with the "politicals" had won out in the international Zionist movement, and new colonies had been established and they survived. International political manoeuvering was sidetracked, and the Jews of these colonies came to depend less on European or American consular protection after the manner of the old settlement than on their own watchmen who stood guard through the night over their clusters of huts.

On the eve of the war, the old settlement is generally portrayed in consular despatches as a decaying community, preyed upon by embezzlers and weakened in its internal structure. The approach of hostilities increased the helplessness of the old residents; yet they remained alien and hostile to the small new settlement that was rebuilding the land with its own strength. The vigor and endurance of this new settlement came to the American consul's attention only when, at the beginning of the world war, it was threatened with annihilation. This was a new Jewish world in Palestine, whose creation and growth American consuls had never taken seriously.

ZIONISM AND THE STATE DEPARTMENT, 1910–1914

Selah Merrill's strictures on Zionism and the Jews were of course not made public, but they cannot be dismissed as the grumblings of an insignificant consul. Many of his arguments found their echo among assistant secretaries and division chiefs in the State Department, whenever Zionism became a subject of discussion among officials who controlled everyday policy.

About 1910, the Zionist Movement in America, though small in number, had become significant enough to force itself upon the consideration of the State Department. It could no longer be disregarded as a movement limited to recent immigrants in our metropolitan areas. Lawyers, professors, businessmen, and a few banker-philanthropists had joined its ranks, and their influence in the American Congress could not be totally neglected. The "Jewish Question" was occupying space in the newspapers, and American diplomacy under Congressional prodding had taken a stand on restrictions against the free movement of American Jews both in Russia and Turkey. Many members of the State Department, especially those in the Near Eastern Division, were annoyed at the interference of what they considered purely Jewish interests in the conduct of the high policy they were devising in the furtherance of American, for the most part, sound business interests involving concessions in Turkey. Since Zionism was a controversial question within the American Jewish community itself and the larger Jewish fortunes were cold, if not hostile to it, the Department could adopt an unsympathetic attitude towards the movement without risking serious protest from a unified Jewry. Restrictions on travel in foreign countries touched the pride of all Jews, and in this field the Department was cautious; Zionism was a political movement repugnant to many powerful Jews in America because it was supposed to raise a problem of dual allegiance.

The ruling elements in the American Jewish population around 1880 were German Jews who usually belonged to the Reformed Synagogue. Their doctrine was based on the principle of a Judaic faith, a religion, as distinguished from any national or racial ties among Jews. This did not preclude charitable activities among other Jews, their co-religionists, persecuted in eastern Europe, but it did eschew any plans for the restoration of the Jews to Palestine. In the eighties it was Emma Lazarus the poetess who expressed dissent from this dominant conception in her Zionist essays, after her conversion from philosophical anarchism. Her writings, in the spirit of nineteenth century nationalism, which approved of both Oliphant's colonization schemes and the nationalist doctrines of Pinsker's *Autoemancipation,* created a measure of interest among Jews both in England and in the United States. There was even an attempt to persuade the strongest Jewish fraternal organization, the *B'nai Brith,* to adopt a program in favor of Palestine colonization. This was defeated, but in a number of cities there were formed organizations for Palestine Colonization and American Jews contributed to the

Montefiore Memorial Fund. The United States was hardly an important center of the Lovers of Zion movement, but it had its stray partisans.

In 1897 a Zionist Federation was established in the United States and it became a branch of the World Zionist Movement; in its first years it played an insignificant role both in the life of the American Jewish community and in world Zionist councils. The upper-class Jews of German origin remained "assimilationist" in the tradition of the reformed synagogue of Germany, and their rabbis were militantly anti-Zionist; the recent immigrant Jews from eastern Europe who were workers in the Atlantic seacoast cities were indifferent to Zionism. Only as a Jewish middle class grew out of these eastern European immigrants did Zionism attract a substantial number of adherents.

The internal State Department memoranda of the period are more expressive of the feelings and opinions of the officials than their public correspondence. In New York a private citizen, Edmund Eliah Frank, an inveterate letter-writer, had for a number of years been sending communications to presidents and secretaries of state on behalf of a Jewish State in Palestine. His efforts had been largely unnoticed, especially his plea that the Government "mediate between Turkey and the Hebrew nation to effect the restoration of Palestine to the Jews"; but Mr. MacMurray of the Near Eastern Affairs Division conceived the cunning idea of "letting this appeal get into print, in order that it might be referred to, in case of need, as an illustration of the purely Hebraic and un-American purposes for which our Jewish community seek to use this government." Assistant Secretary Adee, with years of experience in the Department, was less clumsy, and answered that it did not need to be dignified with a reply.

The Zionists of that period, in the tradition of Herzl's politics, always in quest of a public statement of approval, however diluted, from one of the Great Powers, wrote to the Secretary of State on February 10, 1912, asking for an opinion by the President to be read to a meeting of the Zion Literary Society. Secretary Knox, following the lines of a memorandum from MacMurray, replied that "problems of Zionism involve certain matters primarily related to the interests of countries other than our own . . . and might lead to misconstructions." In his memorandum to the Secretary MacMurray had related Zionism to the propaganda against the treatment of the Jews of Russia. While the Zionists had described the movement as one "for the regeneration of Turkey, for the Jews, with the goodwill of Turkey," MacMurray's realistic comment was, ". . . The fact is that the movement has not the goodwill of Turkey, but rather is a matter of some soreness."

The number of communications to the State Department from individual Zionists, seconded by Congressmen, and from the American Zionist Federation, especially over Turkish immigration laws, was continually on the increase. Though the final replies to the correspondents were bland and non-committal, the men in charge of policy, as they passed these communications around among Department officials, jotted down comments of firm antagonism to Zionist "chimeras." Assistant Secretary Adee, in an extended note which included some rather fantastic misinformation about Palestine and Zionist aims, exemplified the prevalent hostile Departmental attitude: "For thirty years and I know not how much longer, Turkey has writhed under the dread of a restoration of the Judaean monarchy. Permanent residence of alien Jews has been restricted in many ways, but without effect. They still get in and stay.

"Our volumes of Foreign Relations are plentifully supplied with correspondence on the subject, from 1884–1898. . . . The Zionist movement in this country is strong. Every few months we are asked to negotiate for the cession of Palestine to the Jewish 'nation.' The project is chimerical. The country is now barren, although in the days of Moses it flowed with milk and honey and produced the grapes of Escheol. If but a tithe of the 12 million or more Jews of the world were colonized in Palestine, they would starve. The area of all Palestine (Hebrew Pelescheth, land of the Philistines) is 11,000 square miles, mostly mountainous. Russian and German Jews have established colonies on the lowland near the coast, which can be made productive by irrigation. The Russian colony at Jaffa numbers 5,000, and there are four German colonies. All Syria, 115,000 square miles, would be included for the Kingdom of Zion."

In 1912 the Department was beginning to receive scattered factual information from Turkey on the growth of the new colonies, though most of the notices were mere clippings from the *Lloyd-Ottoman* in Constantinople. These described the tremendous success of the Jewish colonists despite hardships. On August 31, 1912, the *Lloyd-Ottoman* estimated the Jewish population at 100,000, divided about equally between the new and the old settlements. The new settlement brought to the land by the Zionist movement consisted of about 40,-000 townspeople and nearly the entire rural population. "The newly arrived population . . . furnishes merchants, manufacturers, doctors, and professors. . . . One has only to look at the Tel-Aviv quarter at Jaffa or the new quarters at Haifa. . . . The rural population occupies about 40 villages; the rural property owned by the Jews in Palestine amounts to 40,000 hectares, of which 30,000 are settled: 8000 in Judaea (15 settlements), 16,200 in Galilee (16 settlements), and 200 east of the Jordan (1 settlement)." The *Lloyd-Ottoman* articles also detailed the various Zionist economic and educational institutions. None of these accounts stirred particular comment in the Department.

On July 21, 1913, Louis Lipsky, President of the American Zionist Federation, sent the Secretary of State of the new Democratic Administration, William Jennings Bryan, a description of Zionist aims and the extent of American Jewish participation in sponsoring new economic developments in Palestine, and asked that certain courtesies be extended the Zionist representative in Palestine by American consular and diplomatic officials. The Department prepared many drafts of a reply and made frequent revisions in its carefully drawn statement; the last draft was specific in its rejection of the request because the "project" seemed to have a "distinct political character, and, so far as it contemplates and would involve American political activity in the Ottoman Empire, could not be promoted by this Government without prejudice to its traditional policy of non-interference in the political problems of the Near East." Apparently the reply was never sent, because in November, Lipsky called attention to his unanswered letter.

When in June 1914 Stephen Wise, Oscar Straus, L. K. Frankel and Louis Brandeis organized a commission to make an objective and intensive social survey of Jewish conditions in Palestine, the name of the new American Ambassador, Henry Morgenthau, was included among the sponsors. The Department indicated its displeasure, and Morgenthau resigned from the group though his original purpose in becoming a member had been quite in harmony with the policy-makers in the Department: "I think it is a splendid scheme to have this investigation made and to give the Jewish and other citizens of the United States an exact report of Palestine's true conditions, which in my opinion are not at all favorable to a large Zionist movement."

Thus prior to the outbreak of the First World War the dominant official attitude in the State Department was unfriendly to Zionism as a political movement and to the increase of the Jewish population of Palestine. To the extent that support of the Jews irritated the Turks who had it in their power to grant or deny concessions, the United States Government considered it contrary to its interests to espouse Zionism. The United States had no strategic plans which involved the Near East and could assume a position of non-interference in the political affairs of Turkey with the expectation that such an approach might be all the more favorable for economic penetration. The Jewish problem in Palestine was extraneous, a nuisance; it had, in the case of the red receipt, come to implicate the United States in a battle of abstract principles with which no hard national interests were associated.

The election of Wilson to the Presidency introduced a powerful new factor in the executive attitude towards the Jews and Zionism which went far beyond any considerations of business concessions and pettifogging legalism. When Wilson appointed Morgenthau to Constantinople he did not see any contradiction between a special humanitarian interest in the Jews of Palestine and American interests. His parting words to the new Ambassador were, "Remember that anything you can do to improve the lot of your co-religionists is an act that will reflect credit upon America, and you may count on the full power of the Administration to back you up." Secretary of State Bryan entrusted to the new Ambassador a less ambitious mission. "Ambassador," he said, "when I made my trip through the Holy Land, I had great difficulty in finding Mount Beatitude. I wish you would try to persuade the Turkish Government to grant a concession to some Americans to build a macadam road up to it, so that other pilgrims may not suffer the inconvenience which I did in attempting to find it."

Morgenthau himself had accepted the post with great reluctance. Both he and Jacob Schiff, with whom he discussed the appointment, were apprehensive lest the mission in Constantinople—where Oscar Straus and Solomon Hirsch had served—come to be considered a distinctly Jewish one and the impression be created that Turkey was the only country where a Jew would be received as an American diplomatic representative. It required the President's insistent urging as well as the intervention of Rabbi Stephen Wise before Morgenthau would retract his original refusal.

Wilson's farewell order characterized his attitude towards the Jews. His interest in Zionism was being slowly nurtured by Louis Brandeis, one of the men who stood closest to him in the early years of the administration and who became the key figure in future American intervention in Palestine. During the first two years of Wilson's administration there was no marked change within the State Department because the President's views had not seeped down through the various levels of the Department; but with the outbreak of the World War, when the Jewish community in Palestine faced extinction, the new Wilsonian approach was decisive. This does not imply that desk men, counsellors, or even Secretaries of State were convinced of the wisdom of America's active intervention in Palestinian affairs. Though they generally obeyed orders, on occasion their divergence from Wilson manifested itself with vigor. As for Morgenthau, since he himself was not a partisan, he did not interpret the President's instructions as support for Zionism, but rather as a humanitarian impulse to succor helpless Palestinian Jews in whatever manner the Ambassador saw fit. Once in Turkey, Morgenthau made a rapid-fire tour of the old and the new settlements with his customary energy and vigor, and left behind him the impression that the new colonies had found in him a devoted admirer. The Jewish community was all the more puzzled at his militant anti-Zionism after the issuance of the Balfour Declaration.

Louis Brandeis's conversion to active participation in the Zionist Movement in 1912 gave the organization in the United States a leader who had already won his spurs in American life and was at the height of his intellectual powers. He devoted the whole of the summer of 1914 to a study of the Jewish problem and on August 30—as the war broke out—accepted the chairmanship of the Provisional Executive Committee for General Zionist Affairs, a job to which he devoted a set portion of his work hours throughout the war. To the organization in America, the only great neutral, now fell the task of sustaining the Palestine settlements, and the Provisional Committee was the instrumentality by which the loose Zionist federations of the various parts of the country, the youth movement, the women's organization, the fund collecting agency, the embryonic right wing (Mizrachi) and left wing (Poale Zion) were centralized to a degree and placed on a war footing. Jacob de Haas, one of the early collaborators of Theodor Herzl, who became Executive Secretary of the Committee, had found in Brandeis the figure to replace his former hero, and he groomed him for world leadership of Zionism.

Brandeis was not a man of half measures. "Zionist affairs are really the important things in life now," he wrote to his brother on April 25, 1915. In his extensive speaking tours throughout the country organizing Zionist units, he developed the doctrine of the basic significance which Zionism would have in inculcating a sense of pride and dignity among American Jews, beyond the practical problem of rebuilding Palestine for settlement. He thrust aside arguments about dual allegiance and proclaimed categorically that loyalty to America demanded that each American Jew become a Zionist. Joined by Dr. Shmaryahu Levin, an experienced Zionist tribune who had come on mission from the World Zionist Executive, Brandeis made political Zionism a powerful force in the American Jewish community instead of the rather feeble intellectual orientation which it had been prior to his day.

Chapter IV

DEFENSE OF THE SETTLEMENT
IN WORLD WAR I

THE GOOD WORKS OF THE STATE DEPARTMENT

To say that the President was an enthusiastic convert to Zionism as the result of Brandeis's preachments would be an exaggeration, but under his direction the whole diplomatic establishment was made responsive to those American Jews who had dedicated themselves to the defense of the Jewish settlements in Palestine, laboriously raised in thirty years of plodding work. That United States foreign policy should serve this purpose was eminently reasonable to a President who, in his own deep conscience was engaged in a humanitarian crusade, whatever significance the more sordid, materialist conflicts of the war may hold for the historian.

There were of course sound military and propagandistic reasons which, before the active participation of the United States in the war, made this diplomatic protectorate of the Jews in Palestine effective both with the Allies and the Central Powers. For the United States it was the free act of a nation which did not have any immediate "interests" involved, in the narrow sense that the term has usually been employed in the evaluation of a country's policy. It was a broad novel view of foreign relations under which each specific act does not have to face the iron test of utility and advantage.

This does not mean that the domestic political implications of the relief of the Jews in the war areas were overlooked by those members of Wilson's administration who counted and tabulated Jewish votes in the metropolitan areas before the close 1916 elections. The State Department in August of that year even issued a special memorandum on its good works among foreign Jews. But in the Wilsonian policy the guardianship of persecuted peoples had a genuine meaning beyond the propagandistic purposes for which it could be utilized on occasion.

During the war years, the internal conflicts over Zionism within the Jewish community first forced themselves upon the attention of United States officials. Brandeis represented one view and Morgenthau another. In the war period the Brandeis conception was the dominant one, as long as the sustenance of the Jews in Palestine remained devoid of political commitments.

Officials in the State Department were sometimes annoyed by what they considered the exaggerations of the American Jewish community whenever there was an attack or threat of an attack against the Jews in Palestine. Historically this vigilance and these protests—even when heightened by occasional hyperbole—have been justified. That the Turks did not destroy the Palestine community was due to a significant extent to their fear of reprisals from what they considered powerful Jewish elements in the United States and throughout the rest of the world. In the final analysis the propaganda and the pressure techniques of the American Jews were effective. In more than one instance local Turkish officials went out of bounds and ordered expulsions, arrests, and confiscations, a few murders. There was starvation in Palestine, alleviated largely by American charity. But the Jewish community survived the war. When Jewish leaders pled for a homeland at the Peace Conference in Paris they could represent a living if decimated settlement in Palestine. This is the ultimate significance of the American diplomatic defense of the Palestinian Jews during World War I.

ABOLITION OF THE CAPITULATIONS

Immediately upon the outbreak of war, Reverend Otis Glazebrook, the American consul at Jerusalem, began to send pleas for the relief of destitute Jews to Ambassador Morgenthau in Constantinople. The conditions he described were not unique. Throughout the Ottoman Empire the frantic attempt of an intricate, corrupt, and confused regime to put itself on a war footing was accompanied by military license against minorities, with or without official sanction. The Ottoman Empire of old Pashas and Young Turks was not an adequate mechanism even in peacetime, and the strains of war aggravated its patent internal weaknesses.

Glazebrook telegraphed the Embassy in Constantinople: "Military authorities seizing supplies of foreigners. Protests unavailing. Violation of domicile continues. Sixteen thousand troops concentrated

Nablous without visible support. Reign of military terrorism. Great distress prevails. American Jewish Community beseeches financial aid and food from America. Will you transmit appeal? Urgent." The Beirut consul reported similar requisitions of food and horses from Jews in the Haifa and Safed areas which were within his jurisdiction. When he had tried to protest on behalf of Americans in the name of the capitulations and the Treaty rights he was told by the governor that foreigners residing in the Ottoman Empire were subject to the laws relative to military requisitions.

A consular agent at Safed described the great fear in Galilee. The Jews in the area were terrified because in addition to outrages committed by Turkish officials, the war rumors had stirred the Bedouin tribesmen who surrounded them. The consular agent foresaw pillage and rape: "The natives and foreigners are suffering from this state of tyranny and misery and are in a bad state of mental worry concerning their safety. Safed and Tiberias are two Jewish towns and consequently are considered to be very wealthy and to contain beautiful girls. The numerous Arab tribes which live in the neighboring districts are quite aware of these two facts."

The Turks took advantage of the circumstance that the Powers were at war to rid themselves formally of the system of capitulations which was so odious to their national pride. Rustem Bey, the Turkish Ambassador in Washington, informed Secretary of State Bryan that beginning in October his Government would abolish the capitulations, which restricted the sovereignty of Turkey in her relations with the Powers. "All privileges and immunities accessory to these conventions or issuing therefrom are equally repealed. Having thus freed itself from what was an intolerable obstacle to all progress in the Empire the Imperial Government has adopted as basis of its relations with the other Powers the general principles of international law."

While American officials in Turkey were agreed among themselves that the continuation of the various *economic* capitulations which involved freedom from business and income taxes and limitations on import duties were hardly defensible in a modern state, the idea that, with the abolition of the *judicial* capitulations, American citizens might be tried in Turkish courts and thrown into filthy Turkish jails was abhorrent to them.

The Great Powers sent an identical protest to the Porte about the unilateral abolition of their treaty rights, but none of the European nations, still jockeying for position in Turkey, was inclined to irritate the Porte, hence the note was weak. The European ambassadors considered the Turkish decision a *fait accompli*. Ambassador Morgenthau, not involved in the European War, delivered a far stronger protest on behalf of the United States, but the Turks would not recede from their position.

Zionist circles in Palestine at first hailed the abolition of the capitulations. They joined in the public celebrations of Turkey's emancipation and made speeches about the dawn of a new epoch. In part this was an attempt to find favor for their settlements. They soon learned the real import of Turkey's "liberation" from the foreign consuls. Alexander Aaronsohn, a member of that ill-fated Jewish family which served as British secret agents during the war, has described the immediate psychological response of Palestinian natives. "Upon the Arabs it acted like an intoxicant. Every bootblack or batman felt that he was the equal of the accursed Frank, who now had no consul to protect him; and abuses began immediately."

The foreign Jews in the Empire suddenly found themselves subject to Turkish law and to officials who for years had deeply resented their privileged status. Jews had always run with complaints to the European consular courts; now the whole legal basis under which the bulk of the Ashkenazic Jewish community of Palestine had existed was overturned.

THE EXPULSIONS OF 1914–1915

When the representatives of the Allies left Turkey the United States took over their interests and thus became the chief protector of thousands of Jews in Palestine who were nominal subjects of Russia, France, and Britain. The office of the sole neutral representative of a great power in Constantinople became one of the key diplomatic posts in the world. That Ambassador Morgenthau was a Jewish philanthropist with important status in the American Jewish community complicated his position. The Ambassador could not avoid being sensitive on the point that State Department officials might consider him too zealous in his interventions on behalf of his co-religionists. Thus it happened, as the despatches show, that on occasion Morgenthau bent over backward in making his protests mild and in toning down the cries of outrage he heard from Palestine. At the same time it was comprehensible that many Jews both in Palestine and in the United States should be critical of a Jewish Ambassador at the very seat of authority in the Empire who did not secure immediate alleviation of the sufferings of the Palestine community. American Jewish leaders who received from the State Department copies or paraphrases of Morgenthau's despatches could not but feel that his profuse assurances of Turkish good-will were excessive in the face of what they learned from other sources, primarily from Egypt under British control.

The first Jewish problem of magnitude after the outbreak of the war was the fate of fifty thousand Russian Jews in Palestine who constituted about half of both the old and the new settlements. Though the Russian consulate had never bothered to extend them much protection, they had not become Ottoman subjects through any formal process and therefore were still considered Russians, now enemy subjects. Their expulsion or internment would have wrecked the whole new settlement.

In November 1914, Acting Secretary of State Lansing informed the New York banker, Jacob H. Schiff, for publication, that the problem of the belligerent Jews in Palestine was solving itself. The Turkish Government, according to a Morgenthau despatch, had decided not to expel the Russian Jews but to allow them to become naturalized Ottoman subjects *en bloc.*

The next month, giving the lie to these assurances, the Turks initiated a mass expulsion of Jews from Jaffa. On December 25th Morgenthau telegraphed without comment that those belligerent subjects still remaining in Palestine would be interned; he had approved a suggestion from Glazebrook that since Turkish facilities for transporting the Jews were inadequate the U.S.S. *Tennessee,* then in the waters of the eastern Mediterranean, should be used to carry refugees to Port Said. It was not until the next day, upon inquiry from Washington, that Morgenthau gave the Department specific details about the expulsions which by this time had aroused the whole American Jewish community. Morgenthau explained that the expulsion order applied only to those Jews who had failed to Ottomanize themselves. Six hundred had in fact already been expelled. Though they had not been maltreated, families had been separated. Morgenthau took consolation in the fact that the Minister of the Interior was considering favorably a suggestion that any Russian Jews who would at least voice their intent to become Turks would be granted a thirteen month period of grace, during which time it was hoped that money enough to pay the naturalization fees of poor Jews could be collected in the

United States and Europe. Five days later Morgenthau reported that the Porte had accorded the Jews a month's delay, not the thirteen months originally indicated. Under the same order all indigent Jews were exempted from paying a naturalization fee.

The Ambassador's bland reports gave hardly an inkling as to the real import of the Turkish orders and the dilemma they created for the Palestinian Jews. As soon as the Ottomanization decree was issued, the leaders of the new Zionist settlement had undertaken an active naturalization campaign in order to keep the community intact. Ottomanization was considered a means of escape from exile. It soon became apparent, however, that Ottomanization was a direct road for the able-bodied into the perdition of the Turkish army, and the campaign aroused resentment against leaders who had sponsored it.

From Consul Garrels in Alexandria the Department heard on January 18th that six thousand Jewish refugees had already been transported from Jaffa to Egypt on the U.S.S. *Tennessee* and that thousands more were expected. This was the first intimation of the size of the movement about which Morgenthau had been silent. A week later, when the pathetic appeal of the refugees in Egypt, who had organized themselves into an Alexandria Palestine Committee, was received the United States had an account of the political, anti-Zionist motives of the Turkish raids on the Jewish settlements which underlay the expulsion orders. "High military authorities pursue systematic destruction our institutions, properties, all our modernizing work in ancient Judea. Thousands of citizens, old men, women, children, flower of Jewish youth, their sweat-irrigated Palestine fields plundered, brutally expelled. . . . Jaffa military authorities openly pronounced that as impossible to raise fellahs to level of Jewish colonies will try reduce Jews to fellah's state. . . . We implore noble, powerful American nation to use influence and save Jewish colonization work in Palestine."

Newspaper despatches from Alexandria via London were already carrying dramatic reports of the attempt to eradicate the Zionist settlements in Palestine, when Secretary of State Bryan, at the behest of Louis Marshall of the American Jewish Committee, wired Morgenthau for official information.

The tone of Morgenthau's reply can be explained only in part by the fact—which later came to light—that Consul Glazebrook at Jerusalem had hesitated to send detailed reports to Constantinople for fear of censorship and of antagonizing the Turkish officials. Morgenthau was thus not as fully cognizant of Palestine events as he might have been; but aside from that consideration, he betrayed a marked indifference to those Turkish measures of which he was aware. Neither Consul Glazebrook in Jerusalem, nor the Grand Rabbi, nor the Zionist representatives in Constantinople had, he said, given him any reports on the destruction of Jewish property. During the hurried departure of the Jews from Jaffa there had been some disorder, "but nothing very serious." Morgenthau himself had succeeded in obtaining a privilege for the Jews of belligerent nations in the Turkish dominions outside of Palestine: there Jews would be allowed to remain in peace even without becoming Ottomans. But with respect to Palestine Jews the Porte was adamant, and they either had to naturalize themselves or leave. According to Glazebrook two-thirds of the Jews either had already or would soon accept naturalization. The great danger of having fifty-thousand Russian Jews either expelled or interned was thus over. For those who refused to become Ottomans the Ambassador had little sympathy: "The few thousand unyielding ones suffer from their own choice." As for the closing of the Zionist Anglo-Palestine Bank—which the Alexandria Refugee Committee had described as basic to their whole agricultural economy—Morgenthau was unperturbed.

There had been enough agitation in the press about the expulsion of Russian Jews from Palestine to prompt Lansing to get a more circumstantial report than the Morgenthau despatch. And there was a man on the spot whose ship was plying back and forth between Jaffa and Alexandria—Captain Decker of the U.S.S. *Tennessee*. Through the Consul in Alexandria he was charged with the mission of making a careful inquiry into the "rumored reversal" of Turkish policy, to consult with the Alexandria Palestine Committee and Palestine Zionists and to investigate particularly American interests including the Agricultural Experiment Station at Haifa. At the same time, Lansing informed Morgenthau that "Brandeis, the Zionists, and others" were preparing help and that Nathan Straus was sending a ship with food supplies for Moslems and Christians as well as Jews in Palestine and Syria. This latter promise—which would have involved a rather sizable vessel—was to fulfill a British condition for allowing it to pass their blockade.

The Zionists in America in the meantime had advised among themselves and the result of their deliberations was a formal statement which Brandeis had Lansing send to Morgenthau, who in turn was to transmit it to the Porte on their behalf. Zionism had become respectable. Wilson's friendship with prominent Zionists had changed the official attitude since the cold snubs of 1912. It was now possible for the American Zionists to use an American envoy to deliver an official communication to the Porte. The Brandeis wire is remarkable in many respects. Its offer of a food-ship to appease the Turkish rage is reminiscent of medieval gifts to cruel barons from their Jews endeavoring to mitigate the harshness of a decree. "Zionists, appreciating traditional liberal policy Turkey towards Jews, and in keeping with their unbroken record, desire to assure Turkey of their unqualified loyalty."

Morgenthau reported back to Washington that when he submitted Brandeis's statement on behalf of the Zionists, the Porte innocently replied that it had never issued orders against the Zionists and doubted whether any had been promulgated by the military authorities in Palestine. If they had, the Porte promised to revoke them. Morgenthau had indeed heard that a "fanatic" secretary of Djemal Pasha, the virtual dictator of Syria and Palestine, had issued a statement that "the Government is most friendly towards all loyal Jews but that they will strongly attack the seditious and intriguing element which under the name of Nationalism is endeavoring to erect a Jewish Government and has already brought into circulation paper money and stamps." But this was not the policy in Constantinople. The Porte ministers promised Morgenthau that all would change for the better and that they would communicate to local officials their wishes that the Jews be accorded favorable treatment. The Minister of the Interior added that any Jewish refugees who would agree to become Ottomans could freely return from their exile in Egypt. The whole attack on Zionism in Palestine, Morgenthau explained rather glibly, was merely the action of overzealous officials resorting to coercive methods to hasten the Ottomanization of foreign Jews. Two days later Morgenthau related that in his very presence the Minister of War had wired the military commander at Jaffa that consideration must be shown to all Jews.

Soothing declarations about Jews to the American ambassador in Constantinople, while local officials proceeded as usual, was a timeworn technique of Turkish administration. Down in Palestine the only immediate effect which the telegrams from the Turkish Ministries in Constantinople seem to have had was a wave of arrests of Palestine Zionists and the confiscation of their correspondence. Dr.

Ruppin wired Morgenthau from Jaffa that leading Zionists who had participated in the World Congress were among those imprisoned. The Alexandria refugees had received similar reports, and utilizing the facilities of the U.S.S. *Tennessee* they had cabled President Wilson that only a direct plea from him to the Sultan could save Zionism in Palestine from extinction. A few days later the Alexandria Committee sent another frantic message warning of an impending massacre of all Jews and Christians in Palestine in a Moslem Holy War. The Turkish Army was fighting the British at Suez, and fear of the outcome terrified the Jews.

CAPTAIN DECKER'S REPORT

A detailed, balanced report on the whole Palestine crisis of December 1914 to February 1915 came from Captain Decker of the U.S.S. *Tennessee*. Decker performed his mission of inquiry with great thoroughness, assembling a substantial amount of supplementary data on the location and extent of the Jewish agricultural colonies; on the history of Zionism; on the Turkish proclamations against the Zionists; and on the incendiary pamphlets preaching a Holy War. He interviewed the Alexandria Palestine Committee; stopped at Haifa in an unsuccessful attempt to visit the American Jewish Agricultural Station there; questioned Protestant missionaries and Consul Glazebrook of Jerusalem; and, at a secret meeting in the office of the American Consular Agent at Jaffa, interrogated Dr. Arthur Ruppin and Hoofien, the Dutch Zionist who was manager of the Anglo-Palestine Bank. Ruppin impressed him greatly, both the man and his learning. Decker's final document, *Report on Conditions in Palestine with Reference to Zionism,* relayed through Navy communications, was factual, conscious of the significance with which Jewish establishments in Palestine had been invested by people throughout the world. His simple conclusion was that Zionism was in real danger and that its destruction would be lamentable.

From the Alexandria Refugee Committee he learned about political conditions in Palestine from the beginning of the war, which served as background for the events of January and February 1915. They fixed upon Behadine Effendi as the official who had been plotting their annihilation. A specialist on Jewish Affairs in Palestine in the Ministry of the Interior, he was appointed governor of Jaffa in September 1914. In the presence of the Chief Rabbi he declared himself to be a bitter antagonist of Zionism. He had studied the problem thoroughly in Constantinople, he said, and had come armed with special instructions on the Zionists. He knew that their prayer book was filled with memories of Zion and that it was their scheme to conquer Palestine after the manner of the Romans, by establishing autonomous colonies. This technique he was resolved to combat with force. Behadine was not of the old school of lazy venal governors. He clamped down firmly on immigration into Palestine, even of Yemenite Jews—fleeing local tribal disorders—who were Turkish subjects. He attacked the Hebrew cultural institutions, symbol of their national renascence. Previous pashas had allowed Hebrew posters to be hung on stores and offices in Jaffa. Behadine ordered all such signs erased, and red and white ones in Turkish and Arabic substituted. The agricultural colonies in his district were subjected to frequent military searches. Tel Aviv, the new suburb of Jaffa, was encircled by armed forces and any valuables discovered in the homes of belligerent nationals were confiscated. At Mikve Yisrael his agents turned the whole settlement topsy turvy in a wild search for arms. The Arab villagers in the vicinity were openly assured that when the Jews were driven out they would inherit their land. Once they became conscious of official protection the Arabs set about harassing the Jewish colonies with impunity.

On December 17th had occurred the first expulsion of Jews from Jaffa, so colorlessly described by Morgenthau. The Jewish refugees who had been the victims were more emotional in their conversations with Captain Decker. Behadine had issued orders that all non-Ottomanized belligerents be deported at four in the afternoon. The police proceeded to round up Jews of all nationalities in the streets and houses of Jaffa indiscriminately; without letting them collect their belongings, they dragged them along to the port. Since Jaffa only had an anchorage they were loaded into rowboats whose Arab boatmen, taking advantage of their plight, beat and robbed the helpless passengers. When they arrived at the ship which was to transport them into exile it was discovered that there was not enough space for all of them and families were broken up, leaving children on board while parents were carried back to shore.

After an inquiry instigated by Morgenthau, formal blame for the unauthorized expulsions was placed on Behadine, and he was dismissed from his post, only to be appointed to a position of even greater power as secretary to Djemal Pasha. Whereas his malevolence had once been confined to the Jaffa district, it now extended over the whole land. It became common knowledge that he was in Djemal Pasha's confidence and that Jewish affairs were completely in his hands. When the Turkish army undertook its campaign against Suez, the General Staff was transferred to Jerusalem. There Djemal Pasha, in his capacity as commander of the Fourth Army Corps, issued and enforced throughout Palestine all the decrees which Behadine had once imposed on the Jaffa district alone. Zionist flags were confiscated; Hebrew signs were forbidden; and anyone found in possession of the subscription stamps of the Jewish National Fund was subject to the death penalty. Hebrew was prohibited as a language of correspondence. The Anglo-Palestine Bank was closed, an order which threatened to force it into bankruptcy because its assets were obviously not liquid enough to meet all demands for payment in a few weeks.

An all-embracing official proclamation against the Zionists had been issued on January 25, 1915; Behadine ordered it published in the Hebrew *ha-Herut* (Freedom) of Jerusalem, and the news of it spread overnight among the native Arab population. "You are to translate literally and to publish without change the following lines: 'The Government—in opposing the acts of those elements which, through intrigues are trying to create in the Palestinian region of the Ottoman empire a Jewish state under the name of Zionism and who are thus harming the sons of their own race—has ordered the confiscation of the postage stamps, Zionist flags, paper money, bank notes of the Anglo-Palestine Company, Ltd. in the form of checks which are spread among these elements and has decreed the dissolution of all the clandestine Zionist societies and organizations.

" 'We have just learned that a few malevolent intriguers, falsifying our words, say that our orders affect all Jews in general. It is evident that there is no injury here to those Jews who are our allies and who are sons of the fatherland along with us, enjoying the same rights. With God's aid they will always be friends of our fatherland. The orders are aimed only at the Zionist organizations and actions. We hope that all other Jews of our country who have no relations with these corrupt revolutionary elements, may rest in peace as before. We, all the Ottomans, are friends and citizens with all our hearts of those Jews who are our allies. Of Zionism and the Zionists—that element of disorder and revolution which has as its aim the foundation of a state in our country, and all other societies which aim or will aim at similar phantasies—we are implacable enemies forever. . . .' "

The Jews of the Alexandria Committee and Dr. Arthur Ruppin explained to Captain Decker the reasons for adopting those economic measures within their community which Behadine had denounced as a revolutionary attempt to create a state within a state. When, at the outbreak of the war, confidence in the Turkish pound vanished, the Jewish settlements were forced to improvise paper money. Turkey had declared a moratorium and cash was often unobtainable even by those who had money in the banks. A small quantity of chits was therefore issued by the Jewish municipal committees for use in the communal stores. The Anglo-Palestine Bank registered checks had the same purpose. To call their Jewish National Fund subscription stamps, which Decker aptly compared with Red Cross stamps, postage was nonsense.

Decker's informants all agreed that the concerted drive to crush Zionism was directed primarily by the Turkish Nationalists in the army. Men such as Djemal Pasha and Behadine had always been enemies of the Zionist colonies, banks, arbitration boards, Hebrew schools and organizations. The influence of European Zionists in Constantinople before the war, especially the Germans, had prevented the army from proceeding openly against the Zionists. With war, the Zionists could be considered separatists and traitors by the military, and it was difficult for civilians in Constantinople to restrain them, especially when the Egyptian front was active.

Dr. Arthur Ruppin was more resigned to the economic realities of war and his testimony before Decker was less emotional than that of the Alexandria refugees. The Alexandria Committee had denounced the requisitions and had described the total breakdown which faced the colonies. Ruppin and Hoofien were less critical of the requisitions than of the overt acts of violence against Zionist leaders and their institutions. Ruppin knew that the confiscation had borne more heavily on the Jewish colonies than on the primitive Arab villages but thought that was inevitable since they were better equipped. It was the arrests that worried him most because they had robbed the new settlements of their leaders. The Hebrew language ban threatened their whole cultural program. Land titles were being called into question and Arabs in the vicinity of the more flourishing colonies were being goaded on to pillage.

Consul Glazebrook of Jerusalem, for his part, was especially fearful of what might happen if the Turks were defeated at Suez and the army in rout made its way north along the Jerusalem-Damascus road.

Decker had been given copies of the incendiary pamphlets which preached violence against all infidels—except the Germans and Austrians—and he telegraphed Morgenthau demanding the punishment of the authors. At a celebration of the Moslems in Jaffa after a false announcement of victory at Suez, Decker detected a mood of wild exaltation which might become ugly overnight. Glazebrook was of the opinion that though the Behadine proclamation of January 25, 1915 had differentiated between Zionists and loyal Jews, the ignorant Arab population would make no such distinction. The declaration of outlawry against the Zionists had had a serious provocative effect on the Arabs.

Captain Decker learned of the techniques whereby local Arab chieftains were being encouraged to turn on the Jews. An order which prohibited the colonists' watchmen from standing guard with firearms had left them defenseless before their Bedouin neighbors. Formerly Jewish police of the colonies had been recognized as an unofficial gendarmerie, and they had customarily brought marauders either to the Turkish or the consular courts. Now the colonies were left wide open to pillage.

Both Dr. Ruppin and the Alexandria Refugee Committee were in agreement that only a direct appeal from the President of the United States to the Sultan could save Zionism. Ruppin further expressed his sad conviction that if the settlements they had raised in three decades of pioneering were destroyed the movement would never be revived again.

Captain Decker's sympathetic conduct during his transportation of the refugees from Palestine to Egypt and the general manner of his inquiry on Zionism won him a tumultuous welcome from both the old community and the exiles when his ship re-entered the harbor of Alexandria upon the completion of his mission.

DJEMAL PASHA RELENTS

Fortunately for the Zionist Jews, their protectors in Constantinople —Morgenthau, the ambassadors of the central powers, the Chacham-Bashi, and the crypto-Jews who were powers in the Committee of Union and Progress—exerted enough pressure to stay the hand of Djemal Pasha.

By March 1915, the wave of expulsions was over, active persecution of the Zionists ceased, and the temper of Turkish officials towards the Jewish settlement changed. The Governor of Jerusalem reported that only two hundred Jews who were enemy aliens had failed to become Ottoman subjects and the Porte assured Morgenthau that even the recalcitrants would be treated with leniency. Early in April funds for Jewish relief and for the protection of Zionist economic interests in Palestine began to reach Dr. Ruppin from the west, from Brandeis in the United States and from the Dutch Zionist Banker Kann at the Hague. There were still intermittent rumors of impending Bedouin raids, but no atrocities were perpetrated.

The *volte face* of the Turkish government appeared to be complete, and a peaceful settlement was even arranged on the use of the Hebrew language for general correspondence. David Yellin, one of the Zionist leaders, became a censor, and he wrote Morgenthau that the situation of the Jews was highly satisfactory.

Meier Dizengoff, the dean of the Zionist settlement and the first mayor of Tel Aviv, has a delightful account in his memoirs of an interview between the Zionist Entabi, a native Sephardi, and Djemal Pasha, after the arrest of the leaders of the Jewish community in January. It provides a humorous *dénouement* to the grave political crisis of early 1915. To this interview Dizengoff imputes the sudden reversal of Turkish policy. No translation can do justice to the quaint charm of the original Hebrew. "Djemal Pasha began with anger and said to Entabi, 'You Zionists are plotting to tear away this province, Palestine, from the Ottoman Empire, and to found for yourselves a separate government under the protectorate of an enemy power. But it will not be! I shall drive you out of here. I shall drive out all of you, and I shall uproot you from this land forever!' Then Entabi got up, spoke with feeling, and answered with firmness, 'As an Ottoman the son of an Ottoman, whose grandfather was killed in the Damascus uprising and whose bones are buried here on the Mount of Olives in Jerusalem—I protest against this accusation. As if I would lend a hand to felons and to rebels who participate in any anti-Ottoman venture. We are innocent. Innocent, your excellency! Even my friends the new Ottomans, once they have become Ottomanized, will not lie in their souls and will not betray their new fatherland. We all still remember what the Ottomans did for the Spanish exiles—and our hearts have always been grateful to Turkey.'

" 'And this Zionism of yours—is not its goal the transformation of Palestine into a Jewish State?'

" 'No, your excellency. Zionism primarily fights against assimilation and strives for Jewish cultural autonomy. It is our desire to revive and to develop our language, to continue our religious and cultural tradition in our holy land and to return to the labor of the soil as in ancient times. We wish to build up the land which is our historic homeland, to renew its youth and to make it into a real homeland for our sons in future generations—all under the Ottoman flag.'

"When Djemal Pasha heard these words his rage subsided and he said, 'If this is the way things are then why do you follow foreign leaders—Herzl and his ilk? I shall give you crown lands on which to establish colonies, and I will even proclaim absolute autonomy for your religion and your culture. And I shall help you to realize the Zionist ideal under an Ottoman protectorate.' Whereupon Entabi recovered sufficiently to reply in jest, 'If so then I proclaim his excellency president of the Zionist organization and I shall be his faithful secretary.'

" 'But according to the reports I have received all you Palestinian Jews are francophiles.'

" 'But your excellency we are only your pupils. Why only a short while ago your excellency was head of the Franco-Ottoman Committee whose aim was the rapprochement of the Turks and the French. And so we walked in your path. If today you have reason to declare war on France then you must have arrived at a different orientation and you have a different goal before you. Now tell us what it is and we shall follow you in the future as we have in the past.'

" 'The goal? We have to conquer Egypt—even now I am sending my troops to the Suez canal.'

" 'Your excellency, conquer Egypt and build a railroad in the desert and we Jews will take the lead and will return to Egypt.'

". . . And Entabi captivated the despot with his witty talk to the point where the commander said to him, 'Well, as a faithful Ottoman, tell me in complete earnest who are these accused whom I summoned and whom I am sending to Angora?'

"When Entabi told him that they were not guilty of anything except misconstruing the true intentions of the Ottoman Government and suggested that nevertheless he and a few of them worthy of some punishment should suffer as an example to others, Djemal Pasha called for the dossiers which contained the accusations and tore them up. Whereupon an exile of fifteen Zionists was arranged to save face: they were to go to Tiberias for two weeks."

To attribute to this curious interview the re-direction of Turkish policy towards the Jews is doubtless an oversimplification. Surely American and German intervention in Constantinople played at least as significant a role. Such somersaults, however, were quite frequent among the capricious Young Turk bosses who in their bewilderment did not quite know what course to pursue.

Djemal's reversal lasted for about two years—a long time for any consistent policy on Palestine among the Powers—and according to Dizengoff, this new convert to Zionism showed his favor to the Jews on a number of subsequent occasions. At one time Djemal Pasha welcomed Dizengoff and Entabi and announced to them that after the war the three of them would form a committee for rebuilding Palestine under the Turkish flag; he even jotted down the outline of a program. He visited Zionist institutions and their agricultural settlements, and presented one colony with twenty thousand dunams of sandy crown lands.

At the time of the outbreak of the Turks against the Armenians in May 1915 there was a natural tendency among the neutral ambassadors to expect that it would be accompanied by atrocities against the Zionists. Morgenthau at first reported that the movement against the Armenians was the signal for a concerted drive on all non-Turkish and non-Union and Progress elements in the empire and that hostile action against the Zionists would follow. Secretary of State Bryan's laconic instruction was, "Urge Turkish Government to protect both Armenians and Zionists."

Morgenthau bent his efforts towards stopping the Armenian massacres and he tried hard to convince the Austrian and the German ambassadors that atrocities against non-Moslems were injuring the moral position of the Central Powers. He failed, and hundreds of thousands of Armenians were slaughtered. But Turkish policy followed the principle of turning against one minority at a time. While the Armenians were massacred the Zionists were saved.

PIERCING A BLOCKADE

The Turkish nationalists' war against their non-Turanian subject minorities assumed two basic forms. The more virulent phase was genocide—deliberate organized extermination of a people. This was the fate of the Armenians. The alternative to bloody slaughter was abandonment of whole peoples to slow starvation and the ravages of disease under the guise of military necessity. Djemal Pasha in Syria and Lebanon systematically pursued this second tactic which, unlike the Armenian massacres in Anatolia, did not engender the same world revulsion against the terrible Turk, since hunger and disease took on the aspect of acts of God during a long-drawn-out war. Moral responsibility for the decimation of the non-Turanian inhabitants of Syria and Lebanon through famine and disease could be spread among all the belligerent powers; the Allied blockade of the Syrian coast could be blamed as much as the wanton Turkish requisitions of animals and foodstuffs. William Yale, who had been a representative of Standard Oil in the Near East and was an objective observer, wrote the State Department in 1917 that in Lebanon Djemal Pasha had prohibited the transportation of wheat and other food supplies with the intent of exterminating the Christian population. He estimated some 50,000 to 60,000 persons had died of starvation by the end of 1916.

The Jews of Palestine were more fortunate. They fared better than any other minority in the Ottoman Empire because of the peculiar realities of Jewish dispersion throughout the world and the economic resources available for aid from the neutral United States up to and even after the break in diplomatic relations with Turkey. The small Jewish minority in Palestine, though it suffered hunger, survived in a blockaded country through four years of war under an administration which not only contributed nothing to their support but at intervals conducted wild and haphazard raids on their meager stores. Cut off from the *Haluka* which ceased to function with the outbreak of the war, the old settlement would have perished without an effective relief organization sustained by Jews outside of Palestine. The new settlement, which lost the European markets for its crops, could never have endured without subsidy from abroad. Viewed in perspective, Jewish survival was due less to any particular sympathy of the Turks for the Jews, or a dramatic change of mind on the part of Djemal Pasha—though their ancient relations of friendship and Jewish insight into Turkish character as displayed in the Entabi intercession were helpful—than to the sheer political might which the Jews of the world were able to bring to bear on the Turkish government. The legend of Jewish power stood the Jews in good stead during the First World War—for the last time.

Before the small Palestinian community of Jews could be fed, an intricate set of contingencies had to come to perfect confluence.

Foremost was the policy of the Turkish government. The wartime economic measures of the Turks were brutal and irrational. They confiscated animals with a recklessness which left none for breeding. They took whatever wheat and petroleum they could lay hands on. The railroads were clogged with troops shipped hither and yon without any over-all strategic plan. Food could not be transported from the agricultural districts of eastern Syria to the urban areas of the coast, either on the old beasts of burden taken over by the army or in the modern railroad crowded with soldiers. The immediate impact of Turkish military policy brought starvation to the cities, the natural result of war in a bankrupt state entering a conflict of great modern powers. The Jews of the old settlement suffered along with other urban communities, perhaps more than the "true" Turks, but far less than the Armenians, the Syrians, and the Greeks.

The new settlement in Palestine had much more to offer the Turks than the old, for here there were animals and the most precious commodity of all, petroleum, which the colonists used to drive their irrigation pumps. Two basic export crops of the new settlement to Europe, wine and oranges, were blockaded in the country and were not very useful for internal consumption since the Turks were officially teetotalers and the oranges could not be transported. The colonists faced ruin.

In the early months of the war the Turks were absorbed by so many military and economic problems—the Allied navy just missed breaking through the Dardanelles—that they paid no attention to the survival of the Jewish settlement. It was not their affair. They had confiscated the animals; the human beings were of no importance. The Jews of the old settlement were not very useful for military service or even for forced labor on the roads. The younger men of the new settlement were conscripted into the army or the labor battalions where they suffered the same fate as the other vermin-ridden, starved, and bedraggled troops of the Empire. Since the government's relief measures for pure Turks were insufficient to feed them, it was hardly expected that they would exert themselves in caring for peoples whom they considered aliens at best, enemies at worst.

But the Jews had friends at court. Salonika Jews had played a role in the uprising of the Young Turks and the Minister of Finance, Djavid, was a Jew by race though a Mohammedan by religion. Morgenthau, the American Ambassador, was at great pains not to appear as the special pleader for the Jews to the neglect of the Christian Armenians, but the Turks, for whom the religious community was in many ways more basic than the national group, refused to believe that he was not really more interested in his co-religionists. In the early period of the war the Turks wooed Morgenthau. The Jews were a small community of at most 100,000, half of whom were pauperized religiasts who offered no political threat to any regime. The other half, the colonists of the new settlement, were a danger only if their ideal of an independent Jewish State should ever take on more material shape. After the initial drive against the Zionists subsided in the early spring of 1915, there was a political truce between Djemal Pasha and the new settlement until March 1917. The number of political Zionists in Palestine was far too insignificant to make even the suspicious Turks compare them to the 2,000,000 Armenians. Hence if means were devised for outsiders to feed the Jews in both the old and the new settlements the Turks could be persuaded, after the inevitable *démarches,* refusals, assents, and reversals, to allow the distribution of food and relief funds. Only at critical moments of military defeat, when the dread of Zionist politics again suddenly possessed them, did they place impediments in the way.

The final mechanics of relief distribution which were agreed upon showed uncommon forbearance on the part of the Turks. They would naturally have preferred to control the doling out of the food or the funds themselves. No Turkish realists could be blind to the possibilities of graft or subtracting a portion of the imports for their war machine if the food and the money came anywhere near their itching palms. Turkish officials were willing to go to any lengths to keep at least a finger in the relief pie. When the United States forced them to agree to the elimination of their central military and civil authorities in the distribution process, they came back with a characteristic subterfuge, calling for control in the hands of municipal authorities, who, they claimed, were not part of the Government. All foreign powers were versed in Turkish ways, Morgenthau as well as any man, and appropriate guarantees were insisted upon. In the end, except perhaps for some traditional measure of baksheesh about which the records are silent, the relief distribution was allowed to take place without major depredations on the part of the Turkish officials. After the breaking off of diplomatic relations with the United States, the organization became somewhat clandestine, but the relief continued, with relatively minor interruptions, until the British occupation.

The bulk of the relief shipments for Palestine had to come from the United States. Turkish Jews in Constantinople were themselves recipients of the same charity. The Russian Government would not permit the export of funds collected by Jews, despite requests from American Zionists transmitted through the embassy. German Jews got some funds through directly, the moneys being brought down in person by German liaison officers in Palestine, but no food came out of the German war machine. Jews in England and the great imperial units of South Africa and Egypt transmitted donations through the American agency. France was too hard-pressed to be a contributor. Thus the only Jewry of significance was the American community, enjoying the great prosperity of the war years. The relief of Palestine Jews, whenever there were attempts to get funds, food, medicine, or petroleum through the blockade, was primarily an American responsibility.

During the war Zionist and non-Zionist groups in the United States collaborated at moments of crisis when the lives of Jews were in jeopardy, but they remained cool to each other because of fundamental divergences over Palestine. Fund-raising and fund distribution were rarely devoid of political implications. While the Joint Distribution Committee carefully allotted its funds to all Jews in Turkey, Constantinople as well as Jerusalem, the Zionists concentrated on preserving their institutions and settlements in Palestine. Competition for the philanthropist's munificence was sharp. The disagreements ultimately worked themselves out, but great energy was wasted in negotiations among Jewish committees, mutual recrimination in rival periodicals, parallel, or what was more unfortunate, contradictory interventions before the State Department.

The agency of the United States government was crucial in the whole transaction. From the very beginning of the war the official hostility towards Zionism which had once found expression among some division chiefs in the State Department disappeared. Brandeis was the key to the transformation. Telegrams and cables between the Zionists in America and the World Zionist representatives in Turkey were sent in cipher when necessary through the State Department and the embassy. American officials viewed Zionism primarily as a work of humanitarianism, though the political implications of many of the messages surely did not escape them. The frequency of the communications—literally hundreds of instructions and despatches—on the relief of Palestine is proof enough that this was no casual aspect of American policy. With rare exceptions, the requests of American Jews to the Department involving preservation of the Palestinian settlements led to formal diplomatic proposals to Turkish, German, Austrian, English, French, or Italian officials. First failures were followed by renewed attempts to get funds transferred and food ships through the blockade. When commercial bottoms were not available, American naval vessels in the Mediterranean were commissioned once the legal difficulties involved in a liberal interpretation of the appropriations acts were overcome.

Most of the negotiations of American officials in London, Paris, Washington, Alexandria, and Constantinople centered around the necessary permission to send American naval vessels through the blockade of the Syrian coast. America was the great neutral, and her humanitarian appeals had a force which the hard-pressed Allies could not ignore. They had to weigh the moral advantages of helping the Jews of Palestine against the military disadvantages of allowing a blockade to be pierced. The pros and cons were enough to drive a comptroller of economic warfare to distraction. Any relief that got through might be requisitioned for the Turkish war machine, would mitigate the internal economic crisis in Turkey by filling hungry bellies, would tend to disorganize the blockade by special naval arrangements which might betray secrets to the enemy. On the other hand, allowing the food to pass would increase Allied prestige among Jews throughout the world and particularly in an area where Allied armies were soon to go into battle. Feeding the Jews of Palestine, like the British feeding of the hungry Belgians, could be expected to have a benign effect on American public opinion. To deny the requests of the Jews would in a sense make the Allies guilty participants in the starving of peoples whom they needed as friends.

A request from Brandeis to one of the Allies was not looked upon as a personal and unofficial plea. The Allies, especially Great Britain, were highly conscious of the importance of winning over the American Jews, for they had started with a handicap: Imperial Russia and Roumania, the lands of the pogrom and discriminatory decrees against Jews, were on the Allied side. English and French slogans about liberty sounded hollow in Jewish ears as long as they were linked with Czarist Russia. American Jews were overwhelmingly immigrants from eastern Europe, and the idea of succoring the Czar from whose lands they had fled across an ocean aroused no enthusiasm. The great majority of American Jews in 1914 were members of the working class, and whatever ideology they had tended to be socialist and pacifist. The German Jews in America who had migrated from the middle of the nineteenth century on were the prosperous leaders of the Jewish communities. They, along with other groups of German descent, were not militant interventionists in the early years of the war, though they moved along with the current. Thus, winning over the American Jewish community to the Allied cause was not easy. This gave Brandeis leverage in his attempts to get the British and the French to allow the blockade to be broken for the relief of the Jews of Palestine.

The Germans' submarine activity in 1917 made their consent as necessary as that of the admirals of the Allied blockade. In the early years of the war the Germans presented no special obstruction, but as the day of American participation approached, they became wary. Officially, they claimed that the Allies might hit an American vessel intentionally and blame German submarines, or that the ship might strike a mine. Behind it all was a growing suspicion of relief distribution under the direction of the neutral, soon the enemy, United States. But since German opposition did not become concrete until 1917, relief was feasible in the early war years.

THE PASSAGE OF THE U.S.S. VULCAN

In December 1914 the notables of the American Jewish Committee began considering the despatch of a food ship to Palestine, but they sought prior guarantees that relief would reach its destination and not be gobbled up in the maw of the war machines. They wanted assurances that the food ship would not be requisitioned by the Turks, would not be intercepted by the allied belligerents, and that the cargo would be unloaded safely in Palestine. The State Department obviously could give them no such pledges.

At the very beginning of the war, Dr. Ruppin in Palestine, with the aid of the American Zionists, made an attempt to keep alive the fruit economy of the agricultural colonies after they had been cut off from European purchasers by selling their products in the United States. But as the Allied blockade tightened and the oceans became infested with German submarines, economic measures for the preservation of the colonies, by shifting their markets, became impossible; and prosperous planters in the colonies were reduced to dependence on the same charity as the rabbis in the old settlement in Jerusalem, while their fruit crops rotted on the trees. The war brought a complete stoppage to what had been a small though growing commerce between the United States and Palestine.

In January and February 1915, Captain Decker and Consul Glazebrook literally besieged Morgenthau, philanthropic Jews in the United States, and State Department officials with appeals on behalf of the Jews, both those left in Palestine and those who had been exiled to Alexandria.

Since the plans for a food ship from the United States were not coming to fruition, the American Jewish Relief Committee, created during the emergency, tried alternate methods; they inquired in Rome whether permission could be obtained to buy food in Italy for immediate trans-shipment, thus avoiding the hazards of an Atlantic voyage. The Italians, vacillating on the decision of war or peace, refused to allow exports from their economy.

After months of seemingly futile negotiations, a food shipment to Palestine was finally made possible by Josephus Daniels, the Secretary of the Navy. The collier U.S.S. *Vulcan* was due to sail on March 4, 1915 with coal for the warships which were in Mediterranean waters transporting refugees from Turkey. Daniels explained to President Wilson that the Jewish Relief Committee was unable to charter a commercial vessel; but he believed that by reducing the space allotted to coal on the collier he could make room for food. Wilson assented; he was delighted "to find that one of our ships was bound in that direction."

The British, tightening the Syrian blockade, inquired minutely into the details of the proposed method of supervising relief distribution in Palestine and "securing" that it did not indirectly benefit Turkish military or naval forces. To reassure the Allies, Morgenthau promised to have the American consuls in Palestine, in collaboration with local committees, direct distribution and strictly limit the quantity allotted to any one person.

In Constantinople a new obstacle arose: to exempt the food from import duties the Turkish parliament would have to pass a special law, they told Morgenthau, entailing further delay. While this extraordinary legislation was presumably being expedited in the Turkish assembly, the French found cause to reverse their original decision and prohibited passage of a relief ship to any part of the Turkish Empire. Protracted negotiations with the French followed, and they were finally persuaded to make an exception in view of the fact that all plans had already been completed for several hundred tons of provisions to sail on the U.S.S. *Vulcan.*

On March 25th Morgenthau reported that the food ship had been discussed at a meeting of the Turkish Council of Ministers and would be allowed to enter Palestine duty-free on condition that the supply be distributed by appointees of the Jewish community under the supervision of local Turkish municipalities. This was an obvious circumvention of a previous promise that the Turkish Government would in no way interfere with relief administration and that control would be vested in the hands of the American consul. The Turks disingenuously wheedled out of their commitment by maintaining that the municipalities were not a part of the Turkish Government. The import of this new twist did not escape the American Jewish Relief Committee, who feared the customary Turkish abuses and urged that supervision be left to American and Jewish officials as originally agreed. Morgenthau was of a contrary opinion; he allowed the distribution to take place with the participation of the Turkish municipal authorities in order to avoid reopening the whole issue with the ministries in Constantinople.

The *Vulcan* finally passed the blockade safely and unloaded its food cargo; distribution began in the middle of May 1915, about six months after the project was first discussed.

PETROLEUM FOR THE ORANGE GROVES

At the height of the political crisis following on Djemal Pasha's anti-Zionist decrees in 1915, Dr. Ruppin reported to the Provisional Executive Committee for General Zionist Affairs in New York that the orange economy of the colonies was in jeopardy. In March Rabbi Stephen Wise and Brandeis submitted to Robert Lansing a memorandum on the petroleum shortage in the Palestinian orange groves. They requested the Department to use its good offices to obtain permission from the British to allow the Standard Oil Company to transport 20,000 cases of two cans each to Palestine. They explained that there was no petroleum available for the pumps which irrigated the groves; the time element was vital since the groves had to be prepared during the months of April to August.

Simultaneously with a *démarche* to the Allies, the Zionists tried to secure necessary guarantees from the Turks and the Germans that any petroleum shipped would not find its way into their war machine. Though all officials in Turkey admitted that the Jewish orange groves needed petroleum for their irrigation pumps if the trees were not to wither and its importation would help the Turkish economy, the Council of Ministers in Constantinople considered it necessary to meet and discuss arrangements under which petroleum would be allowed to be imported. Their decision was conditional: if it were distributed gratis, the petroleum would be exempt from customs duty; if it were sold, it would have to be in the open market, available to all growers, not exclusively Jews. Though the Minister of Commerce was pleased with the idea of petroleum imports for irrigation, he made the point that the Government did not like to see favors from foreigners intended for any special race. The Turks may not have known how to run a modern economy, but the political implications of every economic act and its effect on public opinion never escaped them.

While the Turks consented to the petroleum imports, with conditions, the French government, which controlled the blockade, refused to sanction the petroleum shipments under any circumstances, regarding pledges of the Ottoman authorities as worthless. The British Jews, on the other hand, thought they were having better luck on the petroleum permits with their government, and they wired the American Zionists, who in turn wrote Lansing, that the British were disposed to consider their request favorably if they could learn the exact nature of the guarantees which the American Government could obtain respecting the petroleum's "freedom from requisition." The American Ambassador in London, however, soon disabused the Zionists of this expectation by reporting that the Foreign Office could not risk any petroleum, of which there was an acute shortage in Turkey, falling into the hands of the military.

Undaunted, Brandeis tried again, and Secretary Bryan asked the British for permission to send small consignments, each succeeding one to be held up until the prior one had been exhausted and the American consuls were satisfied that previous allotments had neither been requisitioned nor tampered with by the Turkish authorities.

The Zionists explored every avenue of approach in their effort to get fuel to the irrigation pumps, and at one point they appeared near achievement of their purpose. Arnold, the American Diplomatic Agent in Cairo, reported that the British authorities in Egypt, after long negotiations, had finally consented to an export of kerosene in lieu of oil, 1000 cans a month. The French still refused to allow any fuels to pass. Once the principle of a shipment was established with at least one of the Allies, the Zionists returned with a plea to raise the allotment, and Bryan requested the British to increase the allowance to 1000 cans a week, with the understanding that any confiscated shipment would immediately put a stop to the operation. By May 28, 1915, the British High Commissioner in Egypt reversed himself and joined the French in categorically refusing any fuel shipment for Syria, since Turkish authorities were seizing all oil and were establishing a submarine base for the Germans. Arnold did, however, wangle permission for a shipment of candles, sulphonated wicks, plaster, and tartaric acid needed for the wine cellars of Rishon le-Tsiyon.

THE TRANSFER OF FUNDS

During the war, international banking transactions became an intricate maze, and World Zionist finances, with deposits in all the major countries of Europe and America, were caught in its complexities. Morgenthau was resourceful and imaginative in proposing new methods for the transfer of funds to Palestine as one avenue after another was shut off.

On April 8, 1915, Morgenthau reported that he had finally succeeded in getting 20,000 pounds transferred to Jerusalem through the Ottoman Bank for the Zionist Jacobus Kann at the Hague where the headquarters of the Jewish National Fund were established. Throughout his mission Morgenthau regularly transmitted to Brandeis the money requests of Ruppin and Lichtheim and Jacobson, the official World Zionist representatives in Turkey, and on occasion he advanced sums of money of his own to the Zionists on condition that the American Zionists refund it through the Department at Washington. Later, at the Paris Peace Conference, Morgenthau was a shrewd antagonist of the political Zionists, but during the long pull of the economic blockade of Syria and Palestine, he helped them diligently.

The British were understandably apprehensive lest the funds which they at first allowed to be transferred through Egypt for indigent Jews in Palestine fall into Turkish hands, and Morgenthau had to send them repeated assurances. In June 1915, it was the Turkish authorities who, in a sudden move, forbade the transfer of all funds from Egypt to Palestine, and another Zionist relief route was cut. It had dawned on some Turkish officials that substantial sums of money transferred from enemy territory to subject minorities in Turkey might be used for purposes other than relief. But influence was brought to bear on the Ministers in Constantinople by Dr. Ruppin, and the Turks changed their minds again. When Dr. Ruppin came to Constantinople payments could be made directly to him for expenditures in Palestine. But civilians, even nationals of friendly powers, were not allowed to move freely from one Turkish province to another with thousands of dollars in specie. In November 1915 Morgenthau renewed his efforts to get relief money in gold shipped directly from Alexandria to the Jerusalem consul in an American cruiser, since it was impossible for him to transfer bullion regularly from Constantinople by the overland route. By the end of 1915 the British began to enforce strict rules against any remittances from Egypt to Syria or other parts of the Ottoman Empire, and this definitively cut that line, leaving open only the approach through Constantinople.

On January 1, 1916 Morgenthau was finally reduced to sending money to Jerusalem by mail, and this became the set method for the despatch of moneys to Palestine during the next eighteen months. From then on there were regular orders to Morgenthau from the United States to make remittances to Glazebrook for the Zionists and for general relief. There was of course a distinct disadvantage to the Constantinople-Jerusalem mail route for the transmission of allotments. In sending the money from Constantinople by mail, Morgenthau risked subjecting the funds to the depreciation of the Turkish pound, because the Embassy could ship only paper money. This led to an ill-conceived complaint from some Jews that they were not receiving the full amount of the allotment.

By March 1916 the Jewish organizations in the United States had put the relief remittances on a definite monthly basis. Morgenthau forwarded Glazebrook's estimate of need, which covered virtually the whole of the Jewish population remaining in Palestine: for 35,000 adult poor, a monthly allotment of three francs each; for 15,000 adults who were ordinarily independent but because of interrupted communications were in actual need, monthly loans of six francs each; food and clothing for 15,000 school children and five francs monthly for each.

When Hoffman Philip, American *chargé* in Constantinople, had an interview with the Turkish Minister of Foreign Affairs on the problem of relief in Syria and Palestine, he was told that Djemal Pasha considered the outcries of the minorities in Syria inspired by the Allies and that the Turks could not therefore encourage this propaganda through any neutral relief distribution. The Turks were keenly aware of the political factors involved in relief for Syria and Lebanon. Even if it were distributed by the neutrals, the minorities would believe that the relief derived from the Allies. The Foreign Minister also commented on the intercepted letters from Palestinian Jews who, he said, were spreading alarmist reports in order to get more relief supplies. While the Syrians and Lebanese were denied relief, the American Consul's work in Jerusalem and the regular monthly remittances to the Jews of Palestine were somehow allowed to continue.

DISEASE AND FAMINE

In the summer of 1916 Palestine was ravaged by disease and Zionist emphasis turned from food supplies to doctors and medicine.

The American Embassy at Berne reported a typhoid fever epidemic in Palestine and the urgent need for medicines. The Zionists tried to get medical supplies shipped to Jaffa from Alexandria. On July 29, 1916, the third assistant secretary, William Phillips, explained to Jacob de Haas that the Department had for months been endeavoring to secure an agreement among the belligerents under which medical supplies could be shipped to Palestine, but the French and English Governments had refused to allow any ship to pass the blockade of the Syrian ports, even for the purpose of transporting medicine.

A few weeks later de Haas was informed by Assistant Secretary Adee that the French had softened and were now willing to permit a shipment to Syria and Palestine "under certain unspecified conditions."

After reports of a cholera outbreak in Palestine were confirmed, repeated communications from de Haas led to constant pressure by American envoys in London, Paris, and Cairo on the Allied governments to allow medicines through the blockade. In September 1916 the cholera and typhus epidemics were followed by acute dysentery; and there was no quinine for the endemic malaria. The Zionist representatives in Constantinople begged for doctors and medicines from the United States. Consul Garrels at Alexandria on September 7, 1916 was able to report that he had finally arranged for the passage of a cargo of medical supplies for Palestine. In six days Josephus Daniels, Secretary of the Navy, informed the State Department that the U.S.S. *Des Moines* was en route to its mission: to carry medical supplies from Alexandria to Jaffa and to transport back such American citizens and other passengers as might be requested by authorized representatives of the State Department. Suddenly a rumor reached the French that the *Des Moines* proposed to land gold at Jaffa in addition to doctors and medical supplies, and they promptly informed the Department that no such shipment could be authorized since it was on the contraband list. Consul Garrels vehemently denied that there was any such intention, and the ship was allowed to proceed to Alexandria.

The French attitude towards the relief of Syria and Palestine became remarkably solicitous towards the end of 1916, especially when Syrian shipments were being prepared, since this was the sphere allotted to them in the secret Sykes-Picot agreement.

Having obtained the right to send the medical supplies on the *Des Moines,* the Zionists proceeded with the next step and initiated a campaign—with the aid of congressional letters to the State Department—to have the American relief ship transfer Palestinian wines and fruit from Jaffa to a port in the Levant for trans-shipment to the United States, thus preserving the economy of the agricultural colonies through the sale of their own products. The French, pliable at this period, agreed to allow wines and brandy to pass back through the blockade on the return trip of the *Des Moines* and the Navy was instructed to transport the goods.

By the fall of 1916 the Provisional Committee of the Zionists in New York was the chief support of the Zionist institutions in Palestine. Transfer of funds from either of the belligerent groups had become almost impossible. Relatively minor details of expenditure in Palestine were controlled in the United States. The Zionist representatives in Turkey sent to Washington their regular pleas and budget estimates, and they usually got at least a portion of what they requested. But despite the transmission of what were then considered large sums, by the fall of 1916 not enough supplies or funds had passed through the blockade to keep Palestine from slow starvation.

In October 1916 Dr. Ruppin was ordered out of Palestine by Djemal Pasha even though he was an Austrian subject. No specific charges were levelled against him, and he was allowed to proceed to Constantinople. There he consulted with Ambassador Abram Elkus, Morgenthau's successor, and dictated for him a detailed report on the general condition of the population in Syria and Palestine. Ruppin described the anomaly of many war-ravaged economies: relative plenty in the agricultural areas and starvation in the towns. Cities which before the war had drawn their grain from the Hauran region, the country east of the Jordan, and the Homs-Hama area, were unable to get supplies because of the dearth of animal transport, the military requisitions, the breakdown of the railway system, and the debasement of the currency. When the Turkish government, in a feeble effort to alleviate distress, took over the supply system it accomplished no more than the private merchants because it had to face the same disruption of communications. In Jerusalem there was a daily ration of about 150 to 200 grams of bread, but even that was irregular. The mortality rate had risen frightfully, Ruppin wrote. "In one Jewish congregation numbering about 5,500 souls, five times as many have died this year as in the year immediately preceding the war. . . . The old people as well as the children suffer terribly."

Ambassador Elkus communicated Ruppin's *Report on Conditions in Palestine and Syria* to the State Department, but he added a confidential note to the effect that "conditions are somewhat overstated, although they are bad enough and getting worse." Like Morgenthau, Elkus too seemed chary of exaggerating reports of the misery of the Jews, lest he appear to be overzealous about his co-religionists.

Two months later, in December 1916, during a dinner conversation with Djemal Pasha in Constantinople, Elkus heard Ruppin's famine reports confirmed by the absolute ruler of Syria himself. Repercussions of the widespread starvation had begun to affect the military position of the Fourth Army Corps. Djemal Pasha promised, on his word of honor, that if supplies arrived from America "not one grain would go to the army or anyone connected with it." He even magnanimously announced that grain imported through American charity would pass duty-free.

That Ruppin had hardly exaggerated in reporting the sufferings of the Jews is borne out by the testimony of a witness less involved in the life of the settlement. William Yale, the Standard Oil representative, later reported to the Department that during the winter months of 1916–1917 the population of Jerusalem "faced starvation from day to day, the daily supply of bread never being sufficient for the daily needs of the population resulting in an increased death rate from starvation and exhaustion." Turkish paper money in Mesopotamia, Syria, and Palestine had fallen to one fourth of its face value and could not be used to purchase food supplies. Of Palestine, Yale wrote that the villages had been tragically depleted by military drafts, famine, and disease; that the great olive orchards had been drawn upon to supply fuel for railroad transportation, and the orange groves had suffered from a locust plague and from a lack of fuel to run the irrigation pumps; that the presence of large bodies of troops involved heavy requisitions of foodstuffs and cattle, placing the civilian population, especially of Jaffa and Jerusalem, in a desperate position.

Dr. Ruppin's grim description of disease-ridden Palestine led the American Zionists to their next project, the despatch of a medical unit to the Jews of Palestine. Since few native-born American doctors available for the mission spoke Yiddish or Hebrew, they had to resort to former residents of Russia or Palestine in recruiting the unit. This would have led to renewed disputes about citizenship with the Turks, who still did not recognize naturalization, and the State Department was anxious to avoid reopening that thorny subject in the midst of a war. If a Palestinian-born Jew on the mission were drafted into the Turkish army against his will, a diplomatic incident would have broken out. When the Department wrote to the Zionists rejecting the new project the citizenship problem was referred to only in passing; the shipment of a medical unit was declared unnecessary because Djemal Pasha had said that the epidemics had subsided, and he had been supported by Dr. Ruppin. De Haas, arguing on the fact, replied curtly, "We are in a position to know that Dr. Ruppin does not corroborate Djemal Pasha's answer."

In November 1916, Jacobus Kann, head of the Jewish National Fund at the Hague, wired the American Zionists through the Minister in Holland, suggesting that they ship gold on an American vessel to Jaffa. Rapid depreciation of the Turkish paper money which the Zionists had to use for transfer from Constantinople to Jerusalem was wrecking their budgetary estimates. In the face of the Allied blockade this notion was as chimerical as Dr. Ruppin's suggestion to Ambassador Elkus that he arrange for regular monthly food relief ships to Palestine, but in the end it was just such effrontery or defiance of simple realities that got the Zionists whatever concessions they did win.

THE U.S.S. CAESAR AND THE U.S.S. DES MOINES

The U.S.S. *Caesar*, with a cargo assembled by the Red Cross and American Missionary Boards for the relief of the Syrians, was running into all the obstacles the ingenious Turks could devise when they wanted to stalemate relief shipments. Jewish relief had also been allotted some space on the same collier, but the U.S.S. *Caesar* was primarily intended for the Beirut area.

In January, 1917, while both the *Des Moines* and the *Caesar* were waiting at Alexandria for final instructions to pass the blockade and proceed to ports in Syria and Palestine, a further hitch developed. On the latest advices from his government the French Admiral of the Blockade refused passage for the *Caesar*. The State Department, in order to get the ships through, held out as further inducement to the Allies the landing of food at Mersina for British prisoners of war. Simultaneously the Turks began to tighten up on the various Zionist activities in Palestine, which went beyond direct food relief and involved the support of educational, health, and economic institutions (probably including land purchases). The Turkish officials in Jerusalem became pressing in their demands for the control of all Zionist moneys. Upon the severing of diplomatic relations between the United States and Germany, the *Des Moines* and the *Caesar* were ordered to remain in Alexandria indefinitely. The protracted international negotiations over the relief of Syria and Palestine seemed to be petering out when a telegram from Elkus showed that the Central Powers had suddenly become extraordinarily conciliatory and helpful. Elkus had received a message from Djemal Pasha himself, stating that all of the *Caesar's* cargo could be unloaded at Beirut, and that the ship would be allowed to take return passengers for Europe. Djemal, who had once been hostile to any relief shipments, requested that a second shipload be sent to Jaffa as the population of Palestine was in great distress. Djemal agreed that the *Des Moines* could go to Jaffa with its medical supplies and return with wine and books. This reversal meant either that the Turks were trying last minute blandishments on the United States or that they wanted food ships to lay their hands on in the event of war.

The Turkish War Office verbally informed Elkus that the Germans and Austrians would allow the *Des Moines* and the *Caesar* to pass without submarine interference. Elkus was cautious, and requested that the commitment be put in writing.

On the eve of war, persistent de Haas was back again on his medical unit proposal. "If Djemal Pasha is in a favorable mood, this concession ought to be obtained from him now," he advised the Department. There was a conscious policy of *carpe diem* to these Zionist tactics, and the Department actually tried to get the unit through.

Elkus's despatch of February 23rd again left in doubt the sailing of the relief ships. The German admiralty had instructed its submarines to allow the *Caesar* and the *Des Moines* to pass "but seeing that errors in the blockaded zone are not impossible their safety could not be guaranteed," nor could they guarantee against the danger from floating mines.

By the middle of March the Germans were no longer in a hurry to grant the necessary written guarantees for the *Des Moines* and the

Caesar. Elkus learned from unofficial sources that the Germans wanted the American Government to require identical assurances from the British and French Governments. The German Admiralty made its agreement contingent upon the continued existence of a state of peace between the United States and Germany, upon the ships' following specified channels both coming and going, their exact route to be communicated four weeks in advance so that all submarines should have ample warning.

The United States Government was not inclined to accept these conditions, and the Declaration of War on Germany rendered them meaningless in any event.

On April 4th, 1917, Jacob de Haas, still trying to persuade the United States Government to get a medical unit into Palestine, initiated a proposal that, under the changed conditions of the British invasion of Palestine, the doctors might go to Alexandria and then along British lines of communication as far as Gaza, their furthest point of advance in the Palestine campaign. With a simplicity which might well have made military men bristle, he added: "Whether there it would be permitted to cross the military lines into Palestine, or whether it would have to withhold itself until the military issue has been settled—these of course are matters which we must leave to the discretion of the Department."

When the new political crisis of March–April 1917 in Palestine finally broke into the open, the American Zionists tried to send emergency funds through neutrals, while the Department debated the new policy problems created by the war. At first there was a tendency to adopt the position that a transfer of funds into Turkish territory would not be countenanced. Urgent appeals for relief came via American Ambassador Morris in Stockholm and the Swedish Foreign Office, and in the end they prevailed.

The final policy decision was favorable to the Jewish settlement, and even after the break in diplomatic relations with Turkey, the United States Government continued to allow the transfer of funds to the subject races of the Empire—Syrians, Armenians, Jews, as distinguished from the Turks. In order to maintain a measure of control over the funds, the Department, after discreet inquiry in Holland through the Minister, approved of Hoofien of the Anglo-Palestine Bank who was a Dutch subject as the sole distributing agent in Palestine, and he acted for both the Zionists and the Joint Distribution Committee until the arrival of the British.

Thus the relief line to Palestine was actually never severed during the war, though after the break in United States-Turkish relations and the departure of American officials, members of local Jewish committees had to be far more secretive about their activities.

THE CRISIS OF 1917

On April 20, 1917 the Turkish Foreign Office advised Ambassador Elkus that relations between the United States and Turkey were broken. American interests were confided to the Swedish Minister, but a state of war never was declared. With the disappearance of the last great neutral from Constantinople, the Jews of Turkey and other subject minorities lost their most powerful protector. The war entered its critical stage, the Egyptian front became active again, and the Turkish attitude towards the Jews went through another somersault.

On May 4th Jacob de Haas, Secretary of the American Zionists, sent a direct query to the Near Eastern Division in the State Department. "Is Department in position to confirm or deny report Djemal Pasha threatens massacre?" The Department knew nothing; moreover it had to be cautious of the agitation invariably aroused by the mere use of the word "massacre" in any communication, as one official noted in a memorandum, hence its reply was laconic: "Department has no information on subject."

Ambassador Page in London, who was instructed to check on the threatened "massacre," traced the story to the *Jewish Chronicle* of London, whose despatches were confirmed by the British Foreign Office. The only actual development which Page could report was that an evacuation of the civilian population of Jaffa had occurred early in April, ostensibly for reasons of military security; there was no information on the number of Jews affected.

Similar inquiries to Cairo and Stockholm confirmed Page's general account. The Department was interested in learning the actual source of the information, but the Ambassador was unable to persuade the editor of the *Jewish Chronicle* to name his informants, though he guessed that they were secret agents in Palestine the revelation of whose identity would be dangerous. By May 14, the Department was convinced of the "deportation and threatened massacre of Jews" and requested the Swedish Government to protest earnestly against the atrocities on behalf of humanity. The American *chargé* at Cairo, repeating the British story, added: "In discussing with the military authorities probable cause and significance of the Turkish treatment of the Jews in Palestine I was informed that the Turks, apprehensive of a British advance at Gaza, seem to have followed their old and customary policy when similarly pressed, of ordering massacres. It is believed that position of the Jews in Palestine continues to be extremely critical and that they will be subjected to cruel treatment probably resulting in innumerable deaths." Garrels, as confirmation, sent in the full text of a Reuters despatch of May 8th: "The order to evacuate Jaffa covered all Jews, even subjects of the Central Powers. On April 1 they were given 48 hours; a week earlier 300 had been deported from Jerusalem. Djemal Pasha openly declared that the joy of the Jews on the approach of the British would be short-lived as he would make them share the fate of the Armenians. . . ." The number of evacuees was fixed at 8000. The Jews were not allowed to take along any provisions, and as they left a swarm of pillaging Bedouin women and Arabs with donkeys and camels swooped down upon their houses like birds of prey. Two Yemenite Jews who tried to resist the looters were hanged at the Jaffa gate as an example. Wealthy Jews were found dead on the sandhills around Tel Aviv. When young men of the Jewish villages organized a road guard for the refugees from Jaffa they were dispersed by the Turkish authorities. The Reuters despatch indicated that there was some truth to the pretext that this was a military measure because it was later extended to the Moslems, but they, unlike the Jews, had been allowed to remain in the orchard areas around the city and to return to their properties from time to time. The British saw cunning in Djemal Pasha's Jewish policy. He did not order coldblooded massacres after the manner of the Armenian atrocities, but drove the evacuated Jews to their death through disease and starvation. The Reuters correspondent suggested that Djemal Pasha might turn next on the Arab pillagers, all a part of his chauvinist plan to exterminate peoples who were not Turanian.

In the face of the "threatened massacre" the Jews in the American community laid aside their party squabbles and made urgent appeals to the State Department for American intervention; Straus, Morgenthau, Louis Marshall, the orthodox Rabbis, and the Zionists were united in this action.

When the Department became fully convinced of the truth of the report that some large-scale expulsion was in progress, it began to devise methods to prevent further atrocities and to use the outrages against the Jews in a psychological warfare offensive. At first they had a limited objective, concentrating on the morale of the Jews in Austria and Germany. With this aim in mind they discreetly suggested to Brandeis that the facts about the Palestine atrocities might be communicated to the Jews of the Central Powers through the Jews in neutral countries like Switzerland and Holland. Four days later the scope of the offensive was broadened into a full-scale diplomatic action.

At this period in the war the Allies were acutely conscious of the moral advantage which they had gained from the German invasion of Belgium and the Armenian atrocities. Highlighting a massacre of Jews in Palestine throughout the world was part of the same pattern. Psychological warfare was practiced in World War I with considerable imagination before special departments were created under the rubric. A conscious exploitation of the incident does not exclude the fact that the humanitarian principles of Wilson were here finding concrete expression in the protection of a persecuted people.

On May 22, 1917 Lansing addressed a formal diplomatic communication to the major neutral envoys in Washington, summoning them to join in protest to the Turks: "During the past few days the attention of the Department has been repeatedly called to reports which have reached this country from Europe and from Alexandria that the deportation of the Jews in Palestine has been begun under the direction of the Turkish officials. The Department believes the reports received to be substantially true, that very great suffering already has resulted therefrom, and that there is danger that these deportations may continue and increase. It has been suggested that the danger might perhaps be averted if a number of the neutral countries would protest in the name of humanity to the Turkish Government against the deportation of the Jews from Palestine, accompanied as such deportations would necessarily be by the suffering and death of countless innocent people, including women and children. . . ."

The United States, not officially at war with Turkey, preserved a measure of temperateness in its formulations. Great Britain, in the midst of a campaign in Palestine, had only advantage to gain from dramatizing the events. On the same day that Lansing addressed the neutrals, Cecil Spring-Rice of the British Embassy sent Jacob H. Schiff a harrowing description of the evacuation: "Jews resisting pillaging hanged. Thousands wandering helplessly on roads starving."

The German Government was sensitive enough to the implications of this diplomatic attack to issue a formal note denying the veracity of the Havas and Reuters reports. According to the German story the evacuation of Gaza was a measure of military necessity, as proved by the subsequent engagements in the area; Jaffa was evacuated because of fear of naval bombardment. "Reports referring to massacres, incendiarism, pillage and rape are entirely disproved. Nothing of the kind has happened either in Jaffa or in Jerusalem, Nazareth and Capernaum, cities mentioned in Havas reports, or in Jewish colonies in Galilee. . . ."

The British and the French had issued lurid versions of the events; the Germans made the evacuation appear neat and orderly; the American note had been cautious, its framers mindful of the fact that the United States was not at war with Turkey and aware of the extraordinary secret diplomatic manoeuvre which was being planned during those very days—the Morgenthau Peace Mission.

THE MORGENTHAU PEACE MISSION

On May 17th Secretary Lansing wrote to Wilson telling of conversations he had had with Alsberg, Elkus's private secretary, who had left Constantinople early in April, and with Morgenthau. Both men were agreed that Turkey might be persuaded to negotiate a separate peace if she could be relieved in some way of the fear of Germany, especially the dread of the two German warships anchored before Constantinople, with their guns trained on the city. Morgenthau thought that by contacting members of the former Turkish cabinet with whom he could talk freely, arrangements might be made to allow submarines to enter the Dardanelles and destroy the German vessels.

Once decided upon, the mission had to have a public cover, and for this purpose the Jewish problem in Palestine was ideal because Morgenthau was a prominent Jew and a former ambassador to Turkey. The mission in reality did not exclude a study of the condition of the Jews in Palestine, but this was a subsidiary part of the plan. Morgenthau knew, however, that in view of his ambiguous attitude towards Zionism, he would stir up a rumpus if he alone went as the representative of the Jews, since, as he wrote sarcastically to Lansing, "the Zionists under the leadership of Brandeis, Dr. Wise and others think that the future of Palestine is primarily their concern." To satisfy the Zionists and to follow up on the Jewish aspect of his mission, he suggested to Lansing that Felix Frankfurter, then attached to Secretary Baker's office in the War Department, and a member of the advisory board of the Provisional Zionist Committee, go along with him as his assistant.

The use of Morgenthau on a mission involving Turkey is peculiar in the light of the fantastic episode which followed his departure from Constantinople in 1916. In a speech before the New York Chamber of Commerce, he was supposed to have made some tactless statements about the Porte which the Turks picked up and which caused their embassies throughout the world to issue formal statements. They denied: (1) that Morgenthau had ever discussed the sale of Palestine to the Zionists with the Porte; (2) that the Chacham-Bashi of Constantinople was to be appointed Minister to Washington to negotiate the details of the sale; (3) that Morgenthau conducted his business with the Sultan over the telephone; (4) that Morgenthau was to be made Turkish Minister of Agriculture while still keeping his post as United States envoy.

Elkus in letters to Brandeis and Tumulty, the President's Secretary, made harsh remarks about the impression which Morgenthau had left at the Porte and the difficulties he had straightening matters out. As for the discussion of the "sale of Palestine," according to Elkus's information there actually was some sort of talk with Talaat, the Prime Minister, around the subject, but it was strictly confidential; hence the resentment of the Turks about the story, since any minister who even alluded to the possibility of alienating Turkish territory would be considered a traitor. The Porte was truly Wonderland, as Herzl said; but so was Washington, to send Morgenthau on another mission to the Turks.

On June 1, 1917, when Morgenthau read in the papers that Arshag Schmavonian, the Legal Adviser of the Embassy in Constantinople, was actually in Berne with Ambassador Elkus he excitedly wrote to Lansing that it was providential and he asked that this ideal "intermediary" with the Turks be allowed to accompany him to the secret Gibraltar conference which was planned with representatives of the Allies. But the Zionists, who were not a party to all aspects of the mission, were patently quite unhappy about the plan. Brandeis was leery of placing Frankfurter's talents at the disposal of Morgenthau to serve his dubious purposes, but was finally reconciled.

On June 14, a "Private and Secret Communication" from the Foreign Office to the British Ambassador was on Lansing's desk: "Armenians and Zionist Jews have called at the Foreign Office to protest against the proposed Mission. From what they said, they seem to have full information as to the scope and objects of the Mission. The London *Times,* and probably other papers, seem also to have information. It is unfortunate that secrecy, on which success depended, and to which was attached so much importance, is no longer possible. Under these circumstances, it appears to be wise to postpone the Mission." But Wilson was not convinced.

Before he departed, Morgenthau advised Lansing that he suggest to Brandeis an abandonment of the proposed American Jewish Congress scheduled for September. Morgenthau feared that such a Congress would pass resolutions denouncing the Turks for atrocities and thus jeopardize his efforts to negotiate a separate peace. Aware of the suspicion with which Zionists regarded him he forewarned Lansing, "But kindly do not mention to him that you are doing this at my instigation." Wilson seconded Morgenthau's efforts. Following an interview with the President, Rabbi Wise was authorized to issue a statement that a temporary postponement of the American Jewish Congress might be necessary "because of the urgency at this time of the public business." The phrase covered Wilson's opposition to the Congress which could not be made more explicit without publicizing the details of the Morgenthau plan.

Upon the departure of the mission it was announced in the *New York Times* that Morgenthau and Frankfurter were going to the Near East on an important mission "having for its main objects collecting information to be used as a basis for a movement to prevent massacres of Hebrews."

The extent to which the plan was compromised is evident from a letter of June 29, 1917 addressed by the Armenian National Delegation in Great Britain to Ambassador Page expressing profound misgivings about any separate peace with Turkey. "Is then the Young Turk clique to be trusted again in the matters of the Armenians, Arabs and Zionist Jews?" Considering the number of deeply hostile forces, it is hardly to be wondered at that the project died aborning.

The end of the Peace Mission did not warrant the air of mystery with which Morgenthau sought to surround it in later years. The United States delegates landed at Cadiz and then proceeded to Gibraltar; there they were met by Dr. Chaim Weizmann, the British representative, who for months had been negotiating with the British Foreign Office about a Declaration on Palestine, and by a Monsieur Weyl who had directed French tobacco interests in Turkey. For long hours they debated the Morgenthau plan in an atmosphere of great secrecy, and in the end they arrived at the conclusion that the time was not opportune for the manoeuvre. Weizmann was clearly not enthusiastic about a separate peace with Turkey at a time when his whole life's work was hanging on a British award of Palestine to the Jews. In reality, the British were only humoring Wilson. The very act of sending Weizmann to the conference as the British representative indicated that they were quite cold to the adventure, and were committed to a far different course in the Near East. Weizmann fulfilled his duty as Balfour had instructed him. "I was to talk to Mr. Morgenthau, and keep on talking till I had talked him out of this mission," he wrote in his autobiography.

A DIPLOMATIC FIASCO

While the Morgenthau peace proposal was still brewing, the Department received reports on the effectiveness of its propaganda offensive among the neutrals. It was Elkus in Berne who first minimized the Palestine atrocity stories. Through the Department he communicated a message from Ruppin to the Provisional Zionist Committee in New York, denying massacres or cruelties, though confirming the evacuation of Jaffa. On June 5th Ambassador Morris in Sweden sent in a report from George Talbot Odell of the *New York Evening Mail*, contradicting massacre rumors. Odell's correspondent in Berlin had interviewed a member of the Turkish General Staff, just returned from Palestine, and had learned that Djemal Pasha was inviting the Spanish, Austrian, and German consuls to visit any place in the land, and that Foreign Minister Zimmerman had obtained permission for three German Zionists to make a tour of inspection.

The neutrals had their own sources of information on Palestine, and the diplomatic offensive turned into something of a fizzle. The Chief Rabbi of Palestine in a message to the Chief Rabbi of Stockholm had contradicted the persecution rumors and therefore the Norwegian government had decided not to interfere. The Danish Minister followed suit, and the Swedish Legation at Constantinople deflated the reports still further. The Swedes reported to Ambassador Morris that according to their information from Constantinople the Turkish Government had forbidden the expulsion of the Jews from Jerusalem, though nobody would vouch for Djemal Pasha's obeying the order. By July 7 the Swedes were flatly labelling as untrue the rumors about massacres and persecutions. Whereas the other neutrals had contented themselves with factual remarks about the state of affairs, the Spanish Ambassador proudly took the opportunity to arrogate to his Government all credit for the subsiding of the crisis. "As a result of the representations made by the Spanish Government to the Sublime Porte, the Turkish Government has ordered the Military Authorities to permit the return to their homes of the Jews who had been expelled from Syria and Palestine."

When the Turks got around to issuing a communiqué in July, it followed the general lines of the earlier German note. In addition it included a detailed account of the facilities which were extended to the evacuees. It was November before the Department got a really authentic account, an official Swedish version of what had occurred in Palestine, and by that time the Allies and the Turks were locked in a new diplomatic struggle over the Balfour Declaration. According to the Swedish story all of the Jewish population of Jaffa had in fact been obliged to leave. Subjects of Turkish allies were allowed to go to Jerusalem, but the bulk of the population had to make the trek to the agricultural colonies in the Tiberias area. There was much hardship but no systematic ill-treatment. No general evacuation from Jerusalem had occurred, though a number of Zionist leaders had been exiled.

According to Arthur Ruppin's authoritative estimate after Allenby's victory, the total number of Jews in Palestine during the war had dropped to 65,000—a sharp reduction in a small community. Other figures run as low as 50,000. But the Jewish settlement had survived, and in large measure through the diplomatic intervention of the United States.

Chapter V

WILSON'S STATE DEPARTMENT AND THE BALFOUR DECLARATION

BRITISH PROMISES

During the years 1916 and 1917 members of the British War Cabinet represented by their director for Near Eastern Affairs, Sir Mark Sykes, and English Zionists grouped around Dr. Chaim Weizmann, an émigré from Russia then lecturer in chemistry at the University of Manchester, conducted intermittent negotiations over the issuance of a declaration in favor of the establishment of a homeland for Jews in Palestine. For the most part these discussions were subsequent to the Sykes-Picot Agreement of May 1916 in which France and Britain had plotted out spheres of influence in the Near East and decided upon the internationalization of Palestine. The talks also post-dated the correspondence exchanged between Sir Henry McMahon and the Sharif of Mecca about the creation of an Arab Kingdom and the loose understandings between St. John Philby, acting for the British Government in India, and Ibn Saud, the Wahabi ruler of the Nejd and the mortal enemy of the Sharif Houssein.

The extent to which the commitments of various British agents overlapped one another making a crazy-quilt of imperial promises is by this time a commonplace. A voluminous partisan literature has grown up around these secret understandings. The original actors in the desert drama have testified as to their intentions at the time the documents were drawn, and scholars in the service of their respective governments have written glosses and interpretations on every particle of evidence. The texts are patently at odds, though not sufficiently to phase the great conciliators of the British Foreign Office with a mission to prove that the word of His Majesty's Government is never broken, especially if tendered to aborigines and nomads. This much may be said for British policy: the men who intrigued in the Near East during the war did not always treat with the Arabs on the basis of hard and fast instructions drafted in Downing Street, Cairo, or

Bombay. Coordination among the agents, many of whom were enthusiasts who had a tendency to fly off on their own with pledges to chosen favorites was, to say the least, inadequate. And ministers with ultimate responsibility may not have borne closely in mind the details of negotiations in a secondary theatre of war. Such is the testimony of Ronald Storrs, Oriental Secretary of the Residency in Cairo:

"Much play has been made by Arab and other critics with ambiguities, mutually incompatible undertakings, and 'betrayals'; without entire justification but not without cause. . . . Until Mark Sykes appeared in Cairo in 1916 we had but the slightest and vaguest information about the Sykes-Picot negotiations for the tripartite division of non-Turkish Turkey . . . and there was far too little realization of Indian operations in Iraq and of Indian encouragement of Ibn Saud. So far as we were concerned it seemed to be nobody's business to harmonize the various views and policies of the Foreign Office, the India Office, the Admiralty, the War Office, the Government of India and the Residency in Egypt."

Whatever worth the apology may have, the discussions with Hussein and Ibn Saud, conducted in that strange manner which the British orientalists had devised for the meeting of the two civilizations, usually left on the Arab chieftains a very different impression from the literal meaning of the English emissaries' words. The Arab chieftains were not the austere men of honor glorified in the romantic tradition which Lawrence fabricated. The British bargained their gold for Arab blood and the accounts could not always be balanced. British agents were not eager to clarify ambiguities. At times there was downright deception—on all sides. During the revolt in the desert, the Arabs of the Hedjaz had tentacles out to their Turkish oppressors which would have sold the British short; and the British also extended peace-feelers to the Turks. As Lawrence wrote in one of his later letters to an American special agent he had known in the Near East, ". . . all is fair in love, war, and alliances." Nevertheless, the character of the Balfour Declaration to the Jews is distinguished from the ceremonial parleys with Arab chieftains in at least one respect: it was the subject of months of discussions in London in which all members of the War Cabinet participated.

The day of reckoning came after the war when those to whom the British had lightly made promises—Arabs, Jews, and Frenchmen—tried to set forth to their own peoples the nature of these understandings. The Arabs and the Jews were in the early stages of a nationalist renascence and their leaders resorted to the facile hyperbole characteristic of such movements. They had to speak with Messianic absolutism to win and hold their adherents; they could not make pronouncements in terms of dependent clauses and contingent promises. Thus the contradictions inherent in the British pledges were sharpened.

ZIONIST OPINION IN THE UNITED STATES

Throughout the early years of the war American Jews remained divided into two primary groupings. The Zionists, under Brandeis, propagandized for the convocation of a great democratic congress representative of all parties and factions in order to imbue the Jews of the United States with an awareness of their historic responsibility for the fate of Jews throughout the world and to assume leadership in securing the Palestine homeland. The American Jewish Committee, a group of wealthy Jewish notables under the direction of Louis Marshall, preferred to use their influence behind the scenes on behalf of the suffering Jews in the war zones, without participating in Jewish mass organizations and without submitting to the rough and tumble of Jewish politics. The notables feared that they would be outvoted during the forensics of a Jewish congress and would thus lose their prestige in the Jewish communities. In general the American Jewish Committee shied away from the Jewish nationalism implicit in the Zionist movement. For two years of the war the Jewish press of the United States was alive with the polemic between the partisans of the congress idea and their opponents.

Dr. Victor Jacobson, the official representative of the World Zionist Organization in Constantinople—motivated by a different set of considerations from the notables—was equally unenthusiastic about the holding of a congress of American Jews at which demands would be served on Turkey for rights of free Jewish immigration and political autonomy for Jews in Palestine. He doubted the wisdom of the emotion-laden public addresses which would be delivered and he frankly feared the reaction which the resolutions of the congress might have on the precarious political existence of the colonies in Palestine. The congress plan prevailed, however, at a meeting of the World Zionist Executive at the Hague in March 1916 and the proposal of the American Zionists to seek firm commitments from Turkey received formal sanction. Subsequently, protracted discussions were initiated between the Zionists and the American Jewish Committee about the mechanics of the assembly; but by time a tentative agreement was reached on the allotment of delegates, the United States had entered the war. It was then that upon direct White House intervention, motivated by the strange Morgenthau peace mission of June 1917, postponement was deemed advisable until after the cessation of hostilities.

Under the aegis of Brandeis and with the help of Dr. Shmarya Levin, a great popular orator with especial appeal to Yiddish-speaking audiences, who had been deputed by the World Zionist Executive to stimulate the rather moribund American movement, the Zionist Federation enrolled several hundred thousand members during the war years. The misfortunes of the Jews in eastern Europe caught on the war front between Russia and the Central Powers lent weight to the Zionist argument that the Jews needed some area of the world which they could call their own. Since the majority of American Jews were only a few years removed from the eastern European settlements they felt keenly the sufferings of their relatives whom they had left behind in the Russian pale; to a far greater number of American Jews than ever before, Zionism seemed to offer an ultimate salvation for the persecuted Jews of eastern Europe. In this period the movement was nevertheless essentially the ideological expression of the middle strata of the three and a half million Jews in the United States. With comparatively few exceptions both Jewish capitalists and the Jewish working classes under socialist influence remained either hostile or indifferent.

Outside of the Jewish communities there was a measure of sympathy for Zionism. Ex-President Taft, in a Washington speech before the National Geographic Society, said that a definitive solution of the Jewish problem should form part of the agenda of the Peace Conference; in May 1916 the Reverend William Blackstone revived his memorial of 1891 and persuaded the Presbyterian General Assembly to adopt a resolution in favor of a Jewish homeland in Palestine; under Samuel Gompers the American Federation of Labor approved of the idea which thereafter became a standby resolution of its annual conventions. Insofar as American public opinion turned an ear to Zionist doctrine it was not unfavorable. It seemed to be a reasonable solution to the pathetic "Jewish problem" at no cost to the United States—a desideratum of foreign policy for the man in the street.

BRANDEIS AND THE FRAMING OF THE DECLARATION

During the war American Zionist leaders grouped around Brandeis were kept informed of the progress of the London talks between Zionists and the British War Cabinet. They accepted Weizmann's *de facto* leadership in the negotiations, even though he had no official status on the Executive of the World Zionist Organization. Prior to April 1917 this American support bestowed upon Weizmann great worth in the eyes of the British hoping for participation of the United States in the war; even after American entry the development of enthusiasm in the United States for the European war was still a major concern of British leaders. The British valued and perhaps exaggerated the influence of American Jews in the formation of American public opinion. Lloyd George, who was Prime Minister at the time, testified before the Royal Commission in 1937, that stimulating the war effort of American Jews was one of the major motives which, during a harrowing period in the European war, actuated members of the cabinet in finally casting their votes for the Declaration. The British were of course even more attracted by the notion that the grant of a Jewish homeland in Palestine would be effective in quieting defeatist propaganda against the war which was sweeping through Russia. The overthrow of the Czar had diluted the bitterness of the Jews against Russia; there were simplists in the British Foreign Office who believed that the issuance of the Balfour Declaration would swerve the Russian Jews from the path of the more extreme revolutionary elements who were plotting to seize power and would keep the Jews in the ranks of the Kerensky war party. A cognate conception was held by Colonel House who wrote Wilson of his plans for organizing the American Jews in an attempt to stem the defeatist tide among the Jews in Russia. T. E. Lawrence, when later ridiculing the Balfour Declaration in a conversation with William Yale, the American special agent in Egypt, referred to it as payment for the support of American Jews and Russian Jewish revolutionaries. Foreign Secretary Balfour himself may not have envisaged the role of Zionism in the Empire in such crass and limited terms but many of the other members of the British government interpreted his policy in that restrictive sense.

In the United States Brandeis had enlisted State Department officials in the complex diplomatic negotiations with all the belligerent powers which war relief in Palestine entailed. He had occasion to mention the London meetings of the Zionists and the British to American officials and to the President. But the extent to which he received from them verbal approval for the Zionist *political* aims as distinct from humanitarian relief for starving and persecuted Jews in Palestine remains highly conjectural. The full political import of the Balfour Declaration was not weighed in the Department prior to its issuance on November 2nd, whatever Wilson may have said in his private talks with Brandeis and Stephen S. Wise. Rabbi Wise reports a June 1917 conversation in which Wilson assured him that the Jews and the Armenians were two nations certain to be reborn after the war—facile promises. Wilson was born in the manse, the son of a Presbyterian clergyman, and on more than one occasion he described his feeling for the Bible as fundamental to his attraction to Zionism. Yet these sympathies alone do not constitute a policy. The record of Wilson's adherence to political Zionism is far more complicated.

While there are no written reports in the State Department files for this period on the meetings between the Zionists and the British government, there is one document describing high Zionist policy in London which was transmitted to the Department by Brandeis with a brief note in May 1917. "I think you will be interested in enclosed formulation of the Zionist program by Weizmann and his associates and which we approve." The document itself, written on stationery of the Provisional Executive Committee for General Zionist Affairs, contains in embryo many of the formulae which later reappeared in various drafts of the British mandate.

"It is proposed that the following be adopted as the heads of a scheme for a Jewish re-settlement of Palestine in accordance with Jewish national aspirations:

"1. *Basis of Settlement.*
Recognition of Palestine as the Jewish National Home.

"2. *Status of Jewish Population in Palestine Generally.*
The Jewish population present and future throughout Palestine is to possess and enjoy full national, political and civic rights.

"3. *Immigration into Palestine.*
The Suzerain Government shall grant full and free rights of immigration into Palestine to Jews of all countries.

"4. *The Establishment of a Chartered Company.*
The Suzerain Government shall grant a Charter to a Jewish Company for the colonisation and development of Palestine, the Company to

have power to acquire and take over any concessions for works of a
public character, which may have been or may hereafter be granted
by the Suzerain Government and the rights of pre-emption of Crown
Lands or other lands not held in private or religious ownership and
such other powers and privileges as are usual in Charters of Statutes
of similar colonising bodies.

"5. *Communal Autonomy.*
Full autonomy is to be enjoyed by Jewish communities throughout
Palestine in all matters bearing upon their educational, religious or
communal welfare.

"*Summary.*
"Palestine is to be recognized as the Jewish National Home. Jews
of all countries to be accorded full liberty of immigration.

"Jews to enjoy full national, political and civic rights according to
their place of residence in Palestine.

"A Charter to be granted to a Jewish Company for the development
of Palestine.

"The Hebrew language to be recognized as the official language of
the Jewish Province."

As far as the State Department is concerned there is no evidence that
this "scheme for a Jewish re-settlement of Palestine in accordance with
Jewish national aspirations" was ever studied by officials. In the early
summer of 1917 the policy of the United States was oriented far more
in the direction of arranging a separate peace with Turkey than in
espousing the causes of the various subject minorities of the Ottoman
Empire.

During his trip to the United States in May 1917 Balfour had discussed Zionism and his proposed declaration with Brandeis. Both
men were impressed with each other and Balfour pledged his personal support of Zionism. Palestine was not a part of the Balfour-
Wilson negotiations on the conduct of the war except indirectly: in
one of his private talks with Wilson, Balfour informed the President
in a "personal," not an official capacity, of the existence of secret
treaties among the Allies. During the same period Brandeis again
raised the subject of Palestine in conversation with Wilson. On May 15
he cabled Louis de Rothschild in London that he had had "satisfactory" talks with Balfour and with the President, but that this news was
"not for publication." Contrary to accepted legend, there is no evidence for a belief that Zionist aspirations had been discussed in detail by Balfour and Wilson, or that Wilson during their meetings on

the conduct of the war, had committed the United States to acceptance of British policy with respect to Palestine.

Whatever discussions about a Jewish Palestine went on were arranged either directly between members of the Brandeis group and the President or through the intermediary of Colonel House, without the knowledge of Secretary of State Lansing. It was not unusual for Wilson to formulate international policy without consulting his Secretary of State; nevertheless, this freezing out of Lansing had unfortunate consequences for the Zionists. The by-passing of Lansing was by no means the sole cause for his covert hostility towards Zionism, but it was a factor of no mean significance in his alienation.

In the months of September and October 1917, when the critical details of the final text of the Balfour Declaration were being debated in London, and the British were making attempts to draw Wilson in as an active partner in the venture Colonel House, not Lansing, carried on the consultations. It is difficult to know whether the British realized the extent to which this device kept the United States technically clear of any pledges on the settlement even in this tiny area of the globe. Lansing could later maintain with complete accuracy that the United States Government had never approved of the Declaration prior to its issuance; he for one had never signed any communications on the subject; and the off the record conversations of a Justice of the Supreme Court with Colonel House about a statement the British Government chose to publish were not in his province. A divided executive policy on Palestine, with the Presidency and the State Department often pulling in different directions, remained a characteristic of American foreign relations for three decades.

On September 4, Colonel House wrote Wilson that he had received the following cable from Lord Robert Cecil: "We are being pressed here for a declaration of sympathy with the Zionist movement, and I should be very grateful if you felt able to ascertain unofficially if the President favors such a declaration." The casualness of this inquiry is hardly congruent with the protracted negotiations which the British had devoted to that one long sentence of the Declaration and the scores of drafts which by that time had been composed by Zionists and British officials.

President Wilson, organizing the nation for its first great foreign war, was not particularly preoccupied with what was, from the viewpoint of American overall interests, a mere detail. Three days after his query Colonel House came back again to prod, reminding Wilson of the Cecil message. This time House took occasion to express his personal misgivings about the whole idea. "Have you made up your mind regarding what answer you will make to Cecil concerning Zionist Movement? It seems to me that there are many dangers lurking in it, and if I were the British I would be chary about going too definitely into that question." Earlier in the year House had written ecstatically to Rabbi Stephen Wise, "I hope the dream which we have may soon become a reality." For the President's Zionist friends Colonel House always had a pleasant mien.

British Jews were sharply divided over the issuance of the Declaration; there was one party represented in the War Cabinet by Edmund Montagu who believed that, whatever the wording, "a Jewish national home" would pose for them the problem of dual allegiance. For many months the issue had hung in the balance and Wilson's final approval was considered crucial by the Zionists in London to outweigh the hostility of the assimilationist British Jews to the Declaration. British policy, they knew, was bending every effort to draw the United States into active participation in a world settlement and was seeking definite American pledges. Sanction for this one post-war plan in the Near East would be a reasonable commencement.

On September 19th Dr. Chaim Weizmann cabled Justice Brandeis a version of the Declaration tentatively agreed upon by the British along with the suggestion that it would be very helpful if both he and President Wilson supported the text. There was a real danger at this time that owing to the hostility of the assimilationist British Jews the solution of the knotty problem of the Declaration would be indefinitely postponed. Weizmann simultaneously wired the American Zionists de Haas and Levi-Epstein urging them to galvanize Brandeis and Frankfurter into action. No specific written approval from Wilson was forthcoming. Instead, Brandeis cabled Weizmann on September 24th, apparently at Colonel House's suggestion, advising him to get the French and the Italians to make inquiry about the President's attitude. On the same day another more affirmative cable from Brandeis stated that on the basis of previous talks with the President and from opinion voiced by his close advisers he could say that "the President was in entire sympathy." This again was only a description, not specifically authorized, of what Wilson thought. The French and the Italians never did ask for Wilson's opinion.

On October 9th Weizmann described to Brandeis the formidable offensive which had been launched by those British Jews who were opposed to the Declaration and this time he called for more than Wilson's general assent; he needed the President's insistence on the specific text, buttressed by telegrams from important Zionists and other American leaders. None arrived. By October 14th Weizmann had to send Brandeis a new formula of the Declaration, this one significantly watered down at the behest of the assimilationist, anti-Zionist English Jews. While the September version had laid down the principle that "Palestine should be reconstituted as the national home for the Jewish people," by October the Declaration referred only to the "establishment in Palestine of a National Home for the Jewish people" (an emendation which formed the basis for Churchill's famous quibble in the White Paper of 1922). In September the British promised to "secure the achievement" of the homeland; by October they would only "facilitate the achievement."

More than a month after Colonel House's original note to Wilson, on October 13th, he received the following breezy reply from the President: "I find in my pocket the memorandum you gave me about the Zionist Movement. I am afraid I did not say to you that I concurred in the formula suggested from the other side. I do, and would be obliged if you would let them know it." On October 16th House dutifully wrote Wilson: "I will let the British Government know that the formula they suggest as to the Zionist Movement meets with your approval." In the meantime, of course, the "formula" had been basically altered, but it is highly dubious from the record whether Wilson was aware of what version he was approving. During this period he was troubled by the Pope's peace offensive and the course of the Russian Revolution; the Declaration was a minor incident. Under the circumstances it is rather far-fetched to consider Wilson one of the progenitors of the Balfour Declaration. The most that can be said is that he allowed it to happen. The British and many Zionists, in the nature of things, interpreted Wilson's agreement as an act of considered diplomacy, not being aware of the manner in which it was bestowed. Weizmann, in any case, considers the House note crucial in the final overriding of the powerful opposition of the Montagu group by the War Cabinet.

According to de Haas, American Zionists were responsible for a final revision in the text of the Declaration. British Jews, troubled about the problem of dual allegiance, had secured an alteration in the October version to the effect that nothing in the Declaration would prejudice "the rights and political status enjoyed in any other country by such Jews who are fully contented with their existing nationality and citizenship." When the American Zionists received a copy of this text they objected to the last clause because it made of Zionism a mere product of discontent. On October 15th they proposed to Colonel House an excision to make it read simply, "the rights and political status enjoyed by Jews in any other country,"—a change which was duly accepted by the British. At the insistence of Justice Brandeis there was another change—the award was made to the Jewish "people," instead of the Jewish "race" of an earlier draft.

Apparently Weizmann had envisaged the publication of a statement of formal approval in the United States almost simultaneously with the issuance of the Declaration. Brandeis disabused him of the prospect; Wilson was not disposed to make a public declaration in connection with the Balfour pronouncement because the United States was not at war with Turkey.

THE AFTERMATH OF THE DECLARATION

During 1917 and 1918 the State Department had a source of intelligence on Palestine and Zionism in Vice-Consul Edelman, who had formerly been stationed in Jerusalem, and who was set up in Geneva in what was called a Near Eastern Intelligence unit. The information he supplied was of an inferior order, dependent for the most part upon his previous knowledge, his simple prejudices, and the available newspapers of the Central Powers for which Switzerland was a clearing house. His reports were in the spirit of a Lansing policy which was soon to express itself sharply. Samuel Edelman was an anti-Zionist; from his earlier Jerusalem despatches and from the Geneva intelligence reports it is quite apparent that he was intensely worried lest the Zionist agitation act as an impediment to his career in the Department by posing the problem of dual allegiance. In November 1917 he described the Zionist immigrants into Palestine as a poor lot, totally unfitted to till the soil. "It is true that here and there a successful orange orchard or vineyard had flourished, but if the books were balanced, it would be found to have returned little or no interest on the money invested." Edelman attacked Zionism on the familiar grounds of the unsuitability of the climate, the sanctity of the Holy Places, and the numerical predominance of the Arabs. The Zionists had flooded the Allies with propaganda, and had even tried to bargain with the Vatican, Edelman "learned," offering to use Jewish financial and political influence to arrange for Vatican representation at the Peace Conference in exchange for Catholic support of the Zionist program. The British Jews were a religious community and were opposed to political Zionism, in Edelman's judgment, and the Balfour Declaration had been most compromising to them. In the American Jewish community he said that the pro-Zionists were recent immigrants led by a few demagogues who exploited the movement for their own advantage and the anti-Zionists were the "upper strata of Jewish thought and leadership" such as Ambassadors Straus and Elkus, Louis Marshall, Jacob Schiff, Otto Kahn. His conclusion was absolute: "A Jewish State should not be tolerated." After Edelman had analyzed the newspapers of the Central Powers he made the prediction that the Balfour Declaration would not exercise the slightest influence on the morale of Jews in enemy countries, with the possible exception of recent Russian and Roumanian immigrants into Germany and Austria. To explain the issuance of the Declaration he credited the success of the Zionists in England to a curious Christian sect of Anglo-Israelites who believed that the inhabitants of the British Isles were remnants of the lost ten tribes. As political intelligence, this was rather extravagant speculation.

Official Washington received the Balfour Declaration without comment. Zionists tried to intimate that they enjoyed great influence in the White House and they considered the Declaration a signal victory, but no formal statement was forthcoming either from the President or his State Department. In the heart of world Jewry, in Russia, there was great jubilation because a rumor had spread that President Wilson had voiced his adherence to the British proposal. The American Consul in Odessa telegraphed that a hundred thousand Jews had demonstrated before his office in gratitude to the government of the United States. There were mass celebrations and huzzas before American consulates in Salonika, in Alexandria, in Sydney, in Shanghai. Scores of telegrams of thanks poured into Wilson from all parts of the world, almost as if *he* had issued the Declaration.

Among American Jews the issuance of the Balfour Declaration forced into the open that great cleavage between Zionists and anti-Zionists which had already divided the Jews of Britain. Former Ambassador Henry Morgenthau wrote a letter to the *New York Times* which was headed, "World Significance of the British Occupation of Jerusalem and Limitations of the Zionist Movement." Morgenthau was not yet as violently hostile to Zionism, the official policy of a wartime ally, as he later became at the Paris Peace Conference, but he was distinctly cold to the movement. To the President he wrote privately: "It seems to me conclusive that the 400 million Christians will assert their interest in Palestine and resent any attempt on the part of the Jews to dominate that province. The Christians, Mohammedans, and Jews must be treated alike. . . ." In the circle close to Wilson, Henry Morgenthau, who had directed the Democratic Financial Committee in the election of 1916, was a counterweight to the Zionist Brandeis. The potency of his influence is recorded in their intimate correspondence over many years. The rival factions of Jews thus had a tug-of-war for the President's support.

The Zionists were restive. More than a month had passed since the issuance of the Declaration and still there was no word from the White House. On December 13, 1917 Lansing took cognizance of the "pressure" of the Zionists in a formal letter to the President, a cautious analysis of the factors of United States policy involved in approval of the Declaration. He was as clear-cut as Wilson was vague; he had never committed himself to this Zionist "formula," neither had anyone in his Department expressed the slightest sympathy for it.

"There is being brought considerable pressure for the issuance of a declaration in regard to this Government's attitude as to the disposition to be made of Palestine. This emanates naturally from the Zionist element of the Jews.

"My judgment is that we should go very slowly in announcing a policy for three reasons. *First,* we are not at war with Turkey and therefore should avoid any appearance of favoring taking territory from that Empire by force. *Second,* the Jews are by no means a unit in the desire to reestablish their race as an independent people; to favor one or the other faction would seem to be unwise. *Third,* many Christian sects and individuals would undoubtedly resent turning the Holy Land over to the absolute control of the race credited with the death of Christ.

"For practical purposes I do not think that we need go further than the first reason given since that is ample ground for declining to announce a policy in regard to the final disposition of Palestine."

The next day at a cabinet meeting Wilson returned the letter to Lansing with a comment which the meticulous Secretary of State carefully noted: "The President returned me this letter at Cabinet Meeting, December 14, 1917, saying that very unwillingly he was forced to agree with me, but said that he had an impression that we had assented to the British declaration regarding returning Palestine to the Jews." It was clear that Wilson did not remember precisely or give great weight to the approval of October 13 to which both the British and Zionists attached such importance. He had only an "impression" that he had assented to the Balfour Declaration.

Lansing's December 13th letter to Wilson on Zionism, not published at the time, became the official State Department position for ten months during the war. There is no reason to imagine that Lansing ever swerved from his viewpoint, even at the Peace Conference. Wilson had general sympathy for "Jewish aspirations"—but it did not always assume material shape. Though Lansing was finally overridden by the President in August 1918 when he first gave public expression to this "sympathy," the Secretary of State had ample opportunity to revert to his own line of thinking on many critical occasions during the peace negotiations.

The day following the cabinet meeting at which the President had acquiesced in Lansing's arguments in favor of official silence on the Balfour Declaration, the State Department sent the London Embassy a request to investigate discreetly and report fully on the reasons for Balfour's recent statement relative to "the Jewish state in Palestine." Thus more than a month after the Declaration, the Department was referring to a "Jewish state" and seemed totally ignorant of real British intentions in Palestine. Ambassador Page called on Lord Robert Cecil, in charge of the Foreign Office during Balfour's illness, to make his "discreet inquiry" in accordance with instructions. He was formally told of an understanding with the French Government that Palestine was to be internationalized, an official hint of the existence of the secret Sykes-Picot Agreement. As for Britain's commitment to the Jews in Palestine, the British Government merely had pledged itself to put them on the same footing as other nationalities. "No discrimination shall be made against them. This is as far as the British government has yet gone." During the informal conversation which followed, Lord Robert Cecil made the further point that internationalized Palestine would have to have some "proctor"; since European powers were too jealous of one another to agree on any one among themselves, he expressed the hope that the United States would accept the task. He was, of course, not speaking officially, "only for himself." For the first time the United States was offered Palestine by the British; it would be tried again.

If State Department officials still had any question as to the highly

circumscribed interpretation which the British placed on the Balfour
Declaration at the time of its issuance, their doubts should have been
dispelled by a formal statement on the immediate policy which the
British occupation forces proposed to adopt with regard to Palestine, transmitted by the British Embassy in Washington. This did not
preclude a broadening of British policy at a later date, but it already
betrayed the wariness of the British military confronted by a vague
Declaration which was reported to be exerting a negative reaction on
the Arab troops who were the right flank of Allenby's army. The
note enumerated nine objectives: 1. Religious equality; 2. Equality
under the law to all Allies of the United Kingdom; 3. Settlement of
the problem of the Holy Places with Moslem and Christian religious
chiefs; 4. Maintenance of a civil police force, recruited from all the
denominations, to safeguard the Holy Places under British control;
5. Return in the near future to Jerusalem of the heads of the religious denominations, though not the consuls; 6. Employment of local
functionaries, wherever possible, without favor to any special community; 7. "The maintenance of Zionism on right lines," safeguarding Holy Places and allowing full facilities for the reconstruction of
the colonies; 8. Removal of German influence; 9. Fair play.

This confidential exposition of the aims of Allenby's army of occupation shrivelled the import of the Balfour Declaration in Palestine.
For purposes of the international propaganda war for the sympathies
of the Jewries of the world, however, the British government inflated
the meaning of its Zionist policy and watched anxiously every Turkish
and German move to neutralize the effect of the Declaration. On
February 13, 1918, the Intelligence Bureau, Department of Information in the British Foreign Office, prepared a detailed *Memorandum
on the Attitude of Enemy Governments Towards Zionism,* which Ambassador Walter Page sent to the State Department a week later. There
British Intelligence outlined details of the Karasso Scheme, a competitive bid by the Turks, at Germany's instigation, to grant certain
autonomous rights to the Jews of Palestine. After a brilliant evaluation of the relative propagandistic advantages of the Balfour Declaration and the Karasso plan, the memorandum concluded that British
Zionist policy still had a distinct edge over Turkish and German
attempts to woo the Jewries of the world. Any American official reading this memorandum would have arrived at the conclusion that the
Balfour Declaration was an improvisation of the war meant to serve
an immediate military situation. The British Embassy in Washington,

keeping the Department fully informed on every new development in its Zionist policy, officially submitted the details of the Karasso scheme to the State Department and drew attention to its dangers, but concluded with the optimist outlook of the British Intelligence Memorandum. The British care to keep the United States posted on every detail of Palestine policy was more than normal courtesy to an Associated Power in the war; at this stage Balfour meant to draw the United States in as an active partner in the Near East.

On February 28, 1918, Lansing wrote to the President for a final decision on two proposals by the American Zionists: one requested passports for Americans to join a commission of Zionists, acting under sanction of the British Government, who were proceeding to Palestine on an inquiry; the other revived the Zionist medical unit project for Palestine to be promoted in the United States. Lansing, holding fast to his original position on intervention in Turkey and on Zionism, objected to both ideas. The United States Government, he wrote, had never accepted Mr. Balfour's pronouncement, was not at war with Turkey, and should not sponsor an organization with distinctly political aims. President Wilson over-ruled him on the Zionist medical unit, which he authorized, but he could find no reply to Lansing's argument against American participation on the Zionist Commission. In the end—with or without Lansing's approval—a compromise seems to have been worked out. A New York lawyer, Walter Meyer, went along on the Weizmann Commission, as it came to be known, but without official status as an American on the Commission; he was sent merely as Weizmann's assistant. The exchange between Wilson and Lansing over the Commission is significant because it emphasized again Lansing's persistent negation of Zionist projects.

THE WILSON LETTER OF AUGUST 31, 1918

On August 31, 1918, the American Zionists won their first concrete diplomatic victory in the United States. Their agent on this occasion was Rabbi Stephen Wise. While Wilson had been hailed as the lover of Zion in a thousand Jewish meetings throughout the world, no American State Department official had uttered a single word or written a line for the public record in favor of the Balfour Declaration at a time when Zionist missions in Europe had already persuaded the French and Italians to write statements in favor of the idea of the Declaration. On August 27, 1918, Rabbi Wise had an interview with the President, during which he tried to allay Wilson's apprehensions about making any statement predetermining the allocation of the territory of a power with whom the United States was not at war. When Wise left the White House he had an after-thought and wrote to the President, renewing his plea for a message of sympathy in time for announcement on the Jewish New Year's Day. His letter stressed the point that the Zionist program contained no plank about the nature of the Turkish suzerainty and expressed no view as to the desirability of a change. "In discussing with you this afternoon the Zionist development, I failed to give you a copy of the so-called Basle Program which is, and from its inception has been, the whole platform of Zionism,—namely, 'The object of Zionism is to establish a publicly recognized, legally secured homeland in Palestine for the Jewish people.' You will note that no reference is made in this platform to the character of the suzerainty which might obtain over such homeland, and that the Balfour Declaration, likewise silent on this subject, involves no challenge of the present suzerainty and leaves that for determination at the Peace-table."

Wilson was finally moved to ignore Lansing's caution and to write a letter to Rabbi Wise. Approval of the Balfour Declaration was not the form which his expression of sympathy for Zionism could take if Lansing's objections were to be met even half-way. Wilson therefore tied his letter to the activities of the Weizmann Commission in Palestine, then purportedly making economic investigations and preparing to found a university.

"I have watched with deep and sincere interest the reconstructive work which the Weizmann Commission has done in Palestine at the instance of the British Government, and I welcome an opportunity to express the satisfaction I have felt in the progress of the Zionist Movement in the United States and in the Allied countries since the declaration by Mr. Balfour on behalf of the British Government, of Great Britain's approval of the establishment in Palestine of a national home for the Jewish people, and his promise that the British Government would use its best endeavors to facilitate the achievement of that object, with the understanding that nothing would be done to prejudice the civil and religious rights of non-Jewish people in Palestine or the rights and political status enjoyed by Jews in other countries.

"I think that all Americans will be deeply moved by the report that even in this time of stress the Weizmann Commission has been able to lay the foundation of the Hebrew University at Jerusalem, with the promise that that bears of spiritual truth."

As Wise had requested, the letter was sent as a greeting to the Jews on the New Year. The long-drawn-out periodic sentence is not in Wilson's style, and it would not be too far-fetched to surmise—though Rabbi Wise has expressed outrage at the idea—that Zionist leaders had to compose their own congratulations. It was the first of a long line of statements of approval which the Zionists received from Wilson and every other American President since then and on which they had to sustain themselves in lieu of more formal diplomatic action. The specific contents of the Wilson letter were soon forgotten, but the Zionists were able to come before their people with the joyous tidings that the President their friend was in favor of the Jewish homeland and, when orators were carried away, they might even say that he was in favor of the Jewish State. The juridical nuances of various stages of independence and suzerainty could hardly be conveyed to an audience thirsting for the land.

Presidential statements such as Wilson's New Year greeting to the Jews in 1918 have a peculiar status in American foreign policy. They are expressions of attitude, and the degree to which they may be formal commitments of any sort, especially when they do not pass through the State Department, remains dubious. There is no section of the Constitution more explicit than the article which confides the treaty making power, hence the framing and direction of foreign policy, into the hands of the President. The problem nevertheless remains whether the President makes foreign policy every time he utters a sentence about it. If he does, United States policy on Palestine was a grotesque for more than three decades.

Wilson's letter of August 31 was clearly executed in the White House, and a draft is still in the Wilson papers along with the Wise correspondence in connection with its issuance. There is no record that Lansing was consulted about its drafting or that its significance was defined in the State Department. The Department refused to recognize this letter as a declaration of policy, and in the years following, officials in their memoranda would ingenuously ask whether and if so where we had formally approved of the Balfour Declaration. Nevertheless the letter had significance—though it was probably not as great as the Zionists claimed. Its publication made it clear to Americans in the diplomatic establishment and in the Department where Wilson stood—sentimentally at least. After its publication,

Justice Brandeis, with enthusiastic abandon, declared that opposition to Zionism could henceforth be considered disloyalty to the United States. And the Washington correspondent of the *London Times* wrote: "This letter is taken as tantamount to a recognition by the United States of an American interest in the Zionist venture, such as France and Italy as well as Great Britain have already given."

AMERICAN ZIONISTS AND THE AWARD TO BRITAIN

One of the subjects of the cable discussion between Weizmann and Brandeis during the period prior to the issuance of the Balfour Declaration had been the identity of the nation whom Zionists would seek as the trustee for Palestine. Weizmann and Lord Rothschild were determined upon Britain while the United States Jewish press was in favor of an Anglo-American condominium. After his meeting with Balfour in May 1917 Brandeis, though still unwilling to commit himself publicly, assured Weizmann that he had accepted Britain and was convinced of her sincerity. The subject was reopened in August 1917 when Professor Frankfurter, at Brandeis's request, discussed the problem with Weizmann after the Morgenthau peace mission had petered out. Weizmann was forthright in refusing any combination of powers in the trusteeship of Palestine as detrimental to the future of the homeland. His reasoning appears to have been that any more than one "trustee" would inevitably entail French participation, and this was considered disastrous. It was a wise policy decision on Weizmann's part since Jewish autonomy in an internationalized area would have been well nigh impossible; such a status for Palestine would have stressed the universal religious character of the land, precluding it from ever becoming a national home for Jews.

Balfour, on the other hand, was genuinely in favor of an Anglo-American protectorate for Palestine and tried to interest Brandeis in the idea in May 1917. His motive was probably to secure American assistance as a counterweight to the French, who had been promised internationalization in the Sykes-Picot agreement. But since by that time Weizmann had convinced Brandeis that the only politic position for Zionists was to espouse a British protectorate, Brandeis explained to Balfour that in his opinion many Americans were still opposed to the war and were reluctant to undertake responsibilities in foreign parts. Balfour's daughter, in her biography of her father, bestows upon the Brandeis-Weizmann diplomacy of this period with respect to a

British protectorate a degree of integration it may have lacked, but her analysis has some basis in fact. "Dr. Weizmann's letters and telegrams were keeping him [Brandeis] shrewdly informed of the British point of view. England, Dr. Weizmann said, was not yearning to annex Palestine, and would hardly care to oppose the internationalisation which would be fatal to Zionist hopes, except for the attraction that the idea of large-scale Jewish settlement was beginning to have for her. Hence, Zionist policy must keep to that simple demand for a British Protectorate, rejecting all other schemes which would tend to raise fresh jealousies, and bring about some joint control. The American Zionists grasped the point. A Jewish national diplomacy was in being."

Balfour often reverted to the idea of American participation in the Palestine protectorate. "Personally," he wrote in a Foreign Office Minute of June 13th, "I should still prefer to associate the U. S. A. in the Protectorate should we succeed in securing it."

On December 16, 1918, when the American Jewish Congress following Brandeis's leadership declared formally that it was in favor of the trusteeship of Great Britain, it gave the British solid American support against French ideas of a condominium with Britain or an internationalized state. This by no means fazed the French. They sent M. Picot with the title of High Commissioner to join Allenby, and in the Chamber of Deputies on December 27 Pichon announced that internationalization of Palestine was an agreed policy.

WILLIAM YALE AND AARON AARONSOHN, SPECIAL AGENTS

By late summer 1917, the State Department had become aware of its woefully inadequate intelligence on the Near East. Although the United States was not at war with Turkey, our top officials realized that the liberated lands of her empire in Asia Minor would become a key area in the general peace settlement; the great loot of the war, it was later called. American consular and diplomatic agents in Egypt, an outpost proximate to Turkey, were not transmitting detailed political intelligence and their stray reports were too meagre for State Department analysts attempting to follow the threads of the drama which was being enacted beyond Suez. The British had an Arab Bureau in Cairo, staffed with brilliant orientalists and political officers who manipulated the Arab desert chieftains and the Syrian politicians in exile. It was therefore reasonable for the United States as an initial move to despatch a special agent to Egypt—and the choice proved to be no mean one, William Yale. A man of thirty in 1917, he had been trained as an engineer at the Sheffield School at Yale, had served in Panama and had worked for Standard Oil of New York in the Near East, first as an explorer and then as a resident agent in Jerusalem from 1915 to 1917. Upon his return to Washington after the break in diplomatic relations with Turkey, he had written an informal report on wartime political and economic conditions in Syria and Palestine which was straightforward, balanced, intelligent. When the State Department sent him to Cairo he was ordered to report directly to Leland Harrison assigned to "special duty" in the Department and was given free rein. While Wilson and his Zionist friends used a language which might be described as vaguely idealist, Yale wrote in the prose of power politics as practiced in the western world.

In Paris en route to Cairo, Yale met a former Jerusalem acquaintance, Aaron Aaronsohn, who had directed the Jewish Agricultural Station at Athlit, an institution supported largely by Rosenwald funds from the United States which then enjoyed close scientific relations with the United States Department of Agriculture. Aaron Aaronsohn had been the chief organizer of a British spy ring among the Jewish colonists in Palestine, his work facilitated by an appointment under Djemal Pasha to direct the war against the locust invasion of 1917. Opinion about him was sharply divided among the more staid Jewish colonists, many of whom saw in his partisan activities on behalf of the British a threat to the existence of the agricultural settlements if he were ever discovered. His arrogance was proverbial. In Cairo, Miss Annie Landau, an orthodox Jewess who had been head of the British Evalina de Rothschild school in Palestine and who was militantly anti-Zionist, later gave Yale a poisonous description of this enigmatic figure: she called him an ignorant uncultured upstart, a selfish and unscrupulous opportunist, who under the cloak of Zionism was working to feather his own nest. The portrait was prejudiced, but many Zionist colonists have been no gentler in their estimate. According to Miss Landau, Aaronsohn stole from a poor Alsatian Christian woman the discovery of wild wheat, to which he owed his fame. Despite his unsavory reputation in some quarters, however, Aaronsohn was said to have a great following in the United States, including Justice Brandeis among his admirers. A reading of Brandeis's speeches on Zionism does in fact disclose a number of eulogies of Aaron Aaronsohn as the type of "new Jew" whom Palestine had developed in recent years.

During his September 1917 conversation with Yale in Paris, Aaronsohn lashed out against the immediate establishment of a Jewish state in Palestine and announced that he was proceeding to England and America to combat the idea. Yale had a more complex view of the import of Aaronsohn's contemplated American journey. He suggested to the Department that the British authorities meant to use Aaronsohn in America to stimulate a demand on the part of American Jews for the separation of Palestine from Syria and the grant of special privileges to the Jews in Palestine under British protection. Thus, if Aaronsohn's propaganda were effective, in the end it would appear to be the United States, instead of Great Britain, which opposed the Arabs, the French, and the many Christian interests hostile to the policy of the Zionists.

After their talk Aaron Aaronsohn gave Yale what he called a letter of introduction to his brother Alex, who had escaped from Palestine after serving in the Turkish army, had made his way to the United States, and was now back in Cairo working with British intelligence. The long letter was written in Hebrew. With an obvious contempt for the enterprise and intelligence of Yale the oil man whom he had known in Jerusalem, Aaronsohn used him as a courier. Yale sent a translation of the letter to the State Department in a report of December 1917. The indiscreet passages about William Yale himself and the American consul in Jerusalem, Reverend Glazebrook (a friend of President Wilson's and a direct presidential appointee), were not likely to have gained Aaronsohn either the friendship of American officials or their respect for his ingenuity as a spy. The letter confirmed Yale in the idea that Aaronsohn was a special agent for Mark Sykes, chief British adviser to the War Cabinet on the Near East, who was not at all popular with the British Arabophiles in the Cairo Arab Bureau.

Aaronsohn's letter described his interview with Edmond de Rothschild, the great sustainer of the pre-war Palestine colonies, who as a Frenchman had been placed in an awkward position by the recent orientation of the Zionists. "He feels as we all do, that if Great Britain would only rule over our land, we could obtain great things." Aaronsohn's introduction of Yale to his brother was: "Meanwhile I have seen William Yale, who knows me from Jerusalem, where he was in the oil Co. He takes a great interest now in Eastern Questions. I spoke to him at great length. Get as pally as you can with him and watch him, for you will be able to get information from him which you need, especially about happenings in Egypt." Of Consul Glazebrook he wrote: "He was especially pleased that I got to Egypt safely. The old man is just as soft as he used to be, so you can understand that I was able to find out from him all that had happened. He saw a lot in our country (Palestine) and after all he believes you and I are working in earnest and with all our might. I am glad that I shall have the opportunity of seeing him again in London and through him I can reach the Ambassador."

The letter was an open window on internal Zionist squabbles: "Mark Sykes came here the day before yesterday. He told me every-thing and showed me what a lot of enemies we have, most of the opponents from among our own people, and that is dangerous to our organization. He told me that my letter to Weizmann was like a thorn in the latter's eye. Mark Sykes begs me to make peace with them and wants me to promise not to quarrel. He says that I should listen to Weizmann and to Sokolow. I told him that I was not going to London to quarrel, only to tell them their mistakes and to show them the way to do things properly."

Aaron Aaronsohn was killed in an airplane accident in 1919, after having been decorated by the British. A strange character was re-moved from the Zionist scene.

YALE'S FIRST VIEW OF BRITISH IMPERIAL POLICY

When Yale arrived in Egypt, there had as yet been no decision in Washington as to what official title he was to assume; he therefore decided, in consultation with the American Diplomatic Agent, Kna-benshue, that since British intelligence would trail him anyway he might as well go directly to Sir William Wingate, the High Commis-sioner, and frankly announce that he was a special agent for the State Department. In Cairo he talked to everybody: Egyptians, Syrians, Arabs, Zionists, anti-Zionists, the British officers in the Arab Bureau; and while he kept his reports factual he did not hesitate to formulate a policy or to recommend a course of action for the United States. In the Department they liked his weekly reports; they were basic to the Near Eastern analyses of the *Inquiry* which preceded the Peace Conference. While his concrete suggestions were not often followed, he had a long term effect on the framing of policy through the steady seepage of his viewpoint into the minds of American officials. He was the only American special agent in the Near East. When grand decisions were being drafted, the United States literally had no other significant source of its own of live political intelligence on Asia Minor.

Yale's weekly analyses, which covered the whole gamut of Near East politics, written in Cairo from November 12, 1917 to June 1918, at which time he was attached to Allenby's army in Palestine as a military observer, have distinction even when they err by exaggerating a momentary crisis. Yale realized, unlike simpler intelligence reporters, that a great empire such as Britain, at the crossroads of its historical development, might well nurture along in the same world area alternative, even flagrantly contradictory policies. He sagely commented in his first report from Egypt: "Towards all the varied interests Great Britain seemingly takes a sympathetic attitude, at times even an encouraging one. The part played by the British has had the tendency to make people believe that they are playing a very deep game, with a very definite aim which will only be revealed at the right moment. However the truth seems to be that Downing Street has no definite policy and have given their agents no clear program to work out. . . ." This was the same lack of coordination to which Sir Ronald Storrs later testified in attempting to explain conflicting British commitments in the Near East. Yale reported further that in his judgment Britain had no cut and dried program for the whole of the Turkish Empire after defeat nor for its several parts—Anatolia, Mesopotamia, Syria, and Palestine. He could discern at most two relatively stable aims: control of Mesopotamia under a regime similar to India or Egypt; and dominion over Islam through the instrumentality of the King of the Hedjaz erected into an independent power. France was the great rival in this plan and the Franco-British war for control was the heart of the power game in the Near East. The British might have to countenance the French in Syria, Yale thought, but in that event they would erect a buffer state between the French area and Suez. Palestine offered itself as a convenient tool for this purpose, since Protestant, Greek and Russian Orthodox, Jewish and Moslem religious bodies would be unanimous in hostility to French domination, for fear of the hegemony of the French clerical party and the Vatican in the Holy Land. Yale believed that the Zionists had fallen in with this policy of the buffer state and favored British control. The British in turn kept close to the Zionist leaders and bestowed official recognition upon them.

In this same report Yale sent a rough outline of the Near East

spheres of influence which had been determined upon by the British
and the French in secret agreements. By this time United States ignorance of these understandings was only "official."

Soon after his arrival in Cairo the Balfour Declaration was issued
and Yale sent a circumstantial account of the attempts of the British
political officers to make it palatable to the Syrians in exile. He reported in detail the attitude of Colonel Symes, an important official
of the British Residency close to the High Commissioner: "He remarked that he was explaining to the Arabs that this was the first
step taken by Great Britain in carrying out her policy of justice to
small nationalities. He went on to say that the aspirations of the
Zionists found ample justification historically to be considered and
recognized under the principles of the declarations of the Allies in
regard to small nationalities. However he had but little to say about
the rights of the present inhabitants of Palestine, who feel that Zionism threatens their very existence, except that he said that as these
people had never shown any great effort to develop their own country
their rights could not be given the same consideration as those of
others." Colonel Symes was not apprehensive about the discontented
Syrians and Arabs; nevertheless Yale felt it important to note that
protest meetings had been held in Cairo and emissaries sent to the
King of the Hedjaz and his son Feisal, and that the "younger and
more hot-headed among the Moslems are laying plans for the future
that bode no good for the peace of Palestine. . . ."

For himself, Yale tried to divest this British Zionist policy of many
of the emotional and quasi-religious considerations which were being
read into it. He adhered to his conception of Zionism as primarily an
instrument of British imperial policy, an idea from which he diverged
on occasion in future months, but to which he always returned: "It
may be that underlying important financial, sentimental reasons for
their attitude towards the Zionists, are reasons of state concerning
French expansion in Syria. The creation of a state in Palestine which
would probably in the future grow to be an almost purely Jewish
state, would introduce a new element in the East, another Power in
opposition to Islam, a Power that would be a protection to the Suez
Canal, a people under eternal obligation to the British." For a first
view of the early intentions of British policy in Palestine as it was
being forged by agents in the Near East, this was incisive. Yale's
formulation is almost identical with the argument which Dr. Weizmann did in fact use in his discussions with Lord Cecil prior to the
issuance of the Balfour Declaration.

THE CAIRO SYRIANS-IN-EXILE

The Syrians-in-exile in Cairo, both Moslems and Christians, who were in turn divided into a score of parties, were initially Yale's chief source of Arab intelligence. They maintained relatively close contact with the King of the Hedjaz and had an underground, with which their ties were more haphazard, in Damascus and Beirut and southern Palestine. They were a vocal urban element in the Arab revolt; they were traders and intellectuals, newspaper owners and writers who often indulged in the accepted hyperbole of the Levant and their profession. Many of them were in the pay of the British, a few were hirelings of the French, some were hangers-on of the more prosperous nationalists of their own community, supporting one or another of the factions wrestling for control in the Near East. Though Yale was cautious to indicate the source of his intelligence, he was not always critical of its limitations. In the early months of his stay in Cairo, his reports were deeply colored by the expressions of these Syrians-in-exile. Since they were the only articulate Arab group in the Near East and were in a position to exert an influence far out of proportion to their numbers, there is some justification for Yale's preoccupation with their opinions. There were times, however, when he fell in with their more hysterical forebodings. He was confronted with the standard problem of evaluating the intelligence and opinion of exiles and émigrés who are rarely conscious of the degree to which they are cut off from the desires of their own people.

In his early reports Yale tended to accept at face value complaints about the Palestine Jewish colonists voiced by the Cairo Syrians. The Syrian businessmen said they feared the encroachment of Jewish finance and Jewish colonists from eastern Europe upon all of the Lebanon and Syria. They had watched Jewish expansion under the Turkish regime and they were terrified by the almost mythical power of Jewish capitalists using the Arab's avarice to buy possession of the country. Yale also credited their malicious tales about the Jewish bands of watchers organized to protect the agricultural colonies from the Arab marauders who surrounded them. In Palestine Jewish history these men are glorified as heroic pioneers. Yale, deriving his opinion from the Syrians, wrote of them as "young, hot-headed Jews who, used to Russian tyranny and oppression, and now possessing a power they never before dreamt of having, have become at times overbearing and arrogant in their treatment of the felaheens."

But irrespective of the biased source of some of his conceptions,

Yale always had a long view; and with the objectivity of a keen outsider he analyzed the catastrophic forces inherent in the Arab-Jewish relationship at a time when most Zionists throughout the world, in the first flush of enthusiasm over the Declaration, hardly mentioned the Arab problem. They dismissed it with the easy assumption that it would somehow solve itself. Yale on the contrary predicted in 1917 that the Arabs would bitterly oppose Jewish possession of Palestine with every means in their power and that the two elements would soon be locked in violent conflict at once economic, cultural, and political. "It can be expected that under a stable and benevolent Government, the Arab population of Palestine will have a large natural increase, such as has been witnessed in Egypt during the British occupation. If such be the case, an ever increasing Arab element will meet the competition of Jewish immigration, and the result will be an increasingly bitter social, economic, and political struggle, which under the stimulus of religious fanaticism and national intolerance, on both sides, will engender fierce antagonisms.

". . . National, racial, and religious feelings will be stimulated to stiffen the resistance of the Arabs.

"If Zionism becomes a success, and the Jewish colonies thrive and increase in numbers and size, two eventualities can be imagined. In the first place, the existence in Palestine of two opposing forces, practically of two states, will result in a struggle accompanied by constant difficulties, disturbances and outbreaks. In the second place, unable to compete with organized Zionism, the Arab land owners, merchants, etc. will give place to the Jews and eventually leave Palestine. The question then arises as to what is to become of the fellaheens. Living on lands owned by the Jews, they will either have to abandon their homes and emigrate to another land, or become as serfs to a Jewish aristocracy, which owns and controls the country. Such serfs will be of a different nationality and a different religion from their masters and will have implanted in their hearts an undying hatred of their overlords.

"The Jews claim that they can and will assimilate the Arabs; but assimilation of the Arabs by the Jews does not seem possible. In order to assimilate the Arabs it would be necessary for the Jews to mix and live with them, which if they did they would run far more danger of being assimilated than would the Arabs. The Jewish colonists will come from many parts of the world speaking different languages and having different customs and habits. To weld these diverse elements it will be necessary for the Jews to live in communities apart from the Arabs, and learn as their common tongue the Hebrew language. . . . Hence it must be concluded that there will exist in Palestine two elements, diametrically opposed to one another, which, as long as they continue to exist side by side, will be in bitter strife one against another."

The Syrians in Cairo had kept Yale informed of their attempts to protest the Balfour Declaration to the British Government. When they were prohibited by the Residency from sending messages to London, their agents penetrated into Palestine for the express purpose of arousing the Palestinian Arabs against Zionism. These agents, Yale noted, were often civil administration appointees of the British, sent from Cairo to Palestine after Allenby's entry into Jerusalem. When Yale raised the issue of Arab hostility towards Zionism with British officials they would glibly reassure him about Houssein: "The King of the Hedjaz is a sensible sort, and we do not expect any trouble from him on that score."

By December the Syrians in Cairo were beginning to tell Yale that they considered protest against the Declaration hopeless, since they had come to realize that it probably had been issued with the prior assent of both the United States and France. But in a few days the situation was altered. The telegrams of the Syrians to Balfour, after having been held up for weeks in Cairo, were finally despatched and reassurances were received in return from Mark Sykes that the Declaration meant a "home" for the Jews, not an immediate state or government. Clayton of the Arab Bureau, in obvious fulfillment of instructions from Mark Sykes, preached a sermon to the Cairo Syrians about the necessity of their joining the Arab-Armenian-Zionist triumvirate of nationalities which was Sykes's grand design for a Near Eastern solution. After being somewhat placated by the message from Sykes about the immediate intentions of the British, the Cairo Syrians took counsel among themselves and reached the conclusion that if Palestine was not to be given outright to the Jews—which had been their first apprehension after publication of the Declaration—they would have a breathing space during which to organize Syrians throughout the world economically and politically to combat the Jews.

The Syrians sent Hakki Bey, a Damascus Moslem, to the Emir Feisal, the leader whom Lawrence had chosen for the revolt in the desert, to discuss the Balfour Declaration and British policy generally. From him Yale learned that Feisal, while unfavorable to the Declaration, was relatively indifferent to the Syrian Arab agitation. Feisal did not believe it wise to send a mission to the United States to propagandize against Zionism, and Hakki Bey had the impression that Hussein his father was bound by an agreement with the British not to interfere with their policy in Palestine. Hakki Bey received a more sympathetic welcome from other Arab leaders, who were not appeased by the British assurances in Cairo and who, Hakki Bey told Yale, were strongly in favor of soliciting protection from the United States, the only power the Arabs of Syria, Mesopotamia or Arabia could look to against the ambitions of Great Britain and France. These Arab feelers to the United States would be extended again.

In February 1918 Yale learned that the British had sent an agent to Jeddah for a discussion with Hussein about Palestine and the grand design of Mark Sykes. Yale's report jibes in substance with the account by the emissary, Commander Hogarth, which the Foreign Office published many years later. It appears that Hussein declared himself ready to accept international control of Palestine and to allow Jews to settle there. But he had a pronounced distaste for sending a delegate from the Hedjaz Government to the Arab-Jew-Armenian Commission organized at London; he distrusted the members of the committee, and indicated that their interference with what he considered *his* interests was incompatible with his claim to be the single spokesman of the Arab nation.

ANTI-ZIONISM, PSYCHOLOGICAL AND MILITARY

In the early months of 1918 the British were pouring intelligence on Palestine and Syria into the State Department and its agents in various parts of the world. While Ambassador Page in London was handed the full text of the British Memorandum on the Karasso Scheme and the Balfour Declaration, Yale in Cairo was fed copies of the *Arab Bulletin,* the secret publication of the Cairo Arab Bureau. Yale established close and amicable relations with Lawrence, whom he had known earlier in Palestine. He was shown many of the Lawrence sketches and reports even in unfinished form. Yale was by no means merely taken in by the Lawrence charm. He had a keen awareness of the manner in which that strange band of orientalists in Cairo and the Near East were exerting a decisive influence on long-range British policy. In February 1918, he wrote: "I am sending this article with my report [enclosing 'fragmentary notes written in 1915' entitled,

Syria, the Raw Material, by T. E. L.] not only because it gives a very vivid picture of Syria, but also because the opinions of British Statesmen on Syrian questions will be formed from the information that their agents in the East supply them with, and in order to understand the British Policy it is necessary to know on what their views are based."

This Lawrence sketch of Syria, including Palestine, drawn in terms of population segments, obviously impressed Yale, who knew some of the country from his oil explorations. The portion which treats of Palestine is of interest for its insights, its gross misinformation about the Jewish colonies, and its dose of contemporary anti-Semitism. Yale's commentary on the description of the Jewish colonies in Lawrence's sketch reveals the marked antagonism towards Zionism which colored his Cairo reports at this period. He too was not above indulging in a primitive sort of racial characterology.

"T. E. L. in a few words suggests the bitterness which exists in southern Palestine against the Zionists. This bitterness of feeling is shared alike by Moslems and Christians, and recent developments tend only to aggravate the natural hatred of the Palestinians for those Jews, who come to Palestine declaring the country to be theirs and acting as if such were the case.

"The concessions made by the British to the Zionists will tend to widen the breach and perhaps to spread this bitterness to northern Palestine and to Syria. A great deal depends upon the Jewish leaders; if, as in the past, the Zionists in Palestine have as leaders that disagreeable arrogant type of their race, who antagonise their own people almost as much as the Palestinians, and in many cases dishonest and ignorant adventurers, the bitterness may grow to such a pitch as to render conditions in Palestine very disagreeable and difficult to handle. On the contrary, if the Zionists' leaders be that broad-minded, liberal high type Jew which western Europe and America have developed, the feeling in Palestine might be ameliorated and the bitterness toned down."

In the spring of 1918 when the Germans mounted their great offensive on the Western Front and Allenby's army in Palestine was stripped of a number of its best divisions, Yale's anti-Zionism assumed another form. He began to fear the military consequences of the Zionist policy, the discontent of the Arabs as expressed by the Cairo Syrians, and the propaganda of the Turks who were making political capital out of the Balfour Declaration and the Russian Bolshevik publication of the secret agreements for the division of Asia Minor among the Allies.

Yale thought that it was time the United States intervened to proclaim the rights of small nations in the Near East because, unlike the French and the British, we would be trusted and believed. He was genuinely perturbed about the military consequences of a possible Arab about-face and realignment with the Turks at a time when Allied fortunes on the Western Front were far from brilliant. Zionism appeared to be a hazardous liability in the East. The conclusion of his intelligence report of early March 1918 might have been written by an Allied political agent worried over Arab defection to the enemy in either the First or the Second World War. Yale posed the dilemma of the Allies in blunt terms: "The Zionist policy is detested by Christian and Moslem alike, and Moslem fanaticism is being greatly stirred by it; the Allies must judge whether they can afford to alienate the Arabs and risk turning the entire Moslem world against them for the sake of the Zionists."

An interview with Lawrence somewhat allayed Yale's fears, stirred by the Syrian exiles, of an immediate Arab reversal of policy, but it confirmed his original judgment about the military risks of the Zionist policy. In a sense Yale's intelligence reports during this period became a mouthpiece for the Arabophile British officers working out of the Cairo Bureau who were also obsessed with the possibility of an Arab desertion of the Allied cause. They saw all their labors in the Near East annulled by a diplomatic decision in London in favor of a few thousand Jewish religiasts in the old settlement and a handful of Jewish agricultural colonists from eastern Europe. To the British military in the Near East Zionism was a political scheme hatched in London which was an immediate liability on the war front. This antagonism to a Zionist policy which may have had some basis in the spring of 1918 was later carried over into the post-war period and was nurtured by arguments which no longer had validity.

In his conversation with Yale, Lawrence pronounced a eulogy on the loyalty of the Arab tribes and expressed his distress at the recent pro-Zionist policy. Balfour in London was Foreign Minister; but Lawrence was directing a war of his own in Arabia and Yale was a good pipe-line to the United States if he needed aid for his private struggle with Downing Street policy-makers. Lawrence told Yale that the Arabs no longer had any faith in the word of England and France and that they now believed they would possess only such territory as they were able to secure by force of arms. As for the Zionist Movement, he stated flatly that if it were announced that a Jewish State and

Government were to be established in Palestine the Arab Movement would collapse. Lawrence expressed the hope that Emir Feisal would soon make a triumphal entry into Jerusalem, after a successful advance by the Arabs east of the Dead Sea, when a juncture with the British right flank would be effected. He expected that such an event would have a beneficial influence on the Moslems of Palestine who had been stunned by recent events and were confused by the policy of the British towards the Zionists. Lawrence considered the activities permitted the Zionists in Egypt and in Palestine foolhardy. With his typical abandon he told Yale: "I suppose that *we* are supporting the Zionists for the help it was thought that they could be to us in Russia and because they brought America into the war."

In contrast with their disillusionment with the Allies, Lawrence declared that the Arabs had great faith in the United States and believed in America's political honesty. He broached the idea of American intervention: "If things should not turn out as well as is expected, and if there should be an imminent danger of the disaffection of the Arabs, a declaration by the United States concerning the future of the Arabs and their country would prove to be a 'trump card' to play against the Turkish-German propaganda, and he feels that such a declaration would have an enormous effect upon the Arabs." Weizmann's description of Lawrence's "positive" attitude on Zionism in his recent autobiography is to say the least unknowing as far as the war period is concerned. In later years Lawrence did utter a number of highly flattering remarks about the President of the World Zionist Organization.

Though Lawrence convinced Yale that for the time being the Syrians' estimate of the situation was exaggerated, he only reinforced his previous misgivings about the establishment of a Jewish State. "If a Jewish State is to be created in Palestine it will have to be done by force of arms and maintained by force of arms amid an overwhelmingly hostile population," was Yale's summary conclusion. He saw no advantage in preserving the ambiguity of Britain's Zionist pronouncements; he "respectfully submitted that it would be wisest to state plainly what their policy was."

THE WEIZMANN COMMISSION

The Zionist Commission under Weizmann, created in the spring of 1918, was apparently an attempt of Balfour's Foreign Office and

Mark Sykes to remedy the disaffection of the Arabs which Yale and British officers had been reporting and perhaps exaggerating. The Commission was hardly likely to be received enthusiastically by the Arabs. But if Yale is an accurate observer, Weizmann's conduct throughout was diplomatic and skillful. It even somewhat softened Yale's antagonism to the Zionists.

When the Zionist Commission—which had been denied official American participation by Lansing—reached Cairo in March 1918, Yale met Walter Meyer, Weizmann's American "assistant," who arranged conversations for him with the chief members of the group. It had been Yale's original intention to visit Emir Feisal's headquarters at Akabah at this time, but he considered the political importance of the Weizmann mission paramount and made efforts to obtain permission from the British to be in Palestine with the Commission. His request was referred to General Allenby, but at this point the British temporized, explaining that representatives of other nations —by which they meant the French—had already been refused permission, hence the presence of an American would be embarrassing.

The Weizmann Commission's work had been described to Yale as the organization of relief in Palestine, the study of its economic potentialities, and the laying of the groundwork for future immigration. Yale was more interested in the political role of the group than in its social and economic functions. He knew that Weizmann, before his departure, had been instructed in London by high Empire authorities, among them General Smuts, to adopt a conciliatory attitude towards the Arabs. Weizmann himself told Yale that Sir Reginald Wingate, the British High Commissioner in Cairo, had advised tact and diplomacy in dealing with the Arabs. Yale was convinced that it was Weizmann's purpose "to meet the Arabs half way" and to win their confidence.

During their interview Weizmann was profuse with generalities about the Zionists coming to help in the development of the country with no designs or intentions against the Arab inhabitants of Palestine. Walter Meyer the "assistant" was more frank, if more clumsy. He indicated that the Zionist Commission would assure the Arabs that no Jewish government would be imposed upon them "at the present time," but no commitments would be made for the future which might restrict Jewish rights under the Balfour Declaration. Meyer explained that the Zionists could not afford to discourage Jewish immigration by conceding that Palestine would not be established eventually as a Jewish state; their strongest appeal to the Jewish people would thus be lost.

Yale detected a certain divergence of opinion among members of the Commission over the Arab problem. One group considered cheap Arab labor indispensable to the growth and progress of Palestine; another believed that the Arabs would be a hindrance. In this connection he recalled Israel Zangwill's proposal to transfer the native population of Palestine to the vast region east of the Jordan.

Weizmann did not conceal from Yale his suspicions of the French and their ambition to maintain their traditional role in Palestine and Syria as the protecting power of all Catholics in the Orient; Yale remarked upon the similarity of Weizmann's views and the British position.

Yale was hopeful that the Commission might be able to ease the political tension among the Arabs and dissipate their growing resentment against the Allies, at least temporarily, so that their hostility would not exert a detrimental effect upon the military situation in Palestine. In long terms, however, he remained profoundly pessimistic of any entente between Zionism and the Arabs. "It cannot be expected," he wrote, "that two such forces, two such conflicting ideals, as Jewish Nationalism and Arab Nationalism, a militant Judaism and a fanatical Islamism, can meet on common ground in dispute between them, namely Palestine, without future friction and unpleasantness. The Zionist ideal embraces the aspiration of a Jewish State and the absorption of Palestine; nascent Arab Nationalism but recently awakened and stimulated by the events of this war is yet incoherent in its aims and ambitions, still it exists today as a force in the East without a definite direction." Yale was of the opinion that the apparent acquiescence of the King of the Hedjaz and his son Emil Feisal in the British Zionist policy gave both the Jews and the British an unwarranted sense of security. Houssein was completely tied to the British by bonds of a monthly subsidy and he had burned his bridges behind him in a revolt against the Moslem Caliph, the Sultan of Turkey. The other Sheikhs in Arabia and the Arabs in Syria had not accepted his policy on Zionism and he could not be considered representative of their sentiments. The ultimate effectiveness of the King of the Hedjaz in quieting the agitation against Zionism was dependent upon the fortunes of the military drive of General Allenby's troops and Emir Feisal's forces. But the successful northward movement of the troops would engender new political dangers, Yale feared, for as the

Syrians were liberated they would become articulate about the disposition of the whole region, and the French—in the sphere of influence laid out for them—would arrive to complicate the political-military situation. The hour of decision was approaching: "Up until the present time the discussions concerning the future of Palestine were of an academic nature; but the situation is now entering upon a new phase, the King of the Hedjaz will soon be no longer content with vague promises, the Zionists will demand something more real than declarations, the Syrians with the force of a large population behind them will not so complacently accept to be now caressed and cajolled, now threatened and frightened, the Moslem Syrians will become more bitter in their opposition to French occupation as it becomes more inevitable, the French whose jealousies have already been aroused by conditions in Palestine, will become more insistent in asserting their rights."

In April 1918, Yale sent the Department his report on the political implications of the successful military operations completed in Palestine. He detailed several versions of the ambitions of the King of the Hedjaz and his sons in Syria and Arabia, who "it can be very well understood . . . are not waging war for '*les beaux yeux*' of the British," but he was not certain of the specific intent of the British in nursing them along. Was it to spur Feisal to more aggressive military action or were they seeking an excuse to keep the French out of Syria? At the same time Yale got the impression—the same one reported by other American representatives in Cairo and London when their British interlocutors were dropping "personal," so-called unofficial hints—that the British were anxious for the United States to assume a greater interest in Syrian-Arab affairs. Yale reasoned: "Britain would prefer that the Government of the United States assume the unpleasant task of curtailing French ambitions in Syria."

After describing the military activities of the sons of the King of the Hedjaz and foretelling the impending destruction of Ottoman power, Yale turned to the specific situation in Palestine. From the letters of Jerusalem Moslems to Syrians in Cairo he deduced an increasing undercurrent of discontent. This was confirmed by the *Arab Bulletin* of the Cairo Arab Bureau, which made little attempt to conceal its discomfiture with the official Zionist policy of the British government, which, the *Bulletin* noted, greatly hampered relations with the non-Jewish inhabitants of Palestine. In the existence of a pro-Turkish party among the city Arabs in Palestine Yale saw indication of the depth of their anti-Zionist feeling. He mentioned the formation of a committee of Moslems and Christians in Jaffa to protect themselves "against the possible aggression of the Jews." He learned of the attempt of the Zionists Hoofien and Thorn [Thon] to establish a central council of Jews at Jerusalem and the difficulties created for them by the rivalries of the Ashkenazic and Sephardic communities, especially over Sephardic participation in *Haluka* money sent from Ashkenazic communities in Europe and America. It was one of Yale's great virtues as a political observer that while he had a sharp eye and a long memory for detail and reported it meticulously, he never allowed it to obscure his vision of the main lines of development into the future. Through all the confusion of events and personalities of Near Eastern politics, he clearly foresaw a polarization of all groups and the emergence of one basic conflict between Jews and non-Jews: "The Jewish factions would end their rivalries and the Christians and Moslems would find common interests to unite them."

In Cairo Weizmann met with the Syrian representatives and gave specific assurances on all issues which were troubling them; he told them to have no fear of the establishment of a Jewish Government or anxiety about the Holy Places; talked of an intellectual home for Jews; quieted their misgivings over large land purchases by announcing that he himself had requested Balfour to suspend the buying and selling of land until the end of the war. The Syrians in their turn suggested that there be proportionate representation of Jews, Christians and Moslems in the future government and an extra-governmental council to settle their differences. Ormsby-Gore, a British member of the Commission, was cold to this latter proposal because it might tend to usurp governmental functions.

The Syrians asked for laws to protect small fellaheen holdings from seizure for debt and for the establishment of an Agricultural Bank, and proposed that the great uninhabited tracts of Palestine be put up for sale to Jews. When the Syrians complained of Jewish clannishness in trade and commerce, Aaron Aaronsohn, now a member of the Commission, apparently forgetting the conciliatory role of the group, vociferously branded such accusations as lies. The Syrians replied that irrespective of the facts, Arabs believed that Jewish exclusiveness was a reality and the Zionist Commission, if it were sincere, should combat that sentiment by a contrary policy. On the whole, Yale thought, the conferences were a success from the point of view of achieving an overt conciliation and he remarked on the fact that after Aaronsohn's impulsive outburst Weizmann shoved him into the background.

The exiled Syrian leaders whom Weizmann saw in Cairo, however, could have little influence on the feelings of the Palestinian Arabs. It was Yale's impression that Palestinian Arabs, with years of training in dissimulation before masters, would, after the manner of the Syrians in Cairo, conceal their true feelings from the Zionist Commission when it arrived, in view of its official status.

Yale sent to Washington confidential excerpts from the *Arab Bulletin*. This was what the British Arab Bureau wanted their officers to believe as official policy—a very diluted interpretation of the Balfour Declaration. The *Bulletin* expressed the hope that Arab apprehensions at the arrival of the Zionist Commission would be allayed by an immediate announcement of the purposes of the Commission, "which is understood to be opposed both to expropriation or exploitation of existing land-owners and also to any Jewish political control of Palestine. For the very moderate number of Jews expected to desire to settle there, it is considered that the almost derelict crown lands and unappropriated marshy and sandy areas will provide ample scope."

In propaganda for the creation of an Arab Empire under a Caliph —including Syria—Yale saw the hand of the British, who were willing to risk alienating the Christian Syrians in the process, because in this way the anti-French aspect of the movement would stand out in sharp relief; the Christian Syrians in their fear of a great Moslem overlordship would have only the French as their protectors. In the fact that Palestine was excluded from this pan-Arab propaganda emanating from Egypt, he recognized another mark of British manoeuvering. There were times when Yale accepted the handouts of the officers in the Arab Bureau at their face value, but he was by no means a British instrument. He could deliver himself of truly magnificent presentations of the scope of British imperial ambitions in the Near East, and there is evidence that at one time his analyses exercised considerable influence on those Peace Commissioners who read his reports.

Yale still saw in Anglo-French rivalry the key to oriental politics, and he knew how to appraise the bizarre alignments and the sacred principles in whose name they were created. "With southern Mesopotamia in their hands; with Palestine under their control and the prospect of an increasing pro-British Jewish population; with a predominating influence along the coast of Arabia at Bassorah, at Koweit, in Hasa, in the Sultanat of Oman and in Hadhramat; with control over the British Protectorate of Aden; with closer relations with the

Idrissi in Asir; with powerful influence over the King of the Hedjaz and with treaties with other Arabian Sheikhs; it can very well be that the British may be opposed to another European Power driving a wedge between Mesopotamia and India in the East and Palestine and Egypt in the West; and such a wedge Syria would be. And it might be supposed that Great Britain would not relish a European power holding Aleppo and Damascus, the northern gates of Arabia and the western gates of Mesopotamia and Persia. And it is quite possible that British statesmen would prefer to see Syria and northern Mesopotamia in the hands of the King of the Hedjaz under an inefficient and backward Oriental Government over which they, the British, would inevitably come to exert an ever increasing influence rather than to see a progressive Syria under the influence of some European rival for colonial power and commerce. . . . One cannot help but feel that the fundamental factor in Oriental politics at present is the rivalry of France and Great Britain, and that the Zionists, the Lebanese, the Druzes, the Christians and the Moslems, the Cherif of Mecca and his son Emir Feisal are but pawns in the game, which these two great Powers move to suit themselves with due caution, however, not to offend if possible the sensibilities of their own people respectively and those of the United States in regard to the free development of small races and nationalities and in regard to colonial expansion."

While Yale was still being kept in Cairo with no reply on this request to visit Palestine or on his proposed cover-job as a relief worker there, he drafted a comprehensive and incisive statement on the history of Zionism and modern Palestine, with a reasonable insight into the forces at play among the Jews of the world. He described Zionism stripped of the emotional phraseology of the orators. He had established relations with members of the Jewish community in Alexandria, including the bitter anti-Zionist Miss Landau, who had so roundly denounced Aaron Aaronsohn to Yale. Yale's conclusion allowed for the rights of Jewish settlement in Palestine, but ruled out any proclamation of a Jewish state at that time.

To Yale it was clear that no matter what the Powers of the world ordained, a Jewish State would be a fiction until the Jews actually colonized Palestine with hundreds of thousands of immigrants and transformed it from the Arab country which it predominantly was in 1918. He believed, further, that it was an act of injustice to impose a Jewish state upon a recalcitrant native population until the Jews proved that Zionism was more to them than a distant ideal. Thus he felt that for the present the Jews should demand only the right to immigrate freely, to settle and acquire land, and to be protected in their rights.

In April 1918 the British in Cairo were once more sounding out American diplomatic agents on the prospect of American participation in governing Palestine. This was a fixed idea of Balfour's foreign policy in the Near East, one to which he reverted again and again despite the coolness of both the Zionists and the State Department. Yale's explanation that it was a means of saddling the United States with the burden of handling the obstreperous French bears credence. Whatever the motives, it was no casual idea of a lone British official in a distant outpost, but a fullfledged offensive that sometimes perplexed Americans to whom it was broached. Our own unresponsiveness only encouraged the British to give us less and less veiled hints. On April 25, 1918, Hampton Gary in Cairo reported the latest of these suggestions. "During the course of several conversations I have had with Sir Reginald Wingate, the British High Commissioner for Egypt, I have been impressed by the fact that he has repeatedly endeavored to draw my attention to the Palestine situation and has pointedly raised the question of the United States 'taking a hand there.' He thinks that it would be fortunate for the people of Palestine if America became the guiding power there, and that it would be agreeable to the powers and prove effective in keeping them on friendly terms among themselves.

"Whether the High Commissioner was simply expressing his own personal views (he said, of course, that he was not speaking officially) or reflecting the wishes of London is uncertain, but he has given me the distinct impression that the British would look with favor upon the establishment after the war of what would amount to an American protectorate over the government to be set up in Palestine."

William Yale sent the Department the full text of Weizmann's speech at a state dinner in Jerusalem, a speech replete with subtle policy nuances. Yale drew from the elegant phrases of the Zionist leader a number of hard propositions: 1. Weizmann's opposition to internationalization or multiple control over Palestine, in favor of one civilized democracy chosen by the League of Nations; 2. the announcement that the Jews would postpone the declaration of their choice until after the war; 3. the stiffening of Weizmann's policy of conciliation towards the Arabs with the warning that "the Jewish communities of the West are not without influence in the councils of the nations." Yale noted also that Georges Picot, the French High Commissioner in Palestine, was not present at the dinner and that Weizmann described the gathering as under the wing of "the mightiest of the world's powers."

Despite the misgivings of the more suspicious members of the Arab Bureau, a delegation of Cairo Syrians was allowed to visit Palestine on the heels of the Weizmann Commission. Ostensibly they were being sent by British Intelligence for the express purpose of persuading the Palestinian Arabs to a compromise with the Zionists. Yale's report on their mission was not encouraging. The fears of the Arab notables in Palestine were not allayed and a rather harmless phrase in a speech by Weizmann had been misinterpreted as a dire threat.

Yale continued to report at length all the Arab complaints transmitted to the Cairo Syrians about the arrogant behavior of the Zionist minority in Palestine. Critical Jewish historians have since commented on the pretentiousness of some of the Zionist leaders in the early months of the British occupation; they were somehow possessed with the notion that the Jewish State was already a reality and that the transfer of the administration from the British to the Jews was only a matter of time. It was the standard technique of the Arabs and the British officials on the spot, who fundamentally considered Zionism a "bluff," to parade the fantasies of these Jewish extremists as basic Zionist policy. Yale made himself a party to the Arabophile sentiments and moralized about the evils of the Zionists. He warned that if the Zionists failed to use restraint in exercising their newly-won power they would arouse formidable forces in Christendom and in Islam against them, and that unless the Powers curbed the fanaticism and intolerance of the Jewish nationalists they would be "nursing trouble for the future."

In one report he delivered himself of a long excursus on the psychological characteristics inevitably acquired by an oppressed people and retained in the early years of their emancipation. At this time he was under the impression that the British Foreign Office policy in Palestine favored complete Jewish control, and he was apprehensive lest governance be entrusted to intolerant orthodox Jews or fierce Jewish nationalists from eastern Europe. "The Judaism of many of the orthodox Jews of Eastern Europe is as intolerant as the Islamism of the fanatical Moslems, as the Christianity of the Middle Ages, and as the Puritanism of the seventeenth century. And the nationalism of many of the enthusiasts among the Eastern European Jews is tinged with wild socialistic and anarchistic ideas and a fierce chauvinism.

"These two elements, the nationalist and orthodox Jews of Eastern Europe, are almost certain to play an important role in the Zionist drama now developing in Palestine; and if these elements are not held in a tight rein by the World Powers not only will Zionism run great danger of arousing a world-wide movement against it but also the powers will risk incurring a far more serious post-bellum problem to deal with than perhaps is contemplated."

When Dr. Weizmann and members of the Zionist Commission returned to Egypt for a short visit in June, Yale again interviewed Walter Meyer, the American "assistant" who, though not particularly perspicacious himself, was regarded by Yale as an adequate mouthpiece for the judgments and decisions of his superiors. From him Yale learned what he believed was the new public position of the Zionists with respect to the government of Palestine. "Mr. Meyer said that the situation had entirely changed . . . and that the Zionists did not wish, *certainly not at the present time,* an independent Jewish State in Palestine."

On Arab-Jewish relations Meyer was ignorant, indifferent, and crassly arrogant in a manner which must have irritated Yale, who for all his realism about the tawdry power politics of the Near East was a confirmed believer in the Wilsonian rights of all peoples. "Mr. Meyer said that as in the south the white population would never submit to a domination by the negroes, so a Jewish minority in Palestine would never submit to a domination by an Arab majority. . . . In answer to a question as to what he thought of the outline of the conditions to exist between Jews and Arabs as given in the program submitted to the Zionists Commission by a certain Syrian Committee Mr. Meyer said that he had heard no further talk of this proposed program, and that he considered them as being more or less ridiculous propositions made by individuals, who represented nobody in particular, and who only wished to arouse discussion and make difficulties; he did not consider that they should be taken seriously.

"In regard to Arab personalities in Palestine, Mr. Meyer said that he had only met the Mufti of Jerusalem (who does not speak either English or French) ; but that he did not have much use for any of them."

Meyer said that the Jews would be able to live in harmony with the fellaheen, whose labor they would use, but not with the land-owners

who oppressed the fellaheen. He thought a million Jews could readily be supported in Palestine.

On the question of a protectorate over Palestine, Meyer expressed
the Weizmann policy pure and simple. He regarded internationalization or dual control as detrimental to Zionist interests, but he was
careful to express no preference as to which country should be entrusted with Palestine. Both Meyer and Cowen (a British member
of the Commission, a long-time Zionist who had been one of Herzl's
agents during the El Arish negotiations with Chamberlain) were critical of the fact that the British military had in their administration
preserved the same group of "crooks" who had been in control under
the Turks because of the Hague Convention with respect to civil
administration in conquered enemy territory.

Meyer expressed the opinion that the United States should declare
war on Turkey, an act which would aid the British in maintaining
control over the Arabs. Yale took special note of this remark and in a
detailed analysis of both sides of the issue advised strongly against
any such course. In the early stages of the war, Yale reasoned, the
Allied offensive was primarily military, aimed at crushing Turkey and
destroying German power in the Orient. This had changed completely.
The purpose of the Allies was now political, to wrest from the Turks
those parts of the Ottoman Empire which they had come to consider
their respective zones of influence: Syria, Palestine and Mesopotamia.
If the United States declared war on Turkey, it might eventually find
itself embroiled with its own Allies. "The peoples of the Ottoman
Empire look to the United States not only to deliver them from
Turkish oppression, but also to protect them from the aggression of
European powers after the war. Thus, in declaring war against Turkey, the United States would be morally assuming such obligations
towards these peoples."

THE NEAR EAST COCKPIT

In June 1918 Yale got himself attached to Allenby's army and many
of his reports during the final drive northward were of a purely military character, but in the fall he resumed his political analyses. His
intelligence on Palestine was no longer second-hand, based on talks
with Cairo Jews, Syrians in exile, and British officers. Now he had
been in the field, had become intimate with the military commanders,
had seen the Jewish settlements again, and had spoken with the Pal-

estinian Arabs. After viewing the scene, he tended to deflate the contribution of the Arab revolt to the final victory, although he never demeaned the personal achievement of Lawrence with the meager forces at his disposal. His doubts about the expansive Jewish nationalism of the Zionists persisted; now he had become equally skeptical about the wisdom of creating a great Arab state.

In September 1918, Yale sent a report entitled *Recent Political Events among the Arabs* which analyzed the main currents of internecine Arab quarrels in Asia Minor. The British manoeuvring with the King of the Hedjaz in the east and Ibn Saud in the west of Arabia had been disrupted by a clash between the rival Arab forces at Taif. Yale, impressed with the religious drive of Ibn Saud's Wahabis, bestowed on his movement greater long term influence than on what he considered the "artificial" uprising of the Hedjaz Cherif, which, he predicted, would collapse immediately upon the withdrawal of British gold. Yale was cognizant also of reported contacts between Feisal and the Turks, and expressed the view that his brother Abdullah— today King of Transjordan—was far more concerned about his struggle with Ibn Saud than about driving the Turks out of Medina. Yale denigrated the capacity of the Arabs to make war: "It would appear from the remark of Jaafar Pasha [one of Feisal's commanders] that the trained force under Emir Feisal does not exceed 2,000 men."

The Syrians were reluctant to accept the rule of a desert chieftain whom they considered a barbarian, and cruel pronouncements from the Hedjaz that the Syrians would be forced by the sword were repugnant to Yale, who wrote: "Should Syria be ruled over by the King of the Hedjaz and should it form part of an Arab Empire, its inhabitants would probably suffer under a worse government and a more oppressive tyranny than under the Turks." These reports from Yale were the basis for the opposition to hegemony of the Hedjaz King over a great Arab State in the first proposals to the American Peace Commission at Paris by the group's Intelligence Division in January 1919. This was before Feisal's magnificence had captivated Lansing and the American Near East missionaries had chosen their man. At the Paris Peace Conference, it will be seen, Feisal swept Lansing and his aides off their feet with the bold affirmation that 100,000 men had joined in his revolt, every man who got a gun; Yale, our special agent in the field, had estimated this glorious insurgent army at 2,000.

A Yale memorandum of this period entitled *Political Situation in the Arab Provinces of the Ottoman Empire,* is a brilliant political and ethnic survey of the whole region. He depicted the inhabitants of Jerusalem in all their ugliness—his disgust was a sentiment he held in common with men as diverse as Herzl, Lawrence, and Weizmann. No admirer of organized religious bodies (which helps explain his later divergence from the heads of the King-Crane Commission, who were imbued with a missionary zeal), he excoriated both Jews and Christians alike for living off the bounty and charity of their co-religionists in other countries and exploiting religious pilgrims who came to the Holy City. As for the relationships among the three religious groups, he observed that the Moslems were inclined to be tolerant towards the Christians and the foreigners, but blind in their hatred of the Jews, in which they were joined by most of the Christians.

Yale did not believe in the existence of a greater Syrian nationality covering the whole of the area from Rafa to the Gulf of Alexandretta and he recognized the distinctness of the Palestine area. He was opposed, however, to the Zionist attempt to include a great area of Transjordania within the boundaries of Palestine, since its inhabitants, with the exception of a few Circassians, were purely Arab. He found no reason to alter his earlier judgment, written in Cairo, on the profundity of Arab-Jewish hostility: "The feeling between the Arabs and the Jews in Palestine cannot be much bettered by speeches and declarations."

While the interest of the top-flight American policy makers was absorbed primarily in the European settlement, he tried to direct attention to the decisions of the Near East. Yale feared the consequences of creating in that area two governments, an Arab Empire in Syria and Mesopotamia and a Jewish State in Palestine, which would be based essentially on religion and would tend to intensify the solidarity of the Moslems and of the Jews in all countries. "The Western World," he wrote, "cannot afford to give its support to two such formidable movements for sentimental reasons, or small political reasons. Should such a step be contemplated the deep significance for the future must be taken into consideration. To make a mistake in the Near Eastern policy would be deplorable; but to allow any small political influence to affect a just settlement of the Near Eastern Problem would be criminal."

After his trip to Palestine, Yale was more than ever convinced of the hostility towards Zionists harbored by Moslems, Christians, and many British military authorities. The Arabs resented the employment of Jews in the administration, the use of Cairo Jewish lawyers to reorganize the judiciary; the soldiers and officers of the British forces were increasingly resentful of the "arrogance of the Jews." His reflections on the attitude of the British military were similar to the opinions expressed by Weizmann in long letters to Brandeis and Balfour in the summer of 1918.

As the months wore on Yale grew increasingly certain about the underlying egotism of British and French Near Eastern policy, and he stated his convictions without mincing words, with a measure of righteous indignation. On December 16, 1918, on the eve of the Peace Conference he wrote: "In plain English, in spite of a widespread camouflage propaganda in regard to the liberation of oppressed races and the rights of small nations, the British and the French are thinking and working only for their own interests in the Near East."

His picture of Palestinian and Near Eastern politics at this period is tinged with a moral repugnance—almost Wilsonian in temper—for the dishonesty and the undercover intrigues that characterized all the principal actors. The Arabs and Christians were bitter against the Zionists and although a strong military government prohibited them from protesting too vocally to the world, they were organizing to resist the policy of a Jewish National Homeland in Palestine. Despite the public love-feast of Weizmann and Feisal at Akabah, the Emir had hired paid agents to stir up bitterness against the British and the Jews in secret and to arouse enthusiasm for the Cherifian Party and the independent Arab Empire. As Yale pointed out, the Arabs of Palestine needed no prodding to oppose Zionism, but the Cherifians were trying to make political capital out of this hatred and win adherents for their own imperial scheme. ". . . In all three Zones, British, French and Cherifian, propaganda is being quietly and more or less secretly carried on against one another."

These Yale memoranda were a realistic set of field reports, written in a tone which sounded decidedly inauspicious for the forthcoming Near East settlement in Paris.

Chapter VI

IN THE CRUCIBLE OF THE PEACE CONFERENCE

THE PITTSBURGH PROGRAM

In June 1918, after the deliberate silence of the early war years, American Zionists held a general convention in Pittsburgh, the city where many minority groups met to formulate programs of national reconstruction for post-war Europe. At this convention Justice Brandeis emerged the unchallenged leader, even though he did not accept the active presidency of the organization; the old stalwarts repressed whatever annoyance they felt at finding themselves superseded. Brandeis himself is reputed to be the author of the brief statement of principles for Zionist action in Palestine which became known as the Pittsburgh Program. Its concise, sharp language bears the earmarks of his style; the advocacy of public ownership and control in the Jewish homeland was similar to the policy he had urged on President Wilson for the United States in the first years of the new administration.

After a short preamble of standard Zionist phraseology, the Pittsburgh Program read:

"First: We declare for political and civil equality irrespective of race, sex, or faith of all the inhabitants of the land.

"Second: To insure in the Jewish National Home in Palestine equality of opportunity we favor a policy which, with regard to existing rights, shall tend to establish the ownership and control by the whole people of the land, of all natural resources and of all public utilities.

"Third: All land, owned and controlled by the whole people, should be leased on such conditions as will insure the fullest opportunity for development and continuity of possession.

"Fourth: The cooperative principle should be applied so far as feasible in the organization of all agricultural, industrial, commercial and financial undertakings.

"Fifth: The system of free public instruction which is to be established should embrace all grades and departments of education."

Such doctrines were a distinct departure from the main currents of European Zionism. There was a left wing in the international Zionist movement based on moderate labor socialism, but before the First World War it was not a weighty faction in World Zionist councils. To the extent that the Jewish working class in Europe was active politically, it spent its vigor in the socialist and revolutionary organizations of Russia and Poland; political Zionism, for the most part dominated by middle and upper class Jews, was often posed as a counterbalance in Jewish life to socialist and communist revolutionary influences. Whenever they allowed general social problems to enter their councils, the social theories of the dominant European Zionists tended to be conservative and *bourgeois*.

The Brandeis conception of the modern state at war with trusts and monopoly was rooted in purely American notions of crusading democracy and had little relationship with European ideologies of the class-struggle. His proposals as formulated in Pittsburgh sounded alien and queer to the bankers and middle-class intellectuals who, *inter alia*, were espousing Zionism as a nationalist alternative to destructive revolutionary tendencies among the Jews. The leaders of European Zionism read the principles of the Pittsburgh Program in the light of European class conflicts and the dominant ideas of the Allied Powers in post-war revolutionary Europe. Men like Weizmann doubted their propriety altogether and preferred to fight for the rights of the Jewish nation without direct reference to social doctrines or, at best, with perfunctory oratorical allusions to the idea of Justice as embodied in the Books of the Prophets.

Many of the formulae of the Pittsburgh Program crop up again and again in the successive drafts which the Zionists prepared for the British mandate; but as the terror of Bolshevism spread over Europe and gripped the British Empire these words, which sounded rather "social democratic" in June 1918, became far too dangerous for incorporation into any formal political instrument. Only a faint echo is found in the final text of the British mandate accepted by the League of Nations.

AMERICAN AND EUROPEAN ZIONISTS

In the fall of 1918, while the American Delegation to the Peace Conference was assembling its staff, the American Zionists conducted a thorough preliminary campaign of "predisposing" members of the delegation to the Zionist program. Their leaders arranged interviews with anyone who, they imagined, might be consulted on Near Eastern affairs. A group of striking figures surrounded Justice Brandeis in the ranks of American Zionism: there was Felix Frankfurter, then a professor of law, in all the alert brilliance of his early thirties, who had been one of the legal lights in the War Department and had wrestled with special problems in labor relations and international politics for the President; Judge Mack, president of the Zionist Organization of America and a respected member of the judiciary; Rabbi Stephen S. Wise, the tribune, who could sway an audience of Jews or a Democratic Party rally with his grandiloquence and sheer lung power; there were also young men in their twenties, among them Horace Kallen and Benjamin V. Cohen, the future braintruster of the New Deal and Byrnes's Counsellor in the State Department. As a group they stood nearer to the source of political power in their country than any other national Zionist organization in the world.

In addition to approaching the members of the American Commission to Negotiate the Peace, the Zionists associated themselves with the aspirations of all the subject European nationalities who were clamoring for independence. They even met with them in a conference of subject minorities awaiting liberation. If the other small nations were allowed to emerge, the Jews too might hope for recognition. At the same time, the Zionists were vigilant over every manoeuvre of Arab or Syrian propaganda which sought to engulf their promised strip of land on the Mediterranean in an Arab empire or a Greater Syria. If they had a failing it was their tendency to accept as commitments the polite interest of American officials expressed in conversation.

The first American Zionist delegation sent to Europe consisted of Rabbi Wise, Mrs. Joseph Fels, Bernard Flexner, Louis Robison; later Jacob de Haas, Frankfurter, and Howard Gans were added. In March 1919 they were joined by Judge Mack at the head of a large group representing the American Jewish Congress. In all, the pro-Zionist spokesmen at Paris were numerous and influential. Justice Brandeis stayed at home and directed the delegation from afar through the cables of the American embassies in London and Paris, the only means of fast communication, until he was summoned during the crisis of June 1919.

The Jews of the world were torn by internal conflicts which reduced their total power in presenting any case before the Great Nations. In this their fate was not unique; all the new nationalities of central Europe and Asia Minor, in the first stages of their independence movements, spawned a host of minor party groupings which often paralyzed their capacity for action as a cohesive national unit. With violence and persistence the parties were locked in deadly embrace over seemingly insignificant side issues, whose solution one way or another was of far less moment than the squandering of their energies on the disputes. The Jews, a people dispersed among all other peoples, could in the nature of things find even more ground for internecine strife than a compact new nationality which had been granted a slice of territory from off the carcass of a dead empire. To non-Jews they were all Jews, identifiable people who aroused in them varying reactions; the Jews of the various countries of the world, however, considered themselves markedly different from one another and there were complicated gradations of snobbery among them of which non-Jews were not often aware.

In the nineteenth and early twentieth centuries French, English, and German Jewish bankers had been the official protectors of the Jews of eastern Europe. They had organized systems of philanthropy, had sponsored propaganda in defense of the Jews, had provided for migration and settlement of persecuted Jews both in the Americas and in Palestine. They regarded the Jews of the Russian pale as their wards and they expected their advice to be followed in the councils of world Jewry. The Jewish intellectuals from eastern Europe considered themselves the soul of Jewry in contrast to the money bags of Paris, London, and Berlin and, as is usual in such relationships, there was a hidden resentment against the philanthropists who doled out the charities and imagined that by virtue of the power of the purse they were the men to decide what was good for Israel.

At Paris in 1919 the balance of world power was shifted across the Atlantic. With President Wilson in the Peace Conference chair, American Jews assumed primacy among world Jewry. This development did not take place without some dissatisfaction on the part of those groups who were losing power and its tokens of pre-eminence. English Jews accepted American leadership with the feeling that the men from across the sea were still raw in the ways of diplomacy, inept in the art of protecting the Jews and winning concessions for them from potentates. Russian-born intellectuals who had migrated to the west and were among the leaders of world Zionism partook of this same sentiment. The German and Austrian Jews, defeated with their Kaiser, had to withdraw from the limelight and wait, though they were soon invited back into Zionist councils to join a European front against the Americans. Eastern European Jews, caught in the turmoil of postwar pogroms and revolutions, were the objects of charity whose opinions on their own salvation were considered in the west to be merely a patient's description of his symptoms.

Before the American Zionist delegates could set themselves up in Paris to influence the Allied and Associated Powers, they had to have some understanding with the European Zionists. London was the meeting place for scores of conferences. On December 20, 1918, Rabbi Stephen Wise, first leader of the American group, sent Brandeis a cable which summarized the status of negotiations with Weizmann who headed the Europeans and until then had been the liaison with the British Foreign Office. Tentative political proposals for Palestine had been prepared by the Europeans for submission to the British Government and the Peace Conference; the Americans had suggested modifications and Rabbi Wise promised that he would send Brandeis the draft they had finally agreed upon. A member of the American group, Bernard Flexner, had been set to work on immediate and long term fiscal problems of the Jewish homeland.

These meetings of the American, the British and a few Russian Zionists were somewhat irregular in terms of the formal Executive of the World Zionist Congress last chosen at Vienna in 1913, where the Germans and Austrians had been the dominant group, but the American and British governments were the real forces at the Conference and their Zionists had *de facto* control. Dr. Wolfsohn and Dr. Tschlenow, two presidents of the World Zionist Organization, had died in succession during the war years and there was an executive vacuum. "Certain extra-legal measures necessary reorganization counting upon later ratification by congress," cabled Rabbi Wise. Hantke and Warburg, the leaders of German Zionism, as was fitting for the representatives of a defeated power, had agreed in writing to ratify any decisions which the London group might make; they gave them their *pleins pouvoirs*. It was decided that London would become the center of world Zionism and that the reorganization of the Executive would include Weizmann, two Englishmen, two Americans and a Dutchman as additional members. Rabbi Wise proposed himself and de Haas as proxies *ad interim* for the Americans. Copenhagen, where the Zionist headquarters had settled during the war, was to become a mere branch office. The Americans and Englishmen were coming out for a status in Zionist leadership commensurate with their economic and political support of Palestine during the war.

Near the end of the Wise message to Brandeis appeared a meaningful sentence: "Weizmann will not continue except as chairman." In theory Weizmann's position was as ambiguous as that of any of the Americans for he had not been elected a member of the Zionist Executive. For the time being the Americans were acquiescent though they would come to resent his predominance.

Rabbi Wise was a figure competitive to Weizmann in high diplomatic negotiations. When President Wilson, during his pre-Conference triumphal tour through England, received the freedom of the City of London, Rabbi Wise was in his entourage. The President introduced him to Balfour, and the next day he was invited to tea at Downing Street. There he announced to Balfour that the American Jewish Congress had just opted for a British protectorate. In reply the British Foreign Secretary said to him: "Your people pay us a very great compliment. It means that all Jews who may at any time in the future wish or require to dwell in Palestine shall be free to do so." Rabbi Wise duly noted the promise in his diary and recalled it twenty-six years later in his testimony before the Anglo-American Committee of Inquiry on Palestine, when the doors of the land were shut in the face of post-war Jewish refugees.

The statutes of the International Zionist Organization, a complex formalized structure, provided for the convocation of annual conferences which, though they did not have all the authority of a World Congress, could under emergent circumstances assume similar powers. Such an annual conference was held in London in February and March 1919 during the Peace Negotiations. It was composed of those Zionists from the various countries who somehow managed to make their way to London despite the transportation problem, hence it was not remotely representative. Before this body, the Zionist leaders, shuttling back and forth across the channel, would report their triumphs and their defeats at Paris. The assembly in its turn passed resolutions, many of them utterly preposterous in terms of the manoeuvrings at the Peace Conference.

At the London Conference there were already indications of the conflict between Weizmann and the American Zionists which later tore international Zionism apart. With fantastic irrelevance to the actual drama at the Paris Peace Conference the American and European Zionist lined up on opposite sides of major economic policies for the future homeland in Palestine. The Americans did not accept seats on a reconstituted Zionist Executive headed by Weizmann and all during the Paris negotiations while the American Zionist Delegation cooperated with Weizmann and a group of European Zionists who had been designated as the official delegates of the World Movement, friction between the two groups was evident. It was not until the annual conference in London in February 1920 that the open break between the Weizmann party and the Brandeis party occurred. But signs of the impending schism can be discerned on more than one crucial occasion during the day to day negotiations in Paris.

THE INQUIRY ON ZIONISM

In 1918 an *Inquiry* had been set up by the United States government which prepared detailed political, ethnic, and economic summary analyses of every nook and cranny of the globe. This was to be background material for the great decisions of the Peace Conference. It brought forth impressive collections of memoranda. The idea was novel in European power politics: a world was to be redistributed in accordance with a sort of democratic geopolitics in which the self-determination of peoples was the guiding force. Its naiveté, and sometimes its cant, are now obvious. In almost every borderline area of the world the desires of peoples who could articulate them were contradictory and the appetites of European imperialism were insatiable.

Into the background reports of the *Inquiry* went expressions of all the groups who concerned themselves with the award of Palestine: the American Protestant Missionaries, the Zionists, the Arabs of the desert, the Syrian Arabs of the cities, the British, the French, the Vatican. The *Inquiry* was ultimately merged in the Intelligence Section of the American Commission which was set up in Paris staffed for the most part with historians from the major American universities. The documents of the *Inquiry* were the source material for the diplomatic struggles which were waged at the Conference.

By the end of 1918 about ten papers had been prepared on Palestine and the Arab problem. David Magie wrote a brief one entitled *Palestine;* Lewis B. Paton, a professor of Old Testament exegesis, prepared an extensive compendium, which began with the paleolithic period, on the *Geography, History, Ethnology, Religion, Economics, Domestic Life and Government of the Land of Palestine;* an anonymous writer, a fervid Zionist, drafted an essay on *Palestine and Jewish Nationalism;* Dr. James L. Barton, head of the Near Eastern Missions, though not a member of the *Inquiry,* had his great design included: *Suggested possible form of government for the Area covered by the Ottoman Empire at the Outbreak of the war, exclusive of Arabia, but inclusive of the Trans-Caucasus;* Howard Crosby Butler compiled a *Report on the Proposals for an Independent Arab State or States,* which synthesized William Yale's reports with secondary sources, as did E. H. Byrne's *Report on the Desires of the Syrians;* Oscar J. Campbell prepared a *Report on Zionism* which covered hundreds of pages and literally combed every recent printed source in existence on Zionism, though for live intelligence he too relied almost exclusively on William Yale. Details on economic spheres of interest in the Turkish empire were compiled by Leon Dominian and Oscar J. Campbell. Finally in January 1919, for the files of the American Delegation the Committee of Reference and Counsel of the Foreign Mission Conference of North America contributed an elaborate listing of all Protestant missionary establishments throughout the world along with maps plotting their precise locations; Palestine and the Near East was not the least of their areas of influence.

The Magie report and the essay on *Palestine and Jewish Nationalism* were entirely in the spirit of American Zionism. Of the Palestine boundaries, Magie wrote: "The boundaries of Palestine have varied at different times and under differing circumstances. Within the larger historical limit, the country extended north to the Lebanon and Mt. Hermon; south to the Egyptian border and the gulf of Akabah; west to the Mediterranean and east to the Syrian and Arabian desert. A less extensive Palestine would leave out old Samaria on the north (i.e., giving Haifa to Palestine but little beyond it) and extend to a little beyond Gaza on the south." He included a most complimentary estimate of the Jewish agricultural colonies, their local self-government, universal adult suffrage, tax system, courts of arbitration, central committees of delegates of all the colonies; he praised their schools, agricultural and medical establishments, banks, mutual loan societies, cooperatives, land purchase policy. All this he contrasted with the backwardness of the native Moslem Arabs and the indifference of the Christian Syrians in Palestine. His conclusions were simple and rather optimist: "The demand of the Zionists for a British or American protectorate would meet with a welcome from all classes, and is the only obvious solution." But he warned against immediate

Jewish Statehood. "Neither Christian (Syrian, etc.) nor Moslem (Arab) populations would accommodate themselves readily to a Zionist State at *present*." Magie included in his report a "Short Statement Submitted by Zionist Committee." On the ultimate disposition of Palestine this "Zionist Committee," obviously American, backed up the Weizmann line on the British protectorate. Its emphasis on economic development of Palestine was in harmony with key Brandeis ideas. "Internationalization, neutralization or joint control (Condominium) are all unsatisfactory settlements, either temporarily or permanently.

"The Peace Conference should delegate to *one* power the control of the country; for many reasons this country should be *Great Britain*.

"Until the population shall have reached the stage where autonomous government can safely be exercised, broad and gradually augmented powers should be committed to a public *Jewish chartered Company,* working solely in the public interest. Its primary function should be the development of Palestine agriculturally, industrially, and commercially, as well as administratively, and the settlement therein of the Jewish people."

For the Holy Places common to more than one religion, the "Zionist Committee" advised joint commissions; for the non-Jewish communities they accepted the safeguards of the Balfour Declaration.

Palestine and Jewish Nationalism is a fervent exposition of the unique significance of Palestine to the Jews throughout the world, despite the absence of physical contact with the land. At times this essay indulges in a nationalist *mystique* which is rare among the papers on territorial settlement. "Judaism knows nothing of a 'new Jerusalem' which exists only in Heaven. Judaism spiritualizes the material, but for Judaism to spiritualize is not to dematerialize. The material remains material; but it derives a spiritual value by virtue of its being regarded as the necessary basis of an idea. . . . What Palestine means to the Jews can be understood only in the light of this Jewish attitude to the problem of body and spirit." Apart from the theology, the paper is replete with dithyrambs on Zionism and its prospects. "Among the surprises of the war there is perhaps none more striking than the emergence of Zionism, the Jewish national movement, from comparative obscurity into the sunshine of popular acclamation and international sanction. . . . Now, almost suddenly, all is changed. Thanks to the breadth and sincerity of British statesmanship, to the inherent justice of its own aims, and to the ability with which those

aims have been presented, Zionism has received the official approval
of the British Government—an approval which, in the circumstances
in which it was given, makes the realization of the objects of Zionism
one of the avowed war-aims of the Allied Powers." If this paper was
Zionist propaganda, it was not of the best.

Of a different character were the memoranda which dealt with the
Syrians and the Arabs. Byrne's chapter on the Syrian attitude towards
Zionism is merely a compilation of their hostile expressions from
Yale's reports. Butler's report makes short shrift of the Jews as in-
truders in the interior of Syria, strangers introduced from the out-
side like the Circassians settled by Abdul Hamid.

Campbell's report on Zionism was a comprehensive, workmanlike
job covering every conceivable aspect of the problem. It was at once
a history of world Zionism, a study of the development of the colonies,
a statement of American Zionist policies, and of Arab-Jewish politics
as gleaned from Yale's reports. Campbell tried to be rigidly objective
and not to propose any solutions. If anything, his report tended to
delete the psychological characterizations of Yale's accounts which
were none too complimentary to the Jews on the subject of their
"arrogance" after the issuance of the Balfour Declaration. Campbell
considered Yale's materials an excellent source of information for
conditions in Syria and Arabia and opinion in Cairo, but noted that
he was clearly anti-Zionist.

There were two documents of Protestant missionary origin in the
Inquiry file. Though the overall reports on Zionism tended to omit
American missionary involvement in the Near East, at the Peace Conference representatives of this "interest," who appeared at Paris in
substantial numbers, played a role equivalent in strength to the Zionists in vying for the favor of the American delegation. In their January 1919 presentation of Protestant missions throughout the world
little Palestine had seventeen stations, many with more than one
establishment. Dr. James Barton of Boston, head of Near Eastern
Missions, had a grand plan for Turkish dominions exclusive of Arabia.
While it was not noticed at first, his memorandum grew in significance
at Paris. Behind its elaborate framework of state mechanics was a
project for the economic control of the whole of the Near East by a
single *protector* which, he hoped, would be the United States working jointly with a great spiritual and educational force, the missionaries of the Near East, whose civilizing influence had already proved
its worth in such institutions as Roberts College in Constantinople
and the Syrian Protestant University at Beirut.

The whole Near East area was to be kept intact, he argued, because any subdivision into spheres of influence would retard its development. He rejected the idea of a Commission of Protectors in favor of one responsible power as guardian for what he called *The Federation*. This responsible power would send in a Governor General and other officials from among its own nationals. His Federation was to have six constituent states: Georgia in the Transcaucasus, Armenia, Syria, the Jewish area centering around Jerusalem, the Turkish area around Konia, and the Greek territory on the West of Asia Minor. His intentions are obvious: at first law courts would be Christian, Moslem and mixed, but he was certain that in a brief time the Moslem courts would be deserted. The protecting government would gradually standardize schools through the Federation. And the state would soon prosper because of its coal and oil resources exploited under the protection of the guardian government.

This was a flexible scheme whose basic concepts could later be transformed to espousal of a great Arab state under the protectorate of the United States. At Paris this American Protestant missionary element was not only Zionism's most influential competitor among the American delegates; at one point it even became the rallying point for anti-Zionist American Jews such as Morgenthau.

It is interesting that, with the passing of the years, as the great plans faded into nothingness, one aspect of the design of the Near East missionary group assumed ever greater proportions—their militant pro-Arabism and virulent anti-Zionism. A few of the same individuals in the group even survived to head, in recent years, propaganda centers of active Arab sympathizers—the Institute of American Arab Affairs, for example.

THE AMERICAN PEACE COMMISSIONERS

In the fall of 1918 when the United States was sounding out Great Britain about its plans for the distribution of the constituent parts of the Turkish Empire, American officials were not told a consistent story. On October 30, 1918, during a conversation between Colonel House, acting as Wilson's Special Representative, and Lloyd George, the British Premier extended feelers along the general lines of the Sykes-Picot Agreement, but in two areas he betrayed a crucial deflection from those war-time commitments to France about the future peace settlement. He indicated that Britain would have to assume a protectorate over Mesopotamia and "perhaps" Palestine. The precise limits of British influence in Mesopotamia provided for in the secret agreements may have been open to interpretation; but Palestine was explicitly marked for internationalization. Lloyd George was thus advancing proposals to the United States in flagrant contradiction to Britain's previous promises to France. A month later, the Foreign Office unofficially communicated to the American Embassy in London an outline of the British Government's peace plans for the Near East which showed that divergences existed within the British cabinet itself. Balfour's pattern in contradistinction to Lloyd George's was Great Britain in Mesopotamia; America in Palestine, Constantinople and the Straits; France "probably" in Syria. This represented a complete scuttling of Sykes-Picot and a frank bid for American participation in control of the Near East at the expense of Britain's European Allies. Whatever imperial considerations may have dictated Balfour's choice in other areas, the offer of Palestine to the United States was consistent with a view he had entertained since the first issuance of his Declaration.

Prior to the Peace Conference, the four American Commissioners Plenipotentiary had not displayed any particular enthusiasm for the Zionist project; on the contrary, at various times they had expressed skepticism and even antagonism. Colonel House may have been amiably pro-Zionist to Zionist officials such as Brandeis and Wise who were friends of the President, but in his memorandum to Wilson he had been chary about the issuance of the Balfour Declaration. While Henry White's opinions were not made public, his private papers show a marked hostility to Jewish autonomy in a Palestine disjointed from Syria. In his mind "Zion" as a geographical entity was a British idea, a bastion in their vast new imperial system. General Tasker Bliss did not trouble himself significantly about the subject, though his papers include an unusual number of the more vitriolic propaganda diatribes against a Jewish homeland in Palestine. Lansing had used his powerful office in 1917–1918 to restrain Wilson from being swept into an emotional expression of sympathy for the Balfour Declaration. By time they reached Paris, Lansing knew well enough what the President's sentiments were, but the Secretary of State was not a man to be moved easily from a fixed position. He would comply when formally instructed by Wilson; for the rest he kept his counsel. A Lansing memorandum of September 1918, intended as a general guide, not instructions, for the American Peace Commissioners, had included provision for the creation of an autonomous Palestine as a separate state unit under a protectorate, but it made no reference to any special Jewish status in the land.

Wilson arrived in Paris, ready to fight for the right as revealed to him by his territorial experts, professors from the major American universities. By now the American Peace Commissioners knew the details of the secret treaties of the Allies and were girded for battle against their iniquities. Palestine was to them only a tiny chamber in the great world structure the Americans were to erect in defiance of the European imperialists and basically it did not absorb them. But it presented problems both in terms of Wilson's oratorical idealism and the *realpolitik* of the European powers.

In December 1918, within a few days after landing in France, Lansing was already troubled about what he called certain phrases or epigrams of the President, especially the word self-determination. In his private notes he wrote that it was loaded with dynamite, might breed disorder, discontent and rebellion. His neat, logical mind saw it leading the President into strange contradictions. "Will not the Mohammedans of Syria and Palestine and possibly of Morocco and Tripoli rely on it? How can it be harmonized with Zionism, to which the President is practically committed?" he asked himself. In a letter to his colleague General Tasker Bliss, Lansing warned that Palestine, among other areas, might be dangled as a lure in the impending diplomatic struggle—to sully American disinterestedness. "I am convinced that the two principal governments, with which we are to deal, have come to a working understanding and will endeavor to frustrate any plan which will defeat their ambitions. We are peculiarly strong because we have no territorial cravings, no selfish interests to serve. If they could succeed in tarring us with that stick, they would gain a decided advantage. I believe that it will be attempted by tempting us with an African colony or starting a controversy in regard to the Pacific islands. Possibly a protectorate over Armenia or Palestine will be the bait. Whatever it is, I feel sure that we will have to be on our guard, since nothing would be so pleasing to the diplomatists of those countries as to be able to point to the United States and say that our unselfishness was a sham and we really wished territorial acquisition. If they can do this our preeminence would be lost and we would be unable to carry our program."

On December 30, 1918, James Brown Scott, on behalf of the Technical Advisers to the Commission to Negotiate Peace, sent Lansing a *Skeleton Draft of Peace Treaty* which had been drawn up for the

American Delegation. On Palestine the advisers made only an indifferent conjecture: "It is possible that an independent State may be created in Palestine, but also possible that all of the peoples redeemed from Turkish domination will desire some connection with existing States."

In summary, of the five Americans who stood at the head of the Delegation, the President had given the Zionists verbal expressions which could reasonably be interpreted as acquiescence; Colonel House, as the President's alter ego, had adopted his attitude without enthusiasm; Lansing and White saw Zionism primarily as an instrument of British imperialism which they were not eager to foster; General Tasker Bliss was unconcerned. The "experts" considered the situation fluid and adopted a non-committal approach pending authoritative guidance.

FIRST PROPOSALS

But a consciousness of the Wilsonian preference for a Jewish Palestine, amorphous though it was, soon seeped through the various levels of the Foreign Service and the junior members of the American staff at the Peace Conference. Vice Consul Edelman in the Near Eastern Intelligence Section which was housed in Geneva, though he was no power in the framing of policy, is typical of this transformation in the lower ranks of the State Department. For months after the publication of the Balfour Declaration his memoranda had been militantly anti-Zionist; towards the end of 1918 there was a metamorphosis. Edelman began to take an autonomous Jewish Palestine for granted. He even thought that official United States policy was in favor of a State of the Jews and he resigned himself to the prospect. Since he regarded the existence of the Jewish State as a *fait accompli* he proceeded to trace its proper boundaries for the instruction of the Peace Conference. On the south he recommended a straight line from Gaza directly east to a point south of the Dead Sea. On the north he drew an arbitrary line beginning halfway between Acre and Tyre on the Mediterranean and running to a point east of the Jordan, before it flows into Lake Tiberias. The eastern boundary of Palestine was to be "some miles" east of the Jordan and Lake Tiberias. He admitted that his boundaries for the Jewish State were rather cramped, but he thought that territorial limitation was necessary in order not to antagonize the Arabs at the outset of the "Zionist venture." His theory of the politic approach to the Arabs was similar in many respects to that which British intelligence officers were persuading Weizmann to adopt and which, in a sense, he practiced. The Arabs, Edelman believed, were far more anxious about saving appearances than about real loss of power in Palestine. If the Arabs were told bluntly that they were ultimately to be ousted from the land they would put up strong resistance to the coming of the Jews; but if they were assured that their majority rights would be protected and that they would remain the "owners," they might make concessions to the Jews on the ostensible ground that they were benefiting themselves. "The more modest and considerate the Jews are in their dealings with the Arabs today," wrote Edelman, "the greater and more lasting will be their work and influence in Palestine in the future." This was a well-meant diplomatic sermon whose precepts might conceivably be taught to individual leaders, but could hardly be communicated to two peoples hot with renascent nationalism.

At Paris, more authoritative plans for Palestine than Edelman's were being drafted by the large staff of experts of the American Delegation. On January 21, 1919, the Intelligence Section of the American Delegation, the most recent label for the technical advisers, presented their first concrete proposals on Palestine and the Near East to the American Commissioners in a few paragraphs of an *Outline of Tentative Report and Recommendations*. The Intelligence Section was an outgrowth of the *Inquiry* and at this stage the report was based upon the pro-Zionist memoranda of the earlier project. In the American Delegation Dr. S. E. Mezes was Director of Intelligence; Dr. Isaiah Bowman, Chief Territorial Specialist; under them there was a Western Asia Division headed by Westermann. Bullitt as chief of Current Intelligence Summaries was a channel from the territorial specialists to the Commissioners.

The *Outline* was the highpoint of fulfillment for the aspirations of American Zionists in their fight to secure a form of Jewish statehood in Palestine. After reaching this pinnacle of success they suffered a fairly steady decline in strength at the Paris Conference as a host of enemy forces converged upon them. The all-embracing paragraph 3 of the recommendation was as broad a statement of policy on Palestine as Zionists hoped for in their most sanguine moments. "That the Jews be invited to return to Palestine and settle there, being assured by the Conference of all proper assistance in so doing that may be consistent with the protection of the personal (especially the religious) and the property rights of the non-Jewish population, and being further assured that it will be the policy of the League of Nations to recognize Palestine as a Jewish state as soon as it is a Jewish state in fact." The proposed boundaries for Palestine, in contrast with the final demarcation, were broad. "As drawn upon the map, the new state would control its own source of water power and irrigation, on Mount Hermon in the east to the Jordan; a feature of great importance since the success of the new state would depend upon the possibilities of agricultural development." The advisers proposed Great Britain as the mandatory for Palestine and spelled out a warning against the pretensions of the King of the Hedjaz to a vast Arab dominion. The American Jewish Congress at its conference in December 1918 had asked for no more.

Sometime in January, Chaim Weizmann saw President Wilson. Of the main purport of their conversation there is no published record, though T. E. Lawrence, in a brief diary fragment, noted that they expressed their common annoyance with French ways in diplomacy. "Weizmann was asked by Wilson how he got on with the British— he said so well that he wanted them as his trustee. Then how he got on with the French. He said he knew French perfectly, but he could not understand or make himself understood by the French politicians. 'Exactly what I find,' said Wilson." Lawrence was at this point in the negotiations boyishly excited about the manner in which his newspaper campaign to obtain America's cooperation in the Near East, against the French, was proceeding. "I want to frighten America with the size of the responsibility, and then that she should run us for it instead," he wrote cryptically. There is no doubt that one British design early in the conference envisioned Anglo-American condominium in Asia Minor, with the Zionists to cement the relationship. It cannot be said to have evoked much of a response among the Americans. Weizmann naturally joined the British with alacrity in their anti-French crusade.

ZIONISM BEFORE THE PEACE CONFERENCE

January 1919 was the halcyon period of public Arab-Jewish relations. Through the intervention of the British, Weizmann arranged a formal understanding with Emir Feisal. On January 7, William Bullitt transmitted a copy of what he called the "Treaty" between Weizmann and Feisal along with an advance copy of the *Zionist Proposals for the Peace Conference* to Professor Westermann, head of the Western Asia Intelligence Section of the American Commission. The "Treaty" was a document of whole-hearted cooperation between the Zionists and the future Arab State; it even proffered the Arabs freedom from British advisers if they availed themselves of Jewish ones instead. The Zionists, still in dire need of expert help themselves for the reconstruction of their small settlement, promised the Arabs a commission, patterned after the Weizmann Commission, to develop their economy. Feisal in his turn expressed himself in favor of the immigration of Jews on a large scale and of close settlement on the land; he agreed to help put the Balfour Declaration into practical effect. Together they dispensed with the Peace Conference by providing for an Arab-Jewish Commission to draw the boundary line between Palestine and the future Arab State. At the end of the "Treaty" there was a critical postscript—with a translation in Lawrence's hand—which made Feisal's fulfillment of the agreement contingent upon the materialization of British pledges to the Arabs. In reality this "Treaty" between Feisal and Weizmann was a pathetic document between two leaders who did not enjoy the complete confidence of the peoples whom they pretended to represent; nor did they have the *de facto* power to dispose of the territory which they were allocating to each other.

In January, the Jews of the world, distant from the maze of the Conference and the anti-Semitic prejudices of British military occupation in Palestine, still naively believed that a State had been bestowed upon them. The Jews of Eastern Europe who had survived the horrors of civilian existence in battlefront areas were impatient for a final ratification of the great decision. At times they were jubilant in anticipation; they were filled with gratitude to all the Allies, and whenever their spirits overflowed they sent messages to France for having been the first country in the world to decree the emancipation of Jews, to England for giving them Palestine, to Italy for having a king who had been Herzl's friend, and to the United States for being their everlasting protector. Their joy was soon to be cut short by pogroms in Poland and the Ukraine, while the Conference debated.

Before long, attacks on Zionism and the idea of a Jewish State in Palestine began to flood the American Delegation. Clayton of the Arab Bureau in Cairo, who had been sending the British a series of telegrams—which were duly paraphrased for the Americans—warning against political Zionism, raised the threat of an army of occupation in the Near East for years if both the Sykes-Picot agreement and the

Zionist program were enforced. Anti-Zionist memoranda poured in from all over the world—from Syrians in Syria and Syrians in America, American pamphleteers, Jews and non-Jews, Christians and Moslems in Palestine, Franciscans in Jerusalem, Orthodox anti-Zionist Jews of the old settlement represented by Agudath Israel, French businessmen, French clerics, an American admiral stationed in Constantinople, American missionaries, and most significantly, from Reverend Glazebrook, the consul in Jerusalem, returned to his post. They followed stereotyped lines of argument, even when they wandered off in many directions with various final solutions for the Holy Land. The Jews who would migrate to a Palestine homeland would be Russian Jews and would bring Bolshevism with them. The Jews would speak a Yiddish jargon and would therefore be under German influence. The Vatican would be unhappy if the Jews ruled over the Holy Places. Ancient Judea had been beset by internal conflicts. The majority rights of the Moslems were being violated by Zionism. It was not fair for one religion to be allowed to dominate the other two. A Jewish State would lead to a revival of anti-Semitism throughout the world. The Zionists were a godless element, unfit to represent the orthodox Jews. French rights in Palestine were historic and had to be safeguarded. The American Commissioners Plenipotentiary never wearied themselves with this welter of protest and petition, but their experts did read them, and each according to his previous sympathies found support in some laboriously contrived memorial.

In mid-January, despite the pro-Zionist *Outline of Recommendations*, W. L. Westermann, the Cornell Professor of Ancient History who had inherited the Western Asia Division from the medievalist Professor Munro of Princeton, wrote a series of memoranda to William Bullitt, expressing his grave misgivings and many demurrers about Zionist policy. Bullitt as head of the Intelligence Reports Section of the American Commission to Negotiate the Peace was the channel through which the advice of the experts was communicated to the American Commissioners. Westermann awoke to see in the whole Near Eastern settlement as it appeared to be taking shape a denial of the basic Wilsonian principles of self-determination. Jewish ambitions in Palestine were advancing far beyond what was implied in the phrase Jewish National Homeland as he had understood it. From the reports of American consuls and agents, Westermann had arrived at the conclusion, confirmed by his own private conversations with Zionist leaders in Paris, that the Zionists were looking towards the establishment of a distinctly Jewish State of Palestine in the immediate future. Under the circumstances he was sorely troubled about the status of the Arabs. If Palestine were established as a separate state, he advised the Peace Conference to exact from the Jews every possible guarantee of equal rights for the Arab majority in the land. Zionism was in Westermann's opinion only one instance of the flagrant violation of the rights of self-determination as proclaimed by the British and the French in the Near East on November 8, 1918. Westermann pointed out that in the division of the zones of military occupation, the British and the French had shown, despite all their promises and in contradiction of point twelve of the Wilsonian theses, that they were still proceeding in terms of the secret Sykes-Picot agreement. Westermann believed in the authority, rights, and initiative of free peoples in a literal sense. He thought Sykes-Picot should be scrapped and that they should follow the advice of Howard Bliss, President of the Syrian Protestant College in Beirut, and appoint a commission which would go to Syria and there determine what the desires of the people really were. As Lansing had foreseen, Wilson's Zionism had hit up against the wall of self-determination of peoples which meant the counting of heads.

This barrage from Westermann was a cue for the emergence of the most potent single force whittling down the maximalist program of a Jewish Homeland at the Paris Peace Conference. From a number of directions, the protestant missionary elements of the Near East converged on Zionism. Dr. Howard Bliss had appeared in Paris as the respected authority on Asia Minor by virtue of having lived there for many years; he propounded an idea which Wilson could not help favoring. Bliss was the most influential American in the Near East. In November 1918, Yale wrote of him: "He is known to be anti-French and although to every appearance he holds himself and the University aloof from all political questions, his ideas are well known and have an undoubted influence upon the people, as all the leaders of the different parties are known to him personally and come to him to discuss the questions of the day.

"The faculty of the College are as a whole opposed to French occupation of Syria and this in itself has an undoubted effect upon the people. For a number of years the Americans have fought against the French Jesuit influence in Mount Lebanon and Syria and a certain amount of friction has arisen on both sides, which affects the political situation here."

Dr. Bliss suggested a Mixed Commission of the Allies to investigate the true will of the Syrians, irrespective of previous diplomatic commitments or promises. The desirability of such a body was hardly debatable once Wilson's epigram about self-determination had become policy. It was as if that will lay hidden, unsullied, somewhere in Syria, to be discovered by the representatives of the great powers who, for the period of the search, would divest themselves of all interest, history, and prejudgment. In Asia Minor the shibboleth of self-determination was often to appear in its most ridiculous guise. As if to give the Mixed Commission its full worth in American eyes, President Bliss proceeded on January 28 to make a detailed prognosis for the American Delegation of what it would find: a universal desire for a united Syria, to include Palestine, under an American protectorate.

By February 1, the idea of a purely American Commission to seek information about the will of the people in Syria and to report back to the American Delegation had received Wilson's approval. He immediately appointed Frederic C. Howe and Dr. James L. Barton, head of the Near Eastern Missions. Barton had of course already presented his viewpoint to *Inquiry* in a memorandum calling for a Federation of subject Turkish minorities under the protectorate of one great power. This did not seem in the least to disturb the President who, in his offhand manner, even seemed to be encouraging Barton's design. On February 1, 1918, he wrote Barton: "The paper is a most impressive one and I am happy to say that there is every likelihood that the matter in which they are so interested will be handled in just the way they suggest. I am very happy to think that you are going as our Commissioner to examine the problems of that very region."

Through Cairo, Professor Philip Marshall Brown of Princeton, an international lawyer, on mission to Palestine for the Young Men's Christian Association, had been sending Lansing reports since mid-1918 to the effect that Zionism was not good for the Jews, for their own sake, and that the Arabs were in a state of unrest. Before his departure for the Holy Land, Lansing had asked Professor Brown to transmit his reflections on Zionism and Palestine. Brown took the request seriously, and on June 8, 1918 sent in his report on Zionism and the Zionist Commissioners through the Cairo office of Hampton Gary. When Brown interviewed Yale, our special agent was somewhat embarrassed at the apparent duplication of his efforts, but he took it in his stride. Weizmann impressed Professor Brown as a striking and forceful personality though "like Disraeli, he occasionally reveals the temperament and the characteristics of an Oriental." Aaron Aaronsohn he considered a man of exceptional ability "but he does not inspire absolute confidence." Walter Meyer was, according to Professor Brown, added to the Commission at Frankfurter's request. He judged that the Zionists would ultimately be successful in unifying the various parties and sects in the Palestine Jewish community, though he was skeptical about the effectiveness of Weizmann's working definition of "national homeland" as a moral and intellectual center in quieting either Moslem or Christian apprehensions. Brown considered Zionism a thoroughly nationalistic movement, and feared that it would act as a deterrent in the process of assimilation and absorption of the Jews throughout the world; thus he regarded it as a movement detrimental to the best interests of the Jews themselves. Though appreciative of the achievements of the agricultural colonies he felt that the Zionists over-estimated the economic potential of the land. He doubted the Zionist contention that the Vatican was sympathetic. And like Yale, he thought that the British might try to thrust a protectorate upon the United States in order to unravel the complications of the warring political interests in Palestine. In his conclusion, he urged upon the United States government a policy of caution towards Zionism. "Certainly any proposition of a nature to embroil us in a problem already possessing complications of the most serious character should be regarded with disfavor. . . . Zionism as a normal process by which individual Jews might return to the land of their ancestors and help in the task of its regeneration is something to which no objection may properly be made. As a *political* movement for the establishment of a *national* home, however, Zionism is open to very serious objection. Its publicity, which its leaders appear to regret, its formidable organization, and its activities in Palestine—all tend to arouse fears and to court an antagonism that does not augur well for the future."

Soon after his letters were received, Professor Brown appeared in Paris in the flesh and lent substance to his contentions in "several interesting talks" with the American Delegation. Lansing thought enough of these conversations to report them to Acting Secretary Polk in Washington. Professor Brown persisted in his antagonism through the years, and in 1944, after his retirement, publicly reiterated his position.

The Great Powers met on January 30, 1919 and agreed to sever

Palestine and all other subject areas from Turkey. Beyond the dismemberment of Turkey they could not proceed without hearing the voices of the interested subject minorities. Therefore they called for a parade of opinion and desire to pass before the Conference of Ten.

The Zionists' proposal, printed on February 3, was in the optimist spirit of the Feisal-Weizmann agreement; it went far beyond any narrow interpretation of the Balfour Declaration. They showed it around among their American friends on the Peace Commission. On February 9, Professor James T. Shotwell, who as head of a historical section in the Intelligence Division held a central position, spent the afternoon discussing the document with Mr. Bernard Flexner, the Chicago lawyer and member of the American Zionist Delegation who had drawn up the first draft of the proposal. Shotwell advised a revision back to what it had been before other members of the "Zionist committee" had contributed their alterations. Flexner assured him that it had already passed both the British authorities and Emir Feisal. "With Arabia and the British satisfied," Shotwell commented in his diary that day, "there seems little for the Peace Conference to do but to register the decree."

The Zionist statement was an amalgam of the conceptions of both the American and the European Zionists; various ideas were interwoven and none too well digested. Whenever there was a difference of opinion among these two major groups the solution tended to be to incorporate both versions after eliminating only their most striking contradictions. They asked broad economic frontiers: on the north of Palestine, the Litany River and the Hermon; in Transjordania they were willing to sacrifice their historic boundaries out of deference to the Arab interest in the Hedjaz railway which runs to Mecca and to seek nothing east of the tracks. Palestine was to be governed in accordance with the terms of a contractual relationship between the Jews and the mandatory, Britain, whom they now formally chose for themselves. The ultimate goal, a Jewish Commonwealth, was to be an explicit part of the agreement, as were priority rights to a Jewish Council in concessions for development projects; close settlement on the land; free immigration; public control of land and utilities; Hebrew education; and observance of the Sabbath. The Jewish Council was to participate actively in the administration of Palestine by side of the mandatory. The signatures on the document are indicative of the weight of various national Zionist federations: Lord Walter Rothschild signed for himself; on behalf of the Zionist Organization of America: Julian M. Mack, Stephen Wise, Harry Friedenwald, Jacob de Haas, Mary Fels, Louis Robison, and Bernard Flexner; on behalf of the Russian Zionist Organization, Israel Rosoff; on behalf of the Jewish population of Palestine, in accordance with a mandate received, and on behalf of the World Zionist Organization, Weizmann and Sokolow signed twice.

While these Zionist proposals now appear over-sanguine, almost visionary, they were denounced as far too timid by the Jewish delegation from Palestine, which appeared in London later in the month. They would have demanded the inclusion of such extravaganzas as a Zionist flag for Palestine and a commitment that the mandatory, Britain, appoint in its cabinet a permanent undersecretary of state for Palestine. Maintaining a semblance of balance among the diverse Zionist proposals was not a minor diplomatic feat.

On February 6, 1919, Emir Feisal appeared before the Conference of Ten and made a formal presentation of his case. Lansing was entranced; that cold legalist later described the appearance of the "noble Arab" with all the enthusiasm of a nineteenth century romantic: ". . . his voice seemed to breathe the perfume of frankincense and to suggest the presence of richly colored divans, green turbans and the glitter of gold and jewels." Still loyal to the treaty with Weizmann, Feisal excluded Palestine from his demand for hegemony over all of Asia Minor. All chiefs of the Allied delegations were present with their staffs; Lawrence served officially as part of the Hedjaz delegation. When Lloyd George asked Feisal how many troops the Hedjaz had put in the war, the Emir, in wild contradiction of all intelligence reports, brazenly replied that it was impossible to give the exact figure, but, including the Hedjaz Army, the Arabs had sent about 100,000 men into the field. There were, in addition a considerable number of Irregulars who were not on his registers. "He thought he could assert that every man of fighting age in possession of a rifle between Mecca and Aleppo had joined the Arab standards. How many that might have been it was difficult to say, as he had no figures of the population."

The next day the British delivered to the American delegation the printer's proof of their official proposals to the Conference for the overall settlement of the Middle East. No other Power ventured to write its views out as concretely. While British officials had in fact seen the Zionist proposals and commented upon them, the Zionist belief that this constituted approval may have been a grave exaggeration. Britain's Palestine was not an answer to any Zionist prayer. In their plan, Palestine was to be a small rectangular area, limited by the depression of the Jordan on the east, the line of Nahr Litani on the north and "the limit between the cultivated or cultivable area and the domain of the Bedouin tribes" on the south. They mentioned no Jewish Commonwealth or any special status for Jews, though they expressed a willingness to give them wastelands for settlement, without "driving the Arabs to the Wall." The mandatory mission which Britain accepted for itself in this statement was "to train the two elements [Arabs and Jews] to work together."

To complicate matters at this point, when Captain Yale, who was now in Paris attached to Westermann's Division, saw Feisal on February 11th for an informal probing conversation, he learned that the Arabs did not want a British protectorate at all in their dominion, despite H.M. Government's willingness; it was America that the Arabs preferred because the United States seemed devoid of self-interest. The British may have looked forward to America's sharing their burden in the Near East; they had never meant the invitation to reach the point where they would themselves be excluded from the tent which they had raised in the desert.

On February 13, Dr. Howard Bliss got before the Conference of Ten with the Syrian and Lebanese delegates to deliver a United Syria plea. For the United States Wilson, Lansing, Westermann, and Shotwell were present. Dr. Bliss formally asked the Conference to appoint a Commission to investigate the wishes of the Syrians whose views, he charged, had hitherto been suppressed by censorship. After him Checkri Gamen, Chief Representative of the Central Syrian Committee, concluding a plea for a greater Syria offered a Palestine proposal in a spirit of compromise with the Zionists; he suggested an autonomous Jewish Palestine connected to Syria by the ties of a federation. Nothing came of his proposal, but the manner of its presentation was indicative of the strength of the Zionists at the time rather than their weakness.

"May we say one word as regards Palestine—although the subject is said to be a thorny one?

"Palestine is incontestably the Southern portion of our country. The Zionists claim it. We have suffered too much from sufferings resembling theirs, not to throw open wide to them the doors of Palestine. All those among them who are oppressed in certain retrograde countries are welcome. Let them settle in Palestine, but in an autonomous Palestine, connected with Syria by the sole bond of federation. Will not a Palestine enjoying wide internal autonomy be for them a sufficient guarantee?

"If they form a majority there, they will be the rulers. If they are in the minority, they will be represented in the government in proportion to their numbers.

"Is it necessary in order to establish them, to dismember Syria, to take from it its means of access and its historic safeguard against invasion (which always took that route) and to constitute a State in the midst of a country which, as a consequence, would be hostile to them."

The American Delegation by this time had listened to so much expert opinion on Asia Minor that they began to doubt the need for sending a special Near East Commission composed of Barton and Howe, since it would only delay a decision; they expressed themselves satisfied to listen to Feisal and Bliss and Westermann of the Western Asia Section and to make up their own minds. On February 26th Bliss had a separate session on Syria with the American Delegation and again espoused the idea of an Inter-allied Commission. For the time being his proposal was left hanging.

At the Zionist presentation before the Conference of Ten on February 27, 1919, Wilson was not present, nor was Lloyd George. For the United States, Lansing and Henry White, David Magie, Frazier, and Leland Harrison sat. Sylvain Lévi, the French Professor of Sanskrit, was officially listed as a member of the Zionist Mission, along with Sokolow, Weizmann, Ussischkin, and André Spire, though he hardly proved to be one. According to Weizmann, de Haas had been invited to represent American Zionists, but "he could not come on time." Sylvain Lévi had been asked as a representative of the French Jews, and Spire was the French Jewish Zionist. To Zionists this was a great historic moment, their first appearance before a conference of world powers, at long last official recognition of their national status.

Sokolow began with a statement on the importance of the Jews among the Entente powers and in the United States, and their contribution towards winning the war; but he made it clear that he was not pleading for Jews in the enlightened countries. It was for eastern European Jews that there had to be a definitive solution, and this could be provided only in a Jewish national centre. Weizmann who followed described the tragedy of the Jews in eastern Europe and the manner in which they were being "ground down by the political machinery which had been set up in Russia." In Palestine, he prognosticated, there was room for a population increase of four to five million without encroaching on the legitimate interests of the people already there. Zionists wanted to establish Jews in the empty spaces of Palestine, organizing the settlements to be created by the expenditure of their own money and the exercise of their own brains. A million Jews in eastern Europe, staff in hand, were waiting the signal to move. Ussischkin then spoke in Hebrew in the name of a National Assembly representing 3,000,000 Jews of South Russia, but the official reporter did not record what he said.

Spire, the French Zionist delegate, admitted that most French Jews were not Zionists, but said that France had nothing to fear from the movement if its ancient privileges in Palestine were safeguarded. Professor Sylvain Lévi announced that he was not a Zionist at all, even though he had participated in the Zionist Commission to Palestine. After a eulogy of the contribution of France in the upbuilding of Jewish Palestine, he proceeded to outline the difficulties of settlement with "the frankness of a historian." He drew the attention of the conference to the type of persecuted immigrants from eastern Europe whom they would have to receive in Palestine. "Those people would carry with them into Palestine highly explosive passions, conducive to very serious trouble in a country which might be likened to a concentration camp of Jewish refugees." He was, as a Frenchman, opposed to the International Jewish Council which the Zionists had proposed as an adjunct to the mandatory because it would appear to bestow upon certain Jews political powers in two countries. Professor Lévi was all for a Jewish philanthropic committee to aid in Jewish immigration from eastern Europe, but he did not want the committee to enjoy political rights. While Sylvain Lévi went on orating about the great French Revolution and the contributions of Jews and Frenchmen to civilization, Lansing interposed to ask Weizmann the correct meaning of the words Jewish National Home. "Did that mean an autonomous Jewish Government?" Dr. Weizmann replied in the negative. "The Zionist organization did not want an autonomous Jewish Government, but merely to establish in Palestine, under a mandatory Power, an administration not necessarily Jewish, which would render it possible to send into Palestine 70 to 80,000 Jews annually. The Association would require to have permission at the same time to build Jewish schools, where Hebrew would be taught, and in that way to build up gradually a nationality which would be as Jewish as the French nation was French and the British nation British. Later on, when the Jews formed the large majority, they would be ripe to establish such a Government as would answer to the state of the development of the country and to their ideals." The speech was a superb diplomatist's formula; it surrendered nothing in ultimate Jewish rights while retaining the spirit of the policy of conciliation with the Arabs. It did not however join the immediate demand for a Jewish Commonwealth which the American delegation of Zionists had espoused. In a concluding statement, Weizmann delivered a dignified but deadly riposte to Professor Lévi's implied belittling of the benighted Russian Jews: "As a Russian Jew, he was entitled to say that the Jews in Russia lived in an atmosphere which was not conducive to quiet thinking. On the other hand the colonies in Palestine which had been described in such glowing terms by Professor Lévi had been created by Russian Jews, and they had succeeded in transforming deserts into flourishing gardens, even under the Turkish yoke."

The Zionists at this Conference session had been represented only by Europeans. Since no American Jews had been heard from, Lansing offered Weizmann time for an appearance by Professor Felix Frankfurter. On March 1, 1919, Weizmann replied that he did not want to impose upon them further—an extraordinary response to the Conference at whose doors every new and ancient nation of the world was clamoring for a hearing. He did ask, however, that arrangements be made for Frankfurter to represent the Zionist case before the Commission when it was appointed to deal further with the Zionist proposals. No great love was lost between the American and European Zionist delegations. Should the Conference listen to such newcomers as Frankfurter, there would have been an implied derogation of the capacity of the old Zionist diplomatists Ussischkin, Sokolow, and Weizmann, who had been prominent in the movement from its inception.

Weizmann came away with the impression that the Zionists' presentation before the Conference of Ten had been a great success. The Zionists construed Lansing's question to Weizmann as a signal indication of favor. Little did they know the man who ever since the landing of the Commissioners in France had been secretly chafing under Wilsonian directives and work methods, with both of which he was in thorough disagreement. Lansing's notation in his desk diary on this meeting was: "Conference of ten listening to Zionists. Clemenceau

attended Council but did not remain. Seemed remarkably well."
Weizmann later described Lansing's interpolation about the Jewish
National Homeland as a crucial interruption of Sylvain Lévi's long
address, which had depressed the Zionists. There was an understandable tendency among the Zionists to exaggerate the import of these
historic moments.

FELIX FRANKFURTER'S MANDATE DRAFTS

At this stage in the negotiations Professor Felix Frankfurter had
assumed active leadership of the American Zionist delegation to the
Peace Conference under the remote control of Justice Brandeis. He
knew many of the American professors on the staff of the Peace Commission and he participated in the drafting of a number of non-Zionist
projects at the Conference such as the International Labor Office.
He could circulate among them with familiarity. He was as possessed with Zionism as Brandeis during this period. Passionately
moved by the fate of the Jews in eastern Europe, he accepted the
Zionist solution with implicit faith in its outcome. The temper of
the European Zionist political leaders, most of them many years his
senior, who went from exultation to despair and back again with
each new Peace Conference rumor, was not easy to accommodate to.
The number of hands who left their mark on each official Zionist
political document, especially the early drafts of the mandate, must
have been disconcerting to him, since many of the draftsmen often
had only an imperfect knowledge of the English language in which
they were composing. The resulting texts, compromises which often
bore Frankfurter's name for identification in the files of the American
Commission, were far from tightly drawn legal instruments.

When Captain Yale and an anonymous critic on the American staff
got hold of a tentative text of the Palestine mandate, which was
labelled Frankfurter's draft, they ripped into its provisions with a
vengeance. The words "historic title" of the Jewish people to Palestine were questioned. Yale and anonymous annotators also disapproved of the assumption that the League of Nations had recognized
the right of the Jews to "establish the foundations of a Jewish Commonwealth." In a provision which read: "It is the wish of the inhabitants of Palestine and of the Jews that the government be conferred
upon Great Britain as mandatory" they crossed out "of the inhabitants
of Palestine." Then followed that play of words which had been

indulged in at the time of the drafting of the Balfour Declaration. The Frankfurter proposal began Section II with the words: "The establishment of Palestine as the Jewish National Home"; the annotator turned it back again to the language of the Balfour Declaration: "a national home for the Jews in Palestine." Section IIa committed the mandatory power to promoting immigration and close settlement on the land. It got labelled "cut out." Sections IIe and f had a passage on public ownership of utilities, public works, natural resources, and land, all of which was in the Pittsburgh Program adopted by the American Zionists. It was a fundamental Brandeis conception for Palestine. This was marked out for identification, "Socialization of land on the lines of the Zionist social views." The order to the mandatory to "work progressively in cooperation with appropriate Jewish agencies" was questioned. They wanted the whole subsection on the special status of Jewish agencies eliminated.

Yale took up the immigration section with the comment that Jewish immigration should rest entirely upon the shoulders of the Jews, without any obligation on the part of the mandatory to promote Jewish immigration. He also underlined for discussion the establishment of Hebrew as one of the official languages and Section IIf which would involve a radical taxation of all inflation in land values since August 1, 1914. These were extreme "socialistic" formulations in harmony with many Brandeis conceptions of public ownership, hardly palatable to conservative members of the delegation with one eye cocked on the rising tide of Bolshevism. Section IV provided access for all faiths to the places holy to them. Though this sounded innocent enough, the annotator was quick to grasp its implication: "This may be dangerous as the Moslems have held for centuries as shrines where no Jews are allowed to enter places holy to the Jews!" Finally the anonymous annotator became irritated by repeated commitments to guarantee rights to everybody in Palestine irrespective of race, sex, or faith. "Let it be sexless!" was his exclamation.

While the so-called Frankfurter mandate draft was being mutilated by the technical advisers of the American Delegation, and the Zionist position in Paris was under attack by professors who had a literal interpretation of self-determination and by the missionaries who had a parochial interest to safeguard in Palestine, Wilson during his brief visit home was making Zionist history on his own in another hemisphere—with a certain casualness. In Chicago on March 2, 1918, he received a delegation, under Judge Julian Mack of the American

Jewish Congress, which had finally met in December 1918, and with the active participation of Louis Marshall of the American Jewish Committee had adopted two sets of resolutions, one on Jewish minority rights in eastern Europe and one on a Jewish Commonwealth in Palestine. Following the interview a statement was issued from Washington in which the President was quoted as follows: "As for your representations touching Palestine, I have before this expressed my personal approval of the declaration of the British Government regarding the aspirations and historic claims of the Jewish people in regard to Palestine. I am, moreover, persuaded that the Allied nations with the fullest concurrence of our own Government and people, are agreed that in Palestine shall be laid the foundations of a Jewish Commonwealth." These words were far more of a commitment than the letter to Rabbi Stephen Wise on August 31, 1918; they outstripped the British promise in the Balfour Declaration. That amorphous word "homeland" had become a Jewish Commonwealth. But the life of the Paris conference was so hectic that nobody in the American Delegation commented upon this statement for weeks.

Wilson's pronouncement, coupled with a letter from the Emir Feisal to Frankfurter a day before, elevated Zionist hopes to the sky once again. On March 23, 1919, Frankfurter, writing from 10, Place Edouard VII, the Zionist Delegation at Paris, sent Professor Westermann the complete text of Feisal's famous letter of March 1, 1919, in which the Emir, to contradict reports of a change of heart, wrote with enthusiasm of Weizmann and the Jews as "cousins in race." The letter contained passages full of warmth, often quoted since during the Arab-Jewish controversy as examples of Arab duplicity. "With the chiefs of your movement, especially with Dr. Weizmann, we have had, and continue to have the closest relations. He has been a great help to our cause, and I hope the Arabs may soon be in a position to make the Jews some return for their kindness. We are working together for a reformed and revived Near East and our two movements complete one another. The Jewish movement is national and not imperialist. Our movement is national and not imperialist, and there is room in Syria for us both. Indeed I think that neither can be a real success without the other." Feisal explicitly approved the proposals submitted by the Zionists as "moderate and proper." Professor Frankfurter was delighted and enthusiastic about the statement. ". . . I should not like you to miss it," he wrote to Westermann. In the same communication Frankfurter enclosed another copy of his tentative draft for the proposed mandate and outlined the considerations the Zionists had in mind in drafting it. "It should fit the structure of the Covenant, it should follow the guiding principles of Balfour's declaration and Wilson's declaration in Washington on March 2." Frankfurter believed that great flexibility had been preserved in the provisions. "In general the detailed structure of government should be left for the mandatory to be worked out between the mandatory government and the appropriate representatives of the people whose trustee they are." This in a sense implied a contract to be elaborated later, but he highlighted the two specific limitations which had to be imposed on the mandatory: "a. the limitations applicable to all mandatory areas, such as non-discrimination and freedom of intercourse, the development of the natural resources and of the land for the benefit of the people, and the prohibition of private exploitation; b. restrictions applicable to the specific area, having in mind the specific purposes which are to be achieved, namely the establishment of Palestine as the Jewish homeland." The end of the letter is in the spirit of exaltation generated among Zionists by Wilson's statement of March 2 to the Mack Committee. Frankfurter, unlike Morgenthau, saw no problem of dual allegiance in his presence at Paris as a Zionist representative. In the light of the welter of forces playing about that narrow strip of land, there is a youthful naïveté in his conclusion: "I do represent an interest here, but it is an interest which has behind it the formal sanction of the Allies and our government. So far as you and everybody else is concerned, I feel confident that I can represent that interest without partisanship."

The Feisal letter was sent to the newspapers in both Europe and the United States. The *New York Times* of March 5, 1919 published it as a cable from Paris with the caption, "Prince of Hedjaz Welcomes Zionists." In later years Feisal rather lamely attempted to cast doubt on its authenticity.

The Zionist Delegation in Paris was not the soul of discretion in dealing with members of the American staff. Because Wilson was their friend, they did not consider it necessary to use caution in what they communicated to the delegates. They never hesitated to speak freely with any American representatives since they regarded Zionism as fixed American policy. On March 12, 1919, the ubiquitous Captain Yale had a conversation with André Spire, French representative on the official Zionist delegation. Spire quoted Weizmann as saying that "he did not gave a damn about the boundaries of Palestine"; he had made his claims only for sentimental and historical reasons, but he had no interest in fighting over what he considered details.

WILSON OVERTURNS THE APPLE-CART

On March 20, 1919, with Wilson back in Paris, occurred the historic session of the Council of Four at which the President overturned the apple-cart full of wartime British and French arrangements in the Near East. During the preliminary debate, among other complaints, Pichon maintained that Lloyd George in December 1918 had asked Clemenceau for Palestine, contrary to the Sykes-Picot agreement. In a formal reply on February 15, 1919, the French had said that though they themselves did not want the responsibility of administering Palestine, they preferred an international administration as had been decided in the secret treaty. This was still their position. After the Allies wrangled long enough about their mutual promises Wilson told them bluntly that he considered none of the secret understandings binding on the United States. Loyal as he was to his associates he thought that their treaties were not the proper method of determining the ultimate division of Turkish territory. The only "scientific basis possible for a settlement"—and he used those words—was to send a commission to Syria to determine what the people desired. That would be self-determination in practice. The Howard Bliss conception won—but not before Clemenceau leaped forward with a neat thrust. If they were to have a Commission why should it be limited to Syria and exclude the British spheres of influence in Mesopotamia, Palestine, and Armenia. And so it was that a Commission to investigate the wills of the inhabitants of all the former Turkish territories was agreed upon. The Council of Four drafted instructions for the Commissioners in the spirit of the Anglo-French pronouncement of November 8, 1918, words dripping with promises of self-determination of peoples, and omitted mention of any special status for the Jews of Palestine. The instructions made a *tabula rasa* of all previous promises and commitments. The Jewish Commonwealth of March 2 was forgotten and within a few days Wilson had selected his two commissioners: the president of a Protestant college in Ohio, Henry C. King of Oberlin who had been a religious director for the American Expeditionary Forces, and Charles Crane, a former Chicago manufacturer of valves and vice-Chairman of the Finance Committee in the 1912 campaign, fresh from a mission to Russia, a man who in later years became a hysterical anti-semite. The British chose two of their star oriental experts, MacMahon and Hogarth; the French delayed.

The end of March, which saw the Wilsonian espousal of the Inter-allied Commission on the Mandates in Turkey, as the new commission was named, and reopened the whole issue of Palestine's status, witnessed fresh dangers to the original Zionist proposals in the emergence into the open of a wide rift in American Jewry. On March 25, 1919 Judge Mack and his committee arrived in Paris to submit a memorial to Lansing in which the December 1918 decisions of the American Jewish Congress were incorporated. They had used the phrase "Jewish Commonwealth" and had made it explicit that in their judgment the whole mandatory policy should be directed toward the achievement, in due time, of a Jewish state. Two days later, the anti-Zionist American Jews, led by Henry Morgenthau, delivered to the American Delegation their petition signed by 299 "prominent American Jews" who bluntly disavowed the Balfour Declaration and attacked the creation of a Jewish homeland, because they believed that, whatever phrases it was buried under, a homeland could only mean a state and would raise for Jews the world over the problem of dual allegiance. They demanded guarantees of equal treatment of Jews throughout the world, no special status in any one country, Palestine or elsewhere. Professor Westermann realized the full weight of this petition and in the memorandum which he addressed to Bullitt for transmission to the Commissioners, he referred to the contention of the petitioners that it was they and not the handful of American Zionists who truly represented the opinion and wishes of the three and a half million American Jews. While Westermann was not impressed with the Morgenthau argument against the Balfour Declaration based on the fear of dual allegiance, he returned to his original idea of the weak point of Zionism which he had developed at length in his memoranda in January: it was in contradiction to the wishes of the overwhelming number of inhabitants of Palestine, a violation of the principle of self-determination. While the American Jews were fighting for their rival points of view before the American Delegation, the English Jews in their Joint Foreign Committee of the Board of Deputies of British Jews and Council of the Anglo-Jewish Association addressed the Peace Conference with still a third approach on Palestine somewhere midway between the attitude of the Morgenthau group and the Zionists. These dominant British-Jewish organizations approved of the Balfour

Declaration because they were good Englishmen and would not oppose a policy upon which His Majesty's Government had pronounced itself; they did not, however, want any special Jewish agency or council empowered to interfere in the administration of the mandate in the name of World Jewry. The interference of Jews from foreign countries with governmental powers in Palestine was contrary to their conception of sound principles of independence. With three divergent Jewish viewpoints presented to the American Delegation within a few weeks—not to mention the orthodox Jerusalem rabbis of Agudath Israel who were hostile to all of them—the Commissioners might well have been somewhat bewildered as to what the Jews of the world really wanted.

The confusion created by the Jewish delegations who had descended upon the Conference strengthened the hand of any American elements hostile to the Zionist program. Otis Glazebrook, the Jerusalem consul of the United States, had earned the benediction of the Jews of Jerusalem for his exertions during the distribution of relief to the starving during the War, but once the political aspects of Zionism came to the fore and he heard the complaints of the Christians and Moslems of Jaffa and Jerusalem against the Zionists he set up a steady flow of reports to the American Commission on the grave dangers of the Zionist policy. His main argument was that Zionism would lead to Arab outbursts and bloodshed. In his despatches he quoted numerous instances of the extravagant boasting of Palestinian Jews in cafés which terrified the Moslems and Christians. There can be no doubt that Jews in the land who had suffered injury from petty Arab officials in the Turkish service avenged themselves with verbal insults which took the form of bestowing a grandiose interpretation on the intent and meaning of the Balfour Declaration. "Of course the Zionistic leaders could not be held responsible for such extravagant statements and no doubt they also would be repudiated by the same element in Palestine; but these statements add fuel to an already existing, if concealed, fire which will take but very little to manifest itself in consuming fury. . . . There is no difference of opinion . . . that the opposition of the Moslems and Christians to granting any exceptional privilege to the Jews in Palestine is real, intense and universal."

Loose and irresponsible talk about what Jews would do when they came to power doubtless frightened the minority of Christian Arab converts of the missionaries whose well-being was a concern of the

Protestant establishments in Palestine, but the missionary ideal for the Near East was far more grandiose than solicitude for the handful of converts they had made in the past. To the American missionaries in the Near East the King-Crane expedition was a triumph which had vast horizons: they had been granted what they regarded as a fresh reconsideration of the whole problem and, as one of the heads of the American section, they had the president of a Protestant college who had been director of the religious work department of the YMCA for France; Howard Bliss was delighted with the appointments and wrote as much to Lansing. According to de Haas, the Near Eastern Missions under Dr. James L. Barton, the missionary William H. Hall, and Morgenthau were at this time actively associated in a scheme, deriving from Barton's original plan, to put the whole of the Near East under an American commission for the development of its economic potential while still keeping the Ottoman Empire, exclusive of Arabia proper, intact.

On April 11 an incident broke in Paris which showed the growing irritation of the American Commissioners with the Zionists. Westermann called Bullitt's attention to a despatch in the Egyptian press which quoted Wilson's purported statement to a delegation of American Jews at the White House [sic] on March 2, that both he and the Allies were in favor of a Jewish Commonwealth. This had aroused dismay among the Arabs in Cairo and placed the American delegation in a quandary. On Westermann's advice, they decided to inquire of Wilson exactly what he had said and, if the statement was not authentic, to suggest pointedly that he should outrightly deny the sponsorship of a Jewish Commonwealth. Wilson's reply was evasive. The statement was not meant to be a quotation, he wrote, and the Jewish Delegation had not issued it as such. All Wilson intended to do was to reiterate his support of the Balfour Declaration; he was specific in stating that the phrase Jewish Commonwealth went a "little further than" his intentions at that time. Since Wilson had been ambiguous and had patently not disavowed the statement, the American Commission decided to leave matters as they stood without further comment. As a consequence, confusion was multiplied. The public use of the term Jewish Commonwealth by the President stood uncontradicted; Wilson had told the Commissioners in confidence that he had not meant anything more than the original Balfour Declaration. Neither the Arabs nor the Zionists had been informed of Wilson's interpretation of his statement. It still seemed to define

American policy before the departure of the Commission which was to view the whole of the Near East afresh.

THE KING-CRANE COMMISSION IN LIMBO

By the middle of April the American Commissioners to Negotiate the Peace had "gotten possession" of a secret French memorandum which indicated that despite Clemenceau's previous approval of the Inter-Allied Commission on Turkish Mandates the French had no intention of going through with the project. The memorandum, destined for the French Foreign Office, was summarized by the Division on Western Asia. It was a characteristic revelation of behind-the-scenes intrigue on the Near East.

"1. The British will be eager to have us come to an agreement with Feisal because it fears the result of the Interallied Commission projected for Syria.

"2. Since the intervention of America the assignment of Syria to France is no longer entirely in England's hands. We can now force England to allow us to create a 'de facto' situation there that will aid us in meeting the Commission, if it cannot be avoided, or in meeting any other procedure which may be adopted in deciding the mandate question.

"3. England must allow British troops in Syria to be replaced by French troops.

"4. England and France must support one another in seeing that mandates are given in accord with the Sykes-Picot agreement of 1916.

"5. Feisal must come to an agreement with us when we have agreed with England, because he knows that he cannot rule certain elements in Syria, which are favorable to us, without our help.

Our Analysis of the Document

"1. The French do not want the Inter-Allied Commission to go to Syria.

"2. They know that the British fear the results of it in arousing trouble in Mesopotamia. (It is for this reason that the French insisted on extending its competence over Palestine, Mesopotamia, and Armenia.)

"3. The French expect to influence our Commissioners to help them obtain Syria.

"4. The mandates of the Near East are to be settled on the general lines of the Sykes-Picot agreement. (The old formula 'zones' and 'zones of influences' is to be changed to 'mandates.')

Our Conclusion

"If the Interallied Commission goes to Syria it will find the cards stacked everywhere. It can do no good and may do much harm.

"All the information requisite to the settlement is already here in Paris. Delay only adds to the difficulties.

"The Near East is the great loot of the war. The fight on the question of division and mandates must be fought out here in Paris— and the sooner the better."

Thus the French had arrived at the conclusion that by extending the inquiry to all British possessions they had forced Britain to side with them in upholding the main lines of the Sykes-Picot agreement, because the Commission would find the same antagonism towards the British in Palestine and Mesopotamia as the French had experienced in Syria. Captain William Yale had gathered supporting evidence on the real French intentions from the political agent Robert de Caix who, in mockery of Allenby's prognostication that there would be an Arab uprising when the French appeared in Syria, suggested that if the British only gave the French the money for Feisal's subsidy all would be peace and harmony with the Arab leader. Robert de Caix was disdainful of a commission of inquiry, asserting that they could get Arabs to testify in favor of any viewpoint at a franc a head.

In view of the obvious French duplicity it was at first decided not to send an American Section of the Commission alone, the other two powers having practically withdrawn from the agreement to participate, but this conclusion was fought in a set of subtle memoranda by Professor Lybyer, a former teacher at Roberts College in Constantinople—another Near East missionary institution—who later became Secretary of the Commission and was subsequently identified with the Institute of Arab American Affairs. Professor Westermann was initially opposed to a separate American Commission, but he apparently changed to favor it when he learned that the sending of an American group might help to quiet the Arab population, whose restiveness was worrying Allenby.

During April and May, while the Interallied Commission came into being and passed away at regular intervals, Professor Westermann's Western Asia Intelligence Unit was dividing and subdividing Asia Minor in accordance with sets of alternatives and variables. In the sections of their memoranda dealing with Palestine they generally took a British mandatory for granted and in setting up the limits of Palestine drew restricted boundaries on the east side of Jordan. Lawrence sent Captain Yale outline maps with notes in support of the delimitation of Palestine as set forth in the British presentation to the conference in February and on the whole the American Intelligence group tended to go along with his basic premises.

At a May 3 discussion of the Big Three, when Lloyd George pointed to the problems which would arise in allocating the mandates for Turkey, Wilson agreed, observing that Palestine might be especially difficult because of the Zionist question, on which the British, the United States, and he thought also the French, were "to some extent committed." He pointed out with facile prophecy, however, that there was plenty of time, since the League of Nations would not be in operation until the Peace Treaty with Germany had been ratified and that would take a long time.

THE WILSON-FRANKFURTER LETTERS

By May the general atmosphere at Paris had become manifestly hostile to the Zionists, who were fully aware of all the inimical potentialities of the King-Crane Commission. On May 8th Professor Frankfurter wrote to Wilson with feeling on the tragedy of eastern European Jews, the uneasiness of the Jews throughout the world over the delay of a Palestine decision, and the heavy historical responsibility which lay upon the President in settling the Near Eastern problem before he departed from Paris. "Conscious of the duty of every American not to take from your time and energy, I am nevertheless compelled to bring to your attention the conditions that now confront Jewry, above all Eastern Jewry.

"You are familiar with the problems and have stated their solution. The controlling Jewish hope has been—and is—your approval of the Balfour Declaration and your sponsorship of the establishment of Palestine as the Jewish National Home. The appointment of the Interallied Syrian Commission and the assumed postponement for months, but particularly beyond the time of your stay here, of the disposition of the Near Eastern questions, have brought the deepest disquietude to the representatives of the Jewry of the world. As a passionate American I am, of course, most eager that the Jew should be a reconstructive not a disruptive force in the new world order. I have assured their leaders, with the conviction born of knowledge of your purposes. They have faith; I venture to think no people in Paris have more faith—the faith of 2000 years. But they also have the knowledge of the suffering of millions of Jews, and the hopes of Jews the world over, which nothing will assuage except the re-dedication, at last, of Palestine as a Jewish Homeland.

"Moreover, it is not merely a Jewish question. An extended delay in the Near Eastern Settlement is bound to intensify the existing unrest by giving dangerous opportunities to Young Turk intrigue and to the stimulation of religious animosities.

"The English authorities are eager to have Dr. Weizmann and me go to Palestine to assure moderation in the Jewish population. We are doing all that can be done and I am confident the Jewish population will maintain restraint. But I dare not leave here while the Turkish issues are undetermined and while you are still in Paris to decide them.

"You will forgive me for writing, but circumstances have made me the trustee of a situation that affects the hopes and the very life of a whole people. Therefore I cannot forebear to say that not a little of the peace of the world depends upon the disposal before you return to America of the destiny of the people released from Turkish rule."

Wilson answered with a perfunctory note which plunged the Zionist delegation into despair and called forth from Professor Frankfurter a dramatic response in which he described the depression of the Zionist Delegation and begged Wilson for a word of solace, a re-affirmation, even at the cost of being repetitious of his Zionist position.

"You know how profoundly words, even familiar words, move people today—how their hopes and their faith are sustained or saddened, by what you say or fail to say. Therefore, I know you will want me to inform you, in all candor, that your note of acknowledgment to my letter of May eight has occasioned almost despair to the Jewish representatives now assembled in Paris, who speak not only for the Jews of Europe but also for the American Jewish Congress, the democratic voice of three million American Jews. I do not fail to appreciate the forces which confront you here, and the circumspection which conditions impose upon you. On our side the task is to keep literally millions of Jews in check. Uncertainty, indefinite delay, seeming change of policy, bring a feeling of hopelessness which only those in intimate contact with the people whose fate is at stake can fully gauge. We are bending every energy to prevent the slow attrition of the spirit of such a people.

"Therefore you will forgive me for submitting to you the wisdom and justice of a reassuring word, written or spoken—even though it be repetitive—that you are purposing to have the Balfour Declaration written into the Treaty of Peace, and that you are aiming to see that Declaration translated into action before you leave Paris."

Wilson seemed surprised. He wrote back on May 16 that he had never meant to be discouraging to them and blandly assured them that he had not met anybody who was opposed to the Zionist principle. "I have your letter of May 14th. I never dreamed that it was necessary to give you any renewed assurance of my adhesion to the Balfour Declaration, and so far I have found no one who is seriously opposing the purpose which it embodies. I was very much taken by surprise that you should deem anything I wrote you discouraging. I see no ground for discouragement and every reason to hope that satisfactory guarantees can be secured."

To the Zionists this note became another triumph, the third commitment from Wilson since August 1918. Professor Frankfurter telegraphed Wilson's reply to Justice Brandeis, sent the whole correspondence along to the American Delegation with a note, and tried to elevate the exchange of letters to the level of a statement of official United States policy.

KING-CRANE DEPART

But while the Zionists received Wilson's fine sentiments, the Near East missionaries got their King-Crane Commission. By the end of May the indifference of the American Delegation towards sending the American Section of the Inter-Allied Commission alone to Palestine was overcome on an order from Wilson; Colonel House, King, Crane, Henry White, and Professor Westermann had all combined to pressure Wilson into action.

At the meetings of the Council of Three on May 21st and May 22nd, the Interallied Commission on Mandates in Turkey became the subject of a full-dress controversy among the Allies. Wilson opened by informing his colleagues that he could not keep his American Commissioners waiting around in Paris indefinitely since they were "important people," and that he had therefore instructed them to set out for Syria and await the French and British members there. Lloyd

George said he would probably issue similar orders. Whereupon Clemenceau replied that he would have to drop out. This set off a long wrangle between Lloyd George and Clemenceau as to who was guilty of prior breach of faith. The next day the bitter quarrel was resumed: Lloyd George and Clemenceau delivered contradictory versions of their various commitments to each other; they debated the relative weight of French and British bloodletting in the war in the Near East; they disputed about each other's interests in railroads, pipelines, and oil. Finally Wilson broke up the argument by reverting to his old contentions. He inquired sarcastically as to what part he was asked to play in this affair. He himself had never been able to see by what right France and Great Britain gave parts of Syria away to anyone.

Lloyd George then said he was quite willing to abide by the decision of the inhabitants as interpreted by the Commission; President Wilson agreed that that was necessarily his own point of view, since he had no other basis on which to form a judgment. He did not think that the subject peoples of Turkey could be left entirely to themselves. They required guidance and some intimate superintendence, but this should be conducted in their interests and not in the interests of the mandatory. The secretary's notes of the end of the meeting are as inconclusive as most of the arguments: "Mr. Lloyd George said he could not send Commissioners if the French would not send any, but the American Commissioners could go alone.

"President Wilson said that the Commissioners were absolutely disinterested. One of them was Mr. Charles R. Craig [Crane], a very experienced and cosmopolitan man. He proposed that the question should now be adjourned for further consideration."

In the last days of May 1919, King, Crane and their technical staff set out alone for a quick six-week inquiry in the Near East. Members of the staff were Albert Lybyer, George Montgomery, Captain Yale, Captain Brodie, Mr. Moore, Sgt. Doriza, Paul Toren, Sgt. Lambing. Professor Frankfurter was acutely conscious of the crisis represented by the Commission, and he telegraphed Justice Brandeis in the United States again and again, urging that he make a trip to Palestine immediately. He obviously wanted him in Palestine at the same time as the Commission to act as a counter-poise to King and Crane. British Foreign Secretary Balfour, who had tried to resist the whole notion of the Commission, was sympathetic to the idea of Brandeis's journey, he was told. Frankfurter's insistence won over Brandeis's objections and he set sail, following closely on the Commission's footsteps. The American Delegation kept Crane informed of Brandeis's movements.

On June 11, Weizmann "confidentially" transmitted to Leon Dominian of the American Delegation his impressions of the complicated relations of the British military, the Arabs and the Jews which he had analyzed with great subtlety and profound insight in long letters to Brandeis and Balfour in 1918; he also enclosed drafts of the mandate as drawn up by the Zionists, with the "toning down" notes of the British Foreign Secretary, and the replies of the Zionists. If these confidential memoranda were meant to win American sympathy for the Zionist viewpoint they did not attain their objective. Members of the American delegation passed them around and sent them to the State Department in Washington as indications of the Zionist plans to establish a Jewish *State* in Palestine.

BRANDEIS ON THE HEELS OF KING-CRANE

In London en route to Palestine at Frankfurter's urgent call, Brandeis had met Weizmann for the first time. Both were impressed with each other. Brandeis wrote his wife on June 22, 1919: "Weizmann is neither as great, nor as objectionable as he was painted [no doubt by members of the American Delegation to the Peace Conference]. But he is very much of a man and much bigger than most of his fellows." Weizmann saw "something Messianic" in Brandeis's face. After surveying the political scene, Brandeis was convinced that his journey was vital to the British and to his own people, who were both in obvious difficulties, with King and Crane dashing through the Near East assembling hundreds of petitions. In Paris Brandeis met and conferred with a galaxy of notables: President Wilson, Colonel House, Lord Balfour, the French cabinet, the Italian ambassador, Louis Marshall, the Baron Edmond de Rothschild. When he reached Cairo he was given a formal welcome by T. E. Lawrence and other officials but at the same time he was politely asked to delay his entry into Palestine until the return of Allenby, the Commander-in-Chief. Brandeis, whose trip had been encouraged by the British Foreign Secretary, at once sensed where the real power lay in the field.

In Palestine Brandeis found ample confirmation of the analysis which Weizmann had made in the summer of 1918 of the skeptical, sometimes cynical anti-Zionism of the British military forces in occupation. General Allenby pointed out that before there could be any large-scale immigration the Jews would have to dry out the swamp-lands; General Money asked ironically what they needed more Jew-ish immigrants for since there were enough poor unemployed in the land without them. The sight of the old settlement of Jerusalem, which during the war had been reduced to the depths of misery without losing any of its fanatical querulous character had repelled the British liberators. It was impossible for them to understand that these *Haluka* Jews of the old quarter of Jerusalem were not the bear-ers of the Zionist standard.

On his return trip to London Brandeis reported to the Zionist Actions Committee on the basic anti-Zionist attitude of the Military Occupation and there were interventions in the Foreign Office in an attempt to make its political directives obeyed in Jerusalem. On Au-gust 4, 1919, the Foreign Office telegraphed the Military Commander in Jerusalem that the Balfour Declaration was fixed policy; but though a small number of colonial officials disappeared after the issu-ance of the new directive there was no revolutionary change in the basic view of most administrators.

Brandeis found no cause for rejoicing about the general tenor of the Peace Conference, even though he believed his own mission rela-tively successful. "I had three busy and profitable days in Paris," Brandeis wrote his wife, August 8, 1919, "where I lunched effectively with Mr. Balfour and breakfasted with the American Peace Commis-sioners and have supplemented work there with two busy and effective days in London. . . . The world is certainly out of joint. I suppose American problems will tend to further delay action on the treaty and thus prolong and intensify the agony here."

Brandeis had been moved by the beauty of Palestine, and he wrote home about it with exaltation. He had made no speeches in Pales-tine, mostly listened, visited all the cities and twenty-three agricul-tural colonies. His conclusion to his wife was optimistic. "What I have seen and heard strengthened greatly my conviction that Pales-tine can and must become a Jewish homeland as promised in the Balfour Declaration. The problems and the difficulties are serious and numerous—even more so than I had anticipated; but there is none which will not be solved and overcome by the indomitable spirit of the Jews here and elsewhere."

When Brandeis returned to the United States he reported to Ameri-can Zionists on his plans for the creation, within a brief period of time, of a safe haven for a major portion of the millions of European Jews. His ideas were not geared to the slow progress outlined by Weizmann to the Council of Ten, an annual immigration of 70,000 to 80,000; he was thinking of a bodily transfer overnight of the Jews of eastern Europe to Palestine. His plans were Herzlian in scope. With the Arab problem he was not impressed—a blind spot in his vision.

MAJORITY AND MINORITY REPORTS

King and Crane were rapid-fire American observers. On June 20, 1919, they telegraphed to the American Delegation in Paris the conclusions drawn from the very first impressions of Palestine and Syria. They were against Jewish immigration and the Zionist program because it caused Arab unrest and would require the support of a large army. King wired to Wilson from Jerusalem, June 20, 1919. "Here older population both Moslems and Christian take united and most hostile attitude towards any extent of Jewish immigration or toward any effort to establish Jewish immigration over them. We doubt if any British Government or American official here believes that is possible to carry out Zionist program except through support of large army."

At a meeting of the Four on June 26, 1919, after the signing of the Peace Treaty with Germany, Wilson expressed himself as indifferent to Turkey's anxiety about what happened to her territory. In his opinion all the Turks needed to know was that it would not belong to them. At some future date they would be informed who their neighbors were to be. Since the United States could not commit itself at the time on whether it would be willing to accept one of the Turkish provinces under its protection it was decided to postpone final distribution of the mandates until after the United States had reached a decision. Leaving the Near East in limbo, as Frankfurter had feared, Wilson sailed home to face his debacle.

While King and Crane were dashing through Palestine and Syria —sixty towns in forty days—Arab hostility against the special Jewish status in Palestine was given new momentum by the chiefs of the Arab movement. Irrespective of Feisal's overt expressions, he did not control the Young Arabs; the urban leaders of Syria in their Damascus Conference devoted three of their ten resolutions to a denunciation of the Zionists. King and Crane assimilated their viewpoint completely. A second telegram sent by the Commissioners on July 12,

from Beyrouth, expressed outright sympathy for a great Arab kingdom under Feisal, with an American protectorate preferred. They
wired Paris dithyrambs about Feisal's deep love for all Christians,
especially for Americans, and, as one of the most telling arguments in
his behalf, they announced that he even seemed willing to allow the
establishment of an American women's college in forbidden Mecca!
No zealous missionary could have asked for more. If the Holy of
Holies were thus opened to them, then they could foresee the whole
of the Arab world coming under their spiritual wing. With the French
and the Vatican beaten, and the Jews out of the way, their missions
would flower in the desert under American protection. Feisal, "a real
great lover of Christians," they wrote, longed to reconcile Christianity and Islam, and could effectively do so because of his great prestige and popularity in the Moslem world. They saw in him a docile
instrument. "Given proper sympathy and surroundings no danger of
his getting adrift or taking big step without Anglo-Saxon approval."

The final King-Crane Report, presented on August 28, 1919, was
in the same spirit as the rather puerile telegrams. Its conclusion on
Palestine was anti-Zionist: "In view of all these considerations, and
with a deep sense of sympathy for the Jewish cause, the Commissioners feel bound to recommend that only a greatly reduced Zionist
programme be attempted by the Peace Conference, and even that,
only very gradually initiated. This would have to mean that Jewish
immigration should be definitely limited, and that the project for
making Palestine distinctly a Jewish Commonwealth should be given
up. There would then be no reason why Palestine could not be included in a united Syrian State, just as other portions of the country,
the holy places being cared for by an International and interreligious
Commission, somewhat as at present, under the oversight and approval
of the Mandatory and of the League of Nations. The Jews, of course,
would have representation upon this Commission."

Probably because of its disregard for all historic ties in Asia Minor
and its outspoken hostility to France and Britain, the report was
kept secret until 1922 and the British request for a copy was refused.
There may of course have been a more fortuitous reason for its
neglect: it reached the White House a day before Wilson's physical
collapse. Yale, who was a member of the commission's technical staff,
had prepared on July 26, 1919 a far more balanced view of the political factors involved in the Near East in what he considered a minority
report, though it never enjoyed any formal status. With respect to the

expressed desires of the people of Syria and Palestine, he came to the same conclusion as King and Crane; the overwhelming majority of the inhabitants did not want the Jews. But he offered the most reasonable justification, from an objective American viewpoint, for the maintenance of the principle of the Balfour Declaration. He drew back the veil and revealed the mechanics of Arab propaganda in Palestine since the coming of the English, describing with careful detail the synthetic manner in which anti-Jewish feeling had been fomented in Palestine by Young Arabs sent down from Damascus and Syria. If Palestine had been a part of a Syrian State with an ancient national consciousness, Yale would have agreed that the intrusion of the Zionists was a violent overriding of Arab national will. But neither during the war years under the Turks nor during the period of Allenby's conquest had the Palestinian Arabs, as distinct from the Beirut Syrians and the Arabs of the desert, shown any glimmerings of cohesive nationalism or expressed any desire for independence. In the light of the novelty of this nationalism and its artificial creation, Yale arrived at the conclusion that, on balance, greater weight should be given to the contentions of the fourteen million Jews in the world for whom the Palestine homeland was a living reality, even though only a small minority inhabited the land at the time. Yale had obviously changed his viewpoint since the time he had first been confronted with the many headed problems of Zionism in Cairo. The recommendations of his report are a significant presentation, like most of his writing:

"Recommendations: it is recommended that Palestine should be separated from Syria and constituted as a National Home for the Jewish People under the Mandate of Great Britain acting as the custodian of the Holy Land in the name of the League of Nations.

"*Discussion:* It is recognized that this disposition of Palestine is entirely contrary to the wishes of the people of Palestine and those of most of the inhabitants of Syria. If Syria was a nation with a national history, with national traditions and with strong national feelings, such a solution would be unjust and unwise. But this is not the case, and whereas injustice may be done to individuals who inhabit Palestine an injustice is not being done to a nation. Furthermore, the wishes and desires of 14,000,000 Jews who have a national history, national traditions, and a strong national feeling must be taken into consideration. The United States and the Allied Governments have made definite and formal promises to the Jewish people. To retract such promises would be unjust and unwise. The promises must be fulfilled and the Jews must be given their chance to found in Palestine a Jewish Commonwealth.

"Jewish energy, Jewish genius, and Jewish finance will bring many advantages to Palestine and perhaps to all of the East. Modern western methods and civilization will be brought to Palestine by the Jews, the country will be developed along modern western lines as it could not hope to be even under the most enlightened mandatory power. With the immigration of the Jews into Palestine, a new element will be introduced into the Orient. An Eastern race well versed in western culture and profoundly in sympathy with western ideals will be established in the Orient. Furthermore, a Jewish State will inevitably fall under the control of American Jews who will work out along Jewish lines American ideals and American civilization. A Jewish Commonwealth in Palestine will develop into an outpost in the Orient.

"There are many difficulties which lie in the way of the realization of the Zionist program. Those which pertain only to the Jews should be left to them to work out; those which concern the inhabitants of Palestine should be carefully considered by the League of Nations.

"At the present time there is great bitterness among the Arabs of Palestine and Syria against the Jews and there is determined opposition to the establishment of a Jewish National Home. In some towns of Palestine the feeling is so intense that it is not safe for a Jew to pass the night there.

"There will be resistance by the Arabs to Jewish immigration and there will be many difficulties to overcome. There is much talk of wholesale massacres of Jews; much has been said of the necessity of maintaining a very large armed force in Palestine if the Zionist program is to be carried out. In all of this there is much exaggeration due in part to the fact that those who make such statements are opposed to Zionism and are in general anti-Semites. When the Palestinians learn that the Western Powers intend to give the Jews their chance to establish a Jewish National Home, and when the Mandatory Power suppressed with a strong hand any disturbances and demonstrations against the Jews, the danger of a widespread uprising will be dissipated. The Arabs may never become reconciled to Jewish immigration, but they will become reconciled to the fact that they must accept it as inevitable.

"It will be necessary to protect the interests and rights of the Christians and Moslems of Palestine. It is essential that the places sacred to Christians and Moslems be scrupulously respected and protected.

"Great Britain is recommended as the Mandatory Power, not only because the Jews all desire the British but because Great Britain is for many reasons more fitted for the task than any other Power. As Great Britain has a very large number of Moslem subjects she will be obliged to see that the Moslems of Palestine are rightly treated by the Jews. The Jewish population of the British Isles is very small and the Jewish question will not play any part in her internal politics. Great Britain is not a Catholic country so will not have the world wide forces of Catholicism reacting upon her to put stumbling blocks in the way of Zionists. Finally, the British are primarily responsible for the promises given to the Jews and British armies delivered Palestine from the Turks. Great Britain is better prepared and better able to aid the Jews in carrying out the Zionist program than any other country."

The British did not take very seriously the gathering of hundreds of petitions by King and Crane in Palestine—they had "seen" the report even though they did not have a copy—because towards the end of July 1919 they initiated discussions in earnest with the Zionist leaders on the text of the mandate. Throughout these negotiations, Felix Frankfurter and Benjamin Cohen for the American Zionists were active, often vital participants in the drafting and emendation of the proposed provisions of the mandate.

THE GRAND DESIGN OF WILLIAM YALE

It was in September 1919 that the great Syrian crisis broke out. Clemenceau brought Lloyd George around to partial compliance with the Sykes-Picot agreement; the British promised to evacuate their troops from a zone in what is now Syria and Lebanon and to be replaced by the French. This change of occupation forces which drew from Feisal the dramatic accusation that the Arab nation's trust had been betrayed and a threat of an uprising appeared at the time to endanger the existence of the whole Zionist plan. The Arabophiles among the English military, who were opposed to the French possession of Syria, prophesied a general conflagration in the East which would engulf Palestine along with other areas of Asia Minor. Their fears, real or feigned, were not decisive and the English went through with their commitments to the French. In the British Aide-Mémoire of September 13, 1919, the boundary lines of Palestine, in the

British zone, were fixed as Dan to Beersheba, which Lloyd George had pulled out of the Bible for Clemenceau during their London conversation back in December 1918, while the experts were busily drawing all manner of barriers based upon ethnic, historical, economic and strategic considerations.

Feisal came to London to forestall the implementation of the George-Clemenceau agreement in Syria. The British were making a reasonable effort to avoid an outbreak of Arab hostilities against the French which would place them in the unfortunate position of having to choose among allies. Yale followed Feisal to London on orders from the American Commissioners to learn what was happening. There he conversed with leading British, French, Arab and Zionist figures in the Near Eastern maze—Ambassador Davis, Rustem Haidar of the Syrians, Steed of the *Times,* Colonel Gribbon of British Intelligence (who said "that all unofficial statements and promises made to Arabs by British officers would be disregarded and denied"), Emir Feisal (who would accept any solution America "imposes upon me"), Colonel Cornwallis, Assistant Chief Political Officer of the Egyptian Expeditionary Force and head of the Arab Bureau 1916–1918, Colonel Stirling and Dr. Gaster, head rabbi of the Sephardic community in London.

In his talks with Dr. Gaster, at whose house the first formal negotiations had taken place between the Zionists and the British War Cabinet, Yale heard strange details about the inner Zionist conflicts. Dr. Gaster was what might be called a maximalist opposed to Weizmann's numerous concessions to the British Government in allowing them to proceed with what he regarded as a diluted interpretation of the Declaration. Gaster accused Weizmann of permitting the British to go back on what was considered the original intent, the creation of a Jewish Commonwealth or a State in Palestine. Reporting on the interview, Yale wrote: "Dr. Gaster was very bitter against Great Britain because he felt that her statesmen had 'euchred' the Jews out of a Jewish Commonwealth. However, he added that the British had made a bargain with the Zionists, and if the Zionists had gotten the worst of it the British could not be blamed for taking their 'pound of flesh'.

"He said that since the Arab Movement had taken such large dimensions, it was impossible to create a Jewish State. He declared that it would now be impossible to include the Hauran and Trans-Jordania in a Jewish Palestine.

"He said Zionism was a dead letter and that Weizmann and Co. were at the end of their rope. He stated that he had written to the American Zionists to give up their plans for a Jewish Commonwealth. He assured me that Palestine and Zionism could no longer stir widespread enthusiasm in the Jewish world. He declared that Weizmann's threats against the British Empire, should the pledges to the Zionists not be fulfilled, were ridiculous."

Gaster's fiery defeatism, although it affected Yale's estimate of the Zionist forces, did not persuade him to abandon the idea of Palestine as a Jewish refuge. From his analysis of the Near Eastern alignment gleaned from his London interviews, Yale evolved a grand design of his own for settling the whole question of Asia Minor. It won the approval of Lawrence and the British cabinet and the implied assent of Feisal. The text on Palestine, which he gave limited boundaries east of Jordan, reads: *"Palestine* set up as a separate political unit, under the mandate of Great Britain, under whose guidance the Zionists will, with due restraint, be allowed to carry out their projects to make of it a National Home for the Jewish People." This was a far less vigorous proposal than the recommendation of his minority report the previous July, but Yale believed that the strength of the Zionists in the world had petered out during the previous year—Gaster himself had said as much—and he felt that the Zionists would accept the limitations of his plan without protest because they were largely impotent. Grew, Secretary General of the Commission to Negotiate the Peace, sent Yale's report to the Secretary of State on October 27, 1919. It was not adopted as a solution, and the United States refused to intervene when all parties were begging for its leadership. Wilson was ill and no one had been designated with the power to make a decision. Shortly thereafter Yale resigned from the staff of the Commission.

THE UNITED STATES WITHDRAWAL

In the last months of the American stay at the Conference, the Arabs made a series of efforts to arouse the interest of Frank Polk, who had replaced Lansing at Paris, in their cause. Polk did not hold out much hope of getting the Conference to change the Anglo-French military arrangement in the Near East, though, of course, the United States stuck by the theoretical position that they were not going to allow any military boundary lines, established for the purpose of military occupation, to affect in any way their ultimate decision on what the "true" allocations of the various mandates should be. In a conversation of October 17, 1919, between Polk and Abdul Hadi, Feisal's representative, the American delegate did comment unofficially that the Arab chances of success would perhaps be improved if they did not take so uncompromising a stand on the claims of the Zionists. Professor Frankfurter had, in the meantime, picked up enough of the rumor of the Anglo-French arrangement to realize that in this military agreement for zones of occupation the boundary of Palestine was being fixed without consulting at all either the United States or the Zionists. On October 20, 1919, Polk, in reply to an inquiry from Frankfurter, played innocent of all knowledge on the subject of the boundary: he claimed that the most he knew was that the French and British had suggested that the United States act as an arbitrator in any demarcation between Palestine and Syria. Feisal himself entreated Polk for American intervention on October 22, 1919, but to no avail. Wilson was losing the main battle against isolationism in the United States and these minor skirmishes did not seem to be of great import. Polk reflected the basic isolationism which had affected even the men of Wilson's own entourage when he wrote to Lansing two days later that he hoped the United States could get out of the "whole disgusting scramble" of the Near East. He knew that the British were after the control of its oil and said so, but he could see no alternative to the British because they were "good administrators."

In Damascus and Syria the Arab drama played itself out with the French occupation and the expulsion of Feisal from Syria. From December 1919 through February 1920, during the last stages of the mandate award negotiations and the boundary fixing for Palestine, American Zionists tried to exert their influence in support of a broad area for the Jewish Homeland, but they had really lost whatever strength they had with the virtual elimination of Wilson after his collapse. The same mechanics were used again and again: letters of despair to the sick President were despatched in time of crisis. Wilson's abstract sympathy for Zionism had even before his breakdown given way on occasion to annoyance at what he began to regard as the importunities of the Zionists. On September 1, 1919, he sent a note to his secretary, Tumulty, regarding a request from Melamed, editor of the Chicago *Jewish Daily Courier,* for a message to the opening of the 22nd American Zionist Convention in Chicago on September 14: "I wish you would handle this for me in some considerate way. Reading the despatches as I do, every day, I know what a delicate and dangerous situation exists throughout the world and the activities of the promoters of the Zionist movement, and I think it would be most imprudent for me to make any public expression of opinion.

"These gentlemen know the helpful position which the Government of the United States has assumed in this matter and are a little too insistent upon a constant asseveration of our interest and sympathy."

THE BOUNDARY SETTLEMENT

Towards the end of 1919, although the Zionists knew that boundary negotiations were in progress, they were not always fully informed of their substance, but their intelligence and liaison were good enough to alert them when crucial days of decision were at hand. On December 29, 1919, Lloyd George received a Zionist plea for the valley of the Litany and the western and southern slopes of Hermon. They had hired their own experts, an English engineering firm, who returned with a report that these boundaries were vital to the development of the economic potentialities of the land.

On February 3, 1920, when the boundary issue was about to be discussed at Paris by the Conference of Ambassadors, the American Zionists initiated their telegram campaign of intercession. Brandeis, Mack, Wise, Frankfurter, and de Haas signed a telegram to Lord Curzon and another to Millerand setting forth that the existence of the Jewish homeland was in jeopardy unless the extensive rather than the restricted boundaries were awarded to them. Wilson, ailing, received a letter in the same sense from Brandeis, with the addition of a paragraph in which the Justice wrote that a denial of the economic boundary lines would be a betrayal of the promise of Christendom. Wilson was touched, and in a formal communication to Lansing he expressed his concurrence and ordered the American representatives in Paris to do their utmost towards the fulfillment of Brandeis's request. "I enclose an impressive letter which I have just received from Mr. Justice Brandeis and which I beg that you will read. I agree with its conclusions and beg that you will instruct Mr. Wallace at Paris to use every means that is proper to impress this view upon the French and English authorities. All the great powers are committed to the Balfour Declaration, and I agree with Mr. Justice Brandeis regarding it as a solemn promise which we can in no circumstance afford to break or alter."

Wilson's letter was not received in the Department with any enthusiasm. Sheldon Whitehouse in the Near Eastern Division wrote a memorandum critical of the Brandeis proposal and maintained that it would entail an intrusion into Syrian territory and arouse great hostility on the part of the Arabs who were opposed even to a small Jewish state. Whitehouse quoted a recent despatch from Jerusalem by Glazebrook, who had emphasized the seething discontent of the Arabs, their dissatisfaction with America's refusal to assume a protectorate, the growth of their secret organizations to combat the Jews, and their imperviousness to Jewish blandishments.

"The frontiers proposed by Justice Brandeis would double the size of the Palestine agreed to under the Sykes-Picot agreement and bring the northern frontier right up to Beirut and Damascus. The Arabs and Syrians are opposed even to the small Jewish homeland. All the telegrams received from our consular officers tend to show that the Arab population is already in a state of unrest on account of French encroachments on territory they consider as belonging to the future Arab state, and this Division cannot but feel that if the territory claimed by Justice Brandeis should be given to Palestine the interests of the Jews themselves might be the first to suffer.

"In this connection I beg to quote the following extracts from a report by Consul Glazebrook under date of December 12th:

" 'Palestine, sandwiched as it is between Egypt and Upper Syria, is in constant danger of conflagration. Sparks are flying over its borders all the time and it may be that on some unexpected day a fire will be started that will sweep ruthlessly over this land.

" 'It is not probable that Jerusalem will be quickly inflamed—Nablous and Hebron are the danger points. . . .

" 'An amicable agreement seems to have been reached between the British and French as far as the Lebanon section is concerned, but the Sherifian party is still in open and sternly pronounced opposition to any agreement countenancing a division of Syria by which they mean all the territory situated between Anatolia and Egypt. But for British diplomatic intervention very recently there would have been an armed conflict between the French and the Arabs.

" ' . . . There is a marked change in the Moslem attitude. Open dissatisfaction is expressed with the British Occupation and great regret and even unkindly criticism are loudly indulged in because

America seems indisposed to assume the Palestinian Protectorate. Secret societies are being organized in considerable numbers, closer relations are being established between such fanatical centers as Aleppo, Damascus and Nablous. . . . The Jews seem disposed to think that it is a huge bluff and that ducats wisely distributed will heal all sores and distempers, but there are those who know that the Moslem population meet this insinuation with the curse "Thy money perish with thee."

" '. . . I am persuaded that the seriousness of the situation . . . is very real, persistent and fraught, certainly not immediately, but sooner or later, with dire consequences.' "

There are a number of drafts of the Lansing despatch to Wallace in Paris which was sent in formal obedience to Wilson's instructions. The one that was finally cabled in a subtle manner toned down the Wilson instructions that the Ambassador "should use every means that is proper" to impress the Brandeis viewpoint upon the Allies; Lansing appended a remark that since the United States was not participating in the discussions the representations of the Ambassador should be oral and informal. The phraseology of the Lansing despatch also made it clear that this was a Brandeis conception in which the President was concurring, and Brandeis was referred to as President of the Zionist Organization in America, not as Justice of the Supreme Court. Lansing fulfilled his formal duty, but there can be no doubt that he was mechanically transmitting instructions with which he had no sympathy. When Brandeis called at Lansing's office he read him the text of the cable to Ambassador Wallace and, according to Lansing's notation in his desk book, the Justice expressed himself as satisfied.

In Paris Wallace called on Sir George Grahame, Counsellor of the British Embassy, in the absence of Lord Derby, and then on Millerand to fulfill his instructions. Reporting to the Secretary of State February 6, he said Millerand adopted a non-committal attitude, stating that he would have to examine the terms of the Balfour Declaration —as if that ambiguous sentence had included anything about the Palestinian boundaries. In general Millerand held that the Zionist demands were excessive, as did Tardieu, although he "favored the aspirations of the Zionists and the plan to set up a home for the Jews in Palestine." He took particular exception to the northern boundaries claimed in Justice Brandeis's proposal, and made no comment on the Brandeis inclusion of the plains of the Jaulon and the Hauran on the east. He also asked that his views be considered purely informal and conversational.

It was unfortunate for the Zionists that the one time Wilson in an official document lent straightforward support to broad economic boundaries for Palestine, he was a sick man, dependent upon a Secretary of State with whom he was to have a definitive break in a few days and with whom he had been at odds for some time.

On the morrow of Lansing's resignation Reuben Fink, a Yiddish journalist, feeling that his disclosure would no longer injure the Zionist cause, published the accusation that before the Peace Conference Wilson had received a letter from his Secretary of State advising him not to support a homeland for the Jews because "the Christian world will not consent to the establishment in Palestine of a government by the people who crucified Jesus Christ." Fink said he quoted the words of the Lansing letter to Wilson "as far as I can remember them." He had obviously seen and misread that Lansing letter of December 13, 1917 in which the Secretary of State had expressed the judgment that "many Christian sects and individuals would undoubtedly resent turning the Holy Land over to the absolute control of the race credited with the death of Christ," as one reason for his refusal formally to support the Balfour Declaration. Lansing in high dudgeon denied Fink's charge as a flagrant fraud. Tumulty, the President's Secretary, issued a statement backing him, as did Polk the Acting Secretary of State; Judge Mack wrote Lansing that not for one moment had the Zionists given the statement any credence in the light of the splendid support they had received from him at Paris. Lansing replied with unction, "Of course I depend upon my Jewish friends to use their influence to protect me from slanders of this sort."

When the Conference of Ambassadors moved to London, the Zionists, fearing that the American envoy in Britain was not acquainted with the President's views on the Palestine boundary, manoeuvred to have Ambassador Davis communicate Wilson's wishes to Lord Curzon, the new Foreign Secretary. Curzon, who was cool to the Zionism of his predecessor, replied blandly that since Britain was the prospective mandatory they were obviously anxious to secure favorable boundaries, but he doubted whether it was possible to secure agreement to the extensive area desired by the Zionists.

The United States had become a mere onlooker at these international conferences and the last formal interventions of the State Department into the Near Eastern settlement did not have much significance. The American Zionists tried to keep the State Department warm on the subject of Palestine and whenever they received a new draft of the mandate they sent them a copy; the Department on its own accord does not seem to have shown the slightest inclination to follow up on the actual clauses of the document during its early stages. Only when there were riots in Palestine, an attack by Arabs, or fighting between Jews and Arabs did the State Department telegraph to its Jerusalem consul for reports, because "influential American Jews were greatly exercized"—the accepted formula. Beyond these incidents there was indifference.

At the San Remo Conference of the Supreme Council of European Powers on April 24, 1920, after a full dress discussion, during which the French made a last ditch attempt to secure a special status in Palestine, Britain was finally awarded the mandate. The United States had instructed Robert Underwood Johnson, American Ambassador at Rome, to serve as an observer. When Johnson was asked by the European ministers what his orders were he replied that his was merely a reportorial function; he would of course be willing to refer to the President any subject on which they might desire his views.

Wilson's moods at this period were not uniformly favorable to the Zionists. On May 5, 1920, after San Remo, Rabbi Wise wrote to the President and simultaneously to his secretary Tumulty, requesting a greeting to the Extraordinary Convention of the Zionist Organization of America summoned to celebrate the award of the Palestine mandate to Great Britain: "At this Convention, Justice Brandeis, Judge Mack and I will make clear again, though it must be well-known, how great and decisive has been your help to the Jewish people throughout the months and years of negotiations which, beginning with the Balfour Declaration and your own approval thereof, have led to the decisive act of San Remo." The rabbi urged the delivery of a message of salutation, however brief. On Tumulty's written inquiry there was a pencilled notation "No. W. W."

By December 16, 1920, the boundary issue was settled in the sense of the old Lloyd George-Clemenceau agreement. The Premier announced in Parliament that the boundaries of Palestine were to be Dan to Beersheba, which did not include the Litany river valley. Seven days later the French and the British signed a convention on the mandates for Syria, Lebanon, Palestine and Mesopotamia. The

United States had elected an isolationist administration, committed to turn its back on Europe. The fate of the Jews of Europe had ceased to be an American problem.

THE BRANDEIS-WEIZMANN SCHISM

A World Zionist Conference was held in London in July 1920, the first truly international meeting since the Vienna Congress of 1913. In the rules governing the World Zionist Organization, the "annual conference," which this was labelled, did not quite enjoy the status of the triennial International Zionist Congress. It was normally only an interim assembly with limited powers, but the accelerated rate of political events bestowed upon this meeting unusual significance. Its 300 odd delegates were called upon to reorganize the World Zionist movement in the light of the vast new responsibilities flowing from the San Remo award. Unfortunately, representation of the various national Zionist federations at the Conference failed to reflect either the economic power or the weight of population of the chief Jewish centers in the world. Neither were the various social and political factions appropriately represented. The United States, upon whom World Zionism was financially dependent in the postwar world which found Germany in the chaos of defeat and Russia in turmoil, had only 29 delegates; Russia, the numerical center of world Jewry, had a handful; the Zionist labor party only 22. Those delegates had arrived who could manage to book passage, a rather haphazard form of selection which favored the more prosperous Jews and those proximate to London.

At the London Conference, the latent hostility between the American Zionist group around Brandeis and the European Zionists around Weizmann flared into the open, with tragic consequences for the movement. Brandeis from the outset was repelled by the politicking at the conference, that normal function of all assemblies. A Zionist conference was imitative of many of the vices of democratic parliamentarism; to aggravate matters, at this period its rules of order were rather flexible. The victors in the parliamentary contest would, on the morrow of the conference, become executive agents. The qualities which made for a great tribune—and the Zionist movement had an array of brilliant orators in every style—were not necessarily virtues in the organizers of a rational system of fund collection throughout the world and its administration.

This was Brandeis's first World Zionist conference; he was a new-comer among old party stalwarts who had wrangled with Herzl in 1897. But so great was his prestige that he was chosen president of the assemblage. Without mincing words, he expressed his viewpoint at the outset that after their two political victories, San Remo on April 25 and the appointment of Herbert Samuel as High Commis-sioner for Palestine, the political epoch of Zionism was over; hence-forth it would be a technical problem. The Zionist Executive should therefore co-opt Jewish experts whether they were Zionists or not.

The Brandeis conception stripped Zionism of the literary national-ism and Hebraism upon which so many of its adherents thrived. He wanted to rebuild Palestine for those Jews who needed a homeland, plain and simple. It was a "Zion without Zionism," his critics said. His absorption with the immediate practical problem of Palestine reconstruction was so absolute that he was even cool to an expendi-ture of effort on winning minority rights in eastern Europe. In his concentration on Palestine he refused strong support for Hebrew education in the countries of the diaspora and was cold to world Jewish relief organizations.

The theoretical controversy crystallized itself in a personal quarrel between Brandeis and Weizmann. According to the Brandeis group, Weizmann had at first acquiesced in the principle of handing over direction of Palestine reconstruction for three years to an economic body, composed of both Zionists and non-Zionists, which would not be responsible to the World Congress; then, under pressure of old-time European Zionists, he had reversed himself, "broken his word," they charged. Weizmann was in a terrible dilemma: a choice between losing Brandeis and betraying the traditions of a Zionist Congress which from the early days of the movement had been jealous of its check on a strong executive.

After his visit to Palestine in July 1919, Brandeis and members of his entourage, in reviewing the totality of the economic operations of the World Zionist organization, had been severe and disparaging in their outspoken criticism of its business and accounting methods. The meticulous Brandeis could not tolerate the looseness of many budgetary practices. No doubt there was substantial validity to some of their charges of disorder in the fund-raising activities and in the colonization policy; but in formulating their objections, the Ameri-cans appeared to have a superior air to the sensitive European Jews; they acted like men of the new world, reared on American methods of efficiency, come to right all the errors of the old Zionists who had controlled the organization for a quarter of a century and had led it to substantial political victories. In many respects, also, the Americans delivered themselves of facile criticisms about past operations without realizing the fantastic handicaps under which the Zionist leaders had had to operate among the Turks, with their government by caprice and their rampant corruption.

Though never formulated bluntly, the conflict was another aspect of the fight between the politico-economic Zionism of Herzl and the cultural Zionism of Ahad Ha'am. The Weizmann group repeated that it was the duty of Zionism to revive the Jewish national spirit in the whole world through propaganda and above all education—"to rouse their hearts," was the slogan. They regularly used all of Ahad Ha'am's phraseology without quoting his name. This meant reviving Hebrew nationalist culture, language and literature. Palestine was to be the center of a great university from which the spirit of a revived nationalist Judaism was to be diffused throughout the world. Since the Americans in the Brandeis leadership were all Jews who had not participated in the Hebrew cultural renaissance, they were accused of preaching a businessman's Zionism, without soul. The controversy took on the form of one of those factitious, yet verbose wars of the body versus the spirit. The Americans were pointedly accused of the characteristic sin of their countrymen, materialism and dollar-worship.

The great conflict between the European Zionists under Weizmann and the Americans under Brandeis hung like a pall over the crucial formative years of post-war Zionism. After a quarter of a century it is difficult to allocate blame in this acrid controversy. As in most party struggles reality is hardly separable from appearance; nor can it be easily determined which of the problems the rival leaders talked about were vital to them and which they considered merely effective oratorical positions to hide other purposes.

In summary, the Brandeis group accused the Weizmann group of not keeping a reasonable accounting of the Zionist funds that were collected throughout the world. By intermingling the costs of economic development projects in Palestine with the expenses of organizing the collections, with administrative outlays for offices in London and Jerusalem, and with expenditures for educational work and health institutes and other Palestine budgets, they made it impossible to evaluate sound and purely economic projects. Brandeis would divorce the charitable and cultural from the economic. He believed the charities should be supported by separate donations and should be clearly distinguished. The administrative expenses of Zionism were to be cut down and the high living of some emissaries curtailed. In general politicking was to be frowned upon. A group of Jewish administrators, English and American, was to be selected to develop the economic potential of Palestine in a short period of time so that it might be made ready to receive a great migration from eastern Europe. The World Zionist Congress would be asked to surrender its powers into the hands of this committee for a period of time and men were to be chosen for administrative posts because they were experts, and not because they were old party stalwarts who had a genius for oratory. Jews who had hitherto refrained from actual affiliation with the Zionist organization because of their distaste for its wrangling were to be preferred when they had technical skill to contribute, or could attract the necessary capital. The socialized agricultural colonies were to be supported only on a minimal basis. Individual initiative was to be developed and the colonies were not to rely heavily on outside subsidy. Quantitative settlement was to be preferred to the establishment of a few fully-equipped colonies.

The so-called cultural work, the publication of Hebrew books and the establishment of institutions which were to revive Hebrew nationalism among Jews in the diaspora was not given much weight. It was considered secondary, good if it could find supporters; it was not a vital part of the Zionist program. The Brandeis group wanted an all-out effort in the upbuilding of a large population of Jews who would be in a position to assume state or commonwealth responsibility in a brief period of time.

In effect the Brandeis group's plea for efficiency meant the ousting from control of the world Zionist movement of those great tribunes who had kept the movement alive and those men of diplomacy who were expert in that art but had little knowledge of economic problems. It meant the virtual elimination of three men—Weizmann, Sokolow, and most significant of all, that intractable man of power Ussischkin, head of the Zionist Commission in Palestine, who was giving the British administration a hard time. It meant the substitution in their place of Dutch bankers and American professors and scientists. It was a plea for the primacy of the expert.

The Weizmann group attacked Brandeis for the autocratic manner in which the group behaved at conferences, unwilling to compromise, criticizing yet refusing to accept full responsibility at moments of decision. Brandeis had rejected the proffered headship of the World Zionist Organization when it meant his leaving the bench of the Supreme Court. The Brandeis group would not join the Executive when its principles were not adopted in full. It threatened the Executive represented by Weizmann that the American funds would be shut off from the international Zionist organization. In general they tried to use the fact that American Jewry had emerged from the war with great riches to dictate policy without subordinating themselves to the will of the majority of the delegates at the annual international conferences.

The Americans, the Weizmann partisans said, did not understand that the Zionist movement was not a business affair and that the work of rousing the diaspora to Zionism stood on an equal plane with the economic work in Palestine, for without the national revival kept alive by the inspiration of Zionist political and cultural work there would be no pioneers and no Jews willing to endure the trials of the first years in Palestine. The Weizmann group charged that the élite Brandeis leadership were distant from the ordinary people in their own country. They did not understand the Jewish immigrant masses in the United States and tried to formulate policy without reference to them. This was a deep cut for Brandeis, the defender of the common man. The Brandeis leadership were attacked as newcomers who pretended to know better than men with years of experience in the Zionist movement. They wanted to give over controls to non-Zionist American and English millionaires. The Weizmann group was not willing to sell their Zionist patrimony for ducats. The Brandeis party underestimated the importance of political and diplomatic activities with the British and with the Arabs. While they exaggerated their capacity to raise funds, their drives actually were not brilliant successes, a fact which the Weizmann group imputed to their distance from the people and their concentration of power in a few hands to the neglect of the local district Zionist organizations.

They did not realize that the immigration of Jews into Palestine required long preparation and that there were dangers in rousing the peoples of eastern Europe to vain hopes that within a short period there would be room for all of them in the land. Only the old Zionist experts such as Ruppin knew in detail the real problems of land settlement in Palestine. The Brandeis people would neglect the *Kibutz*, that unique form of cooperative labor on the land, and concentrate almost completely on settlers with individual means. They had no feeling for the idealism of the pioneers.

The controversy took the form of debates about the relative powers of the various national Zionist federations. The Brandeis group was accused of refusing to submit the American federation to the decisions of the international body and of creating an almost autonomous rival Zionism in America. This had dangers for the breakdown of the basic structure of the World Zionist Organization whose soundness had been proved by its survival even during the war. The Weizmann group had disdain for the experts who though they may have been specialists in the United States had no conception of the peculiar conditions of life and work in Palestine.

Brandeis was defeated at the London Conference. Weizmann became President and an unwieldy eighty-eight man Actions Committee was chosen to appease all national units and party factions. Under Brandeis instructions, no American delegate was allowed to become a member of the Executive.

Weizmann journeyed to America with his most potent orators. He fought hard and Ussischkin used all the normal tricks of partisan battle in ousting the Brandeis group from American leadership at the Cleveland Convention of 1921. Brandeis, and many of his friends with him, abandoned the organized Zionist movement, though he held firm to its doctrines until his death. The departure of the Brandeis group left a great void both in American and World Zionism. Whatever the merits of the controversy his successors in the United States were men of smaller stature.

Chapter VII

THE ANGLO–AMERICAN TREATY OF 1924

OIL IN THE NEGEV

Oil in the Negev was one of the first major economic interests of the United States in Palestine. For the pre-Peace Conference *Inquiry* of 1918 a memorandum had been prepared on *American Interests in Turkey* which included a brief section covering the most recent attempts of the Standard Oil Company of New York to gain a foot-hold in Palestine. Shortly before the war the company had bought seven concessions from Ottoman subjects for the exploitation of oil in the Negev and the sulphur, bitumen, and phosphate in the area around the Dead Sea. After having exercised a six-month working option the company engineers, in the spring of 1914, reported favorably on prospects and the company signed a contract for a twenty-five year lease. Standard Oil set aside funds for further surveying and testing in the area and contracted for a carriage road to be built from Hebron to their concessions. When the War broke out, boring machinery and equipment had already been shipped from the United States. In his *Report on Zionism* during the same period Oscar J. Campbell referred to a confidential study in their Princeton files which claimed that along the Jordan valley, between the Sea of Galilee and the Red Sea, the oil deposits were as rich as any in the world.

After the British occupied Palestine they displayed great interest in these oil concessions. In the summer and fall of 1918 William Yale who, it will be remembered, had been employed by Standard Oil in Jerusalem from 1915–1917, was acting as a military observer for the United States attached to Allenby's army. Yale learned that both General Money, the Military Governor of Jerusalem, and Colonel Storrs had endeavored to ascertain the precise location of the oil concessions from local Palestinian notables who had been associated with Standard Oil. The British even brought direct pressure to bear on these notables to force revelations from them and, when they failed, resorted to interrogating Yale himself for data. He reported the incident to

American Military Intelligence and through them the State Department was advised. Yale wrote a memorandum in which he generalized from the Palestine incident and stressed the importance of securing an open door policy for American oil companies in the Near East. He reminded both the War and the State Departments that in the British colony of Burma where there were great oil fields, American companies were not allowed to participate. Should Mesopotamia and Palestine fall under British rule, Yale thought it probable that the same exclusive regulations would apply unless the United States took precautions to protect American interests, insuring American capitalists a part in the exploitation of the oil resources. The fact that British petroleum interests were acquiring properties in California, Oklahoma, Mexico, and South America, while American interests were prevented from working oil in British colonies was, he felt, a subject of grave concern because of the military importance of the petroleum industry.

By March 1919 a detailed report of the incident in Palestine had reached the Standard Oil Company; their officials complained to Frank Polk, the Under-Secretary of State, that the British had actually forced their agents in Palestine to show them the maps of their claims —which the British had proceeded to copy.

Mr. L. I. Thomas of Standard Oil appeared at the Paris Conference in person and protested that the Foreign Office had prohibited them from proceeding with their geological survey in Palestine. The Americans, reasonably enough, believed they were being blocked by British oil interests. Since to their knowledge British geologists were actively at work in Mesopotamia, the Americans were not satisfied with the excuse that oil surveys in Palestine had to be delayed until after the award of the Mandate. When Thomas inquired further about the cause for British interference from his Constantinople agent, he was told that it was due to great pressure from the "Zionist Party" intent on hampering outsiders in order to preserve the concessions for themselves. He demanded United States intervention in London. To William Yale, their former employee who was attached to the American Delegation, they delivered a copy of the detailed map of their oil claims which just about blanketed the south of Palestine below the Jaffa-Jerusalem railroad. In October 1919 during Yale's quixotic attempt to persuade British officials and military leaders of the virtues of his grand design for the Near East, he had frequently emphasized American uneasiness at British pre-emption of the oil resources of the whole area. Most of his interlocutors, including Allenby, feigned ignorance or astonishment.

All this was the real prelude to the Anglo-American Treaty of 1924.

PRELIMINARY NEGOTIATIONS

On May 12, 1920 Ambassador Davis delivered a note to Lord Curzon, the British Foreign Minister, which took cognizance of the award of the mandates for Palestine and Mesopotamia to Great Britain at the San Remo Conference, and then, in a formal manner, repeated American charges "that the authorities of His Majesty's Government in the occupied region had given advantage to British oil interests which were not accorded to American companies, and further that Great Britain had been preparing quietly for exclusive control of oil resources in this region." In the light of what the United States considered principles generally agreed upon at the Paris Peace Conference, Davis expressed the hope that the mandate texts would include adequate provision for equal economic rights to all nations. As for the validation of Turkish oil concessions, the United States affirmed that it was entitled, as a matter of right, to participate in any negotiations which involved her citizens and their enterprises. These views of the United States Government were reiterated in July 1920, since, after two months, no response had been received from Great Britain.

Lord Curzon's reply, finally transmitted on August 19, 1920, denied that Britain had initiated oil exploitation in its mandated areas except for such minor developments as were necessary to meet military requirements. Moreover, in a tone of hardly veiled sarcasm, the Foreign Secretary expressed doubt whether "American oil supremacy," with more than 80% of world production under its control, was seriously threatened by British exploitation in the mandated areas, since prophecies as to the oil-bearing resources of countries not yet explored or developed had to be accepted with reserve. Curzon made pointed reference to the exclusive United States oil policy in "territories amenable to their control" in the Western Hemisphere. With respect to any formal consideration of the text of the proposed mandates, he felt that the issue could properly be discussed only by signatories of the League Covenant.

Secretary of State Bainbridge Colby took direct issue with this latter contention and again made a diplomatic request, on the basis of rights deriving from a common victory over the central powers, that the draft mandate forms be communicated to the United States Government for study before submission to the Council of the League.

In August 1921, with the growing deterioration of Britain's position in the Near East, Lord Curzon changed his tune and now expressed a willingness to open a general discussion of the problem of the United States and the mandates. A memorandum was thereupon delivered to the Foreign Office on the *Position of the Government of the United States Concerning Mandates,* in which the right of the United States to be safeguarded against discrimination in the mandates for Turkey and the theoretical foundation for this contention were set forth in detail:

"With respect to mandated territories other than those which were formerly possessions of Germany, while it is true that the United States did not declare war against Turkey, still opportunity of the Allied powers to secure the allocation of mandates and the administration of territories formerly under Turkish rule was made possible only through the victory over Germany, and the United States assumes that, by reason of its relation to that victory and of the fundamental principles recognized by the British Government as applicable to the administration of mandated territories, there would be no disposition in relation to any of these territories to discriminate against the United States or to refuse to safeguard equality of commercial opportunity."

Turning to specific issues in the drafts of the so-called "A" Mandates, the United States made a number of technical observations urging provisions both for a continuance of the capitulatory rights of the consular tribunals in Palestine until adequate courts were established and for their revival after the termination of the mandate regime; prohibitions against discriminatory practices involving American societies and associations; the protection of American missionaries in separate articles; and finally, inclusion of an understanding that the consent of the United States would be necessary to any modification of the mandate after it had been agreed to.

In this early diplomatic interchange, the interest of the United States was clear. Having enjoyed extensive capitulatory rights under a treaty with Turkey, the Republican administration which had just come into power did not mean to surrender them without guarantees. Though the concessions which the Standard Oil Company had held from the Ottoman Empire in the Negev were not mentioned by name, it is evident both from the company's earlier communications to the

American Peace Commission and from informed British sources that oil was the major consideration dictating American interest in the negotiations. At this stage of the discussions there is not the slightest indication that the United States Department of State had any desire to concern itself either with the administration of the mandate or its general purposes as outlined in the Jewish Homeland provisions of the preamble. On the contrary, in the spirit of isolationism, which the elections of 1920 confirmed, there was a general consensus in the Department to remain free of Near East politics. The legal rights of American businessmen had to be safeguarded; the bewildering intrigues of the French, British, Jews, Arabs, the Vatican, and Italy were to be avoided. These "rights," moreover, were to be granted to the United States not as a concession or favor by Britain, but in view of America's contribution to the winning of the war. Great Britain, while now willing to negotiate on the guarantee of American business rights, never lost hope during this period of tying the United States, by however tenuous a thread, to the Near Eastern settlement and thus, remotely at least, to the League of Nations.

A novel element—though not reckoned with in the early negotiations with Great Britain—intruded when both houses of the Congress in June 1922, in the face of covert hostility in the State Department, passed a Joint Resolution embodying the terms of the Balfour Declaration with slight modifications. This independent action gave comfort to the British position and caused the State Department a good deal of embarrassment. It is one of the ironies that the father of the Senate Resolution was Lodge, spearhead of American isolationism in the post-war period.

The complicated record of the negotiations of the Palestine Convention with Britain and the intra-departmental memoranda on its meaning, coupled with the Joint Resolution on Palestine passed by the Congress and signed by the President, do not lead to any definitive conclusion as to precisely what Palestine policy the United States Government was following in the early twenties. Basic ambiguities were allowed to remain. This is the source of that murky stream which runs through United States relations with the Palestine mandatory for a quarter of a century.

Towards the close of 1921 Great Britain was anxious to secure approval for the text of the mandate for Palestine which her officials had prepared for the League of Nations, despite the fact that Turkey had not yet signed a peace treaty alienating her territory. Britain, faced with the agitation of the Arabs, had an urgent need for a definitive political settlement to replace the vague juridic status of Palestine. American consent to those provisions of the mandate which affected United States rights might expedite its consideration among the European powers. British diplomats hoped to use prior American approval as a goad with which to prod recalcitrant members of the League of Nations into ratifying the text.

The United States had asked for an open door policy in Palestine, equal commercial opportunity to all nations. The British found it difficult to furnish guarantees to non-members in a League of Nations instrument but were willing to assure United States citizens and companies equal treatment with League nations in an exchange of notes. Absolute equality to all potential concessionaires was, however, not feasible because of the very purpose for which the mandate was granted and the special status of the Jewish agency in its operating articles. "The mandate expressly provides," the Foreign Office noted in December 1921, "that the administration may arrange with the Jewish agency, mentioned in article 4, to develop any of the natural resources of the country in so far as these matters are not directly undertaken by the administration. The reason for this is that, in order that the policy of establishing in Palestine a national home for the Jewish people should be successfully carried out, it is impracticable to guarantee that equal facilities for developing the natural resources of the country should be granted to persons or bodies who may be actuated by other motives. The general spirit of the Palestine mandate in the view of His Majesty's Government seems to render unnecessary the insertion of an especial provision preventing the mandatory from developing the natural resources of the country for his own benefit."

In the same note the Foreign Office agreed, without objection, to the American demand that the consent of the United States Government should be obtained to any modification of the mandate once agreed upon. This was a broad commitment, amounting in effect to a United States veto over any change in the provisions of a mandate. The phraseology in which an article on mandate modifications was later embodied in the text of the Convention had a very different connotation.

THE BALFOUR-HUGHES CORRESPONDENCE

In January 1922 when Balfour was in the United States at the head of a delegation to the Naval Conference, he and Hughes exchanged letters which, they agreed beforehand, would be considered unofficial, on the various points of contention outstanding in the Palestine mandate negotiations. Balfour wrote in an informal style expressing the hope that the American government would lighten Britain's load in Palestine; he recalled his own advocacy of a United States mandate at Paris; and he reaffirmed his view of the ultimate central role of the Jews in Palestine. "We have got in Palestine to deal with a country in which the majority of the population are Arabs, in which there is an important Jewish minority to whom we desire largely to entrust the task of fitting the country, with the help of outside Jewish assistance, to be a home for the Jewish race; and we have Christian ecclesiastical interests—Greek, Roman and Protestant—divided not merely by theological, but also by national differences, and jealously watching anything which can be twisted into interference with their position or their traditional interests in the Holy Places. If such a situation is to be dealt with successfully by the civilian Government, the position of that Government must not only be secure, but must *seem* secure in the eyes of the populations concerned." When the State Department printed the Balfour letter in an official publication, *Mandate for Palestine,* curiously enough it excluded this paragraph, without mention of the deletion. For the rest, Balfour regretted the long delay in the ratification of the mandate and diffidently requested Secretary Hughes to give his early attention to the instrument under discussion between them.

Hughes, in his reply, avoided all reference to the complex problems of the administration of Palestine upon which Balfour had dwelled and rigidly confined himself to the narrow legal questions involved in protecting American interests. The United States had enjoyed capitulatory rights in the Ottoman Empire by Treaty; these rights could be modified or abrogated only by Treaty. Hence a mere exchange of notes such as the British had suggested would not be a sufficient guarantee for the United States. Hughes ceded a point in the administration of justice; he was willing to agree on a provision in the proposed Constitution of Palestine under which the nationals of the United States would accept native judges in trivial cases and would be satisfied with a right of appeal to a court composed of a majority of British judges. But he insisted upon explicit provision for the revival of the original capitulatory rights of the Treaty of 1830 with Turkey upon termination of the mandate regime. "Even in case a Jewish State should survive, it would still be necessary for the United States to reach a decision for itself on the question at that time." Thus, theoretically, the United States could have raised the issue of its ancient capitulatory privileges upon the creation of the State of Israel. In one respect this is an extraordinary sentence from the pen of the meticulous lawyer, Hughes; in using the words "Jewish State" he revealed his private thoughts that British policy at that time was oriented in the direction of Jewish statehood, not a mere homeland.

In the same letter to Balfour, Hughes withdrew from his absolute requirement of an open door economic policy in the Palestine mandate, though he reserved the right to ask for such a provision in other mandates. Without mentioning the specific goal of the Palestine mandate, the Jewish national home, he made the exception in view of the "paucity of the resources of Palestine, and particularly in view of the special conditions there prevailing to which reference is made in the British note. . . ." As for prior American assent to any modifications in the Palestine mandate, Hughes for some reason belabored a point to which the British had already agreed in their December 1921 note. His emphatic tone is all the more incomprehensible in the light of the later reversal of State Department policy in this respect. He wrote:

"An undertaking on the part of the British Government that it will not propose nor accept any modifications in the terms of the mandate without previous *consultation* with the Government of the United States would not, I fear, adequately meet the wish expressed in the memorandum of August last that the *consent* of the United States shall be obtained before any alteration is made in the text of the Mandates." [my italics]

An American communication embodying the main points of the Balfour-Hughes correspondence was not sent until April 3, 1922; and the British Government acknowledged the American note as a satisfactory basis for the negotiation of a treaty. Thereupon matters were left hanging while Great Britain faced the problem of getting its text of the mandate ratified by the League of Nations. Great Britain had obtained in effect what it needed most, a form of diplomatic approval by the United States of the Palestine mandate text which she could then use in a presentation before the League of Nations. The United States for its part had won the point that participation in this review of the mandate was a right, not a privilege. The Government had in fact examined the mandate before it was debated by the Council of the League of Nations. At no time had the United States expressed any positive interest in the Jewish homeland provisions; the most that can be said is that it made a concession to the idea in not insisting upon an absolute effectuation of the "open door policy," and thus allowing Jewish interests in Palestine a measure of preference.

THE NEAR EASTERN AFFAIRS DIVISION AND THE ZIONISTS

The official attitude towards Zionism had noticeably cooled in the last year of Wilson's administration, though Bainbridge Colby, the new Secretary of State, had at least continued to send telegrams of inquiry to the Jerusalem consul whenever there occurred what the Zionists called outrages in Palestine, such as the Easter period riots of April 1920. But the whole tenor of communications between Jews and the State Department about Palestine changed abruptly with the coming into power of the Republican administration in the spring of 1921. Louis Marshall, not a Zionist, wrote almost apologetically to Secretary of State Charles E. Hughes on May 25, 1921 that he hoped means could be found "of having it understood that the confirmation of the mandate over Palestine would not be looked upon as opposed to the interests of our Government." The Hughes reply was curt and non-committal: "I cannot at this time make any statement regarding the matter which of course you will understand is under careful consideration."

On November 22, 1921 Dr. Nahum Sokolow, one of the diplomatists of the World Zionist Organization, was coldly received when he called on the State Department in the company of Senator Spencer of New York in the hope of obtaining another "expression of favor" for the Balfour Declaration—that perennial goal of the Zionist Movement, and one of Sokolow's special missions to popes, presidents, and princes. This is apparent from an intra-departmental memorandum record of the conversation. It sounded as if the whole issue were a subject for study *de novo*. "Mr. Fletcher replied that as regards making an expression of approval and sympathy for the movement of the Jews towards acquiring a homeland in Palestine, he would first wish to submit the matter for consideration to the Secretary of State." No statement was forthcoming.

Under the Hughes administration of the State Department, Zionist delegations seeking interviews with the Secretary of State were considered a nuisance. The technique of the new Zionist administration which followed the defeat of the Brandeis group at the Cleveland Convention was simple; in time it wore itself thin. The mere reception of a committee by the Secretary of State was considered a diplomatic triumph which could be announced in the newspapers and commented upon in public meetings. The State Department was not unconscious of the use made of these interviews, devoid of content. On March 9, 1922, for example, Hermann Bernstein wrote the Secretary of State: "In view of disquieting rumors that reached us from abroad concerning outbreaks in Palestine due to sinister propaganda, I would greatly appreciate it if you will be good enough to receive a delegation of representative American Zionists. . . ." In the Department, a renewed telegraphic request for an interview was passed around with notes of varying degrees of acerbity. "Mr. Robbins [Warren Robbins, Chief of the Near Eastern Affairs Division] says there is no earthly reason why the secretary should take time to receive this Delegation. Besides they tried to 'put something over' by not telling me they had been received by the others . . ." The Zionists received a brief reply to the effect that the Secretary would not be able to see them since they had already been to the Under Secretary and the Chief of the Division of Near Eastern Affairs.

The Department of State and the Congress, of course, never thought alike on Palestinian affairs under any administration, because they moved in different orbits. When a question of the State Department approving the Joint Resolution expressing sympathy for the Jewish people in their efforts to establish a national homeland in Palestine came up for discussion in the Congress in the fall of 1921, Hughes asked Warren Robbins for an opinion.

Robbins wrote a memorandum expressing doubt as to the wisdom of any commitment. "It seems to me that neither Congress nor the State Department can hasten matters for the Zionists by urging a certain detail which will of necessity be only settled in the Treaty of Peace with Turkey." Hughes's letter to Senator Curtis followed the lines of Robbins's memorandum. It was cautious and negative: "Permit me to say that, apart from the merits of the Zionist Movement, I am inclined to doubt the propriety of the passage of such a Resolution at this time." As was his custom he used legal arguments: "The question really turns, in the present situation of affairs, upon the mandate for Palestine and this mandate necessarily awaits the Treaty of Peace between the Allies and Turkey. The Treaty of Sèvres has not come into effect and therefore such matters as the ratification of mandates and other readjustments affecting the former Ottoman Empire cannot for the moment be given definitive action."

In March and April 1922 repeated Zionist attempts to elicit expressions of approval for a Jewish Homeland in Palestine from Secretary Hughes were futile. In May 1922 when the Congress again had under consideration the resolution of sympathy for a Jewish homeland, and in the League Council the British mandate, with the inclusion of the Balfour Declaration in the preamble, was under continual attack by the Vatican, the Arabs, the Italians, and the French, both openly and secretly, Allan W. Dulles, the new head of the Near Eastern Division, initiated a series of memoranda to top officials in the Department forewarning them against succumbing to Zionist pressure. He set the tone for a departmental policy of strict non-intervention in the Palestine issue during the period when the award of the mandate with its Balfour Declaration preamble hung in the balance of European power politics.

"NE [Near Eastern Affairs Division] feels strongly that the Department should avoid any action which would indicate official support of any one of the various theses regarding Palestine, either the Zionists, the anti-Zionists or the Arabs. To commit the Government to the support of Zionists at this particular moment would be especially unfortunate.

"The Zionists are an influential and a noisy group but while their claims undoubtedly have a certain sentimental appeal, the cold fact remains that the Jews in Palestine now constitute about 10% of the population and that the 90% majority bitterly opposes Zionism.

"From our point of view the Balfour Declaration and the ratification of the Mandate over Palestine are political details of the Near Eastern settlement, which is still in abeyance. If our policy is to let alone the political and territorial phases of that settlement, I see no reason why we should become pro-Zionists—the least of all why we should take the ground that this detail of the Near Eastern settlement be disposed of in advance of the rest.

"I thought it best to bring this matter to your attention in view of the Senate Resolutions regarding Zionism which may result in added pressure on the Department to take some stand in the matter. As a matter of fact we have recently been deluged with protests against this resolution from both Arab and Jewish sources." Of this particular deluge, only three stray Arab communications are preserved in the archives.

In a memorandum of May 26, 1922, to the Under Secretary, Allan Dulles renewed his campaign against any Zionist commitments. He summarized the status of formal American expressions of policy on Zionism in a negative manner that was grossly unhistorical: The Lodge Resolution in the Senate was never formally approved by the Department, although the Department stated that it did not have any "objection to its adoption." Harding is said to have written a letter of approval of the Palestine Foundation Fund, but he in the Near Eastern Division did not have a copy. "Apart from the above, I find no record," Dulles concluded, "that the Government has ever formally been committed to Zionism unless such commitment is interpreted as resulting from our agreement to approve the British mandate under certain conditions. Ex-President Wilson is understood to have favored the Balfour Declaration, but I do not know that he ever committed himself to it in an official and public way."

Three days later Dulles wrote again: "The publicity which the Palestine Mandate question is receiving indicates how important it is that the Department should keep clear of any of the racial and religious complications which are involved in this question." Balfour, at the opening of the session of the Council of the League of Nations, had referred to the American Government and the American Senate as unanimously expressing approval of the whole principle of the mandate; Dulles filed a demurrer in an intra-departmental memorandum. "These statements seem to me rather more emphatic than the situation warrants." But Balfour had foxed the State Department; in the light of the Senate Resolution on Palestine, the Department could not issue a disavowal.

Hughes had the same difficulty with Harding that Lansing had had with Wilson; they kept roaming off the reservation with their Zionist policy. The Department was meticulously avoiding the utterance of a single word of public approval for Zionism, when the President nonchalantly wrote a letter on the Palestine Restoration Fund as if it were a church charity bazaar of which he could not disapprove. The most Hughes could do was politely to request a copy. Such presidential letters did not change State Department opinion or action any more than Wilson's letters converted Lansing.

On June 27, 1922 Allan Dulles again advised silence on the Palestine mandate, which was experiencing an even more trying period than the May offensive against the British mandate text: defeat in the House of Lords, accentuated Vatican opposition, French failure to obtain American agreement to a Syrian mandate, an assent on which the Palestine mandate hung. Mr. Dulles was still incensed at Balfour's announcement that the United States had approved of the British Palestine mandate and he had no desire to aid Britain or the Zionists in their discomfiture. ". . . [T]he quieter we keep from now on, until the mandate is accepted or rejected, the better it will be for us, in my opinion."

A JOINT RESOLUTION OF THE CONGRESS

On July 5, 1922, the British Embassy handed the State Department a draft of the proposed treaty with the United States on the Palestine mandate drawn up "in consultation with the French Government." The British still had not received League of Nations approval of the text of the mandate (it was granted later in the month on July 24) but they had been successful in quieting both Vatican and French opposition.

In the new British text of the Anglo-American Convention, under Article 5, appeared an entirely new conception of the conditions under which modifications in the mandate would be allowable under the Treaty. "Nothing contained in the present Convention," it stated, "shall be affected by any modification which may be made in the terms of the mandate as recited above unless such modification shall have been assented to by the United States." This was a fundamental alteration of the principle which had been explicitly agreed upon in the Hughes-Balfour correspondence and in previous formal notes. The early draft had given the United States virtual veto power over modifications of the mandate; the new text can only be read to mean that nothing in the *operating articles* of the Convention proper is to be affected by any changes in the mandate, whatever they might be, unless the United States gave its approval, but in no sense does it imply that the United States shall have any right to control modifications in the mandate. The new version of Article 5 was accepted by the United States without comment in a note of July 12. This new formulation seriously weakens the Zionist argument that the United States had the right to pass even on modifications in the mandate which did *not* affect "American interests" in the narrow sense as set forth in the operating articles of the Convention. The earlier draft had given the United States that right in no uncertain terms; the later one withdrew it just as explicitly. This sudden shift can only be ex-

plained by the accentuation of State Department isolationism with
respect to Palestine, a reaction against the involvements inherent in
the Congressional Resolution on Palestine which had been adopted,
in somewhat variant versions, by the Senate on June 3 and the House
on June 30.

The United States comments on the British draft, while passing
over Article 5 on mandate modifications in complete silence, singled
out for negative criticism those portions of the text which appeared
to involve the government even remotely in approval of the principles
of the Balfour Declaration as set forth in the preamble to the mandate.
The congressional resolution had increased awareness on the subject
and the Department was determined not to allow itself to be committed obliquely in a Convention. While the United States agreed to
have the operating articles of the mandate quoted in the text of the
Convention it *specifically* requested that the preamble, which included the Balfour Declaration, be excised. Manifesting no interest
in the Zionists, the American reply concentrated on the inclusion of
a special article guaranteeing the rights of American educational,
philanthropic, and religious institutions in Palestine. This insistence
was not motivated primarily by fear of British discrimination in this
field; the United States wanted an article in the Palestine treaty so
worded that we might be able, with good grace, to secure its inclusion
in the treaty on the Syrian mandate with France. The interest of the
Department was concentrated on the key American missionary institution in the Near East, the Protestant College at Beirut which, it was
feared, might not fare well under French Catholic hegemony. At Paris,
Howard Bliss, President of the college, had written to Lansing, quoting Mark Sykes just before his death, to the effect that if France
received a Syrian mandate, the United States should exact specific
guarantees to protect its college.

The cynical attitude of the State Department towards the Joint
Congressional Resolution on the Jewish Homeland was blatantly re-
vealed to a representative of the Italian Government on July 20, 1922.
This occurred at a crucial moment in the European discussions over
the text of the Palestine mandate before the League Council. Mr.
William R. Castle of the Division of Western European Affairs sent
Mr. William Phillips the following account of his interview with an
Italian diplomat:

"Mr. Celesia, of the Italian Embassy, came in to see me yesterday
morning to ask whether the Congressional Resolution favoring the

Jews in Palestine could be taken to represent the views of the United States Government on the mandate.

"When he asked this question, I only smiled, without answering, and Mr. Celesia then burst out laughing and said that he remembered very well that Congress had also passed a resolution urging recognition of the Irish Republic and that that did not represent the view of this Government. He said, however, that his Government had been rather puzzled as to our attitude in the matter and had asked for information.

"I told Mr. Celesia that on the whole question of mandates, so far as this Government was concerned, we were working to protect American interests and that if there were anything specific to be given out on the Palestine or any other mandate, it must of necessity be given out by the Secretary himself; that this was not the kind of thing on which I could make any comment."

When the Council of the League of Nations finally approved the British draft of the mandate (though its formal effectiveness was to be delayed until the French and the Italians came to an agreement on Syria, which confused the legal status of Palestine for more than a year), Louis Lipsky, President of the American Zionist Organization sent Hughes the traditional telegram, "in deep appreciation of services rendered to a just cause by State Department under your guidance." This was either colossal ignorance on the part of Zionist officials of the true sentiments which prevailed in the Department or it was abject submissiveness before power. From Hughes, Lipsky received in return a one-sentence acknowledgment.

In approving the British draft for the Palestine mandate, the League had amended it to include a special International Commission on the Holy Places. The British extended feelers to the United States as to whether we would be willing to accept a position on the body. Over this issue there was a minor difference of opinion in the Near East Division: H. G. Dwight argued in favor of at least considering acceptance because the United States was a great Catholic power and a great Israelite power and American Protestant religious establishments in Palestine were substantial. He was of course fully cognizant of what he considered the British motive—their interest in dragging us into the Near East to make us less shy of the League of Nations. Allan Dulles, however, was as reluctant as ever to be tainted by Near Eastern politics and under his guidance the Department resisted the British offer.

The final text of the Joint Resolution of the Congress of sympathy for the Jewish homeland was passed on September 11, 1922, when the House accepted the Senate version, and the State Department was faced with the problem of advising the President on approval or disapproval. The Resolution read:

"Resolved by the Senate and House of Representatives of the United States of America in Congress assembled, That the United States of America favors the establishment in Palestine of a national home for the Jewish people, it being clearly understood that nothing shall be done which may prejudice the civil and religious rights of Christian and all other non-Jewish communities in Palestine, and that the Holy places and religious buildings and sites in Palestine shall be adequately protected."

The record of the April hearings before the House Foreign Affairs Committee and the debate on the floor of the Congress do not give comfort to those who would read into this resolution an explicit assumption of responsibility on the part of the United States Congress for the creation of a Jewish Homeland in Palestine. A number of congressional expressions of intent are forthright in a contrary direction; they argued that the resolution was only an expression of sympathy and would not involve us in any foreign entanglements—the great bogey of the period.

The Resolution was, however, a distinctly annoying document to the Near Eastern Affairs Division which had striven so resolutely to shy away from Zionist politics. H. G. Dwight's memorandum of September 19, 1922, to Allan Dulles is the frankest available inside formulation of the Department's reading of the Resolution and its implications, *at the time of its adoption.* It may be that Mr. Dwight's understanding of the text was more in the direction of a Zionist commitment for United States policy than that of other members of the Department; but this much is certain—it was not viewed as the completely empty gesture which the State Department tried to make of it during the thirties. It may well have meant less than the Zionists believed, but it was not as devoid of legal significance as State Department officials, in 1936, for example, interpreted it to be. The final paragraph of Dwight's frank memorandum is of particular significance.

"Re the Joint Resolution on the National Home for the Jews, Mr. Sidney Smith says that Joint Resolutions, unlike Concurrent Resolutions have to be signed or vetoed like bills. Or the President can simply do nothing, and at the end of ten days they become effective in spite of him.

"As to wording, the Resolution roughly follows the Balfour Declaration, which is reproduced in the Treaty of Sèvres and the Mandate. But 'Christian and all other' non-Jewish communities is a Congressional gloss, as is the final phrase about Holy Places, etc.

"It is most unfortunate that the thing has come up at all, and that it has come up before our Mandate Treaty is settled. For it is a species of intervention in the Near Eastern settlement, at a point where we really have no interest at all and where we stir up the very active sensibilities of the Moslem majority to say nothing of the Catholic Church. But the Secretary approved of it in principle, as per his correspondence with Senator Lodge last spring. And for us to hold it up now would probably raise more rumpus than to let it go through. Also, if it is held up on our advice, the Senate may make trouble over our Convention.

"Note, however, that the Joint Resolution more or less commits us not only to the protection of the Holy Places but to that of the National Home itself—if a turn of the whirligig should turn the British out." [Italics mine.]

The letter in which Mr. William Phillips in the Department formally advised the President to sign the Joint Resolution goes a vital step further in relating the Congressional action to the draft of the Palestine Convention with Britain then under discussion, even though the Department did not conceal its coldness to the Resolution. The last paragraph of this letter, perhaps more than any other text, refutes later State Department contentions that in the Palestine Convention they had nothing else in mind but the protection of "American interests" in the narrow sense of the term. The letter, addressed to the President's Secretary, George B. Christian, Jr., on September 21, 1922 reads:

"In reply to your inquiry I beg to return herewith the Joint Resolution regarding the establishment in Palestine of a national home for the Jewish people.

"I find that the Secretary had discussed this matter with Senator Lodge and in reply to his written inquiry had stated that while he did not propose such a resolution he had no objection to its adoption. While it is not clear from the correspondence whether the Secretary had contemplated that the resolution would be joint resolution rather than concurrent, which would not have required the President's signature, I feel that, under the circumstances, the Department should not raise objection to its signature by the President should he favor it.

"The proposed convention between the United States and Great Britain in regard to the Palestine Mandate will quote as a part of the preamble the full text of the Mandate which embodies a statement very similar to that of the Joint Resolution."

THE FINAL TEXT OF THE TREATY

The Resolution of the Congress placed a trump card in the hands of the British in the very midst of their negotiations with the State Department on the Palestine Convention. The British Foreign Office note of October 2, 1922 insisted on inclusion of the preamble of the mandate (with its quotation of the Balfour Declaration) in the text of the convention, against which the State Department had expressed itself in a previous communication. The British note was not at all squeamish in stating that it drew support for its argument from the congressional resolution. In a spirit of *quid pro quo* the British government accepted the American "consent" for "concurs" in Article 1 of the operative provisions of the Convention. This apparently minor word substitution must be considered an important concession in any analysis of the source of British authority in Palestine. By using the word "concurs," the United States perhaps would have admitted that the mainspring of the British mandate was the League of Nations. In winning the word "assents" the United States, with Britain's approval, became one of the original powers awarding the mandate.

The Near Eastern Affairs Division, in the meantime, remained firm in its anti-Zionism. In view of the compromising congressional resolution, Allan Dulles stood watchful guard to keep the Department, as distinct from the Congress, from making even the most innocuous utterance on Palestine. The Jewish Correspondence Bureau had asked for a statement on the fifth anniversary of the Balfour Declaration. Dulles was opposed: "As it is not without the realm of possibility that the British might withdraw from Palestine," he wrote in a memorandum to the Secretary of State, "I feel that it would be well to avoid any statement which might later be used by the Jews to indicate responsibility on our part for their coreligionists who would certainly be left at a sorry plight if the British should be forced to quit the country." In a memorandum on the *Status of the National Home for the Jews,* Mr. H. G. Dwight of the Near Eastern Affairs Division, after reciting the chronology of events on the changing legal status of Palestine, concluded skeptically: "So far as the Mandatory and the Zionists are concerned the National Home for the Jews would appear to be an established fact. Whether it will be a permanent one remains to be seen."

Early in October 1922 Allan Dulles drafted a memorandum comparing in detail the most recent American and British versions of the Convention under negotiation. Dulles emphasized the numerous points of difference: the attempt of the British to make their status in Palestine dependent upon assignment by the League rather than a peace with Turkey so that their dominion might immediately become effective; omission of reference to American participation in the defeat of Germany's allies in the British text; the apparent British desire "that we swallow the preamble of the mandate with the text of the Balfour Declaration," despite the fact that the American draft had pointedly omitted the preamble of the mandate; omission in the British text of Article 5 on the protection of educational institutions (which would affect its insertion in the Syrian mandate) ; the inadvisability of surrendering the capitulatory rights until the full legal force of the mandate had become effective.

Allan Dulles was in no hurry to complete the Convention in the fall of 1922; he advised its postponement until after the Lausanne Conference. The Department wanted Britain's juridic status in Palestine firmly established before it went about signing conventions on mutual rights in Palestine. On October 4, 1923, after the convention negotiations had been suspended for almost a year, Hughes informed Post Wheeler, the *chargé d'affaires* in London, of the complicated interim arrangements for legal process involving American nationals which had been agreed upon between the American Consul at Jerusalem and the British Chief Secretary in Palestine, but which were not being respected in practice by the Chief Justice of Palestine. Hughes instructed Wheeler to secure through diplomatic intervention the respect of American consular justice by the British Government. At the same time he indicated that, in view of the signing of a treaty with Turkey, the United States was prepared to reopen negotiations on the mandate convention. Since France and Italy had come to an understanding on Syria, the League Council Resolution of July 24, 1922 was in full operation and the British mandate in Palestine had complete legal sanction.

Post Wheeler in London cabled the Department that the British

Government was indeed most anxious to proceed with the Palestine Convention and was willing, during the period of negotiations, to insure American citizens "all privileges accorded to foreigners by the Palestine Order in Council." But this was not complete recognition of our capitulatory rights.

Another five months passed before the State Department had the American Ambassador in London deliver a communication to the Foreign Office with comments on the last British text of October 2, 1922. In the interim we had signed a Convention with France for the Syrian mandate, placing us in a strong position for asking at least an equivalent set of concessions from Britain. Skillful manoeuvring had been displayed by the State Department in this delay of the British convention. Having gotten the French to agree to an article protecting American educational and philanthropic institutions in Syria, Hughes did not see how the British could raise any valid objection to an identic one for Palestine. A noteworthy American concession was our willingness to agree to some verbal horse-trading: the inclusion of the preamble to the mandate (which contained the Balfour Declaration), if the American text of the preamble to the whole convention were accepted by Britain.

The applicability of the mandate in Transjordania became a special problem. On September 23, 1922, the Council of the League had approved a British memorandum on those articles of the mandate for Palestine which were not to be made applicable to the territory known as Transjordan. In substance this cut off that area from the "Jewish homeland" provisions of the mandate. The United States therefore added this significant comment to its note of April 28, 1924: "Upon the conclusion of the convention between the United States and Great Britain with respect to Palestine it is my Government's understanding that the convention will be applicable to such territory as may be under British mandate to the east as well as to the west of the River Jordan and that in view of the provisions of Article VII as proposed no further change would be made with respect to the conditions of the British administration of the territory known as Transjordan without the previous assent of my Government. I am instructed to inquire whether the British Government is in accord with this view."

In assenting to Article 25 of the mandate and the League Resolution on it, the United States agreed to a modification of the original mandate draft with respect to the "Jewish homeland" preamble and provisions, which were made inapplicable in Transjordania. The key point in the note, however, is the American reading of Article 7; it implied a broad interpretation, far more extensive than the common sense meaning of the words, that no further change in British administration would occur without American "assent." It is difficult to understand how this interpretation could be forced upon the language of Article 7. But if Article 7 could be cited as authority for a form of administrative review of British action in Transjordania by the United States, then it follows that Article 7 would allow for similar review in Palestine west of Jordan.

In the main the British reply accepted American emendations; they were careful, however, to take exception to the "interpretation put by the United States on article 7 of the draft convention as regards changes in the administration of Transjordania, as it is essential that they be allowed latitude to make changes in the administration of that territory in such manner as may appear necessary, provided that such action does not conflict with the terms of the mandate."

Hughes's instructions to Kellogg, the Ambassador in London pursuing these negotiations, apparently conceded to Britain on the interpretation of Article 7, but in a manner which still left ample room for ambiguity. The United States made it clear that it had never intended to suggest consultations on minor administrative changes in Transjordania. However:

"[It] is my Government's view, as briefly set forth in my communication of April 30 last, that it would be entirely consistent with the general policy which is followed by States enjoying mandatory administration over territories relinquished by the Central Powers as a result of the late war to consult with this Government as well as with the States represented by the Council of the League of Nations in connection with any general changes in the form of the Mandatory administration of Transjordania.

"My government had, however, noted the statement contained in Your Excellency's communication that the Palestine Convention shall be applicable to territory under the British Mandate to the east as well as to the west of the River Jordan and the further statement, that the changes which may be made in the administration of the territory will not be of a character to conflict with the terms of the Mandate. My Government is not therefore disposed to delay the conclusion of the Palestine Convention for the purpose of entering into a further discussion of the questions relating to Transjordania, since the essential points in which my Government is interested appear to be safeguarded by the assurances already given, which are understood also to embody the undertaking that the changes which may be made in the administration of the territory will not be of such a character as to conflict with the terms of the Convention."

This winding statement still leaves a host of questions about the rights or responsibilities of the United States in any modification of the mandate and its effectuation. Does it mean that the United States here surrendered all right to assent to substantive changes in the mandate? The United States had insisted, in the general preamble to the Convention, upon a paragraph to the effect that the United States had the right to participate in the award of the mandate by virtue of her contribution to the defeat of Germany "and the defeat of her Allies." The United States as well as the League of Nations is thus a party to the award. Article 1 of the Convention reads: "Subject to the provisions of the present convention the United States consents to the administration of Palestine by his Britannic Majesty, pursuant to the mandate recited above." Does this mean that an administration which was not "pursuant to the mandate recited above" could bring from the United States withdrawal of its participation in the award of the mandate. On the other hand, Article 7 clearly envisages the possibility of modifications in the mandate and yet does not explicitly require either consultation or approval, as the early drafts of this article (then number 5) had set forth.

In the exchange of notes both sides skirted around, but never joined issue on prior United States consent to mandate modifications. Did Article 2 of the Convention, which gave the United States the same rights and benefits as were secured to other nations bestow upon it any supervisory jurisdiction over the mandatory similar to the League? What was the purpose of Article 4 which provided for the communication to the United States of a duplicate of the annual report to the League of Nations? Was it only to see that the operative articles of the Convention were being adhered to or was its additional purpose to check on the manner in which the mandate was being complied with? None of these thorny questions can be answered definitively on the basis of the record of the negotiations. They seem to have been left vague almost by intention.

When a powerful influence in the United States was strong enough to merit protection—business-interests for example—the Government made its position clear beyond cavil, as in Article 3 on the respect for "vested American property rights." Similarly, when a religious-philanthropic interest, the missions of the Near East, wanted guarantees, Article 5 on the free maintenance of educational, philanthropic, and religious institutions was incorporated, even though it involved a certain derogation of Britain's role as an enlightened, impartial ruler. Thus certain American interests were explicitly protected in operative articles of the Convention which clearly could not be modified without the consent of the United States. As for the general "Zionist" character of the mandate, at no point in the negotiations was the State Department positively interested in becoming attached to its preservation despite the Joint Congressional Resolution. On the contrary, we would have omitted the preamble of the mandate if Britain had not actually forced the Department to accept it by referring to the Joint Congressional Resolution.

The fact that some of the inner circles of the Department saw in this Convention nothing but a guarantee of purely American interests does not however justify the assumption that it was devoid of Zionist overtones in its general spirit. In the only two formal communications to the President in which this Convention is mentioned the State Department both times highlighted the inclusion of the "Jewish homeland" principle in the text. When these communications to the President are read together with the Joint Congressional Resolution of 1922, the conclusion is inescapable that the President, the Senate and the people understood in the signing of this Convention some degree of American participation in responsibility for the goal of the mandate as set forth in the Balfour Declaration. It is hard, in view of the record, to make of all this nothing more than an expression of sympathy. At the same time full United States responsibility was not clearly undertaken. It was in essence muddled, evasive, even dishonest policy-making.

RATIFICATION

By October 1924 it was the State Department which had become impatient over the delay in the Convention negotiations; there were a number of cases pending in Palestine where British courts had tried American nationals in contravention of our capitulatory rights.

Kellogg finally transmitted the reply of the British Foreign Office, stating that we were prepared to proceed promptly with the signature of the Convention. In passing, the British made the following commitment on mandatory policy: "In that note [September 2, 1924] you state that the United States Government desire an assurance that His Majesty's Government will consult them as well as the powers represented on the Council of the League of Nations regarding any alteration in the administration of Trans-Jordania for which His Majesty's Government may decide to seek the approval of the Council; this assurance His Majesty's Government have no hesitation in giving." It is noteworthy that the Foreign Office did not extend this promise to the whole of Palestine. Was this implied or taken for granted? Furthermore, Britain is specific that it will refer only such issues as "His Majesty's Government may decide."

On November 14, 1924, in requesting the President for full power authorizing Kellogg to sign the Convention, Hughes said that it was *mutatis mutandis* the same as the Conventions with France on Syria and Lebanon which the Senate had approved without opposition. He did not wish to burden the President with details of the negotiations, but he noted: "This draft quotes in full, as part of the preamble, the text of the Palestine Mandate which, as you will recall, contains certain provisions with respect to the establishment in Palestine of a homeland for the Jews." On the implications of this fact Hughes was silent.

After numerous petty changes in the text, Kellogg announced on December 3, 1924, that he and Chamberlain had signed the Palestine mandate treaty.

There followed another year of negotiations about picayune details concerned with the liquidation of the eight cases involving American nationals in which the courts of Palestine had handed down decisions contrary to the American Consul's interpretation of his rights under the system of capitulations. When Great Britain gave the United States satisfaction in these individual cases ratifications were exchanged and the Convention came into effect.

Technically, this Treaty was the fundamental law underlying United States relations with Palestine for almost a quarter of a century.

DIPLOMATIC AND CONSULAR INTELLIGENCE OF THE 1920's

The Arab riots on the *Nebi Moussa* (a festival in honor of Moses which occurs about the time of Easter and Passover, making this period the critical one for fanatical outbursts) in Jerusalem, 1920, and the indifferent manner in which the police measures of the military authorities were applied raised immediate doubts in the minds of American officials about the forthrightness of British policy. Secretary of State Colby was interested enough to inquire of the American Ambassador in London whether the British government was in fact reconsidering its Balfour Declaration or whether Palestine was becoming a subject of contention between the military in the Near East and the Foreign Office.

In Parliament on April 19th Sir Cecil Harmsworth had affirmed that British policy stood squarely behind the Balfour Declaration. But Lord Curzon, in his interview with Ambassador Davis three days later, was more equivocal. He said they had no choice but to support it, and then proceeded to deprecate the Declaration and to express his great repugnance to the Palestine mandate. When the Department in Washington received Ambassador Davis's despatch on his conversation with Lord Curzon, Warren Robbins commented that they should refrain from giving this information to the "Zionist interests here." The Department continued to act cautiously, in the spirit of the Lansing policy, even after his resignation. The days when Brandeis had ready access to sources of information on Palestine were over. Now the Department was exercising care to keep from the Zionists news pointing to a reversal of British policy in Palestine.

What Washington learned from its consular representative in Palestine only confirmed subordinate officials in the Department in their anti-Zionism. The Reverend Glazebrook's report on the Islamo-Christian Conference at Nablous in April 1920 was filled with foreboding of dangerous outbursts in Palestine. The court trials which followed the *Nebi Moussa* riots, at which Jews and Arabs, the victims and the aggressors, in a spirit of impartiality were sentenced to equal terms of imprisonment, were noted with approval by the American consul.

When in his May 5th despatch Glazebrook embarked upon an analysis of bewildering Zionist parties dividing the Jewish settlement in Palestine, the worthy old preacher, far beyond his depth, produced an amazing hash of political nonsense. The Central Zionist Organization, in reality the Zionist moderates hostile alike to the Revisionist Jabotinsky group and to the Zionist socialists as well as to the minority of Communist "provocateurs" who had been introduced into the land, were, in Glazebrook's account, depicted as violent radical Russian Jews, militant against those who would propagate Christianity. He used strange, politically incoherent language in explaining the doctrines of these sedate middle class Zionist centrists: "They would turn Trotsky if they do not get Palestine. Their essential motive is revanche; to establish a state over against the states in which they have fared so ill. . . ."

Sir Herbert Samuel's arrival to assume office as the first High Commissioner for Palestine was described by Glazebrook with his customary ominous tone. ". . . Under heavy military escort, eight armored cars with machine guns surrounding automobile as he passed through Jerusalem. . . . His coming pregnant with grave possibilities on account of persistent and consistent opposition to Palestine being made a national home for the Jews on the part of both Christians and Moslems."

When old Dr. Glazebrook was replaced by Addison E. Southard at the Jerusalem post, the political intelligence reports became somewhat less naive in tone, but essentially they were no more penetrating. By 1921 the American consulate in Jerusalem had become nothing more than a distant observation post in an area of the world in which the new Republican administration was determined to avoid any political commitments. Southard did send home a detailed trade study because that was the core of United States interest. The adequacy with which the routine intelligence functions of the consulate were performed depended upon the perspicacity of the incumbent, and the consuls were far from being brilliant political analysts. At best they jotted down factual descriptions of incidents or the latest gossip current among British officials whom they frequented. In bulk the despatches were colored by a rather constant antipathy towards the Jewish colonists. In 1921 this undercurrent of antagonism towards the new Jewish immigrants from eastern Europe into Palestine was derived less from any doctrinaire anti-Zionism or romantic pro-Arabism than that fear of Bolshevist world revolution which then possessed the United States. More often than not mediocre men in the field wrote what they thought the Department officials in Washington wanted to hear. This led the consuls to lump together all eastern European Jews as tainted with the Bolshevist virus. The sharp distinctions between socialist Zionists and Bolshevists, between the Zionists of the left and the anti-Zionist revolutionaries in Russia who had proscribed the movement, completely escaped them. What impressed Consul Southard as it had Dr. Glazebrook was that the European revolutionary ideologies were worming their way into the Holy Land.

On May Day 1921 occurred the second post-war clash between Arabs and Jews. Southard's first telegraphic report was characteristically sim-plist. "Last evening May day procession Jewish colonists Bolshevik so-cialistic demonstration aroused Moslems at Jaffa rioting looting resulted, thirty reported killed, more than hundred wounded mostly Jews." In his despatch a few days later Southard labelled the Zionist colonists "potential troublemakers of Bolshevist tendencies." Such con-sular intelligence was not atypical of the early twenties; it did not correct the vulgar prejudices in the Department.

Southard possessed no key to British policy in Palestine, any more than many of the officials who were putting it into effect, but he reported the complexities of the situation as he saw them. At the Arab congresses in Palestine, he thought he discerned the hand of French agitators. He stressed the virulent anti-Zionist policy of the Catholic Church in Palestine. British leniency towards the Arabs after the May Day riots he interpreted as a consequence of their uneasiness over Abdullah's intentions in Transjordania, their own creature. When Arab disturbances were renewed on November 2, 1921, Consul Southard fell in with many earlier American views of Palestine that only if the Jewish settlement divested itself of its political character would it be able to survive Arab hostility. He wrote to the Secretary of State: "Arabs and Jews can live in peace in Palestine and the Arabs would probably offer no objection to the carrying out of all excepting the political phases of Zionism and the Balfour Declara-tion which, as at present interpreted, means that the country will be ruled by a Jewish oligarchy supported by Great Britain. . . ."

The publication of the Haycraft inquiry into the May Day riots of 1921 brought from Consul Southard an encomium upon its accuracy and equitableness. This report had devoted itself to a sharp attack on the methods of political Zionism in Palestine; he was especially pleased with those sections which denounced the practices of the Zion-ist Commission as a cause of Arab restiveness. "This Consulate is con-vinced," he wrote, "that the members of the local Zionist Commission have, possibly in order more emphatically to justify their existence as such and their somewhat luxurious rates of compensation, grown even more tactless in their tinkering with the Palestine situation. Palestine very much needs the Zionists with their money and real ability for its proper economic development, but little is likely to be accomplished in that respect until the Zionist leaders are brought to see the light and adapt their methods and activities more nearly to meet the somewhat peculiar exigencies of the local situation."

In January 1922 Southard perceived a suddenly changed, far more conciliatory attitude on the part of Abdullah of Transjordania towards both the French and the Zionists. He considered this a consequence of the British elevation of Feisal, his brother, to the throne of Iraq, an advancement of which Abdullah was keenly jealous. The appeasement of the Jews, Southard reported, was the result of tactful advances made by the Zionists, met by Abdullah "with the usual financial considerations in view."

On March 15, 1922, he detailed the elaborate police preparations taken by the British government for the annual Easter period riots in Palestine. A month later he reported on the effectiveness of the preventive measures; there were no Arab-Jewish clashes that spring. He had learned of further Zionist subventions to a few Palestinian Arabs who were thus induced to advocate an *entente cordiale,* but that was not in his mind the chief cause for the truce; an Arab Delegation was in London negotiating and they did not want to create an unfavorable impression with disturbances in Palestine. In general Southard remained profoundly skeptical about the long-term effectiveness of Zionist bribing of individual Arabs.

During his last months in Jerusalem, Consul Southard was critical of what he called the growing intolerance and arrogance of the leaders of the Zionist movement in Palestine. He singled out for special comment the "persecution" of the orthodox Jews in the old settlement by militant hoodlums among the new immigrants. While no doubt there was a measure of truth to Southard's characterization of the political techniques of some leaders of the Zionist Commission—especially the intractable Ussischkin—it is noteworthy that in more than a year of regular despatches, the American consul did not include a single appreciation of the economic activity of the Zionists in the reconstruction of the land after the devastation of the war years.

George C. Cobb, who succeeded Southard in the consulate, was on the whole a more impartial observer. The Bolshevik menace, moreover, had temporarily faded. He analyzed the reaction of the population of Palestine to the fast succession of major political events in British and international circles involving the legal status of the land. Even the orthodox Jews, he noted, had participated in the universal Jewish jubilation over the ratification of the British mandate in the League of Nations on July 24, 1922—a new departure in the old settlement which had been traditionally inimical to political Zionism.

Arab hostility to both the Churchill White Paper of 1922 and the mandate approval had at first appeared ominous. At this time of crisis a senior British official tried to convince Consul Cobb that, in the wave of assassinations which he considered inevitable, the United States would also be dragged in because of Congressional approval of the Balfour Declaration. The unnamed British official had predicted not only massacres of Jews, but a "replica of the carnival of assassination of British officials as has taken place in Egypt and Ireland," and aggressions against Americans, Jewish and non-Jewish, particularly American representatives.

The British uneasiness communicated itself to the American consul when he saw lithographs of the Mosque of Omar topped by a Zionist flag being distributed by Arab propagandists. "The suppressed feeling which exists among Jews, Arabs, and Government officials is decidedly hectic," Cobb wrote on July 15th; and two days later he said that there were certain to be disturbances. But by the end of August the hysteria died down in Anglo-American circles. When the Arab Congress which had convened at Nablus to hear the report of the Arab Delegation to London met, a representative of Abdullah was conspicuously absent. In September Cobb foretold the failure of the boycott against the Jews which had been adopted with great fanfare by the Arab Congress.

The petering out of the threatened Arab revolt about which he had reported so dramatically brought Cobb to a complete revision of his earlier conception of the Arab unrest. On September 6th he reported: "It is hard to conceive what the Arab really wants unless it be the life of innocuous desuetude under which he lived with the Turk. The effendi class who have lost the most prestige are the most sorely troubled by the new scheme of events and it is this class that stirs up the trouble amongst the peasant and low class city dweller. It is the opinion of this Consulate that not until the Arabs can get together on a real sound economic basis, with capable leadership, can they ever hope to make their majority in numbers felt from a political point of view." From all his reports it is evident that the character of Palestine as a promised Jewish homeland had already long since been forgotten.

During the early months of 1923 Cobb's view of the relative weight of the Arab and Jewish forces again shifted with the tide. He noted growing anti-Zionist and anti-Semitic tendencies in Great Britain; and by May 17th he came to the conclusion that the Zionists were continually losing ground.

On June 20, 1923, when Cobb reported Sir Herbert Samuel's departure on leave, he explained its purpose as an attempt to secure a realignment of British policy compatible with Jewish interests— barring that, to resign. Clayton, who was left in charge in Palestine was disgusted with the general situation and he and other higher officials made known in consular circles that in their opinion the mandate with its undertaking to establish a Jewish National Home was impractical. Weizmann in his autobiography has sketched a very different impression of the sympathies of this former head of the Arab Bureau.

In general Cobb recognized depression among the Jews and buoyancy among the Arabs who expected an early renunciation of the "Homeland" policy. In the midst of negotiations of the Anglo-American Convention on Palestine, Cobb spoke out for the retention of our capitulatory rights because of the inadequacy of the native public servants in Palestine, especially in the courts. He saw British administration fast becoming oriented in the direction of a crown colony, slowly abandoning the Zionism of the Balfour Declaration for an imperial policy based on purely strategic considerations. "To assert that Zionism, as heretofore understood, is an exploded ideal would be premature but the trend of events certainly indicates such. Therefore, in our opinion, the future possession of Palestine by Great Britain, whether under guise of a Mandate or by conquest, is based on the premise of strategic necessity and not due to a sentimental desire on its part to provide a haven for an oppressed people. That Great Britain has enjoyed and will continue to enjoy the very acceptable backing of those likely to be interested in Jewish welfare may be a contributing factor to the retention of certain Zionist policies goes without saying.

"With the premise in mind that Great Britain needs the territory of Palestine for strategic reasons compatible with her imperialist designs, in the protection of her hold on the Suez Canal and her lines of communication to Bagdad and beyond, it would appear that should the United States Government forego its capitulatory privileges that substantial guarantees must be given that American nationals resident in Palestine will not suffer thereby."

During the first years of British occupation the American Consul continued to exercise his capitulatory rights of justice. The investiture of Sir Herbert Samuel on September 11, 1922 was not considered legally perfect in the eyes of the United States because the mandate for Palestine was only to become formally effective when France and Italy had reached agreement on their mutual rights in Syria. Secretary Hughes had instructed the American Consul to continue to insist on his judicial powers under the Treaty of 1830 with Turkey.

The formal ratification of the mandate by the League of Nations in September 1923 created a mild legal flurry in Anglo-American relations; Palestinian courts became restive with consular exercise of capitulatory justice. Hughes had wired London for an immediate reopening of negotiations on the convention, but was firm on the interim preservation of the capitulatory right, a concession the French had made in Syria. The British on November 5, 1923 wanted to regularize the status of Palestine as soon as possible but they could not admit error by amending an Order-in-Council which had superseded the temporary arrangement agreed upon between the Consul and the British legal secretary. It was a juridic kettle of fish in which both the State Department and the Foreign Office were none too conciliatory. Ostensibly it was an American defense of the judicial rights of its citizens to *bonne justice* in a backward country; actually the Department was less worried about the exercise of the police power of the mandatory than the preservation of the 1913 Standard Oil Company concessions from Turkey. Until these business interests were protected in a ratified Convention with Great Britain, the United States would not allow the Jerusalem consul to be stripped of his judicial functions.

A vice-consul, George Gregg Fuller, shed a gleam of light amid the rather hazy political despatches of the 1920's. In 1924 he sent the Department a series of special reports on Zionism which, though uneven in spots, are far above the run-of-the-mill intelligence from the Jerusalem post. He delved into the sub-surface detail of the intra-Arab fights in Palestine between the Husseini and the Nasashibi families. His study of *Communism in Palestine* was perhaps less successful; he delivered himself of a premature categoric verdict on the *kibutzim*, today flourishing by the score: "The general tendency for the communistic settlements is to gradually disintegrate." For the rest he allayed fears on the number of Bolshevik Communists, as contrasted with what he called the non-political communist agricultural experiments. Communism in Palestine was not to be feared, was his judgment.

Fuller's overall review of the political situation at the close of 1923 showed some insight. He saw the Jews moderating their political program and the Arabs becoming more unified in their obstinacy towards a government under a mandate which included the Balfour Declaration. "Great Britain, having failed to secure the cooperation of the Arab population, has proceeded to take the administration in her own hands and is striving to give a good government on *Colonial lines.*"

Britain's general attitude towards Palestine he summarized as follows:

"Perhaps the most surprising element is the number of sympathizers which the Arabs have gained in Great Britain. In this they have been aided by the anti-Zionists and by the need of political leaders for election material.

"However the government's view seems to be supported by a majority of the population. It feels that the Suez Canal is an essential part of the British Empire and must be protected at all costs. Palestine is an important bulwark against possible attacks from the north, especially since the advent of aeroplanes and the entrance of France into Syria. Added to this military reason is the political situation in Egypt at the present time. Britain wishes to be free to withdraw if possible, but if she withdraws from Egypt she must hold Palestine. It is cheaper to maintain a small force in Palestine than to hold Egypt by military measures. By supporting Zionism and encouraging the flow of Jewish wealth into this country, Palestine may soon become self-supporting and Britain will have gained a territory of great strategic and political importance which she can hold without further expenditure. She will continue to encourage the investment of Jewish money, but will grant gradual self-government as fast as Arabs show their ability and can force it from her. Convinced of the necessity of remaining in Palestine, Britain defends her position by asserting that she is ruling the country for its own good, and is bound by her pledges to the Jews and to the other nations of the world to continue. She will give self-Government as fast as the country is capable of exercising it. If the Arabs refuse to participate, she will govern as though it were a colony conquered by war."

In analyzing the reverse of the coin, the attitude of Palestine towards Britain, he concluded that the Arab opposition was directed against the mandate policy, not against Britain, while the Jews believed that Britain paid too much attention to influential Arab families and too much heed to the Arab agitators who did not represent the average inhabitant.

In his last report Fuller produced a broad theory about the evolution of Zionism which saw beyond the day to day reports and can stand as a provocative generalization for the movement in the 1920's. He divided its post-war development into three phases: political, economic, and religious. In his judgment it had passed the first and was now struggling in the second phase; religious Zionism he believed would be the final result.

Political Zionism was the phase which came to an end in 1923 when it appeared that the Jews of the world were not returning to Palestine in great numbers and the Arab contentions won wide sympathy. Up to that time a large share of world opinion had actually believed that a Jewish state would immediately spring into being. After the failure of political Zionism, came the period of economic Zionism: an attempt to gain economic control of the land mainly through funds from the United States. But this too Fuller felt would soon pass with growing Arab hostility and the drying up of the stream of funds. Zionism would then become religious and cultural and the Arabs would not oppose it. . . . "Jerusalem may one day become the Paris of the Jewish culture and the Vatican of Jewish religion."

The theory is not too far-fetched. When the specter of Hitlerism appeared over Europe in the early thirties, Zionism was in reality fast lapsing into that third cultural phase.

Chapter VIII

THE CHANGELING POLICY

ISOLATIONISM AND A MORIBUND ZIONISM

Before Hitler's seizure of power Jewish Palestine had become nothing more than a minor settlement project of about one hundred and eighty thousand, dependent for existence upon the plodding collection of Zionist funds throughout the world. Russian Jewry, originally the vast potential reservoir for Jewish pioneers in Palestine, was isolated from the main body of world Jewry and seemed to have been assimilated among the nationalities of the Union of Soviet Socialist Republics. The Jews of the central European states brought into being or revived at Versailles—Poland, Roumania, and Hungary —were acclimatizing themselves to the endemic anti-Semitism of those lands. Jews in Germany and Austria, France and Great Britain were for the most part prosperous; they regarded native anti-Semitism lightly, and the idea of migration to a barren land on the Mediterranean was far from their serious consideration.

Jews in the United States, numerous and rising in the economy, had become the official protectors of world Jewry, but the overwhelming majority of them were too absorbed with their own comfort to pay much heed to the seemingly minor incidents of persecution in eastern Europe. A tiny fraction of a percent of the annual income of American Jews fell into the coffers of the Zionist organization as it might into any charity box. When the depression came, it sharply reduced these eleemosynary contributions.

The Zionist organizational forms had remained intact throughout the twenties and early thirties. There were solemn conventions and world congresses in their appointed periods and a running political debate among a host of parties imitative of the European alignment from the extreme rightist nationalism of the Revisionists to the left wing of the Zionist Workers' Party. There were crises and block formations and all the paraphernalia of modern parliamentarism.

Only the land was not theirs. Jewish immigration was a mere trickle, while the Arabs multiplied prolifically. In 1927, the climax of three years of economic depression in Palestine, Jewish emigration exceeded immigration.

Arab leaders began to demand rights of self-government in Palestine and the Jews seemed destined to remain another minority in a Middle Eastern colony of Great Britain. As the prospect of a Jewish state receded, the "spiritual center" ideas of Ahad Ha'am gained greater vogue among the Zionists, and there came into being new groups inspired by a Judaic mysticism whose basic doctrine implied the elimination of Zionism as a political force. Though these spiritual Zionists never won majorities at any world congress their principles and verbiage represented Zionism to many of the ordinary people who contributed their pittance.

This does not mean that the Zionist leaders, whose whole being was wrapped up in the movement, had surrendered their political conceptions. The keenest of the younger group, realists such as Dr. Chaim Arlosoroff, saw in Europe a new cataclysm impending, and thought in terms of a holding action until Zionism as a political program would again attract millions of Jews, victims of another international war.

The virtual failure of Zionism in the twenties had changed the whole Near Eastern view of the British. By 1929 the Arabs had shed their great fear of Zionist domination. The paltry number of settlers was hardly a threat. The pogrom of 1929, contrary to the general view, was probably more an exercise of the Arab sense of absolute superiority than an attempt to beat down a formidable enemy. Great Britain continued to tolerate the Jews as a useful minority who would prevent the too rapid grant of extensive rights of self-government to the Arabs, but Zionism was no longer an important element in Middle East imperial calculations. An Arab world under British tutelage was an accomplished fact of Middle Eastern strategy: this was the British point of departure.

American Zionists could not accept the fact that British imperial policy, having found Zionism a far weaker prop than had been conceived by Balfour, had now reoriented itself around an Arab policy and regarded the Zionist pretensions as a nuisance. The Zionists wrote petitions, held conferences, obtained appointments with officials in the State Department. They railed against immigration restrictions, the failure to award crown lands to the Jews, the leniency of the British administration toward Arab *provocateurs*. But American Zionism in the twenties and early thirties was not a force to be reckoned with seriously.

On the second day of Arab rioting over the Wailing Wall incident of August 1929 American Consul General Knabenshue in Jerusalem was quick to telegraph the State Department that the "Moslem attacks were precipitated by provocative acts of the Jews." When a Zionist delegation arrived in Washington with the customary protest against British laxity in protecting the Jews, Secretary of State Stimson received them with the usual blandishments. "The Secretary said that he had many old and dear friends among those interested in the Zionist Movement," observed the Chief of the Division of Near Eastern Affairs in a memorandum record of the interview. The disturbances were of serious enough character for General Dawes, our Ambassador in London, to broach the idea that an American cruiser might be moved nearer to Palestine for the protection of American lives in case of a renewed outbreak, but Secretary of State Stimson discouraged the proposal lest it offend the British.

Upon the appointment of the British Commission of Inquiry into the riots—which in Hebron had taken the form of a brutal massacre of a small unprotected orthodox rabbinic school—the question arose as to whether a counsel for American Jewish interests should be allowed to testify. Consul Knabenshue, conscious of the "influence" exerted by American Jews, expressed the view that their criticism of the United States Government's indifference to the plight of the Palestinian settlement might be mitigated by permitting an American attorney to participate in the presentation of the Jewish case, but he was adamantly opposed to any official American representation in the inquiry. He did not want to stir resentment against the United States in Moslem countries.

Knabenshue reflected the prevailing sentiments in the State Department. In a conversation between Stimson and Rabbi Wise, American aloofness to the Jews of Palestine was again made official. The two men had met to discuss the appointment of an American Jewish lawyer to prepare the Zionist case before the British Commission. Stimson saw no objection to the sending of a lawyer, American, German, or Polish—that was an internal Zionist affair—but he emphasized that the attorney would enjoy no official American status. "Why should the American Government assist in presenting either the Jewish or the Arab side?" was his query. The inclusion of the Zionist preamble of the mandate in the Anglo-American Treaty was declared to be virtually meaningless. If anything, far from sponsoring Zionism, the American Government regarded it as a negative factor in the development of American commercial enterprise in the Near East because of Arab hostility.

While the State Department remained pointedly indifferent to the Zionist character of the Palestine mandate and was not noticeably exercised over the murder of eight or twelve American Jews in the Wailing Wall riots (there was some discussion about the accurate figure), the previous year it had been far from apathetic about the award of a contract for the construction of the Haifa harbor works, another facet of the British mandate policy. Secretary of State Kellogg had written the American ambassador in London that he considered the virtual exclusion of American bids a violation of the Anglo-American Convention of 1925. The British replied that there was a general misunderstanding about the whole affair and that it had been decided subsequently to abandon the idea of a single general contractor and to utilize the services of the local Palestine Public Works Department. This change of plan was obviously the result of a strong protest by the United States and other powers vigilant to detect any violation of the open-door economic policy in the mandated areas. Intervention in this Haifa case was in the main current of United States policy of the isolationist period: to spurn complex situations which entailed political commitments and to back to the hilt the rights of expansive American business in foreign countries. It was a highly selective isolationism.

After the 1929 riots the League of Nations Mandates Commission severely criticized the relations of the mandatory with the Jews. The United States, unmoved by dramatic literary presentations such as *The Great Betrayal* by Rabbi Wise and Jacob de Haas, remained officially silent. There was even a marked decline in the number of conventional greetings by the Chief Executives to Zionist meetings.

HITLER AND THE REVIVAL OF ZIONISM

The rise of Hitler is the sharp turning point in the history of modern Zionism. Nazism re-educated in the realities of anti-Semitism one of the most prosperous and self-satisfied Jewish communities, the Jews of Germany. It was a long lesson and the piece-meal manner of its communication was such that many of the Jews did not really capture its meaning until the eve of their extinction. Virulent hatred of the Jews spread like a contagion throughout the world. A violent anti-Semitism suddenly flared in eastern Europe, while a slow flame was fanned in France, Great Britain, and the United States.

When the German Jews began to emigrate, the United States and Britain were usually their first choices, but there were groups who because of the immigration laws of the Anglo-Saxon countries or because Hitler's bitter teaching was taking root in their souls chose Palestine as a refuge. Immigration from Germany into Palestine jumped precipitously. At the new annual figure there was a real prospect that in a few decades Jews might become a majority in the land despite the high Arab birth rate. The new immigration had a different character, composed as it was of bourgeois German Jews coming to join the pioneers of the earlier migrations from eastern Europe, and the amalgam of the two elements was not always immediately successful. But this was not the chief obstacle to the creation of a new Jewish center of population in the Near East.

To the British and the Arabs, the renewal of Jewish immigration from Germany in the thirties and the increase in the collection of Zionist funds in the United States, a barometer of Jewish persecution, meant a serious upset in the whole *status quo* of the early thirties in Palestine. The Arab-Jewish conflict was brought to a head during the riots of 1936–1937, when under the Grand Mufti they made a serious attempt to annihilate the Jewish settlement and the British had to use major weapons to suppress disorders which threatened their prestige in the Arab World.

The uprisings of 1936 initiated a new period fertile with British investigatory commissions. Thousands of words of testimony were taken and a sea of documents was let loose on every economic and social aspect of this tiny country. White Papers were composed and superseded almost before they had received respectable distribution.

After each successive White Paper and each new turn of British policy in Palestine American Zionists and non-Zionists who had agreed to participate in the broadened Jewish Agency for Palestine, thundered their denunciations of the British Government and its curtailment of promised Jewish rights. They were joined by a substantial number of Congressmen and a segment of the metropolitan press. But the outbursts against Britain had no bearing on the conduct of American foreign policy during this period.

ROOSEVELT'S NON-INTERVENTION POLICY

Fundamentally, during Roosevelt's first three terms, the State Department adhered strictly to the basic position of the Hughes period, that the Jewish National Home provisions of the mandate were not an "American interest."

In 1936 seven Jewish organizations in the United States submitted a joint memorandum to the Palestine Royal Commission entitled, "American Interest in the Administration of the Palestine Mandate." The Palestine Economic Corporation, an American development company in Palestine, had presented to the State Department a paper which argued that the United States had obligations to the Jewish Homeland under the Anglo-American Treaty. Neither the President nor the State Department gave weight to these contentions. The permanent officials of the department resented what they considered the unwarranted intervention of American Zionists in the conduct of foreign policy. This feeling was expressed with a vehemence of language hardly defensible. If the Zionists acted as special pleaders, the State Department officials were writing with extravagant hostility and distorting a historical record of American interest in Palestine in glaring fashion. Into the innocuous Zionist memoranda they read veiled threats to American-British relations.

The first significant American diplomatic intervention on Palestine in many years came in the summer of 1937. The Peel Commission, created to re-examine the whole Arab-Jewish problem, recommended a form of partition into Arab and Jewish areas which might conceivably affect United States interests as defined in the Anglo-American Treaty. On July 6, 1937, therefore, Ambassador Bingham asked Foreign Secretary Eden whether the United States Government would be consulted with respect to innovations which might be proposed by the British Government in Palestine as a consequence of the Report of the Royal Commission. Eden replied that the rights of United States nationals, as laid down in the Convention, remained inviolate unless the United States assented to a change. But that was as far as American interest could be sustained in the disposition of Palestine. The consent of the United States Government was not required for any revision of the Palestine mandate unless the specific rights of its nationals, in the operating Articles 2 to 6 of the Convention, were infringed. With respect to other aspects of the mandate Eden maintained that since the United States had approved of the mandate as a whole, it had by inference accepted Article 27 which provided that, with League of Nations consent, the mandate could be modified. In closing Eden made a gesture of courtesy; beyond its legal obligations to the United States Britain appreciated and indeed welcomed United States interest in the solution of the Palestine problem and would keep us informed.

Ambassador Bingham's reply of August 4 to the Eden note developed a most complicated juridic position. First, the United States, without emphasizing its divergence from the British, did not accept completely either their viewpoint or interpretation. The United States clung to the same position it had adopted with reference to the end of the mandate in Iraq in 1932: "Since the termination of a regime in a mandated territory necessarily involves the 'disposition' of the territory and affects the interests of American nationals therein, the right of the United States to be consulted with respect to the conditions under which the territory is subsequently to be administered is on precisely the same basis as its right to be consulted, with regard to the establishment of a mandatory regime." Hence the ambassador requested that proposals which Great Britain prepared for the League of Nations should be communicated to the United States Government in ample time to enable it to determine "what, if any observations it may desire to make with a view to the preservation of American rights in Palestine."

In this portion of the note the United States seemingly insisted on its right to be consulted *generally* with respect to the future of the administration of Palestine. The moot question was whether this consultation was still limited only to changes which affected American "interests" in the narrow sense of the term or whether the United States would have a voice, should it so desire, in the character of the regime to succeed the mandatory.

In a subsequent paragraph of his note, however, Bingham reverted to the propositions outlined during the negotiations of the early twenties. He assured the British that *active* American interest still was "based exclusively on its obligation and purpose to provide for the protection of American interests in Palestine on a basis of equality with those of other Governments and their nationals." A certain legal ambiguity about the source of the mandate's authority was preserved, but the main direction of American policy was clearly stated. This correspondence between Eden and Bingham was published by the British, obviously with United States consent. It seemed to render futile direct pressure of American Zionists on their government for active intervention on general Palestine policy.

In a public memorandum of October 1938 just prior to the biennial elections—the month of good auspices for the next decade of Zionist politics—the State Department, under Zionist pressure, eulogized the role of American capital and intellect in the upbuilding of Palestine, but its juridic interpretation of the Anglo-American Treaty of 1924 was as circumscribed as it had ever been under any postwar Republican administration. "None of these articles (the Convention of 1924) empower the Government of the United States to prevent the modification of the terms of any of the mandates. Under their provisions, however, this government can decline to recognize the validity of the application to American interests of any modifications of the mandates unless such modification has been assented to by the Government of the United States." And "American interests" did not include Zionism in the Roosevelt administration of the thirties, no more than they had in the days of Hughes or Stimson. A Roosevelt letter to the Mayor of Hartford repeated the State Department formula in precisely the same terms—thus bestowing on this obfuscated language the highest constitutional authority in the realm of foreign policy. After praising the remarkable accomplishments of the Jewish settlers in Palestine and delivering assurances that the United States would be kept "fully informed" of any changes in the mandate the President concluded with a clear-cut statement of United States legal impotence in the affairs of the Jewish homeland in Palestine. "I understand . . . that under the terms of our convention with Great Britain regarding the Palestine Mandate, we are unable to prevent modifications in the Mandate. The most we can do is to decline to accept as applicable to American interests any modifications affecting such interests unless we have given our assent to them. You may be sure that we shall continue to follow the situation with the closest attention."

There was no official reaction to the British White Paper of 1939 from the White House. In Congress, as usual, it was another story. An attack was made by 15 of the 25 members of the House Foreign Affairs Committee, and twenty-eight senators publicly protested the White Paper, which restricted Jewish immigration into Palestine at a most critical moment for the salvation of the lives of German Jews. The British had promised the Arabs that even the reduced Jewish quotas would terminate by 1944. The Congressmen made their own interpretation of Article 7 of the Anglo-American Treaty of 1924 on mandate modifications. They called the defense of Jewish interests in Palestine a "moral obligation of the United States" and labelled the new British policy a Treaty violation. Since the League of Nations Mandates Commission refused to validate the policy of the White Paper of 1939, it could be legally argued, if such by-play had meaning, that even under Eden's restrictive interpretation of the Treaty the United States could also refuse to honor so fundamental a change in the whole concept of the mandate.

Justice Brandeis, who had long maintained silence and had kept free of Zionist politics, was stirred by the White Paper of 1939 to write a simple moving note. "What does the world propose to do with the Jews for whom exile is enforced? Unless civilization has so reverted to primitivism as to wish the destruction of homeless Jews it must encourage the proved medium to solve in great measure the problem of Jewish homelessness."

Roosevelt affectionately called the old justice Isaiah, but did nothing. The Evian Conference, that gathering of the nations at Roosevelt's invitation to discuss the fate of the Jewish refugees, had been pathetically ineffectual. Seven years later the American Zionist, Emanuel Neumann, appearing before the Anglo-American Committee of Inquiry on Palestine, had a mournful reflection to make on this White Paper: "No one can say how many hundreds of thousands of Jews who have perished since 1939 would have been alive today if their legal right to enter Palestine had been respected."

THE WARTIME DILEMMA

In the domestic crisis of the thirties and then in the great world conflict with Germany which was taking shape, the fate of Palestine seemed irrelevant. The Jews in the United States were lined up as a body to fight the evil of the Nazis and followed Roosevelt in his laborious wrestling with the blind isolationism of the country. In the general holocaust of World War II, the problem of Palestine as well as the fate of the six million Jews in eastern Europe tended to become mere details. It was difficult to view the Jewish problem as unique, deserving of special consideration. If the forces of good triumphed then the Jews too would enjoy the liberties of the new era of mankind; if evil conquered then the Jews would be destroyed along with other free peoples.

During World War II no great promises were made to the Jews about Palestine. Unlike the period of the First World War, when Jews were divided among the belligerents, during the Second the Jews had no choice. They were in mortal combat with Hitler and their sympathies did not need to be prevailed upon. Lukewarm elements, those who could play neutral, like Spain and Turkey and the Arab peoples, had the advantage. They were wooed assiduously because they were potentially hostile. There was no politic reason to give the Jews promises about Palestine at the expense of the pro-Hitler or cautiously indifferent Arabs; it would not increase the Jews' thirst for a Nazi defeat and might be useful to German propaganda among the Arabs. Hitler's anti-semitism had overflowed the banks of the German Reich and had reenforced native anti-semitism in the Ukraine, Lithuania, Poland, Roumania, Hungary, and France. Proclamations in favor of the Jews would play in with the German propaganda line that the war was essentially a struggle against world Jewish plutocracy and the Russian Bolshevists.

Thus in terms of the propagandist's accounting of friendly and hostile elements, there were apparent reasons why no Jewish "angle" of the world conflict should be stressed.

For a variety of political reasons the Zionists eschewed direct public pressure on President Roosevelt and turned to the Congress, whose members from major urban areas were acutely sensitive to the Jewish problem. In April 1941, the American Palestine Committee was reconstituted; it included 68 Senators and 200 representatives. In 1942, the twenty-fifth anniversary of the Balfour Declaration, the legislators issued a statement against the British White Paper. Executive silence continued. In 1943 there were more resolutions by even larger groups of Congressmen but their strong language never raised any significant response in the State Department, which steadfastly pursued a policy of strict non-intervention in the affairs of a war-time ally.

Breckenridge Long, Assistant Secretary of State, appearing before the House Foreign Affairs Committee for a discussion of Jewish refugees in November 1943, finally conceded that Palestine had a larger significance beyond the jurisdiction of the mandatory authority which controlled it. ". . . The American Government is not entirely obtuse about Palestine or is not disinterested in the situation that is developing there." The State Department still clad its pronouncements in a multiplication of negatives; but even this acknowledgment of interest was novel.

In the meantime the war and the early accounts of the horrible fate of the Jews in eastern Europe—only a faint echo of what the State Department had heard officially about the ghetto massacres of 1941–1942—brought about a strong recrudescence of Zionism in the United States. The Biltmore Program, adopted by an Extraordinary Zionist Conference in New York on May 11, 1942, read: "The Conference calls for fulfillment of the original purpose of the Balfour Declaration and the Mandate which 'recognizing the historical connection of the Jewish people with Palestine' was to afford them the opportunity, as stated by President Wilson, to found there a Jewish Commonwealth."

This was a renascence of Herzlian Zionism and the dominant political conceptions of the movement in 1918 and 1919. Essentially it represented a break with the half-measures of the thirties, the haggling with the British over a few thousand immigration certificates, and the diplomatic circumlocutions which came to be identified with Weizmann's name. The American leaders of most Zionist parties, whatever their past differences, again raised the standards of political Zionism: independence for Jews in Palestine and the building of an economy capable of supporting a vast influx of European Jews. Americans were the protagonists of this policy throughout the war years. They did not hesitate at crucial moments to shout down the aging president of the World Zionist organization when he wavered on a clear political solution and still hoped for a *modus vivendi* with the British. American Zionists were the most powerful political and economic body in the world movement and they intended to brook no compromises. The balance of power in the American Jewish community had become so altered that even the notables of the American Jewish Committee, reluctantly, and with a due number of provisos, were ultimately swept along in support of the Jewish Commonwealth thesis which they had traditionally opposed.

On January 18, 1944, Secretary of State Cordell Hull publicly reaffirmed his adherence to a policy of non-intervention in this "British responsibility," except insofar as the Government was generally troubled by the magnitude of the Jewish tragedy in Europe. "In compliance with your request for information," he wrote Senator Maybank, "as to the attitude of the American Government toward this matter, I may say that Palestine is a British responsibility. Nevertheless, the Department maintains a close interest in the Palestine problem and follows closely all developments having a bearing upon the tragic plight of the Jewish people in Europe. You are familiar with the sympathetic attitude which the Department harbors towards the Jews in their present terrible circumstances, and it is doing everything possible, through the Inter-governmental Committee and otherwise, to alleviate their plight. Every aspect of this general problem is a matter of immediate interest to this Government. The Department is accordingly keeping in touch with the different phases of this situation, in Palestine as in other parts of the world, and is doing what it can to be helpful."

In the early months of 1944, as the period contemplated by the White Paper of 1939 for shutting tight the doors of Palestine to further Jewish immigration drew near, the Congress was moved to intervene on its own, breaking the dead silence of the Executive. Identically-worded resolutions were introduced into the House and Senate which for the first time called for concrete *action* on the part of the Government of the United States. This was no longer an expression of vague sentiment as the resolution of 1922 had been. "Resolved that the United States shall use its good offices and take appropriate measures to the end that the doors of Palestine shall be opened for free entry of Jews in that country, and that there shall be full opportunity for colonization so that the Jewish people may ultimately reconstitute Palestine as a free and democratic Jewish commonwealth."

It was a revolutionary departure; in simple terms it meant American intervention to help achieve Jewish statehood. It seemed to presage an end to the policy of mere lip-service, and most American public opinion backed it.

Suddenly, on March 17, 1944, in the midst of the hearings before the House Committee on Foreign Affairs, a letter arrived from Secretary of War Stimson, a brief statement which cut short the debate, for no one could contradict the considered judgment of the War Department "that without reference to the merits of these resolutions, further action on them at this time would be prejudicial to the successful prosecution of the war." In fact there may well have been valid reasoning behind the fears of the military commanders about to launch the Normandy invasion that any disturbance in the Near East might force a deployment of troops away from the main effort. Skepticism about the Arab threats does not signify; at the time the Arabs were an incalculable factor, and the extra measure of precaution at that moment in the war may have been warranted.

As it turned out, Roosevelt's interview of the day before with the

two Zionist Rabbis, Wise and Silver, had been an attempt to mitigate
the blow of the War Department letter. On March 16, the Rabbis,
emerging from the White House, had been authorized to say in the
President's name: "The American Government has never given its
approval to the White Paper of 1939. The President is happy that
the doors of Palestine are open today to Jewish refugees and that
when future decisions are reached, full justice will be done to those
who seek a Jewish National Home, for which our Government and
the American people have always had the deepest sympathy, and
today more than ever, in view of the tragic plight of hundreds of
thousands of homeless Jewish refugees." The statement may also have
been a subtle attempt to persuade the British not to implement that
provision of the White Paper of 1939 which Churchill had once
denounced and which completely cut off Jewish immigration into
Palestine in March 1944.

During the 1944 political conventions, both the Republican and
Democratic parties included fulsome Zionist planks in their platforms.
The Republicans, in a somewhat more favorable political position
as the "outs," condemned the President for his failure to insist that
the mandatory carry out the provisions of the Balfour Declaration.
The Democratic plank vied with them by inserting the "Jewish Commonwealth" of the Zionist "Biltmore Program" into their text. For an
October Convention of the American Zionists in 1944, President Roosevelt went even a decisive step further; he sent a message through Senator Wagner which was a personal reiteration of the Democratic party
platform commitment. It was as clear-cut as the Zionists could have
asked in time of war: "Efforts will be made to find appropriate ways
and means of effectuating this policy as soon as practicable. I know
how long and ardently the Jewish people have worked and prayed
for the establishment of Palestine as a free and democratic Jewish
commonwealth. I am convinced that the American people give their
support to this aid; and if re-elected, I will help bring about its
realization." The constitutional framer of our foreign policy cannot
be presumed to make fortuitous proclamations even during an election
campaign. This pronouncement, like the abortive Congressional resolution, was important for its basic departure from previous presidential salutations to the Zionists. It was not a mere expression of sympathy or favor; it was a promise to find ways and means to fulfill a
policy plank of the President's political party.

Immediately after the elections in November the Zionists arrived on Capitol Hill once more to garner their reward, perhaps somewhat prematurely. In October 1944 the War Department had declared that the military situation was no longer of such a character as to interpose an objection to the Congressional resolution on Palestine. But this time the State Department was the obstacle. It took upon itself the task of staying the hand of Congress and the argument of military necessity was replaced by the vague formula, "unwise from the standpoint of the general international situation." This veto created a crisis in American Zionism which led to the temporary resignation of Rabbi Silver, who wanted to push the resolution, despite the State Department, against the judgment of Rabbi Wise.

The Zionists had hopes that at Yalta, as the war in the west was approaching its final stages, they would receive an international guarantee. This was doubly denied them. Churchill declared in the House of Commons that a decision on Palestine would be postponed until after the war. Then the Zionists were shaken by the ceremonial reception accorded Ibn Saud by the President on his cruiser in the Mediterranean and by his cryptic aside to the Congress when he returned: "Of the problems of Arabia, I learned more about that whole problem, the Moslem problem, the Jewish problem, by talking with Ibn Saud for five minutes than I could have learned in exchange of two or three dozen letters." It was difficult to surmise what deep insights the wily desert chieftain revealed during those five minutes to the ailing President.

Their meeting was not a sudden improvisation. A destroyer had been put at Ibn Saud's disposal to travel eight hundred miles from Jidda through the Suez Canal. "The destroyer decks were covered with rich oriental rugs, while gilded chairs gave added touches of unusual splendor, as, also, did the flowing robes and accessories that make the Arabian dress so strikingly picturesque. . . ." read the White House release. "The President and the King continued their talks long after the luncheon hour." Part of the negotiations were devoted to American air bases in Saudi Arabia; the President gave enthusiastic hints of the help that might be expected for various internal projects in Arabia; and the King vented his rage against the Zionists in Palestine. The head of the Wahhabi religious movement made his opposition to Zionism resound with passages from the Koran which brooked no diplomatic rejoinder. Hopkins later wrote in a memorandum that his show of unalterable hostility to the Zionists had "overly impressed" the President during their interview.

The Arabs embroidered the meeting with oriental tales and fantasies. The American officials who arranged this solemn interview between the desert king and the commander-in-chief of the most powerful army in the world on the eve of victory, were not blind to the possibilities of the encounter, the legends which would grow up around it in the east. Typical of the extravaganzas inspired by the meeting is the account by Azzam Bey, Secretary General of the Arab League, reported in a United Press despatch of August 25, 1945: " 'If Palestine is given to the Jews,' the King told President Roosevelt, 'I will never rest until I and all my sons have been killed in the defense of Palestine.' . . . Ibn Saud then stood and placed his hand in Roosevelt's hand and told him, 'Swear that you will never support the Zionists' fight for Palestine against the Arabs' and Roosevelt shook Ibn Saud's hand and pledged he would not support the Jews against the Arabs." In a sense this meeting fortified Arab sentiment against the Zionists as no other single act since the issuance of the White Paper of 1939.

During the War United States military missions had been established in Egypt, Iran, and Iraq. President Roosevelt sent at least four personal envoys to make independent surveys in the Middle East— Bullitt, Colonel Hoskins, General Patrick Hurley, General Royce. American advisers were engaged to reorganize local police, public works, and general administration in a number of states. Lend-lease became a powerful wedge which penetrated with ease into the oldest spheres of British and French imperialism. In 1939 great oil concessions in Saudi Arabia had been awarded to the Arabian-American Oil Company after major political negotiations. During the war the President was in favor of buying the concessions of the oil companies outright; when they bridled at the idea, his Secretary of the Interior announced that the government would build a pipeline to the Mediterranean for them. The complexities of our Middle East wartime oil policy, however, cannot be discussed here except insofar as they relate to Palestine. Subsidies from the United States and Britain paid directly to Ibn Saud are no longer either secret or startling aspects of war policy. The mystery remains whether political commitments were involved incident to the discussions of air bases and oil fields which affected Palestine beyond promises of mere consultation with the Arabs.

At various times during the War and after members of Congress have denounced the intrigues and betrayals of State Department offi-

cials. Congressman Emmanuel Celler in August 1943 named names—
General Hurley, Colonel Harold Hoskins, and Wallace Murray, an
adviser on political relations in the State Department who for many
years previously had been chief of the Near Eastern Affairs Division.
In retrospect this is a misplaced emphasis, part of a legend which
tends to raise the wartime President above error or the more mundane
ways of diplomacy. The decisions were his, and the Middle East was
a world area of whose significance President Roosevelt was profoundly
aware. He may not be held responsible for every stupid despatch
contrived by a desk man in the Near Eastern Affairs Division, but he
was fully conscious of the main lines of policy towards both the Arabs
and the Zionists.

A few days after Roosevelt's speech to the Congress there was balm
for the Zionists. On March 16, 1945 Rabbi Wise, who in his long life
had become the repository of so many intimate promises of support
for Zionism from Presidents and officials, was handed still another
pledge. He was authorized by the White House to announce that the
President stood by his October 1944 commitment.

The Roosevelt record on Palestine and on the tragic annihilation
of the Jews in eastern Europe will remain cloudy for many years.
Bartley Crum, whom Truman appointed to the Anglo-American Commission of Inquiry on Palestine in 1945, has published what he calls
revelations from a secret file handed to him by State Department
officials on the *Queen Elizabeth* during the Commission's voyage to
Europe. "According to this file," he wrote, "since September 15, 1938
each time a promise was made to American Jewry regarding Palestine,
the State Department promptly sent messages to the Arab rulers dis-
counting it and reassuring them, in effect, that regardless of what
was promised publicly to the Jews nothing would be done to change
the situation in Palestine." The Department refused to publish the
documents upon Crum's later challenge.

One letter of President Roosevelt to Ibn Saud, written April 5, 1945,
shortly before his death, was made public by Secretary of State Byrnes
six months later. It was used by the Department to prove that the
Government had consistently held to the position that it would not
support a final decision affecting the "basic situation" in Palestine
without full consultation with both Jews and Arabs. In this letter
Roosevelt assured "his great and good friend" Ibn Saud that he was
mindful of their interview in the course of which he had an opportunity to obtain so vivid an impression of His Majesty's sentiments

on the question of Palestine. "Your Majesty will doubtless recall that during our recent conversation I assured you that I would take no action, in my capacity as Chief of the Executive Branch of this Government, which might prove hostile to the Arab people." Roosevelt promised full consultation with both Arabs and Jews and renewed his previous reassurances on Palestine.

It could be argued, of course, that the President did not regard a Jewish homeland as "hostile to the Arab people"—a standard contention of the Zionists for decades. Nevertheless, the general impression created by the communication is out of harmony with the precise commitment to the Zionists in October 1944 that he would move to bring about the realization of their goal. The promise to the Jews had been definitive and not contingent upon more Arab conferences which could only be delaying actions, though it could be argued that the Jews were never told explicitly that there would *not be* Arab consultations. Near Eastern Division men in the Department might have considered this astute wartime diplomacy instead of what it really was, a rather clumsy imitation of the British way in the Middle East for thirty years.

It is noteworthy that the British members of the Anglo-American Commission did not take this diplomatic double-dealing nearly as seriously as did Crum. "Really, the Jews are not the most important factor at all," they said to him. "The important thing is Anglo-American cooperation. Since these promises of yours have put both nations in the dock together it only serves to bring us closer in the world ahead."

Sumner Welles has attempted an apologia of the Rooseveltian Zionist policy in his eloquent book *We Need Not Fail.* "He believed," Welles reports, recollecting intimate conversations with the President, "that the creation of the promised Homeland would not only afford security and an assured future for many hundreds of thousands of Jews who would otherwise be homeless, but that such a Commonwealth would also provide a most valuable demonstration to the peoples of the Near East of an advanced form of democratic state, and that the example given and the influence exercised by such a state would be bound within a relatively short time to raise living standards in the adjacent countries." According to Welles, Roosevelt was deeply interested in the possibilities for industrial and agricultural development in Palestine, and the President hoped that once a Palestine Commonwealth was established, the neighboring states of Syria, the Lebanon, and Trans-Jordan would be persuaded of the manifest advantages of a federal union with their neighbor.

Roosevelt was apparently always optimistic about a negotiated settlement with the Arabs in his discussions with his Under Secretary of State.

As for the interview with Ibn Saud and their exchange of letters after the President's return to Washington, Welles believes that they have been misconstrued by "malicious misrepresentation." The letters were prepared by the Department of State for signature during those last weeks of Roosevelt's life when he was unable to devote much time or thought to official correspondence. "Even so," Welles maintains, "open to misinterpretation as some of the phrases used may seem to be, there is in those letters no commitment which is at variance with the views which the President had previously maintained."

Weizmann's published account of his relations with Roosevelt shows the President to have been polite and friendly, but their discussions, even when "affirmative," remained theoretical. In his recent autobiography there are shadowy allusions to a bizarre scheme which involved Ibn Saud, St. John Philby his adviser, Colonel Hoskins whom Roosevelt had sent to the Middle East, the President himself, Weizmann, and Churchill; it was to make Ibn Saud the "boss of bosses" in the Near East if he "settled" with the Jews. But no one seems to have taken the plan too seriously. Weizmann's concluding estimate leaves unsolved the riddle of Roosevelt's Zionist policy. "There was a definite cleavage," he writes, "between the White House and Mr. Sumner Welles on the one hand, and the rest of the State Department on the other, a situation not unlike the one we faced in England." This explanation would sound more convincing for the present administration; Roosevelt was far too much his own world strategist to have been swerved by the anti-Zionists in the Near Eastern Affairs Division from any course he had mapped out.

Roosevelt was confronted by the same world maze that had bewildered Wilson, and despite his superior perspicacity he too was at once a pragmatist and an emotional idealist who initiated a vast complex of wildly contradictory movements. During the war years—and they begin in 1939—without jeopardizing the security of the United States, he might have called for more energetic measures to save at least a portion of the six million Jews who were slaughtered in the ghettos of eastern Europe and to make real provision for the survivors of the massacre in Palestine. Without ignoring the political and military obstacles to bold intervention in this sphere, one can still find the late President wanting.

THE CONTRADICTIONS OF AMERICAN FOREIGN POLICY

The overwhelming majority of the Jews in eastern Europe were killed early in the war, towards the end of 1941 and the first half of 1942. Although the facts were known in great detail long before to the Office of Strategic Services and to Jewish leaders in the United States, the full record of annihilation was not published until 1945. To most Americans the opening of the concentration camps with their gruesome revelations was a shock. But in fact the greater horror had long since been buried in the pits of eastern Europe; the inmates of the camps were only a remnant of the Jewries of Europe.

The ghastly tragedy of the six million Jews of central and eastern Europe penetrated the consciousness of American Jews as no other historic event in modern times. The vast number of American Jews are only a generation removed from those European centers which the Germans wiped out with systematic brutality. When the macabre details became known, even the most complacent Jews in the United States had at least a fleeting thought: "But for the grace of God I too might have been tortured and burned. . . ." This deep feeling is a key to the understanding of our recent political relations with Palestine.

Zionist and Jewish relief budgets which in the past had been limited to a few million dollars a year were expanded to hundreds of millions. Before the war, the notables of the American Jewish Committee had been cool to Zionism; by 1945 only a handful of Jewish diehards dared to hold out in a small anti-Zionist stronghold. The idea that Palestine must be established as a haven for those Jews who survived the rule of Hitler in Europe and the few hundred thousand Jews scattered throughout the Moslem world, permeated every stratum of American Jewish society. For the first time there was a formidable unity among American Jews on the question of Palestine. The new Zionism was qualitatively different in its vigor from any of its past forms in the United States, even in the days of Brandeis.

Nurtured by the considerable political and economic power of four and a half million Jewish citizens and the sympathy of millions of non-Jews, a strong public sentiment in favor of granting the Jews a land was created. President Truman, as well as any man, reflected the ordinary feelings of average Americans. He was subject to their sentimentalities and their prejudices. He had Jewish friends. If he could help displaced persons in Europe and secure the existence of those Jews who were already in Palestine, he would intervene on their behalf. It was a popular idea. The people wanted it, and it was a right thing to do.

But from the very beginning, the President's straightforward convictions, revealed in his first moves after the war, were balked by the realities of world military and political strategy as represented to him by men who professionally thought only in terms of maximum power and maximum military strength. It was equally impossible for the President either to ignore their dire admonitions about the national security, or to maintain publicly the harsh view that the Palestine Jews and the displaced persons must be sacrificed to major policy considerations involving appeasement of the Arabs. Hence the waverings, inconsistencies, and contradictions in American policy as one or another pressure was ascendant. When the international crisis became so grave that armed conflict with Russia appeared imminent, the fate of the few hundred thousand Jews was pushed into the background. When there was a temporary easing of tension in the world, or when the biennial election periods gave American Jews bargaining power, the administration, in the nature of things, was more responsive to Zionist appeals.

In analyzing the forces which drove United States policy alternately in different directions, it would be misleading to attach paramount importance to British opposition to the Zionists. Paradoxically, in the final stages, the character of Bevin's attacks upon the President buttressed his anti-Foreign Office, pro-Israel stand. Britain throughout has been the instrument rather than the motive force of post-war policy in Palestine. Basic military strategy for the west on the general staff level has been in the hands of the United States and not Britain. It is evident, particularly since our belated firm stand has brought an abrupt alteration of British tactics, that if the United States had arrived at an irrevocable decision to take the necessary risk on a Jewish Palestine, Great Britain could not long have offered effective opposition. The cold fact is that until the close of 1948, Great Britain was abetted in its dog-in-the-manger policy by officials in the United States military and diplomatic establishment.

THE ANGLO-AMERICAN COMMISSION

At the United Nations Conference in San Francisco in May 1945, the Zionists made a feeble attempt to secure the immediate recognition of a Jewish Commonwealth. Neither the six million dead in the ghettos of eastern Europe, nor the weight of Jewish participation in the war effort of all the United Nations, nor the sturdy performance of the Jewish colonists of Palestine in the field and in their shops and factories could outweigh Arab hostility represented by Egypt, Saudi Arabia, and Iraq who had proclaimed their war against the Axis as late as January and February 1945. The Zionists did contribute to the phrasing of Article 80 of the Trusteeship Charter which they construed as protection of their rights to a Jewish Homeland granted in previous international instruments.

In the United States, the new President seemed ready to assume responsibilities for the fate of the Jews immediately upon the consummation of victory over Japan. Earl Harrison's investigation of the pitiable condition of the Jews in the displaced persons centers of Germany had momentarily aroused public opinion. His report was a condemnation of the American military establishment. "As matters now stand, we appear to be treating the Jews as the Nazis treated them," he wrote, "except that we do not exterminate them." Harrison in his conclusions had accepted the substance of a Jewish Agency plea for 100,000 immigration certificates to Palestine, and the President announced that he was communicating directly with the British Government in an effort to open the doors of Palestine to those displaced persons who wished to go there.

According to Sumner Welles, the Truman statement on the admission of 100,000 Jews into Palestine was preceded by a rumor that Governor Dewey was about to offer an ambitious plan for their relief. Whatever his immediate motivation, Truman wrote a letter to Atlee which was specific and clear-cut. Like most Americans he was still under the spell of the revelations of the crematoria and the concentration camps. ". . . I concur in the belief that no other single matter is so important for those who have known the horrors of the concentration camps for over a decade as is the future of immigration possibilities into Palestine. . . . As I said to you in Potsdam, the American people, as a whole, firmly believe that immigration into Palestine should not be closed and that a reasonable number of Europe's persecuted Jews should, in accordance with their wishes, be permitted to resettle there. . . . If it is to be effective, such action should not be long delayed."

His plea was rejected by the British "because of conditions in Palestine," they said; they proposed instead that an Inquiry be instituted, to which the United States acceded.

On the surface this Inquiry had a tempo and character distinct from the Royal Investigatory Commissions of the twenties and thirties. In drafting instructions for an Anglo-American Committee, Secretary of State Byrnes was explicit in asking for a report within 120 days. The frame of reference of the Inquiry was broad, covering political, economic, and social conditions in Palestine; the fate of the Jews still remaining in Europe; and the desire of the Jews to migrate to Palestine. The Committee was authorized to make recommendations on the provision of facilities for the settlement of Jews in countries outside Europe.

The Zionists received the new committee with weary skepticism, but they nevertheless proceeded once again to prepare their long briefs of historical and economic data, masterpieces in their way. After ten formal inquiries on Palestine, not many Jews expected this one to be the means of salvation, though it had an element of novelty in the participation of American members who for the most part were not State Department officials. In the displaced persons camps there was wild despair. The months after liberation had dragged on, and Jews were still detained in Germany while successive commissions heard the same arguments again and again.

In the meantime Congress backed up the President's request for the admission of Jewish immigrants with a resolution adopted on December 19, 1945 which enjoined the Government of the United States to secure the opening of Palestine for "free entry of Jews into that country . . . and that there shall be full opportunity for colonization and development, so that they may freely proceed with the upbuilding of Palestine as the Jewish National Home."

Reviewing the work of the Committee of Inquiry, of which he was a member, Bartley Crum concluded: "I find it painful now to admit that Dr. Albert Einstein, Dr. Abba Hillel Silver, the American Zionist leader, and others who characterized the committee's appointment as a device to postpone action were correct." Einstein in his inimitable bland manner had told the Committee that it was worthless before it started at its first hearings held in Washington: "So I may add that I believe that the frame of mind of the colonial people of the British is so rigid that I am absolutely convinced that any counsels will not have any effect. I think commissions like this are a smoke-screen to show good will."

To men of perspicacity it was apparent that no dearth of facts was responsible for postponing a wise and just settlement of the Palestine issue. Indeed, the dreary compilations of commissions, committees, boards and inquiries since the twenties had become an ever widening sea of paper, a barrier which effectively kept the Jews from their promised land of refuge.

At its sessions in Washington the Anglo-American Committee heard Jewish and Arab arguments which had been digested scores of times before. The representations of only one group are worth particular examination. The Foreign Missions Conference of North America, in conjunction with the Federal Council of Churches of Christ in America and the Home Missions Councils of North America, had conducted an investigation—in New York—of the whole Jewish refugee problem and the political situation in Palestine. Their report had been approved only by the Committee of Reference of the Foreign Missions Conference. The Conference spokesman at the hearings of the Anglo-American Committee made a statement in the direct tradition of the anti-Zionist arguments paraded by the Near East Protestant missionaries ever since the Paris Peace Conference. He was followed by Canon Bridgman, who had been official representative of the American Episcopal Church in Palestine working with the English missions from 1924 to 1944. Bridgman indulged in that variety of anti-Semitism which seeks to destroy Jewish unity on Palestine by encouraging the disaffection of Western European Jews. "The acuteness of the Palestine situation," he testified, on January 12, 1946, "is due to a large extent to rabid Jewish nationalism. Many fine things have been done by Jews in Palestine with genuine sacrifice for noble ideals, but the type of nationalism developing in a dominant section of the Jews of Palestine is so blatant, so self-centered, and so intolerant even towards Jews in their midst who dissent from the official policy that it must not be confused with the liberal democratic ideals so ably represented by fine Jews in American and British public life, save in the case of some when they are treating of Palestine, which seems to be their blind spot.

"This is an East European variety of democracy which according to the testimony of the liberal Jews alarmed at the developments, seems to have taken whole pages from totalitarian systems. It is Jewish nationalism which has enflamed the feelings of the Arabs of the country because they see in it a threat to their welfare.

"News of what has been happening in Palestine and the exportation of Palestine Jewish ideas to the Jews of the neighboring countries has rendered insecure the multitudes of Jews who have lived in peace and security in Arab lands for centuries."

This apparent concern for the Jews of other Arab lands cloaked an anxiety which for decades had nurtured the missionaries' opposition to Zionism—fear that the so-called "Jewish spirit" might regenerate the whole Near East and a cultural upheaval undermine the vested interest of the missionaries with their own particular brand of Christian civilization.

Testimony of the missionary groups before the Committee provoked an internal Protestant controversy over the stand of the Federal Council of Churches of Christ in America. Dr. Poling of the *Christian Herald,* representing a Christian committee in favor of a Jewish Homeland in Palestine, sharply dissociated himself from the views of Canon Bridgman. One thing was clearly revealed by this clash of the Protestant "interests" before the Committee: the foreign mission element was consistent in its time-worn hostility to Zionism and there was a strong body of Protestant opinion which dissented from them. As recently as January 31, 1949 the associate director of the Methodist Board of Missions, Dr. Garland E. Hopkins, denounced the recognition of the State of Israel.

The testimony taken by the Anglo-American Committee and the recommendations which it drew up are of less interest than its general character and its revealing informal discussions. Early in its voyage to Europe, a State Department official from the Near Eastern Division sent along to coach the American Delegation, confided to Bartley Crum: "If the committee reaches a decision which could be interpreted as too favorable to the Jews an aroused Arab world might turn to the Soviet Union for support. That is a matter the committee must consider seriously."

Crum was chagrined to find that State Department policy diverged sharply from the public pronouncements of the President and the major political parties, and that the issue of a Jewish National Homeland was not to be judged on its merits but was to be manoeuvred as a pawn on the board of post-war global strategy. He found that the State Department had assimilated the British Foreign Office estimate of the situation as presented by its official on the Committee:

"The Palestine issue must be seen in the framework of strong Soviet expansionism. The Soviet planned to move down into the Middle East. The United States, therefore, would do well to join Britain in establishing a *cordon sanitaire* of Arab states. If Palestine were declared an Arab state it would be a strong link in this chain."

In April 1946 after long conferences and debates on three continents, the Anglo-American Committee presented a unanimous report which recommended the admission of 100,000 Jews into Palestine as the President had originally suggested. They rejected partition as a long-term solution and proposed a trusteeship agreement under the United Nations until the hostility of Arabs and Jews should be transformed into friendship. Their all-embracing political formula was a banality: "Jew shall not dominate Arab and Arab shall not dominate Jew."

The report attempted to divert attention away from the central issue —the opening of Palestine as a refuge to the remaining victims of Nazi persecution—with such extraneous considerations as alternative places of refuge, education, and law and order. Stripped of its pious hortatory section, the report meant at best a continuation of British rule, with an allowance of 100,000 Jewish immigrants, only a minority of those begging for admission to the Holy Land.

The President promptly grasped at the 100,000 immigrants provision, exceeded the Committee in bromidic expression of good wishes and deferred the long-term proposals for further analysis.

The Prime Minister of Great Britain in his turn evaded the recommendations. He announced in the House of Commons that the execution of the report of the Anglo-American Committee would entail very heavy commitments, and the British Government therefore wished to ascertain to what extent the United States Government would be prepared to share the resulting additional military and financial responsibilities. Mr. Attlee also said that it was clear from the facts presented in the report regarding the illegal armies that it would not be possible to admit 100,000 Jews until these military formations had been disbanded and their arms surrendered—by which he meant dissolution of the *Haganah*, leaving the Jewish settlement defenseless.

Despite President Truman's call for the *immediate* implementation of the 100,000 immigrants recommendation, on the 17th of May the Arab States were still being assured by Dean Acheson, Acting Secretary of State, that "it was the intention of the Government of the United States to consult with the Arabs and Jews before taking any definite decision relative to the Committee reports." Such contradictions were not dispelled by categoric announcements like that of May 22 "that there is no conflict and can be no conflict in the two statements. It must be clear that the President's statements are controlling upon all the departments of government." The independent action of the State Department on at least two subsequent occasions belied this in practice.

On the 21st of May, to fulfill the promises of consultation, the Department of State sent out a Memorandum with a copy of the Anglo-American Commission report to all the Arab States, to the Arab Higher Committee, to the League of Arab States, the Institute for Arab American Affairs and also to the whole gamut of Jewish organizations, Zionists of a number of parties, non-Zionists and anti-Zionists. The memorandum announced that the report was advisory, not binding, and literally begged for criticism. The memorandum is interesting, only from one point of view. For the first time it spelled out the legitimate basis for United States "interest" in the whole problem of Palestine.

Consciously or not, it summarized the conflicting motives of American foreign policy. First it recognized a humanitarian interest in the victims of our enemies. This interest was cautiously declared to be general, not limited to Jews. Second, the interest of American Jewish contributions to Palestine was declared to be a subject of legitimate governmental "interest." Third, reference was made to the whole complex of American participation in the Near East beyond Palestine: American missionary schools, government technical missions, the oil developments, and American civilizing functions. The fourth item was a platitude about the contributions of Arab countries to world peace and to the United Nations organization. A cynic might have interpreted this as American interest in the bloc of Arab votes in the UN.

It is significant that the memorandum makes no mention—either directly or by inference—of the fact that there was ever a specific American *governmental* commitment or promise to participate in the establishment of a Jewish national home in Palestine.

On July 2, 1946, after the British Government had imprisoned members of the Jewish Agency Executive in Palestine, Truman received the American members, Wise, Goldmann, Lipsky, and Silver. He expressed regret at the developments, assured them that the United States had not been consulted, again reiterated his demand for admission to Palestine of 100,000 immigrants. He added that the United States was prepared to assume technical and financial responsibility for the transportation of the immigrants from Europe to Palestine.

This was an interim answer to a six point questionnaire received from Britain in June, a pointed and searching inquiry which attempted to pin the United States down to specific commitments in implementing the report of the joint committee and to frighten United States policy makers with the magnitude of the task. What would the United States do to help quell disorder arising from the immigration of 100,000 Jews? How should the displaced persons be selected? How would transport be obtained? Who would furnish transport? How would immigration be financed? What method should be used to provide materials for temporary housing for the new immigrants?

This request for data was met by the establishment of another joint Anglo-American committee to review and pass upon the feasibility of the recommendations of the first committee. The new group was to be distinguished from the earlier one by its "technical" character. In the United States the so-called technical experts, under Henry Grady, derived their powers from a special cabinet committee on Palestine which Truman created to render treatment of the problem more cohesive.

After the new committee had been in existence for about a month, Secretary of State Byrnes announced that a plan for the partition of Palestine had been proposed by the American representatives at the technical talks. This brand new plan, which did not bear the remotest relationship to the first committee report, received the unanimous support of both the American and British delegates and was promptly approved by the British cabinet. It was a complicated cantonal scheme which was ultimately dubbed the Morrison Plan. The country was to be divided into an Arab province and a Jewish province, each with a measure of administrative autonomy, a Jerusalem district and a district of the Negev administered directly by the Central Government. Final control of immigration was to remain in the hands of the Central Government, though district recommendations within their "economic absorptive capacity"—that unvarying immigration shibboleth of the British—were normally to be accepted. The plan, which left the British in authority, was palatable to nobody but the British. The Jews, the Arabs, and the United States Government, whose experts had co-authored it, all rejected it. Each successive commission climaxed its labors with a proposal causing greater dissatisfaction than the preceding one.

August and September saw further temporizing. Truman sent to London a new partition scheme proposed by the Jewish Agency Executive, with the comment that it seemed to merit serious consideration. Representatives of the Arab states accepted invitations to a Conference in London to discuss British plans; the Jews, angered by the Draconian measures adopted against even their moderate leaders in Palestine, refused to participate in what they regarded as futile discussions.

In October 1946 Palestine again became an issue in the congressional campaign. There is nothing ignoble about making contestants commit themselves in hard and fast language on problems about which they have had a normal human tendency to tergiversate. The Zionists availed themselves of this opportunity. In 1946 the two rival party leaders, Truman and Dewey, outdid each other. The President's statement, released to the press on October 4th, rehearsed the complete record of his administration on Palestine since his assumption of office. He did not think that the immediate immigration of a substantial number of Jews into Palestine could await a definitive solution of the whole problem. Should a workable program be adopted he offered economic assistance by the government to move the refugees from Europe and to help develop the new land. As for an ultimate solution, he expressed favor, though he did not explicitly adopt, the Jewish Agency proposal for the "creation of a viable Jewish state in control of its own immigration and economic policies in an adequate area of Palestine. . . ." The precise extent of his commitment was embodied in the following sentences: "From the discussion which has ensued it is my belief that a solution along these lines would command the support of public opinion in the United States. I cannot believe that the gap between the proposals which have been put forward is too great to be bridged by men of reason and good-will. To such a solution our Government could give its support."

The fat was in the fire. In addition to a reprimand, still diplomatic, from Prime Minister Attlee, came a letter from Ibn Saud. The desert king wrote, he explained, in an endeavor to preserve "the friendship of the Arabs and the East towards the United States," of which, by implication, he was the guardian. Stripped of its ceremonial language, the message was a blunt accusation that the President had broken his promises to the Arabs. Ibn Saud wrote with fantasy of Jewish aggression, not only against Palestine, but against neighboring Arab countries, "not even excluding our holy cities."

Truman stood his ground. His reply of October 26th was firm in upholding his previous position: there had been pledges of consultation with the Arabs and these had taken place on numerous occasions; the admission of Jews into Palestine was not an expression of hostility towards the Arabs; he did not believe that the Jews planned an offensive against the Arab states. The most striking aspect of this letter was the introduction of a new element of diplomatic policy: for the *first time* an American president formally assumed a "certain responsibility" in the disposition of Palestine. The letter became the *first diplomatic document* to a foreign power in which the United States, in however circumscribed a manner, stated its historic obligations towards the Jewish Homeland: "The Government and people of the United States have given support to the concept of a Jewish National Home in Palestine ever since the termination of the first World War, which resulted in the freeing of a large area of the Near East, including Palestine, and the establishment of a number of independent states which are now members of the United Nations. The United States, which contributed its blood and resources to the winning of that war, could not divest itself of a certain responsibility for the manner in which the freed territories were disposed of, or for the fate of the peoples liberated at that time. It took the position, to which it still adheres, that these peoples should be prepared for self-government and also that a national home for the Jewish people should be established in Palestine. I am happy to note that most of the liberated peoples are now citizens of independent countries. The Jewish National Home, however, has not yet been fully developed."

Just as the State Department clung to the anti-Zionism bequeathed to it by Lansing, the President derived his Palestine policy from Wilson. In direct contradiction to the position taken by Allan Dulles and the Near Eastern Division in the twenties and thirties, Truman interpreted Wilson's casual endorsement of the Balfour Declaration as the official policy of the United States Government, and with a turn of phrase he acquiesced in what had been a Zionist claim for twenty-five years, that the United States had a *legal responsibility* for the disposition of Palestine and the fate of the Jewish people. The signal failure of the British to bring peace to the area, our overwhelming sympathy for Nazism's victims, the exigencies of an electoral campaign, and our growing commercial and strategic interests had combined to bring a belated recognition that Palestine was not simply a "British responsibility," as Cordell Hull once phrased it.

Governor Dewey, in a spirit of competition with the Democrats, raised the proposed quota of Jewish immigrants into Palestine to several hundred thousand.

When the World Zionist Congress met at Basle in the closing weeks of 1946, it was animated by a militant uncompromising spirit. Led by a combination of American Jews under Dr. Silver and the Palestinians under Ben Gurion, it refused to toy further with the mandatory. The Zionists rejected the Morrison Plan and came out squarely for a Jewish Commonwealth and free Jewish immigration. Weizmann was not re-elected President since he symbolized the spirit of concession to the British and control was vested in the hands of a coalition of parties.

BEVIN BLOWS HIS TOP

In February, with Palestine visibly slipping from their grasp, and Arabs and Jews growing angry and intransigent, the British made another try: they concocted a "Bevin scheme" which in fact gave substantial concessions on immigration to the Jews. But it was too late for compromise and the plan was immediately rejected. In desperation, Bevin announced in Commons that the Government was referring the whole problem of Palestine to the United Nations. The Anglo-American venture at a solution had been a dismal failure. Britain could no longer afford to bear the onus of the Near East debacle which fell chiefly upon her as the mandatory and prime mover in that area of the world. The British resolved to retire to the sidelines and heckle, or hope that in the end their invaluable administrative talents would be called for once again.

But the act of surrender was executed with incomparable ill-grace. Foreign Minister Bevin delivered himself of a vehement denunciation of the American President and the Jews of New York in a crude and brazen speech which the British Information Service distributed in the United States. Appearing in Commons on February 25, 1947, Bevin threw the whole blame for failure of his efforts to secure an arrangement between the Arabs and the Jews squarely on President Truman: ". . . I think we might have been able to do more for the Jews, and have increased this rate at that time [in 1946] if the bitterness of feeling which surrounds this problem of immigration had not been increased by American pressure for the admission of 100,000.

I do not desire to create ill-feeling in the United States . . ., but I should have been happier if they had had regard to the fact that we were the Mandatory Power, and that we were carrying the responsibility. But, instead of that, a person named Earl Harrison went out to their zone in Germany collecting certain information, and a report was issued. I must say it really destroyed the basis of good feeling that we—the Colonial Secretary and I—were endeavoring to produce in the Arab States, and it set the whole thing back."

Bevin never let up on the New York Jews, reverting to them again and again with vituperation. British power in the Near East had fallen apart with the weight of its own contradictions, and he was looking for a scapegoat. It was a technique which Bevin's late enemies, the Nazis, had practiced with ingenuity. For the Jewish Agency's refusal to participate in another London conference, he blamed only the New York Jews. "I know—and I do not want to set one section of Jews against another—that those who have been trained in England and grown up under English customs and practise, wanted to come in, but the Jewish Agency, very largely dominated by New York, would not really come in, and it was with gentlemen from there that I had to deal so much. . . ."

Bevin pretended that he was on the point of securing Jewish participation in the London Conference when Truman issued his statement of October 4, 1946. "My right hon. Friend the Prime Minister telephoned me at midnight, and told me that the President of the United States was going to issue another statement on the 100,000. I think the country and the world ought to know about this.

"I went next morning to the Secretary of State, Mr. Byrnes, and told him how far I had got the day before. I believed we were on the road, if only they would leave us alone. I begged that the statement be not issued, but I was told that if it was not issued by Mr. Truman, a competitive statement would be issued by Mr. Dewey. In international affairs I cannot settle things if my problem is made the subject of local elections. I hope I am not saying anything to cause bad feeling with the United States, but I feel so intensely about this. . . . However, the statement was issued. I was dealing with Jewish representatives at the time, and I had to call it off because the whole thing was spoilt." After decades of discussion, Mr. Bevin's *moment juste* had been ruined!

If President Truman was ever shown a full copy of this Bevin speech it could hardly have filled him with enthusiasm for the British

Foreign Secretary. The period marked a low point in Truman's popularity as measured by the polls which were then in great vogue, and Bevin saw an opportunity to belabor the President with impunity. It seemed unlikely that he would be in a position to retaliate.

Bevin's outburst in the House of Commons on the very eve of the Moscow Foreign Ministers Conference where Britain and the United States were supposed to line up firmly together created a diplomatic flurry. The White House called his chronicle of events "unfortunate and misleading." Senators of both parties denounced it. Representatives of the Jewish Agency characterized Bevin's assertion that they had been close to a solution in October as "fantastic nonsense." The speech was an incredible insult to the President of a foreign state which was still an ally, and a stubborn refusal to recognize the realities of Britain's post-war position. The speech was the more extraordinary in that it was not a rejoinder delivered in anger at the time of the incident. In a fit of surliness almost five months after the events which purportedly had "spoilt" his delicate diplomatic web, he made a cowardly attempt to lay elsewhere the blame for his own ineffectual policy. The derogatory references to the New York Jews were not taken lightly by the Jewish community in the United States. Bevin's anti-semitic slurs raised a wave of indignation; he was regarded as having fallen heir to Hitler's mantle. In Bevin's tirades, the President and the Jewish community were linked—a circumstance which served the Zionists well.

PARTITION IN THE UNITED NATIONS

On April 28, 1947, the First Special Session of the United Nations on Palestine convened. Great Britain publicly washed its hands of the issue and its diplomatists went underground. The United States now assumed active leadership in reaching a definitive solution and fought for broad terms of reference in instructing the Special Committee of the United Nations which was to end the impasse by a report to the second regular session of the Assembly in the fall. The widest possible scope for an expression of opinion by all interested parties was agreed upon, despite Arab opposition which sought to exclude the fate of the Jewish refugees in Europe from consideration as extraneous to the Palestine problem. In the interim all governments were called upon to refrain from any action which might create an atmosphere prejudicial to an early settlement. The creation of the Special

Committee, in a relatively brief session, with American and Soviet consent, gave observers the impression that the cumbersome mechanism of the United Nations Assembly was actually workable.

When the Assembly met in October 1947 the United States was virtually committed to the basic provisions of a Partition Plan which the Special Committee had adopted after listening once more to the same chief witnesses for the Arabs and Jews who had been performing for decades. The great innovation in United States policy was the tenor of the speeches before the Assembly by the American representative, Herschel V. Johnson. In the *ad hoc* Committee on Palestine he re-interpreted three decades of American foreign relations with Palestine, setting forth American responsibility in terms which had been common in American Zionist pamphleteering since 1918. The United States had now plunged in to support a Jewish state and it was helpful to maintain that the government had always supported such a state. The public record was cloudy enough to provide documentation for almost any view. Johnson's narrative of events was a history of what American foreign policy might have been rather than what it was.

"It may be recalled that as a result of the First World War, a large area of the Near East, including Palestine, was liberated and a number of states gained their independence. The United States, having contributed its blood and resources to the winning of the war, felt that it could not divest itself of a certain responsibility for the manner in which the freed territories were disposed of, or of the fate of the peoples liberated at that time. It took the position that these peoples should be prepared for self-government and also that a national home for the Jews should be established in Palestine. . . .

"It may be recalled with regard to Palestine that in 1917 the Government of the United Kingdom, in a statement known as the Balfour Declaration, announced that it viewed with favor the establishment in Palestine of a national home for the Jewish people and that it would use its best endeavors to facilitate the achievement of that object, it being clearly understood that nothing should be done which might prejudice the civil and religious rights of existing non-Jewish communities in Palestine or the rights and political status enjoyed by Jews in any other country. In 1923 the objectives stated in this Declaration were embodied in the League of Nations Mandate for Palestine which was entrusted to the Government of the United Kingdom as mandatory. As the United States was not a member of the League of Nations, a Convention was concluded between the United States and the United Kingdom in 1924 with regard to American rights in Palestine. The Palestine Mandate is embodied in the preamble to this Convention. The United States consented to this Mandate."

The United States made one important emendation in the Special Committee's territorial plan; at its suggestion Jaffa was included in the Arab state. It required Truman's direct telephonic intervention with the American delegation to prevent a sizable portion of the Negev from being excised from the Jewish area. Though preserved in November 1947, the Negev later became a source of controversy when an Anglo-American attempt was renewed to cut off the Jewish state from the rumored oil and mineral resources of the area.

The United States obligated itself in a far-reaching manner to implement the partition proposals which were adopted during the debate in November. We expressed a readiness to assist through the United Nations in meeting economic and financial problems in Palestine and in preserving internal law and order during a transition period, even if this entailed the establishment of an international constabulary. Turning to Arab threats of violence from outside Palestine, the American delegate ingenuously affirmed: "We do not refer to the possibility of violation by any member of its obligation to refrain in its international relations from the threat or use of force. We assume that there will be Charter observance."

According to Granados, the Guatemalan delegate, during the early discussion of mechanics of partition in the committees of the General Assembly the United States stubbornly clung to the belief that Great Britain would be persuaded to accept responsibility as the interim authority. On November 13th, Britain finally announced that it would take no part in a partition program and would do nothing to further its effectuation, a promise, or a threat, which was rigidly adhered to.

The next month the British announced that they would terminate the mandate on May 15 and would leave Palestine by August. What was their motive for haste? Why did they refuse to assume any transitional responsibility? Was it solely a desire to be rid of a costly embarrassment which was causing losses among their troops, lowering their prestige, and raising a wave of indignation at home? Did they expect or hope to be coaxed back? Were they seeking proof of their indispensability? Or was this simply an attempt to sabotage partition by promoting chaos which would interfere with putting the plan into practice? Was it a means of keeping their record clear with their Arab allies? García Granados asserts that until Israel's Declaration of

Independence on May 14 the United States delegation never abandoned the hope that the British would ultimately return to Palestine as rulers.

THE GREAT REVERSAL

During the bitter debate within the United States Government which was engendered by the partition decision the most powerful arguments marshalled against a Jewish State in Palestine were those based on the safeguarding of American economic and strategic interests. Both considerations were merged and made to reinforce each other in public presentations.

After the Treaty of Lausanne, when Austen Chamberlain was asked what had been decided about the oil of Mosul he primly replied that he did not even know of its existence there. Since that time the effect of oil upon the framing of major political decisions has been discussed with far less hypocrisy, but it is still usually relegated to the sphere of secret diplomacy. As a consequence, the influence of oil politics, the exertions of those corporations which, in order to operate in distant countries, seek the support and protection of their government, have often been exaggerated by writers seeking easy catchword solutions to complex problems of international diplomacy. The exploitation of oil in the Middle East is now a major factor—though only one factor—in our foreign policy, and it does not have to be discussed in a tone of political prurience.

During the course of World War II it became increasingly clear that tangible American interest in the Middle East, strategic and economic, as differentiated from the cultural involvement of the Protestant missions and their universities and the racial and humanitarian ties of the pro-Zionists, was to be an important new feature of American foreign policy. It has been compared with our nineteenth century proclamation of a stake in China. Saudi Arabia became a virtual American protectorate. On January 8, 1946 a concession was awarded to the Trans-Arabian Pipeline Company, a subsidiary of the Arabian-American Oil Company which in turn was owned jointly by the Standard Oil Company of California and the Texas Company, to construct a pipeline from the Persian Gulf across Arabia. The existence of a United States Army air base at Dharan highlighted the strategic importance of this greatest single oil area in the world, a barren uncivilized corner of the globe nominally under the power of a desert sheikh called king. The area was no longer a political vacuum and the United States was in the Middle East to stay.

The factors which shaped United States diplomacy in the Middle East were political in the broadest sense of the term: they involved the life and security of the nation as the policy-makers understood it. While once it was part of the cant of our foreign relations that far-flung bases and distant oil fields under United States control were associated with imperialist adventures which we eschewed, the nation has slowly come to accept them as a normal aspect of our international position. Any political or social disturbances in the Middle East, wars or revolutions, were naturally regarded as negative factors in a military estimate of the situation. To the strategists the most desirable condition for Arabia was the endless peace and silence of the desert, traversed by a 30-inch pipeline from the Persian Gulf to the Mediterranean. At the two extremities of the pipeline, a relatively small native population, trained by American engineers, was all that was necessary. To keep the desert tribes at peace instead of at constant war as they had been for centuries, the Wahhabi King was worth enough royalties and other assistance to maintain an "army" which could assure him easy supremacy.

During World War II specific military arguments dictated a pro-Arab policy. Any disturbances engendered by an expression of favor to the Jews in Palestine, the strategists reasoned, would have endangered the oil supplies in the Near East and might have diverted additional troop reinforcements to that area. When the war was over Russia became a potential enemy, and the oil fields of Iran the first diplomatic battleground of a conflict between the Western powers and the Soviets. Again the simple military argument ran: why disturb the Arab status quo by insisting on the introduction of intractable Jewish elements from eastern Europe into the Middle East.

American strategists were well aware that the inhabitants of Palestine were overwhelmingly eastern European Jews. The remnants of the Jews in Europe for whom a refuge was sought were usually the toughest of the survivors of the ghettos of eastern Europe. These Jewish immigrants into the Near East would not be as readily amenable to western control as Arab fellaheen. The very tenacity and blind heroism of the terrorist Jewish bands were evidence to military staff analysts that this was not the human material on which to base a stable political and strategic system for the United States. Without the Jews, staff officers reasoned, a political pattern might be created to render the Middle East quiescent. With them it would become one of the trouble spots.

The thinking of American military strategists, called upon to advise on the repercussions of the Palestine conflict, was thus not complex: The Middle East, because of its proximity to Russia, was a potential base for future military operations against the Soviet. For this purpose Palestine was endowed with advantages not possessed by any other politically dependent state in the region. It had a coastline on the Mediterranean, an excellent harbor at Haifa where a great naval base could be constructed, a landing place on the Red Sea at Akabah; it was proximate to Suez in the event the British situation in Egypt became untenable; there was an oil refinery at Haifa, the end of the pipeline from the Mosul fields; there were broad expanses of fairly level ground in the Negev where air bases could be established; sanitary conditions were superior to most sectors of the Middle East. Palestine had a unique combination of strategic characteristics. Abstraction of vital portions of it from the defense system of the western powers as represented by Britain, and the establishment of an independent Jewish State was undesirable from the viewpoint of an American general staff officer.

In a base of military operations it is best to have the majority of the natives peaceful, cooperative and friendly, at least indifferent—certainly not hostile. Zionism had aroused Arab resentment throughout the Middle East against any country which espoused it. The volumes upon volumes of pseudo-historical analysis about the causes for this condition—whether it was artificially stimulated, whether the British were honorable—were irrelevant. The fact was undeniable that there was Moslem hostility, and it was feared that this enmity was of a religious, fanatical character, which a soldier does not like to cope with. If the United States supported Zionism, it alienated the Arabs, created insecurity throughout an area of potential military operations, and thus endangered national security.

In all of this thinking, there was of course a basic presupposition: that in the inevitable clash between Jews and Arabs, the Arab armies could easily drive the Jews into the Mediterranean. Support for Zionism therefore would have meant military intervention on behalf of the Jews and continual turmoil stirred up by unreconciled Moslem elements. Despite scores of contrary reports Secretary Forrestal remained unconvinced of the military inferiority of the Arab armies.

Tied in with the strategists' overall view of the area was their reckoning on the oil resources. Arabian oil could be shipped most economically to the Mediterranean if the pipelines which the Navy and Secretary of the Interior Ickes had first proposed during the war were completed. Officials in the National Defense and State Departments readily reached the conclusion that the objective of amicable relations between the Arab States and the oil companies was symbiotic with their own strategic determinations and far outweighed any sentimental and domestic "political" considerations associated with the Zionist movement in the United States and the fate of Jewish refugees. If there were Arab resentment the pipelines would not be constructed, or they would be sabotaged by Arab tribesmen. The concessions themselves might be abrogated. In the strategists' global view of an American defense system, the pipelines and their oil were vital, and the basic judgment was made that the Zionist dream was not worth endangering the oil and the telecommunications and the airports of Arabia.

As a corollary to this determination, the extremists among the global strategists adopted the position that partition of Palestine would serve only to further Russian schemes for penetration into the Middle East. Kermit Roosevelt, central figure in pro-Arab propaganda in the United States, gave voice to a viewpoint which in private found favor on the highest political and military levels: "They have tried in Greece, in Turkey, and in Iran to advance towards it. Only the most determined opposition by Britain and the United States has held them in check. It seems logical to conclude that the Soviet support of the partition of Palestine represents Russia's most recent move toward that long established end.

"If this conclusion be correct, as many observers believe, the Russian decision on partition was calculated to achieve three objectives: to strengthen the Soviet Union among Zionists everywhere; to gain a military foothold in the Middle East, on the assumption that partition must be imposed by force and that force used for this purpose by UN must involve Russian participation; and most important, to ensure chaos and confusion in the Middle East by creating, against Arab opposition, a Jewish state surrounded by Arabs."

If the strategists and diplomats in the State and War Departments needed to fortify their rationalist calculations, there were traditional antipathies and allegiances upon which they could draw. Many of them indulged in an ancient sentiment with a worn phraseology, anti-Semitism. The Zionist delegations who beleaguered the Departments at moments of crisis were importunate, emotional and "unreasonable."

Officials had to brace themselves for these interviews in order to maintain their diplomatic calm during the torrent of strong words. The techniques of pressure politics which the American Zionists used with striking success were resented as an invasion of the inner sanctum where the policy-makers were supposed to chart our course immune from such vulgar influences. Personal antagonism made the Palestine debate within the government acrimonious.

The convictions of the diplomats were also in harmony with a sentimental and historical pro-British orientation. Working diplomacy in the Middle East during and after the war meant cooperation with the British, who for more than a century had led in the exploration of that area and the romantic idealization of the Arab natives. The British general staff had intended to make Palestine their strategic base in the Near East after the withdrawal from Egypt. It was essentially the only other dependent area on the Mediterranean which was close enough to oil and to Russia. This clutch of the British on Palestine was not a policy of pigheadedness; it was a policy of desperation.

To our own diplomatic analysts Great Britain was a vital political force from the western world whose status had to be preserved as long as possible. Any influences which made the dominion of the British difficult was inimical to United States requirements in the Middle East, as these officials judged them. The British had been the successful administrators in the past and even if they were ultimately constrained to withdraw it was best that they be allowed to depart gracefully, leaving the aura of their influence behind, as in India. Jewish terrorists were making the position of the Government of Britain in Palestine untenable. They were literally driving the British out of the land through a type of political action which could be imitated elsewhere. Support of British prestige meant putting the quietus on the more militant Jewish parties.

There are elements in the United States whose emotional attachment to Britain is so profound that they believe survival of those islands as the center of an empire is a prerequisite for the preservation of western civilization. Possessed by such sentiments, which have of late been reinforced by a broad strategic alliance, there are few lengths to which they would not drive the United States in defense of the remnants of the imperial tradition. These professional Anglophiles, many of whom are in the State Department, have so entwined themselves with British interests that a defeat for Britain, a mere loss of face in the east, becomes for them *ipso facto* a humiliation for the

United States. There are times when the blind pursuit of such extra-territorial allegiance has its national dangers.

Joined to the other emotional influences which fed anti-Zionism were spiritual and religious interests, defended by the missionaries of the Near East and the sons of the missionaries who came to pursue more worldly careers in the ranks of the Foreign Service. These men bridled at the possibility of what they called Jewish civilization as a seminal force in the Near East. They wanted to maintain the primacy of their own spiritual Christianizing influence on the Arab upper classes. It is immaterial that in origin this may have been a mere idealist superstructure for economic penetration, the classical role of the missionaries. Their arguments carried weight.

Not necessarily less patriotic than the military men and the diploma-tists, the oil men who dabbled in Middle Eastern politics were moved by more immediate and simple aims—to earn profits in a system of free enterprise. It was not their fault that a "quirkish geography," as Frank W. Abrams, chairman of the Board of Standard Oil of New Jersey, lamented, had placed oil in areas of political and social unrest.

By the time World War II broke out, American and British oil interests had roughly marked out their respective spheres of influence in former Turkish territories and were moving to subsidize a few Arab chieftains. The oil companies wanted a maximum of United States economic support—government subsidies to existing rulers, free pipeline construction, higher prices, an assured purchase agreement by the naval and military establishments—and a minimum of direct government participation in their business: witness their violent reac-tion to wartime attempts by the Government to purchase Middle Eastern companies outright or even to buy a portion of their stock.

There are no great American oil company mysteries affecting United States policy in the Middle East. The basic facts were published dur-ing long and extensive Senate hearings over proposed pipeline con-struction in Arabia and national petroleum policy. The major Ameri-can oil companies control by themselves some of the richest fields with the greatest reserves in the world. In other fields they are part-ners with French, Dutch, and British companies, with an Armenian, and with the British Government. They enjoy extensive concessions in Arab countries and pay royalties many times greater than all the other revenues of these countries combined. They hold transit rights for their pipelines in other Arab countries. Upon the oil companies de-pend the national budgets of the Arab states and the employment of thousands of workers. Relations of the companies with the Arab rulers with whom they negotiate as equals are intimate and dependent upon good will.

The companies are of course apprehensive, as are all corporations who engage in vast enterprises in distant lands, and they look to their government to support them in their negotiations and dealings with the Arabs. At least they expect that the Government, taking account of their prodigious labors to supply oil for the Navy (at exorbitant prices, to be sure, as the Senate Hearings conclusively revealed) and oil for the Marshall plan piped to the Mediterranean (in a pipeline built by the Government, it was hoped at one time) would not commit any act which might jeopardize their investments and along with their own fall bring catastrophe to Europe, America, and western civilization. They want United States policy to be so conducted that their production is not for a moment interfered with. Until the intrusion of the Palestine problem, the American oil companies had maintained ideal relations with the Wahhabi King; they did not want a wholly extraneous issue, settling the refugee problem of European Jews, to spoil their business. When top military and State Department officials demonstrated that the success of oil operations was crucial to our global system of defense, it was grist for the oil interests propaganda mill.

The diplomats, the strategists, the oil men, the Anglophiles and the missionaries thus marched as a solid phalanx against Jewish aspirations in Palestine. They said or implied that they were the true spokesmen for American interests, that they alone took the broad view which encompassed American security and the American way of life, and that those Americans who espoused Zionism were placing their own narrow aims above the totality of the national welfare or were the dupes of those who did. The anti-Zionists supported their contentions with an impressive array of arguments, with stirring patriotic appeals, and with a logic that was superficially flawless.

At public hearings in Washington early in 1948, before congressional committees studying United States oil policy and the requirements of the armed services, representatives of the Arabian-American Oil Company and of the National Defense establishment expressed themselves in terms more or less bold, depending upon their status, against the proclaimed position of the Government on partition. The Zionists had become conscious of a new scent in the air even before, in December, within a month after the great decision.

During Secretary of National Defense Forrestal's appearance before a Special Subcommittee of the House Committee on Armed Services on January 19, 1948, Congressman Dewey Short asked him pointedly about Saudi Arabia. "Has not the decision of the United Nations on the division of Palestine rendered more insecure our position there? That is more or less a political question, but it is one we must consider: The whole Moslem world, 350,000,000 people from Pakistan to Morocco, from Karachi to Rabat or Casablanca, backed by the Arab League, which places us more or less in danger of having the pipelines cut."

To which Forrestal replied: "The answer is 'Yes' to your implied question."

"There is no question about that, is there?"

"None."

In other words, the Secretary of National Defense was testifying to the Congress that a political decision of the United States at the UN two months before was inimical to American interests.

On January 21, 1948, Vice-Admiral Robert B. Carney, Deputy Chief of Naval Operations for logistics, did not hesitate to venture out of his field with a lecture on foreign policy to the House Armed Services Committee. In the Admiral's forthright testimony in executive session, though the text was later published, the great reversal was presaged. "Of very particular logistical interest at this time, as I see it, are the possible withdrawal of the British forces from the Near East, and the byproducts of any partition of Palestine insofar as the possible introduction of United Nations forces is concerned with attendant implications of 'their protecting'—and I use that in quotations, sir—oil fields in the Middle East.

"In the event of serious disturbance in the Middle East, there is cause for grave concern for the fortunes of American oil facilities throughout that area, and to those who might desire to deny the oil of the Middle East to us, such disturbance could afford nice opportunities for interference."

It was not difficult to translate what he meant into simple English: that Russia would fish in the troubled Near Eastern oil; that it appeared inevitable as a result of the political decision.

James Terry Duce, the vice-president of Aramco, just returned from the East, took the opportunity of his appearance before the House Armed Services Committee on February 2, 1948, to announce: "The construction of the Trans-Arabian pipeline and to a certain extent the

Iraq Petroleum Company's line has been affected by the riots and the civil disturbances consequent upon the United Nations' decision for the partition of Palestine."

"The Nation Associates" presented to the President detailed memoranda on the activities of Mr. Duce of Aramco. According to their account he was the courier and active agent for a renaissance fabric of intrigue in which the Arab League and State Department officials, working together behind the Chief Executive's back, plotted the negation of the UN decision on the very morrow of its adoption.

Regarding our diplomatic support of a Jewish State as a negative factor in their expansion, the American companies who were exploiting the oil resources of the Persian gulf used all the normal instruments of public persuasion in order to secure a reversal of the policy. In February 1948 *World's Oil,* a trade journal, featured an article by Henry Ozanne entitled "Palestine Partitioning Endangers Middle East Pipe Line Program." The points made by the writer were succinct and telling, cautiously devoid of any psychological involvement in the civil conflict in Palestine. Arab belligerence had already delayed the pipeline projects of American and British oil companies which were to increase the flow from the fields to the Mediterranean and thus had retarded world recovery. The camp of the Iranian Petroleum Company at Mafraq, Transjordania, had been raided by Arab tribesmen and work on the new pipeline from the Persian fields had been abandoned at the Palestine border instead of being continued on through Haifa. The new pipeline was to have been inaugurated late in 1949, with a daily flow of 90,000 barrels in prospect. Each day's prolongation of the delay meant just that much loss to European recovery. Similarly the Trans-Arabian Pipe Line Company, affiliate of the Arabian American Oil Company, which was constructing a line from the South Arabian fields to Sidon, Lebanon, 1030 miles away, had discontinued all work on the project in Syria, Transjordan and Lebanon and had evacuated employees to Beirut. This line was expected to carry 300,000 barrels a day when in operation. As retaliation for American participation in the United Nations decision on the partition of Palestine, Syria had withheld transit rights to the pipeline company. Favorable action from the Syrian Parliament, the writer warned, would probably be delayed as long as the United States supported partition. Middle East Pipe Lines, Ltd., which was owned jointly by the Anglo-Iranian Company, the Standard Oil Company of New York, and the Socony-Vacuum Oil Company had postponed their opening of negotiations until the Trans-Arabian Company had been awarded its concession. In summary, the whole oil policy in the Middle East was in jeopardy. The Palestine partition had put the Middle East pipelines program "back in a mere project stage."

This was not only a loss to the oil companies, Ozanne argued, but it was undermining the Marshall plan, the basic foreign policy of the United States. The European Recovery Program was drawn up with the prospect of a supply of a million barrels of oil a day from the Persian Gulf by 1952. The program's total pipeline construction had called for 3000 miles of pipe, some of it 30-inch. A mill rolling three miles a day would require three years to complete the pipe. The breakdown of the program in February 1948 already reduced the estimates for 1952 to 200,000 barrels a day. Oil men had become skeptical about the whole enterprise. They were agreed that the full impact of Arab resistance to partition was yet to come, with disastrous consequences for the West, which needed the oil.

It is not far-fetched to believe that such arguments, forcefully presented, weighed with military and political authorities in the United States. At a crucial moment in March 1948, the very next month, the oil men saw these arguments translated into diplomatic action, the reversal of the United States stand on partition.

By the spring of 1948 there had already been a number of specific signs that the United States was beginning to regret its forthright espousal of partition. In Secretary Marshall's reply to Congressman Javits, a member of the House Foreign Affairs Committee who had directed sharp questions at the Department, the old diplomatic circumlocutions replaced the broad promises which the American Delegation had made to the General Assembly of the United Nations in November 1947. The Congressman had called the Secretary's attention to British arms shipments into Arab countries fulminating that partition meant war. The Secretary replied that he had no reason to believe that British arms delivered to Arab states under previous contracts would be used in Palestine. Javits's inquiry, "What is the United States prepared to do to help in the implementation of the United Nations decision?" brought a hazy response, "Until the Security Council has received and studied the report of the Palestine Commission on security and enforcement and has reached a decision it is not possible for this Government to determine in advance the steps which may be necessary to carry out such a decision."

Towards the end of February symptoms of the wavering were even more pronounced in Ambassador Austin's statements before the Security Council. There was a growing tendency for the American delegation to seek refuge in such legal interpretations of the United Nations Charter as would limit the powers of the world organization in adopting concrete enforcement measures for the November 1947 partition decision. "The Charter of the United Nations," Austin said on February 24, 1948, "does not empower the Security Council to enforce a political settlement whether it is pursuant to a recommendation of the General Assembly or of the Council itself. What this means is this: The Council under the Charter can take action to prevent aggression against Palestine from outside. The Council by these same powers can take action to prevent a threat to international peace and security from inside Palestine. But this action must be directed solely to the maintenance of international peace. The Council's action, in other words, is directed to keeping the peace and not to enforcing partition."

In the meantime, while the Arabs in Palestine were being armed by neighboring states and were introducing "volunteers" into the land the United States made Jewish self-defense more difficult by imposing an arms embargo of its own accord. Arab military supplies were pouring into Palestine and individual British officers were settling a few old scores with Jews, but the Security Council did nothing.

It was not until February 1948, more than two months after the General Assembly partition decision that the Security Council, upon frantic pleas by the Palestine Commission, placed a discussion of the realities of Palestine on its agenda. A progressive abdication of United States responsibility which culminated in the strange reversal of March 19 was portended when the Security Council suggested that the mandatory be consulted as to whether there was a threat to international peace. To alert diplomatic ears, this sounded like a proposal to scuttle partition, and a cry went up that such a move was impending, until it was silenced by a denial from the American delegate, the Secretary of State, and the President. Instead of action, a proposal by Austin was adopted that the five permanent members *consult* as to whether there was a threat to the peace. The full import of these advance symptoms of a less ardent espousal of the partition proposal were, however, far from obvious to most people at the time. Finally a United States resolution was placed before the Security Council which Austin interpreted to mean: ". . . The Security Council will do everything it can under the Charter to give effect to the recommendation of the General Assembly." After various amendments had been attached to this resolution the United States and Russia, voting together, secured its adoption 8 to 0 on March 14, 1948—though not without the exertion of strong diplomatic suasion on reluctant members.

Then, on March 19, 1948, to the amazement of the unknowing among nations of the world, the United States announced its reversal on the partition decision which only five days before the Security Council, at American insistence, had agreed to implement. This somersault brought forth cries of moral indignation among the smaller delegations on the Council who, though they had become accustomed to being led, found such abrupt movements jarring to their dignity. The newspapers in the United States used it as proof of the unsteady hand at the helm of our foreign policy. To the Zionists outside of the inner circle it was a bewildering blow, especially in view of the fact that on March 18, a day before the announcement, Chaim Weizmann had been received by President Truman who, despite rumors to the contrary, assured him that no change in American policy was contemplated. The historian is faced with a choice between the following two interpretations of the reversal: either President Truman was deceiving Weizmann or, what seems to be the fact, he was not informed by his own State Department of the import of the orders which had been issued to the United Nations delegates.

Ambassador Austin's speech before the Security Council presenting the new United States version of its policy was tortuous, filled with a Byzantine logomachy which attempted to explain the *volte face* in terms of Palestine conditions alone, a thesis which no one was simple enough to believe. If quoted as legal precedent, it virtually reduced the United Nations to a vain debating society: "We think it clear that the United Nations does not succeed to administrative responsibility for Palestine merely because the latter is a mandate. . . . No proposal was made by the United Kingdom to the General Assembly that the United Nations itself undertake responsibility for the government of Palestine. . . . The [partition] plan proposed by the General Assembly was an integral plan which would not succeed unless each of its parts could be carried out. . . ."

In the course of its reversal of policy, as Benjamin V. Cohen, former State Department Counsellor, has pointed out in his brilliant analyses, the United States abandoned a score of hard-won positions bestowing broad powers on the Security Council which had been maintained successfully during the great Iran debate.

The United States ostensibly founded its reversal on the sudden realization that the November 1947 decision could not be implemented through peaceful means. Reports to Secretary Forrestal that the Jewish army in Palestine, fighting for its existence would, if granted the barest opportunity, withstand the mercenary or primitive Arab troops, again met with the official opinion that in open warfare the Jews would be annihilated or driven into the sea.

Instead of enforcement of the November decision the United States proposed a temporary trusteeship for Palestine under the Trusteeship Council of the United Nations and a new special session of the General Assembly to debate the latest American contrivance. The Palestine Commission of the United Nations, which had been proceeding with the implementation of the previous decision in the face of Arab hostility and a British boycott, was to be directed to suspend its labors forthwith. Repeatedly Austin dwelt upon a factitious summary of the impasse: "The Palestine commission, the mandatory power, the Jewish Agency, and the Arab Higher Committee have indicated that the partition plan cannot be implemented by peaceful means under present conditions." This forensic turn was supposed to create an impression of almost universal unanimity among all parties in the dispute. The Jewish Agency, viewing the situation realistically, had in fact said that any United Nations decision would require a measure of force behind it.

No diplomatist was of course naive enough not to grasp the elementary fact that Soviet Russia had failed to send a representative to the Trusteeship Council and would thus theoretically be excluded from the new Palestine regime under the United States proposal. But this was a situation which the Soviets could, and promptly did, proceed to rectify. Realists argued that a new trusteeship, in the agitated state of Palestine, with a group of Jewish terrorists sworn to attain their nation's liberty at the cost of their lives, would likewise require the exercise of force. As Zionists interpreted it, American reversal was merely a switch from force against the Arabs to force against the Jews.

A partial clarification of the United States reversal lies in what is now known, at least in general terms, about the gravity of the international crisis in the early months of 1948 from the Hoover Commission revelations of an "intelligence analysis" which, if it had been followed, might have transformed the cold war into the final catastrophe. It was a period of confusion in the whole international policy of the United States. The President was jostled hither and yon by frenzied reports and by sensational stories of new diplomatic alignments. Perhaps the wildest tale was one which received serious consideration and deeply affected our Palestine policy. This was an analysis of world politics which maintained that if war broke between the United States and Russia, Great Britain would remain aloof and neutral.

Truman's appearance before the Congress on March 17th with a request for broad powers which fell just short of mobilization, was a relatively calm response to the "critical nature of the situation in Europe." The next day Secretary Marshall appeared before the Armed Services Committee to deliver testimony on the relation of military strength to diplomatic action. In his explanatory statement of March 20th, as vocal opposition and mockery of the partition reversal spread through the country, which somehow failed to be impressed with the full seriousness of the international danger, the Secretary of State firmly attached the new Palestine policy to the "crisis." The grave international situation, he said, had emphasized the compelling importance of preventing the outbreak of open warfare in Palestine. "The interest of the United States in a peaceful settlement in Palestine arises not only out of deep humanitarian considerations but also out of vital elements of our national security."

As the tide of criticism in the country mounted still higher, President Truman himself offered an explanation on March 25. The spectre of American soldiers dying on the soil of Palestine was raised. "Unfortunately, it has become clear that the partition plan cannot be carried out at this time by peaceful means. We could not undertake to impose this solution on the people of Palestine by the use of American troops, both on Charter grounds and as a matter of national policy. The United Kingdom has announced its firm intention to abandon its mandate in Palestine on May 15. Unless emergency action is taken, there will be no public authority in Palestine on that date capable of preserving law and order. Violence and bloodshed will descend upon the Holy Land. Large-scale fighting among the people of that country will be the inevitable result. Such fighting would infect the entire Middle East and could lead to consequences of the gravest sort involving the peace of this nation and of the world." The President declared that trusteeship was not a substitute for partition, only an effort to fill the vacuum created by the termination of the mandate.

In the month following Ambassador Austin had recourse to strange arguments to preserve the political *status quo* in Palestine, once open war had become a reality. In his speech of April 7, 1948, he used Article 80 of the Trusteeship Charter, which the Zionists themselves had framed: "I understand that this article was suggested at San Francisco by the Zionists in order to assure continued recognition of their national home in Palestine. But the text equally protects the rights of Arabs to maintain the continuity of the unity of Palestine in their civil and religious rights in the territory protected by the mandate." Among the legal phantasies resorted to, after the United Nations had been debating the Palestine problem for a full year, was the specious argument that when Great Britain surrendered her mandate, responsibility for Palestine reverted to the remaining members of the Allies of World War I, Great Britain, France and the United States. These pseudo-juridic arguments used during the debate to give the administration of Palestine over into the hands of the three western powers did not carry conviction.

The reversal was followed by dismal performances before the Second Special Session of the General Assembly convoked at the behest of the United States to discuss the trusteeship plan. An invasion of Palestine by seven states was threatened. On April 20, 1948 Austin cautiously announced that the "primary reason" for the failure of the November partition resolution was Arab resistance, backed "in part" by aid from the outside; then to balance the censure he denounced Jewish terrorism as an obstacle to a solution. A truce order of the United Nations followed, while the United States kept reiterating its new policy: "a political and military standstill to save human life."

Before the General Assembly, Professor Jessup had to avail himself of all his learning in international jurisprudence to dig up the historic formulae which had once clothed the British mandate to cover the nakedness of the newborn Trusteeship Plan. Immigration was the paramount issue for the Jews in any political solution; for this problem he found a measuring rod in the old British Royal Commission reports of the thirties, "the absorption capacity of Palestine"; only now it was to be determined by the Governor-General of the Trusteeship instead of the British High Commissioner. On April 27, 1948, in his appearance before the Political and Security

Committee of the Assembly, Professor Jessup was forced virtually to plead for debate in order to obtain diverging opinions from other nations on how they would solve the thorny problems of immigration and land settlement should the trusteeship plan be accepted. Disillusionment and apathy had settled like a pall over the delegates.

The Arab invasion, whose threat the United States had used as pretext for abandoning partition, was launched despite the truce and American appeasement. But while the Arabs defied American displeasure in the military sphere, the Jews of Palestine, meeting in solemn assembly, refused to be intimidated by direct warnings that they should desist from precipitous political action. They declared the independence of the State of Israel.

RECOGNITION OF ISRAEL

The behind-the-scenes influences which led the President of the United States to grant immediate *de facto* recognition are still shrouded. It was the second about-face. The proponents of the Trusteeship idea had not surrendered without a struggle. The United States Delegate to the United Nations tried hard to round up all the Latin Americans behind the Trusteeship plan at a dinner party on April 26, 1948 "to lobby for votes," as García Granados put it. "I cannot accept the contention that trusteeship is impossible of enforcement," said Austin in a neat little speech, "I still hope that Great Britain will keep her forces in Palestine, and use them to enforce trusteeship with the cooperation of the United States and such other nations as may be willing to help."

As Trusteeship got bogged down, President Truman apparently came around to the decision that if no other solution were found before the end of the mandate and a Jewish State were in fact proclaimed his government would recognize it. This story is not inconsistent with continuance of American pressure on Jewish leaders—even direct threats—against the final declaration of independence. The United States made every reasonable effort to abort the State of Israel, but once born it was accepted *de facto*. Up to the very last minute of debate before the United Nations on May 14 Professor Jessup was still concocting formulae for some sort of interim regime for Palestine under a Commissioner.

In the midst of the debates appeared a *deus ex machina* from the White House—recognition. During the pandemonium on the floor of the Assembly following Jessup's formal announcement of the President's position, members of the United States delegation could not hide their disgruntlement.

Eliahu Epstein, Agent of the Provisional Government of Israel, on May 14 made formal request for recognition of Israel within the boundaries of the United Nations resolution of November 29, 1947: "With full knowledge of the deep bond of sympathy which has existed and has been strengthened over the past thirty years between the Government of the United States and the Jewish people of Palestine, I have been authorized by the provisional government of the new state to tender this message and to express the hope that your government will recognize and will welcome Israel into the community of nations."

A statement by President Truman was then released to the press under the dateline May 14: "This Government has been informed that a Jewish state has been proclaimed in Palestine, and recognition has been requested by the provisional government thereof.

"The United States recognizes the provisional government as the *de facto* authority of the new State of Israel."

We were the first country in the world to recognize the new State. The political vacuum in a part of Palestine had been filled.

THE MEDIATOR

Three days later, on May 17th, Austin opened his remarks before the Security Council with the superfluous reflection that it now had "adequate information to demonstrate that its earlier efforts to bring an end to the fighting in Palestine have been unsuccessful."

The General Assembly on May 14th had passed a resolution providing for the appointment of a United Nations Mediator in Palestine. His functions were to cover the operation of common services in Palestine, protection of the Holy Places, cooperation with a Truce Commission of the Security Council. His final mandate was "to promote a peaceful adjustment of the future situation in Palestine." There was not the vaguest reference in his designation to any change in the partition plan, nor did any of the preliminary discussions indicate that the mediator's province was to include the proposal of novel plans for the disposition of the territory of Palestine. There can be no doubt as to this.

By May 22, during the discussion of a cease-fire order, Ambassador Austin's extempory remarks revealed the American reaction to the invasion of Palestine by the Arab states under the new post-recognition policy.

"I think the time has come when we cannot ignore the international character of this breach of the peace. Probably the most important evidence and the best evidence we have on that subject is the admissions of the countries whose five armies have invaded Palestine and are carrying on war. Their statements are the best evidence we have of the international character of this aggression.

"There is nothing in the resolution about aggression. It did not occur in the wording of the resolution. But it has occurred in the statements of these aggressors, for they tell us quite frankly that their business there is political, that they are there to establish a unitary state, and of course, the statement that they are there to make peace is rather remarkable in view of the fact that they are making war. . . . We have evidence of the highest type of the international violation of the law here—an admission by those who commit the violation."

The cease-fire order was followed by a four-week truce resolution which called upon all governments to refrain from introducing arms or fighting personnel into Palestine, Egypt, Iraq, Lebanon, Saudi Arabia, Syria, Transjordania, and Yemen. The next month the United States could inform Secretary-General Trygve Lie of the various steps which it had taken in conformity with the Security Council Resolution. The departure of "fighting personnel" to the Near East had been prevented by appropriate authorities; since November 1947 a rigorous arms embargo covering the shipment of all war matériel from the United States had been imposed; and the Mediator Count Bernadotte had been supplied with military observers, aircraft, communications equipment, and naval patrol vessels.

In less than two months after his appointment, on July 4, 1948, Count Bernadotte released a fresh set of proposals on the partition of Palestine which, to the amazement of neutral observers, appeared to be an award of territory to those Arab states which had not only defied a United Nations resolution and peace plea but had been roundly beaten on the field of battle. It was a basic revision of the November 1947 plans; the Negev, on which the tiny Israeli state depended for population settlement and the development of its economy, was abstracted and a portion of Galilee offered as compensation; Israel was to become a member of a dual state joined in a Union with Transjordania; Jerusalem was wholly included in Arab territory;

Haifa was declared a free port and Lydda a free airport; and, what was most offensive to the Israelis, immigration policy was to be subject to review by both members of this strange new political creature, thus curtailing Israel's freedom in the sphere most vital to its existence. This proposal was widely denounced as a scheme of the British, using the count as their mouthpiece to maintain a stranglehold on the area. The United States met it with official silence.

Jewish refugees detained in Cyprus, under British control, were not allowed to move into Palestine. Eliahu Epstein sent the United States a lucid analysis of the language of the Security Council order of May 29, 1948 which had specifically prohibited only the *mobilization* of men of military age who might immigrate into Palestine but, as appears unequivocal in the record of the debate, did not prohibit their movement into the land. In reply on September 3, 1948, Charles E. Salzmann, Assistant Secretary for Occupied Areas in the State Department, took a contrary view in harmony with the tendency to bestow upon Count Bernadotte more extensive powers, far beyond those contemplated in his original appointment: "The instructions provide for the continued prohibition of the exit of emigrants for Israel identified as fighting personnel, and authorize the departure of those men of military age for whom accredited representatives of the Provisional Government of Israel submit to the zonal military authorities advance clearance for emigration obtained from the Mediator by such representatives."

The assassination of Count Bernadotte in Jerusalem occurred on September 17, 1948 and represented a sharp momentary set-back to the Israeli Government in United States public opinion. The conclusions of his final report on a territorial partition in Palestine were released the very next day, while the feeling of outrage was still hot, and within three days Secretary of State Marshall gave a blanket approval of the new territorial partition, essentially the same as Bernadotte's preliminary proposal of July. The major concession to Jewish protests was the internationalization of Jerusalem instead of its incorporation in an Arab state.

A relatively well documented record from unofficial sources maintains that the Bernadotte plan was concocted through the joint efforts of the British Foreign Office and the State Department. Marshall's hasty public acceptance, without any wide discussion of the report or consultation with the Israelis, was the third major switch on Palestine within a year. Once again, the approval of the Secretary of State, then in Paris, does not seem to have been preceded by the acquiescence of the President.

The Zionist forces in the United States were galvanized into action against this abrupt decision. Maps of Palestine appeared in the major newspapers of the country showing graphically the progressive whittling down of the Jewish Homeland area since it was first offered to the Jews by Balfour. The Security Council kept re-issuing its cease-fire orders, while the 650,000 Jews of Israel had to live in a state of intermittent warfare and armed truce which was sapping their manpower and effectively hampering the reconstruction of their state and the assimilation of the refugees from Europe who were being rushed into the land.

THE FINAL STAGE

Palestine became a frank and open election issue in 1948 and once more, as in 1944 and 1946, both major political parties had to compete for votes among Jews in metropolitan areas who were deeply resentful at the manner in which the little state had been dealt with even after its recognition. The origin of the fourth stage in Israel's progress towards final *de jure* recognition is as complicated as most other turns and twists of United States policy. While at the Paris meeting of the General Assembly the State Department-Foreign Office scheme for a mutilated State of Israel ran into the opposition of "outsiders" such as Evatt of Australia and the arrogant rejection of the Arab League whom it was designed to appease, the American President was being taught the facts of a struggle for political survival in the terms he understood.

In the last days before the balloting, President Truman issued a new commitment which once more tore the final policy decision out of the hands of the State Department. The Israeli Government was assured by the President that it would not be constrained to surrender territory which had been a part of the original award without its explicit agreement. It is revelatory of the reluctance with which the State Department accepted the President's new policy that in the official weekly Bulletin of the Department which during the long Palestine crisis had published every major pronouncement, a Truman promise of *de jure* recognition to Israel after its elections was not included. Along with many other Americans, the permanent officials in the Department awaited a new incumbent.

After the November election came Israel's reward. Some commentators have decried the use of election periods as moments of opportunity to wrest a foreign policy favorable to Israel from the President or his opponents. The propaganda methods of the Zionists have often been blunt. But at least they have been overt, a merit which cannot be claimed by all the groups who have fished in troubled Middle Eastern waters. The Zionists have often engaged in tough, though effective political bargaining, but the moral stigma should attach to those who made recourse to such methods necessary rather than to those who, when driven to the wall of despair, struck out with the only power they could command.

By November 20, 1948 Professor Jessup, appearing before the General Assembly of the United Nations, had abandoned the Marshall position of September in support of the Bernadotte plan, and in debate considered it preferable that the United Nations refrain from fixing specific boundaries for the two parts of Palestine. He proposed that the drawing of the lines be left to the belligerents themselves working with the aid of a new Conciliation Commission. Bernadotte's final report had become, in the language of the American Delegation, only a "basis of negotiation."

The President's pre-election promise about Israel's territory was repeated with a somewhat peculiar twist in a formal statement by the American Delegation to the General Assembly of the UN. "If Israel desires additions, it would be necessary for Israel to offer an appropriate exchange through negotiations." This interpretation is by no means implicit in the President's original speech, and, at this late date, appeared to be another attempt at whittling down the executive formula.

On December 2, 1948, Professor Jessup supported the Israeli application for membership in the United Nations in terms reminiscent of Herschel Johnson's espousal of the original partition plan a year before: "No one doubts that Israel has a government. I think the world has been particularly impressed with the way in which the people of Israel have organized their government and have established a firm system of administration and of lawmaking under the most difficult conditions. . . . The Jewish community in Palestine which created the state of Israel expressed its willingness and readiness a year ago to accept the General Assembly resolution of November 29, 1947, and to cooperate loyally in carrying it out. Members of this body in reflecting upon the efforts of this body over the past year to maintain peace in Palestine will recall the degree to which the Provisional

Government of Israel has extended its cooperation to the implementation of proposals made by the Security Council and by the Mediator. . . . The United States has watched with sympathy and interest the birth of the state of Israel and the development of its political and social institutions."

There had been many turns of the circle and the end was not yet in sight. The United States accepted membership on a Conciliation Commission of three. From the White House came renewed assurance of formal *de jure* recognition, and it was granted after the January elections in Israel. An Export-Import Bank loan was arranged.

STRATEGISTS' ERRORS

During the post-war period dominant military and political thinking in the War and State Departments proceeded from assumptions which later events proved invalid and which a few livelier minds, many of them in those very agencies, set forth in the course of the Palestine debate.

There were realists who pointed out that Arab appeasement was not a *sine qua non* for the exploitation of Middle Eastern oil, that the Arab states needed the oil companies for revenue and could not conceivably risk shutting down the oil wells without courting revolution in their own countries. In 1947 Herbert Feis, former Economic Adviser in the State Department, who in the early years of the war had headed an Interdepartmental Committee on Petroleum, made this sage reflection about Ibn Saud and the proposed pipeline from the Aramco oil fields along the Persian Gulf to the Mediterranean: "There appears to be no doubt of the consent of Ibn Saud, ruler of Saudi Arabia. It is conceivable that he might, should events in Palestine offend, reject this prospect of great revenue. But it is not likely; Arab rulers, no matter how absolute of demeanor, are not exempt from the charges of their followers." Feis's forecast was later borne out by the oil men themselves. James Terry Duce, vice-president of Aramco, testified at a Congressional hearing that he had a promise from Ibn Saud that he did not intend to revoke the oil concessions even after the partition award. Despite Arab fulminations, *World's Oil* was able to report in October 1948, in flagrant contradiction of its propagandistic forebodings of the previous spring, that production in Saudi Arabia had jumped from 305,000 to 420,000 barrels a day in eight months, an increase of 38 per cent.

The oil companies were of course always confronted by this

dilemma: if they exaggerated Arab threats, they might emphasize the vulnerability of their whole operation and the government might withdraw their priority for allocations of vital steel; if they discounted Arab threats, partition might be allowed to stand and they would, they feared, face Arab hostility and a turbulent new element in the Middle East.

There were dissenting voices among the strategists, who, quite apart from the question of the good-will or hostility of Arab chieftains, realized that the Arab lands were seething, and were dismayed to find that Middle Eastern oil figured so crucially in our defense calculations. Even the desert does not stand still. The backward Arab countries of the Middle East beneath the surface have been agitated with all manner of political cabals, and the internal structure of their societies has been shaken by rising discontent among the masses in the coastal urban areas. The movement is inchoate, confused, making the area ideal for Russian and communist intrigue. In this fluid environment could the Arab chieftains guarantee stability?

There were observers like General Leroy Lutes who dwelt on the vulnerability of Middle East oil concessions. He expressed his view to the House Armed Services Committee that the United States owed it to future generations to remain independent of foreign oil. There were obvious alternatives in synthetic production and in more intensive exploration in the Western Hemisphere. And even Vice-Admiral Carney, Deputy Chief of Naval Operations for logistics, who had warned the Congress against partition and voiced his conviction that "our foreign policy . . . must be firmly and resolutely shaped toward insuring our access" to Middle East as well as Western Hemisphere oil resources, in almost the same breath admitted that Middle East oil was unreliable from a military standpoint under any circumstances: "The fields are vulnerable to attack; pipe lines and pumping stations are vulnerable to sabotage and attack; and I think it would be assuming too much to insure full availability of the capabilities and capacities of Middle East oil. . . ."

The whole conception of United States strategic policy in the Middle East as centered about a military defense of the oil fields bordering the Persian Gulf was thoroughly discredited in a senatorial investigation in the spring of 1948. In time of war, there were overwhelming military problems in holding that insecure area, and it would have been folly to allow our war machine to be dependent on Middle Eastern oil. As for an overland pipeline, experts in logistics observed that it was subject to easy sabotage in time of war, was not to be preferred to the construction of a tanker fleet. In short, the absolutism of the argument that Middle East oil is a vital link in our chain of defense and the use of this argument as a point of departure for day-to-day decisions on Palestine was simply not warranted by the facts.

Our Palestine policy would not jeopardize the concessions, and in any case Middle East oil, though abundant, was a highly conjectural factor in our national defense, subject to all the hazards of internal disorder and foreign attack—without reference to whether the United States fostered or frustrated Jewish aspirations in Palestine.

It was never seriously doubted by the United States military that in the Zionist-Arab conflict, the Jews would not be able to defend themselves effectively; that if the United States took up their cause, it would mean sending United States troops to push back the Arabs and to maintain the Zionist regime thereafter, or it would mean an international constabulary with Russian participation. Without such intervention, it was believed, the Jews would promptly make peace with the Arabs at any price, or they would be driven into the sea. The threat of Americans dying in Palestine was "scare propaganda" of the type which had paralyzed United States diplomacy in the past.

In fact, there was no rational basis for the confidence in Arab supremacy or belief in their fanatical zeal. There was a susceptibility to romantic tradition bequeathed by Lawrence, and an acceptance at face value of the mighty oaths and bombastic phrases of the Arab chiefs. For centuries the Arabs had dwelt in apathetic servitude to their Turkish overlords, and even during that British-led and British-financed glorious revolt of World War I, they had made an indifferent showing. The British have regularly put down their insurrections without vast outlays. The urban Arabs of Syria, Lebanon, and Egypt were the talkers of the Arab League; the desert warriors of Iraq and Saudi Arabia could not use modern weapons; of all the troops, only the Arab Legion of Transjordania was a military force to cope with and it was under British control.

Nor was there any basis for underestimating the military capabilities of the Jews, in the face of the record of Jewish soldiers in two world wars, except a clinging to the stereotype of the Jew as the shrewd bargainer, the manoeuvrer, the wheedler who used the backdoors of diplomacy.

Now that the Arab armies have crumbled before a small body of soldiers, imbued with a high morale and the mechanical skill to use modern weapons, now that the "united Moslem world" has shown itself to be divided and subdivided by the ambitions of its rulers, now that the Arab chieftains have shown how easily surrender comes to them when the tide of battle appears to turn against them, the foresight of the military strategists can be judged. Their erroneous estimate of Arab military might and tenacity was in no small measure responsible for the original outbreak of the Palestine war. If the military in the United States had supported partition firmly and consistently, the Arab states would not have ventured to invade Israel in May 1948, and if we had been as clear-cut with the British in 1947 as we have apparently become in 1949, their intrigues with the Arab chieftains would have been definitively discouraged and they would have had no choice but to withdraw their moral, economic, and military support. The Moslem "Holy War" would have collapsed before its opening gun was fired. The whole Palestine problem would have been contained within the limits warranted by its size instead of being expanded to the dimensions of an international diplomatic crisis. In a sense we created and gave life to the Arab bogey around which we constructed our Middle Eastern policy.

Our post-war Palestine policy is in large measure the story of a concerted attempt on the part of two great departments of the government to override the will of the vast majority of the American people. Those who participated in anti-Zionist intrigues may have acted in what they considered to be the best interests of the nation, but they were hardly conducting foreign policy in a democratic fashion.

Remote from humanitarian considerations and under no necessity of subjecting themselves and their policies to the verdict of a critical electorate, officials of the War and State Departments could maintain a so-called impersonal point of view. This impersonal point of view, however, has often been the constricted point of view. Apparent detachment has sometimes masked a calloused indifference to any but the grossest material considerations. In the end, the stubborn refusal to deal with moral imponderables, while it may have served the short-term aims of some interests in the country, has been damaging both to the prestige and to the security of the United States.

In this case the common sense sympathies of the simple American in the White House and the hard bargaining of American Zionists won out over the alarmism of State Department officials, war strategists, oil men, Anglophiles, anti-semites of several varieties, a small though intense group of Protestant missionaries, and a few romantic pro-Arabists. The major factor which in the end altered the balance of forces was the victorious Israeli army, which gave the lie to arguments of Arab supremacy, showed the reasoning of the diplomats and the military men to be a flimsy structure, and broke the deadlock in United States foreign policy.

AMERICAN-ISRAELI RELATIONS

The United States must adopt a realistic attitude on Israel's territorial boundaries. Professor Jessup's public declaration to the United Nations in November 1948 that Israel would be called upon to surrender land in exchange for areas acquired during the Arab War beyond the limits of the original partition award is not an adequate formula. Armistice negotiations between the Israelis and the various Arab states will probably establish definitive boundaries. Unless land is wrested from the Israelis in renewed warfare and military defeat they will not relinquish any part of either the Negev or Galilee. Jerusalem is a far more intricate knot to unravel, but this much appears likely: the new city will be retained in Israeli hands.

Areas won by the Israelis after partition should not be regarded simply as war booty. During the initial discussion of partition sectors at the United Nations, the American delegate Herschel V. Johnson conceded to Moshe Sharett, present Foreign Minister of Israel, that the proposed lines were militarily indefensible, but he maintained that UN Charter observance and peaceful acceptance of the partition decision by the Arabs had to be presupposed. The Arab invasion proved this illusory, and the Israelis are now faced with the prospect of existence as an island in the midst of seven hostile states, even though they may cease to be enemies in a technical sense. The twists and turns of hundreds of miles of irregular frontier, allowing for numerous enclaves, make territorial defense a heavy drain on the embryo economy of Israel. The United States must support the rationalization of these boundaries in order to reduce the burden.

Underscoring the boundary issue is the threat of Arab rearmament. Without raising any question as to the independence of the several Arab countries, one can nevertheless maintain that their effective military strength is largely dependent upon United States diplomatic and economic action. Living on its own national income, not one of these countries could afford vast military expenditures. If the Arab states amass arms and train a disproportionate number of men, the *matériel* must be derived primarily from our Allies in the North Atlantic Pact to whom we will extend economic and military aid.

There is no prospect that the present generation of Arabs, even if extravagantly armed, would be able to play a significant role in withstanding Russian military penetration of the Middle East. If either Soviet or United States intelligence had any illusions on this score they have been dissipated by the recent war performance of the Arab nations. Thus, in the near future, Arab military strength can be directed to only three possible objectives: preserving the security of existing regimes, inter-Arab dynastic warfare, or aggression against Israel. The maximum police requirements of these states are not extensive enough to warrant some of the recent British allocations to Transjordania. Arab royal family blood feuds have found adequate expression with less deadly weapons than our newest armaments. Therefore the building up of great military reserves menaces the new State of Israel.

It is within the power of the United States to curtail and regulate the flow of armaments to the Arab states. The diplomatic procedures available for such action are multiple. Directly or indirectly we will pay for these armaments, and unless we revert to the naive doctrines which were held in the first decades of this century, we have a responsibility for their employment.

If the Arab countries were not flooded with arms, the Israelis would be able to devote their limited manpower to reconstruction and to the absorption of refugees from Western Europe and from the Moslem countries. Israel's birthrate is low compared to its Arab neighbors, and for years to come, despite immigration, it will have a population well under two million. Its aggressive potentialities can be discounted. The technical skills of the Israelis and the capital supplied for the most part from America make them agents of modern industrialism in the Middle East. It would be unfortunate to waste this potential upon a large military establishment. In the context of Point 4 of the President's program as set forth in his inaugural address, the Israelis are a technological reservoir in an industrially arid part of the world. If our phrases are not devoid of content, we have an obligation to assist them not only by curbing Arab military plans, but by helping to initiate broad-gauged projects in the Jordan Valley.

Widespread sympathy has been aroused by Arab civilian refugees from Palestine, who fled at the direction of their leaders with the assurance of a speedy return when the Israelis had been driven into the sea. These homeless people require a solution beyond the mere distribution of temporary relief. Their repatriation to former homes in Israeli territory is no longer feasible. In a world shaken by minorities it would be egregious folly to re-introduce still another national problem when it has been eliminated through the fortunes of war. The Israelis are prepared to indemnify the Arabs for their abandoned lands and homes, and the resettlement of the refugees in the unpopulated areas of Transjordania is the only disposition conducive to ultimate peace. If the oft repeated concern of the United States for peace in the Near East is more than verbal we should move directly towards the implementation of a transfer of population. Unless assuaged, the bitterness of civilian refugees uprooted by war can rankle for generations.

American interest in the Near East is no longer remote, and it calls for a lasting re-orientation of American policy on all levels of the State Department and in the Foreign Service in consonance with the Israeli military victory and the establishment of a new sovereign state. Though minor permanent officials may still at times defend outmoded conceptions to which they have long clung, there is reason to believe that such a re-evaluation is taking place.

SOURCES

It would be superfluous to duplicate the comprehensive bibliographies on Zionism and modern Palestine presented in William Zeitlin, *Bibliotheca Sionistica 1852–1905* (Frankfurt a.M., 1909); Getzel Kressel, *Erets Yisrael ve-Toledoteha. Madrik Bibliyografi* (Tel Aviv, 1942/1943); Abraham Levinson, *Bibliyografia Tsiyonit* (Jerusalem, 1943); and *Palestine. A Study of Jewish, Arab, and British Policies* (New Haven, 1947), vol. II, pp. 1238–1280. Nor has any attempt been made to compile the vast periodical literature on the subject. *Palestine and Zionism*, a bibliography issued periodically since January 1946 by the Zionist Archives and Library, New York, has an exhaustive coverage of publications in Hebrew, Yiddish, and most European languages.

The following lists include only such manuscript records, published sources, and secondary works as have special bearing on the subject matter of each chapter.

CHAPTER I

I. FROM THE STATE DEPARTMENT FILES IN THE NATIONAL ARCHIVES:

Despatches from and instructions to Ministers Resident in Constantinople and members of their staffs: David Porter, chargé d'affaires, 1831–1839; Ministers Resident: David Porter, 1839–1843; Dabney S. Carr, 1843–1849; George P. Marsh, 1849–1853; Carroll Spence, 1855–1858; James Williams, 1858–1861; Edward Joy Morris, 1861–1870; Wayne MacVeagh, 1870–1871; George H. Boker, 1871–1875; Horace Maynard, 1875–1880; James Longstreet, 1880–1881.

Despatches from and instructions to the Jerusalem consuls: John Warren Gorham, 1856–1860; William R. Page, 1860–1861; Franklin Olcott, 1861–1862; Isaac Van Etten, 1863; Albert Rhodes, 1863–1865; Victor Beauboucher, 1865–1870; Richard Beardsley, 1870–1873; Frank S. de Haas, 1873–1877; J. G. Willson, 1877–1882.

Despatches from J. A. Johnson, Consul at Beirut, for the years 1868–1869.

The Miscellaneous Letter Books of the Consular Agencies at Jaffa and Haifa.

Personnel Files on David Darmon, a Consular Agent at Jerusalem in 1832, and Warder Cresson, confirmed by the Senate as Consul at Jerusalem, 1844.

II. BOOKS, PERIODICALS, AND GOVERNMENT PUBLICATIONS:

Auerbach, Meyer and Salant, Samuel, *An Open Letter Addressed to Sir Moses Montefiore* (London, 1877).

Baron, Salo W. and Jeanette M., "Palestinian Messengers in America, 1849–1879. A Record of Four Journeys," *Jewish Social Studies* (1943), vol. V.

Bermann, Simon, *Masaot Shimon, Reisebeshreibung im Hailegen Land* (Cracow, 1879).

Cohn-Reiss, Ephraim, *Me-Zikronot Ish Yerushalayim* (Jerusalem, 1933/34), 2 vols.

De Sola Pool, D., "Some Relations of Gershon Kursheedt and Sir Moses Montefiore," *Publications of the American Jewish Historical Society* (Philadelphia, 1947), no. 37.

Finn, James, *Stirring Times. Records from Jerusalem* (London, 1878), 2 vols.

Frankl, Ludwig August, *The Jews in the East*, transl. by the Rev. Patrick Beaton (London, 1859), 2 vols.

Fuerst, Aaron, *Yerushalayim ha-Hadasha* (Jerusalem, 1945/46).

Ha-Magid, a Hebrew weekly, published in Lyck, Poland, for the year 1868.

Hyamson, Albert M., *The British Consulate in Jerusalem* (London, 1939), 2 vols.

Kaznelson, Reuben, *L'immigrazione degli ebrei in Palestina nei tempi moderni* (Rome, 1931).

Klein, Samuel, *Toledot ha-Yishuv ha-Yehudi be-Erets Yisrael* (Tel Aviv, 1935/36).

Kohler, Max J., "Some Early American Zionist Projects," *Publications of the American Jewish Historical Society* (Philadelphia, 1900), no. 8.

Malaki, E. R., "Perek be-Hitpathut ha-Haskalah be-Yerushalayim," *Luah Erets Yisrael* (Jerusalem, 1915).

Montefiore, Moses, *A Narrative of Forty Days Sojourn in the Holy Land* (London, 1877).

Rabinovitz, A. Z., *Toledot ha-Yehudim be-Erets Yisrael* (Jaffa, 1911).

Samuel, Sydney M., *Jewish Life in the East* (London, 1881).

Shuv, David, "Toledot ha-Yishuv ba-Galil ha-Elyon," *Luah Erets Yisrael* (Jerusalem, 1912/13).

Sneersohn, Hyam Zvee, *Palestine and Roumania. The Labours of the Author in the United States* (New York, 1872).

Sousa, Nasim, *The Capitulatory Regime of Turkey* (Baltimore, 1933).

Trivkes, Yizhak and Steinman, Eliezer, *Sefer Maiyat Shana* (Tel Aviv, 1939/39).

Ubicini, M. A., *Letters on Turkey* (London, 1856), 2 vols.

U. S. Department of State, *Papers Relating to Foreign Relations* (Washington), volumes for the years 1861 through 1881.

Yaari, Abraham, *Masaot Erets Yisrael* (Tel Aviv, 1945/46).

Yebaneli, Shemuel, *Sefer ha-Tsiyonut. Tekufat Hibat Tsiyon* (Tel Aviv, 1943/44), vol. II.

Yellin, Jehoshua, *Zikronot le-Ben Yerushalayim* (Jerusalem, 1924/25).

Zitron, S. L., *Toledot Hibat Tsiyon* (Odessa, 1914/15).

CHAPTER II

I. FROM THE STATE DEPARTMENT FILES IN THE NATIONAL ARCHIVES:

Despatches from and instructions to the envoys extraordinary and ministers plenipotentiary and members of their staffs: Lewis Wallace, 1881–1885; Samuel S. Cox, 1885–1887; Oscar S. Straus, 1887–1889; Solomon Hirsch, 1889–1892; David P. Thompson, 1892–1893; Alexander W. Terrell, 1893–1897; James B. Angell, 1897–1898; Oscar S. Straus, 1898–1899.

Despatches from and instructions to Jerusalem consuls and members of their staffs: Selah Merrill, 1882–1885; Nageeb J. Arbeely, 1885; Henry Gillman, 1886–1891; Selah Merrill, 1891–1893; Edwin S. Wallace, 1893–1898; Selah Merrill, 1898–1907.

II. FROM THE DIVISION OF MANUSCRIPTS, LIBRARY OF CONGRESS:

The Papers of Oscar S. Straus.

III. Books, Periodicals, and Government Publications:

Adler, Cyrus, *Jacob H. Schiff. His Life and Letters* (New York, 1928) , 2 vols.

Bein, Alex, *Toledot ha-Hityashvut ha-Tsiyonit* (Jerusalem, 1943/44) .

Ben Yehuda, Eliezer, *Kol Kitve Eliezer Ben Yehuda* (Jerusalem, 1941/42) .

Cazalet, Edward, *England's Policy in the East* (London, 1879) .

Gelber, N. M., *Zur Vorgeschichte des Zionismus* (Vienna, 1927) .

Ginzberg, Asher, *'Al Parashat Derakim* (Berlin, 1921) , 4 vols.

Havatselet, a Hebrew fortnightly, published in Jerusalem, for the years 1882–1898.

Herzl, Theodor, *Tagebücher* (Berlin, 1934) , 3 vols.

Malaki, Eliezer Rafael, *Ha-Itonut ha-Yerushalmit* (Jerusalem, 1910/11) .

Medzini, Moshe, *Ha-Mediniyut ha-Tsiyonit* (Jerusalem, 1934/35) .

Oliphant, Laurence, *The Land of Gilead* (London, 1881) .

Straus, Oscar S., *Under Four Administrations* (Boston, 1922) .

U. S. Department of State, *Papers Relating to Foreign Relations* (Washington) , for the years 1882 through 1899.

CHAPTER III

I. From the State Department Files in the National Archives:

Despatches from and instructions to the Ambassadors Extraordinary and Plenipotentiary and members of their staffs: John G. A. Leishman, 1906–1909; Oscar S. Straus, 1909–1911; William Woodville, 1911–1913; Henry Morgenthau, 1913–1914.

Despatches from and instructions to the Jerusalem consuls and members of their staffs: Selah Merrill, 1898–1907; Thomas R. Wallace, 1907–1910; William Coffin, 1910–1913.

Intra-departmental memoranda and correspondence on Zionism, File Nos. 867.55/11 through 867.55/29.

II. From the Division of Manuscripts, Library of Congress:

The Papers of Oscar S. Straus.
The Papers of Woodrow Wilson.

III. Books, Periodicals, and Government Publications:

Burstein, Moshe, *Self-Government of the Jews in Palestine since 1900* (Tel Aviv, 1934) .

Eisenstein, J. D., *Otsar Zikronoti* (New York, 1929) .

Havatselet, for the years 1897–1898.

Morgenthau, Henry, *All in a Life Time* (New York, 1922) .

Shiryon, Yizhak, *Zikronot* (Jerusalem, 1943) .

U. S. Department of State, *Papers Relating to Foreign Relations* (Washington) , volumes for the years 1900 through 1913.

Wallace, Edwin Sherman, *Jerusalem the Holy* (New York, 1898) .

CHAPTER IV

I. From the State Department Files in the National Archives:

Despatches from and instructions to the Ambassadors in Constantinople and members of their staffs: Henry Morgenthau, 1914–1916; Abram I. Elkus, 1916–1917. Series Nos. 711.673; 763.72; 763.72115; 840.48; 867.40; 867.48; 867.4016; 867N.01.

Despatches from and instructions to the Jerusalem Consul, Otis A. Glazebrook, 1914–1917. Series No. 867N.01.

Despatches from W. Stanley Hollis, Consul at Beirut, 1914. Series No. 867.48.

Correspondence between the State Department and the American Zionist Organization, the Provisional Zionist Committee, and representatives of American Jewish Relief Organizations. Series Nos. 867.48; 867.4016.

Despatches from and instructions to Garrels, Consul in Alexandria. Series Nos. 840.48; 867.4016.

Despatches from and instructions to Arnold, American Diplomatic Agent in Cairo. Series Nos. 867.48; 867.4016.

Copies of Reports of Captain Decker of the U.S.S. *Tennessee* to the Secretary of the Navy, 1915. Series No. 840.48.

Reports of William Yale, a representative of the Standard Oil Company in Jerusalem, to the State Department, 1917. Series No. 763.72.

Despatches from and instructions to the American embassies in London, Rome, Paris, Berne, the Hague, Stockholm. Series Nos. 867.48; 867.4016.

The Post Records of the Embassy in Constantinople for the period of World War I.

II. From the Division of Manuscripts, Library of Congress:

The Papers of Woodrow Wilson.
The Papers of Ray S. Baker.
The Papers of Robert Lansing.

III. Books, Periodicals, and Government Publications:

Aaronsohn, Aaron, *With the Turks in Palestine* (Boston, 1916).
Adler, Cyrus and Margalith, A. M., *With Firmness in the Right* (N.Y., 1946).
Brandeis, Louis Dembitz, *Brandeis on Zionism* (Washington, 1942).
Dizengoff, Meier, *Im Tel Aviv ba-Golah* (Tel Aviv, 1935/36).
Djemal Pasha, *Memories of a Turkish Statesman, 1913–1919* (London, 1922).
Elmaleh, Abraham, *Erets Yisrael ve-Suriyah be-Yeme Milhemet ha-'Olam* (Jerusalem, 1927/28), 2 vols.
Joffe, Hillel, *Dor Maapilim* (Tel Aviv, 1939).
Luncz, Avraham Moshe, *Luah Erets Yisrael 1914–1916* (Jerusalem, 1914–1916).
Morgenthau, Henry, *Ambassador Morgenthau's Story* (New York, 1918).
Ruppin, Arthur, *Milhemet ha-Yehudim le-Kiyumam* (Tel Aviv, 1940).
Shalosh, Josef E., *Parashat Hayai* (Tel Aviv, 1931/32).
U. S. Department of State, *The Lansing Papers* (Washington, 1939), 2 vols.
U. S. Department of State, *Papers Relating to Foreign Relations* (Washington), volumes for the years 1914 through 1917.
Yale, William, "Ambassador Morgenthau's Special Mission of 1917," *World Politics* (1949), vol. I.

CHAPTER V

I. From the State Department Files in the National Archives:

Documents on the Balfour Declaration. Series No. 867N.01.
Reports of Vice-Consul Edelman, Near Eastern Intelligence Section. Series No. 867N.01.

Reports of William Yale, Special Agent of the State Department. Series No. 763.72119.

II. FROM THE DIVISION OF MANUSCRIPTS, LIBRARY OF CONGRESS:

The Papers of Woodrow Wilson.
The Papers of Ray S. Baker.
The Files of the *Inquiry*, Acquisition 2206. These include a set of memoranda by William Yale; duplicates are also in the House Collection in the Yale University Library.

III. BOOKS, PERIODICALS, AND GOVERNMENT PUBLICATIONS:

Adler, Selig, "The Palestine Question in the Wilson Era," *Jewish Social Studies* (1948), vol. X.
Baker, Ray Stannard, *Woodrow Wilson; life and letters* (New York, 1946), 7 vols.
De Haas, Jacob, *Brandeis* (New York, 1929).
De Haas, Jacob, *History of Palestine* (New York, 1934).
Dugdale, Blanche E., *Arthur James Balfour* (New York, 1937), 2 vols.
Gelber, N. M., *Hatsharat Balfour ve-Toledoteha* (Jerusalem, 1938/39).
Lawrence, T. E., *Secret Despatches from Arabia* (London, privately printed, 1939).
Mason, Alpheus T., *Brandeis* (New York, 1946).
Spring-Rice, Cecil, *Letters and Friendship* (London, 1929), 2 vols.
Storrs, Ronald, *Orientations* (London, 1937).
Tcherikower, Elias, ed., *Geshichte fun der Yiddisher Arbeter Bavegung in di Faraynikte Shtatn* (New York, 1943), 2 vols.

CHAPTER VI

I. FROM THE STATE DEPARTMENT FILES IN THE NATIONAL ARCHIVES:

Records of the Paris Peace Conference, a separately indexed collection.
Intra-departmental memoranda on Palestine. Series Nos. 867N.00; 867N.01.

II. FROM THE DIVISION OF MANUSCRIPTS, LIBRARY OF CONGRESS:

The Papers of Woodrow Wilson.
The Papers of Ray S. Baker.
The Papers of Henry White.
The Papers of General Tasker Bliss.
The Papers of Robert Lansing.
The Files of the *Inquiry*.

III. BOOKS, PERIODICALS, AND GOVERNMENT PUBLICATIONS:

Antonius, George, *The Arab Awakening* (Philadelphia, 1934).
Baker, Ray Stannard, *Woodrow Wilson and the World Settlement* (New York, 1922), 3 vols.
Boehm, Adolf, *Die Zionistische Bewegung* (Jerusalem, 1937), 2 vols.
Garnett, David, ed., *The Letters of T. E. Lawrence* (New York, 1939).
Howard, Harry N., "An American Experiment in Peace Making. The King Crane Commission," *The Moslem World* (1942), vol. XXXII.

Lansing, Robert, *The Peace Negotiations* (Boston, 1921).
Medzini, Moshe, *Eser Shanim shel Mediniut Artsi-Yisraelit* (Tel Aviv, 1928/29).
Perlmann, M., "Chapters of Arab-Jewish Diplomacy, 1918–1922," Jewish Social Studies (1944), vol. VI.
Shotwell, James T., *At the Paris Peace Conference* (New York, 1937).
U. S. Department of State, *The Paris Peace Conference* (Washington, 1942–47), 13 vols.

CHAPTER VII

I. FROM THE STATE DEPARTMENT FILES IN THE NATIONAL ARCHIVES:

Correspondence, intra-departmental memoranda, reports, despatches, and instructions on Palestine and Zionism. Series Nos. 867N.00; 867N.01.
Records of the Paris Peace Conference.

II. FROM THE DIVISION OF MANUSCRIPTS, LIBRARY OF CONGRESS:

The Files of the *Inquiry*.

III. BOOKS, PERIODICALS, AND GOVERNMENT PUBLICATIONS:

Andrews, Fannie Fern, *The Holy Land under the Mandate* (Boston, 1931), 2 vols.
U. S. Department of State, *Mandate for Palestine* (Washington, 1927).
U. S. Department of State, *Papers Relating to Foreign Relations* (Washington), volumes for the years 1920 through 1927.
Wright, Quincy, *Mandates under the League of Nations* (Chicago, 1930).

CHAPTER VIII

I. FROM PRIVATE MEMORANDA:

The author has had access to memoranda prepared after interviews with key American officials engaged in formulating recent policy on Palestine.

II. FROM THE LIBRARY OF CONGRESS:

Anglo-American Committee of Inquiry. Typescript of Hearings in Washington, January, 1947.

III. BOOKS, PERIODICALS, AND GOVERNMENT PUBLICATIONS:

American Jewish Conference, *Report of the Interim Committee* (New York, 1946).
Arabian-American Oil Company, *Summary of Middle East Oil Developments* (s.l., 1947).
Crum, Bartley C., *Behind the Silken Curtain* (New York, 1947).
Fanning, Leonard M., *American Oil Operations Abroad* (New York, 1947).
Feis, Herbert, *Petroleum and American Foreign Policy* (Stanford University, 1944).
Feis, Herbert, *Seen from E.A.* (New York, 1947).
Fink, Reuben, *America and Palestine* (New York, 1945).
Friedrich, Carl J., *American Policy Toward Palestine* (Washington, 1944).
García-Granados, Jorge, *The Birth of Israel* (New York, 1948).
Great Britain. Foreign Office: *Correspondence with the United States Government regarding United States Rights in Palestine, London, July 6–August 4, 1937, Command Paper 5544* (London, 1937).

In Di Yorn Fun Yiddishen Khorbn, a collection of documents (New York, 1948).

Jones, S. S., and Myers, D. P., editors, *Documents in American Foreign Relations,* January 1938–June 1939 (Boston, 1939).

Middle East Journal (Washington), a quarterly, 1947–1948.

Mikesell, R. F., and Chenery, Hollis B., *Arabian Oil: America's Stake in the Middle East* (Chapel Hill, 1949).

Revusky, Abraham, *Jews in Palestine* (New York, 1945).

Robinson, Jacob, *Palestine and the United Nations* (Washington, 1947).

Roosevelt, Kermit, *Partition of Palestine. A Lesson in Pressure Politics* (New York, 1948).

Royal Institute of International Affairs, *Great Britain and Palestine, 1915–1945* (London, 1946).

Sherwood, Robert E., *Roosevelt and Hopkins* (New York, 1948).

United Nations. Special Committee on Palestine, *Report to the General Assembly* (New York, 1947).

U. S. Congress. House of Representatives, Armed Services Committee, Special Subcommittee on Petroleum, *Hearings* (80th Congress, 2nd session, Washington, 1948).

U. S. Congress. Senate, Special Committee Investigating Petroleum Resources, *Final Report* (80th Congress, 1st session, Washington, 1947).

U. S. Congress. Senate, Special Committee Investigating the National Defense Program, *Hearings,* part 41, "Petroleum Arrangements with Saudi Arabia" (Washington, 1948).

U. S. Congress. Senate, *Statement of the President of the United States together with the Report of the Anglo-American Committee of Inquiry on Palestine as Submitted to the President and to the Government of the United Kingdom* (79th Congress, 2nd session, Senate Document no. 182, Washington, 1946).

U. S. Department of State, *Bulletin,* for the years 1939 through 1948.

U. S. Department of State, *Papers Relating to Foreign Relations* (Washington), volumes for the years 1928 through 1932.

Weizmann, Chaim, *Autobiography. Trial and Error* (New York, 1949).

Welles, Sumner, *We Need Not Fail* (Boston, 1948).

World Petroleum, a monthly, New York, for the year 1948.

World's Oil, a monthly, New York, for the year 1948.

Ziff, William B., *The Rape of Palestine* (New York, 1938).

INDEX